STARR SOFTWARE INC.

About the Authors

Joe Weessies

Joe Weessies has been involved with business software for over 20 years. He has seen the progression from MRP To ERP to Optimization. He has worked on small private companies to large fortune 500 corporations. Joe joined with PeoleSoft in March of 1996 to be one of their first manufacturing consultants. By the end of the year, Joe had earned the 1996 Consultant of the Year Award. In 1997, Joe earned 3 top Performer awards from PeopleSoft Consulting. Joe was not only considered one of the top functional consultants within the Supply Chain area but also a top-notch technical consultant.

Joe left PeopleSoft to pursue other goals but still continued to do PeopleSoft consulting working with smaller consulting firms, including forming his own company. Joe then accomplished a long term goal, completing the first book on PeopleTools version 8 which has sold around the world.

Steve Bollinger

Steve Bollinger has been working as an independent consultant doing custom business software design and coding for over 20 years. His primary focus has been on Supply Chain and ERP implementations. Steve has been involved with programming PeopleSoft Supply Chain custom modifications since January of 1997.

ACKNOWLEDGEMENTS

Joe Weessies

This is the second book in a series covering the PeopleSoft 8 Tools Suite. The first book was such a hard effort with many ups and down but this book seemed to flow much better as I had more control from the start. My friends were still helpful in keeping me motivated yet help me still take some time off to have fun. Mark Neal for encouraging me to keep going and exploring new opportunities. Wendell and Marie Mitch for their prayers, encouragement and faith in me. And lots of responses on email from all over the world.

Special thanks to my editor, Melanie, without whom I would have had hundreds of misspellings and totally bad grammar. She spent many of her hours alone with a dictionary making this book possible. Her efforts are more than appreciated.

There are also three other special names to recognize who read the book and helped with readability and finding errors: Marc Polley, Nasir AliKahn and Nirav Vyas. These three took time off their business schedules to read and give their input. Thanks!

Finally, I hope each reader of this book finds something new to learn.

ACKNOWLEDGEMENTS CONT...

Steve Bollinger

I would like to thank Joe Weessies who invited me to participate in this book with him by writing a few chapters for him. His enthusiasm and high energy for this task is a real inspiration to me. His editing of my work was both a trial and a reward in learning how to write. Although my participation is this book has been small (primarily writing the Set Processing Chapter), I have gained a great deal in the experience.

The several years I have worked together with Joe consulting on PeopleSoft projects, have been a real learning experience for me. His technical expertise and knowledge of both the PeopleTools and the PeopleSoft applications has been very helpful to me. His humor and up beat approach have made the task of consulting a lot of fun. Thank you, Joe!

DEDICATION

Joe Weessies

This book is dedicated to my family. For without the encouragement of my wife, Melanie, and the hugs from my children, Christine and Stephen, I might never have finished.

Steve Bollinger

I dedicate this book to all the programmers and IT folks out there who get excited about their technology and have a philosophy of sharing their knowledge with others. I have learned countless things from others along this journey both technical and about life. It is my hope that I have and will give back in kind.

Table of Contents

Introduction

PeopleSoft has been evolving their set of tools for some time now but with the release of version 8 they have taken a giant step forward. This is especially true for the Application Engine Program. This latest version from PeopleSoft makes Application Engine a powerful tool with a wide range of capabilities.

PeopleSoft has also expanded the role of the Application Engine tool now. It has not replaced all the COBOL and SQR programs but it has come very close. There are new ways to use this tool in PeopleSoft and all of these will be discussed within this book.

First, you will learn how to move around the new programming interface. Application Engine is now part of the Application Designer program with a new interface that is really helpful to review and update code. You will learn a great new capability in that you now have PeopleCode that you can use within the Application Engine program. This solves a lot of problems with the earlier versions of Application Engine and makes this tool so much more powerful. After learning all of this, you will jump right into modifying some of the existing programs. You will cover all that you need to know as well as some tricks and shortcuts you can use to help find the right place to make your modification.

Now with a lot of knowledge about Application Engine, you can begin to create your own programs. Modification is difficult because of the need to find the right place to modify the code but the core of the program is already written. To create your own Application Engine program, you start with a blank slate. There are some issues that you need to be concerned about to create a good Application Engine program and you will learn them all.

You move up to the issues of the new File Layout object, next. Here is another new area that PeopleSoft has greatly enhanced within Application Engine. Before, if you wished to do flat file processing, you were limited to using SQR from Brio but now PeopleSoft recommends using the new Application Engine. PeopleSoft has even re-written most of their flat file processing to use the new Application Engine and the File object.

Then you will learn the key to Application Engine – Set Processing. Set Processing is a new way to think in how to process based on sets of data. There are benefits as well as drawbacks to using this process and you will learn all of these. Many programmers will need to concentrate here to get the most benefit of Application Engine because this is a new way of thinking that is not the same as creating a SQR report.

With all of the structure learned, you will finally get to where you can read and modify an Application Engine program. Your learning will then come to a peak when you create you own Application Engine including one using the File Layout object.

The last things to learn are some of the debug and review techniques. These too have changed in the new tool with some greatly enhanced capabilities. You will learn not only the prescribed format but also some tricks used by consultants. Finally, you will learn what to do when your Application Engine program crashes and does not complete successfully. You have some restrictions and issues when this happens but all is not lost. It is simple to handle these issues once you know what you have to do.

Purpose of this Book

This book was written for a specific target audience. It is assumed that you have been already working in PeopleSoft tools version 6,7 or 7.5. You do not have to be working on PeopleTools version 8 to fully understand this book but of course it does not hurt either. You do need however some skill in using the Application Designer tool since Application Engine is now created, updated and maintained in this tool. This book will explain any special issues with the new release of PeopleTools 8 specific to the Application Engine but will not cover all of the features.

You should also have a fairly good skill at creating new database records and understand their relevance. There are good books on the market, at the time this book was written, that can help with this skill if you need to polish up a bit. Another required skill is the use of PeopleCode. PeopleCode is now allowed in the Application Engine program and brings with it a whole set of fantastic capabilities. This book will not try and teach you how to code in PeopleCode but will show you how to use PeopleCode here in the Application Engine program.

Finally, the last and most important skill is SQL. You must fully understand how to write proper select, update and insert statements to make the best use of the Application Engine program. Since PeopleSoft is a data storage and analysis product, you must be able to select the data from tables, manipulate to other formats and insert into new tables in potentially different structures. This all requires good SQL skills. Again there are many good books available on this subject if you need to work on this skill.

History of the Application Engine

Application Engine changed a little during the earlier revisions, 5 thru 7, but with the release of version 8 Application Engine took a quantum leap forward. Rumors would abound with each version on how the Application Engine was being used to do all sorts of things and how it was going to take over the world. Developers were pressured to re-write their COBOL programs into Application Engine programs back in earlier versions when the tool was just not ready to handle it.

The current understanding of where this tool came from is that a few developers got together seeing the lack of a good SQL programming tool. They came up with the construct for Application Engine based on this need. It was crude, but you could put a series of SQL statements in and have it process very quickly – faster than any SQR program.

Application Engine was a tough program to use in earlier versions. It did not have a good development tool to help understand the program flow as well as having key constructs missing. The program was hard to visualize seeing how it went from one SQL to the next and why it would do so or not.

Application Engine also had missing simple logic constructs such as "IF" statements. You could not re-direct the program based on a logic choice – you had to use SQL statements to drive the logic. This was a hard to grasp concept for many developers. Many developers got lost on this "IF" concept especially when they saw the way the SQL worked.

The largest problem for Application Engine was that although Application Engine could run SQL very quick, it was best used on processing sets of data. Application Engine had issues when it had to process on a single row of data within a set of data (this is called row-by-row processing). Many times in complicated programs you had to do this row-by-row processing to validate, summarize, or collect other necessary data. This caused the performance of the Application Engine program to be worse than SQR programming. So if proper SQL statements were written using the strength of Application Engine, processing in sets of data, you could have a very quick and powerful program but this way of handling set data was usually very difficult for most developers to write. Even PeopleSoft developers struggled with this problem. Many times, a program written in SQR out performed Application Engine due to this row-by-row problem. But when an Application Engine program was written correctly (you had to use all of your SQL skills), you had a program that could rival COBOL in performance.

With this latest release (8) you will find that not all the issues are gone – but many are removed or lessened with the new capabilities. Of course with all new versions you gain some new features and you lose a few as well. Each of these will be discussed in detail later in the Chapters.

Purpose and Uses of Application Engine

Now that you have read all the issues and concerns about Application Engine you need to see why it is a good tool to use and in what places PeopleSoft now recommends this tool as the primary tool for developers.

First, Application Engine is not for reporting. If you need any type of reporting output, this is not the tool for you. Yes, technically, you could force this program to output a flat file in HTML format but why struggle when there are much better tools available to you.

Application Engine programs do cover two main areas. First is the batch update capability. SQR, COBOL and Application Engine can do these types of programs. Although in the past most developers would use SQR to code these programs, PeopleSoft now recommends to use the Application Engine tool. A developer, in the past, used SQR since this was an easy tool to use, had good debug capability and was not bad on performance. SQR was also a simple language to learn and readily available to everyone. COBOL programs within PeopleSoft are not known for their ease of use, so most developers tended to stay away from this program. COBOL also required the use of a compiler and special language skills that a lot of PeopleSoft developers just did not learn. Application Engine was also not that easy to use and did not have a good tool to help understand the process so many developers never gave it a chance to try and learn the tool. The problem was key in that COBOL and Application Engine was tough to use while SQR was just so easy. Most developers took the simple way out and went with SQR. Now with this new release, Application Engine can move closer to the ease of use of an SQR and still maintain the performance of the COBOL programs. You will find in version 8 that PeopleSoft has converted more SQR and COBOL programs into Application Engine because developers are spending the time to learn this new tool.

The second area that Application Engine is to be used for is flat file programs. Before, your only option was the SQR tool, as COBOL could not create these needed files. Now, with release 8 and the new File Object capability you can create Application Engine programs to handle all this processing. You will find that PeopleSoft has spent a great deal of their own time to follow their own recommendation. You will find that many programs that handle flat file processing are now Application Engine programs. So you can see why it is important to learn this new tool not only for today but also for the future.

You should now be able to see that PeopleSoft is placing a greater emphasis on this new tool. They have greatly expanded its capabilities while still keeping the performance level high. This is their tool of choice for all background and flat file processing. You can still use the SQR tool if you wish but you will not be following PeopleSoft guidelines and recommendations. If there ever was a time to learn this tool it is now, as it is being used heavily and the plans are for more improvements.

Future designs for Application Engine

Although the future of the Application Engine tool cannot be predicted it can be inferred by its history to this current release. In the beginning the tool was difficult to use, at best, but now it is used a great deal. You can also see that this has been taken to heart by PeopleSoft developers themselves, in that they are creating new programs for this tool as well as converting old SQR and COBOL programs.

Newer versions of PeopleSoft tools will be made and you can bet that Application Engine will be a tool that will remain in the set. It has come a long way and is poised to be a major tool within the PeopleSoft tool suite.

Next

Now that you have learned all the history and uses of the Application Engine tool, it is time to start actually learning the tool. The next chapter starts right off in how to open, read and move around the new tool interface. This has changed greatly from the previous version of PeopleSoft so there is a lot to learn here.

Chapter 1

Understanding the Design Tool

With the new release of version 8 there have been some dramatic changes to the tool used to develop the Application Engine programs. First, Application Engine is no longer in its own tool but uses the Application Designer. This new capability not only brings about a new way to develop but also a host of other new capabilities that will be explored in each further chapter. Since so much has changed you first need to learn all about the design tool itself and how to move around to read the program. Then, you will dig in a bit further to understand some of the new syntax and use of common statements. You should, by the time you have completed this chapter, be able to review and read all Application Engine programs.

Application Designer

To review an Application Engine program you first have to start the Application Designer. This should only be launched from the Windows client in either 2 or 3-tier mode. For Application Engine it does not matter which tier mode you use so you can launch the Application Designer as you have done in the past. On standard PeopleSoft installations, the Application Designer would launch from the Windows menu: Start – Programs – PeopleSoft 8 – Application Designer. Once you have the Application Designer open you should see the three main areas; the project area, the message area and the working area, as shown in figure 1.1 below.

To open an Application Engine program you use the menu: File – Open or click on the file open icon . In either case, you will see the Open Object window, as shown in figure 1.2. This window is where you open any object, as you are about to do with your Application Engine program.

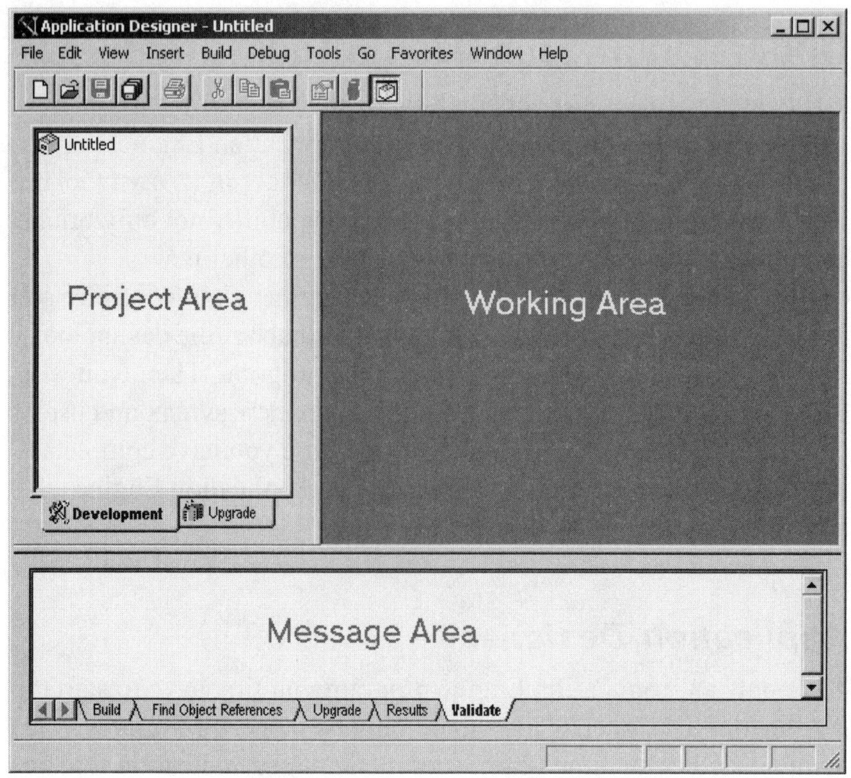

Figure 1.1 Application Designer areas

First, you have to set the object type. You use the drop down to find the object, or you can type the first letter of the object to set the type. If you type 'A', you will see that the type is set to Activity. This is the first object encountered in the list starting with A. If you type 'A' again, you will then be set on the Application Engine type. Now, you can type in the name of the Application Engine program you want to open in the Name field in the Selection Criteria area, type in the beginning letters or you can leave it totally blank. Once you have this input, you can then click on the Open button or type the Enter key to have the display area below filled in, based on your selection. The objective here is to find the Application Engine program you wish to review or edit.

You can also use the other fields in the Selection Criteria area (as shown in figure 1.2).

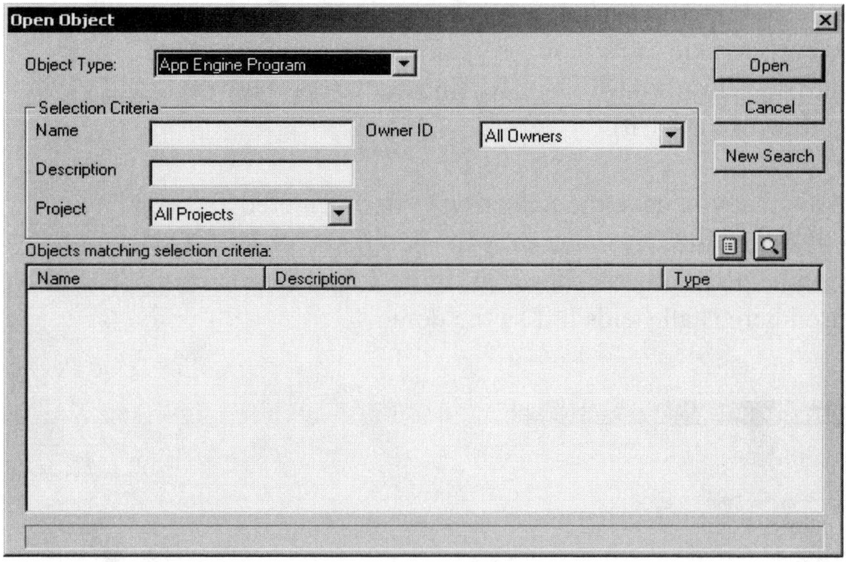

Figure 1.2 Open Object window

The Description field can be used, but note that some Application Engine programs do not have any descriptions and it must be spelled accurately or you will not find your program. The Owner ID field can also be used to show only those Application Engine programs owned by a specific owner. This is mostly used when you are using the owner feature within PeopleSoft development to find your own Application Engine programs. The Project field will open any Application Engine program assigned to a specific project. The problem with this is that you can only find it by selecting All Projects (which is the default) unless you have already assigned the Application Engine program to a specific project.

Once you have your Selection Criteria entered, you can only click on the Open button to see the list of the Application Engine programs listed in the display area below. There are two small buttons on this window that control the look and feel of the display area. The default normally shown in the display area is the Detail View. This Detail View is the button with the magnifying glass. The other view is the List View (the notepad button) and shows only the Application Engine name. The List View is used to show more programs in the same space and to help move quickly through a long list (most developers use the Detail View and never change it).

Now that you have the Selection Criteria entered and you have clicked on the Open button, you should see a list of Application Engine programs, as shown in figure 1.3. The Selection Criteria used here is all fields left as the default.

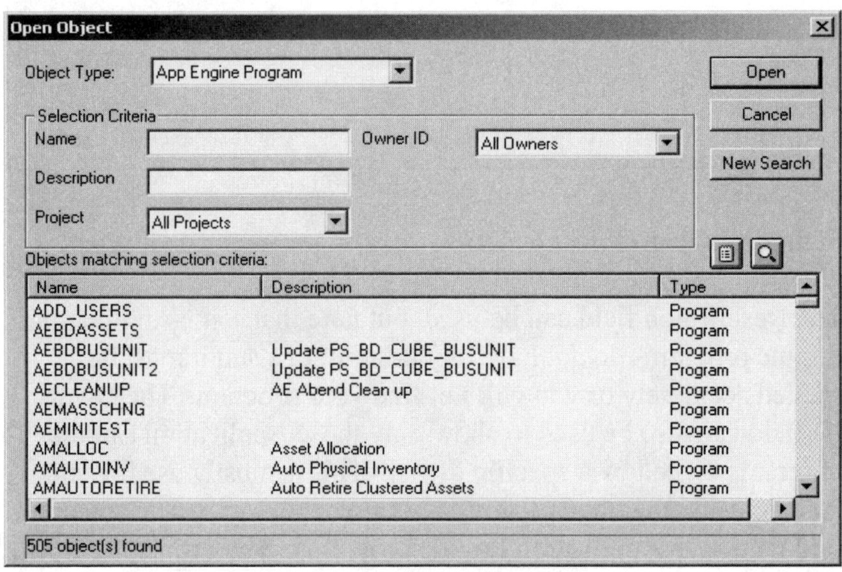

Figure 1.3 Open Object Application Engine selected.

You can now scroll up and down through the list by the use of the scroll bar on the far right on this window. You can scroll till you find the Application Engine program you are wishing to work on. For our example here, scroll through the list to find the Application Engine program, PO_POSTAGE. Once you find this in the list, you can click on the name once and then click the Open button; or you just double click on the Application Engine name. In either case, the Open Object window will close and the Application Engine program will open a new window within the work area of the Application Designer, as shown in figure 1.4.

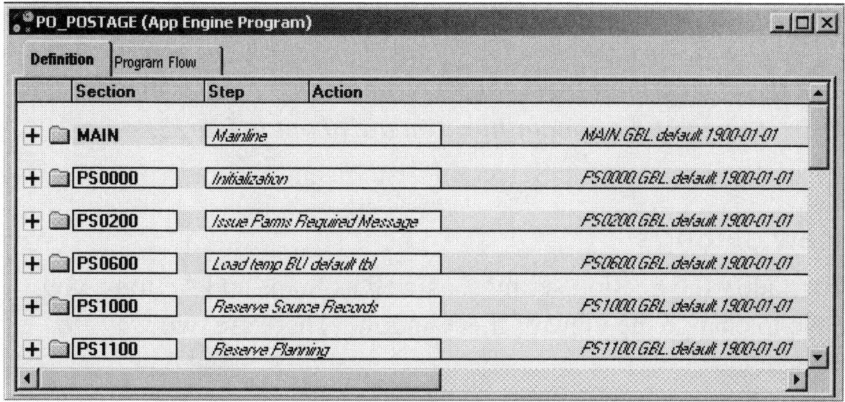

Figure 1.4 Application Engine Program window.

Application Engine Program – Definition window

You can now see the new Application Engine programming window. You need to fully explore this window so that you can learn all of the new capabilities.

You are first presented with the Definition view where all the Sections have been collapsed. This is the base starting point. Listed across the top of this window you see the column titles of: Section, Step and Action. These column headings are used only when you expand one or all of the Sections. The only column that lines up now is Section – the Step and Action columns are not visible at this point. Each line you see now shows the Section name (in the correct column) followed by the Section description. The information on the far right is some detail information about this Section.

New terms have been introduced here; Section, Step and Action. These are just blocks or sections of work and are all fully defined later in this Chapter.

NOTE: *If you have object locking turned on; you will need to lock the object to work some of the following controls. If you do not lock the object, the system thinks you can only review and will restrict some of the capabilities you are about to learn.*

View settings

To modify the Section settings, as well as Steps and Actions, you have to change the view of this window. There are two ways to change the view.

View Menu

First, you can use the View menu of the Application Designer by clicking on the menu: View. This will give you a drop down, as shown in figure 1.5.

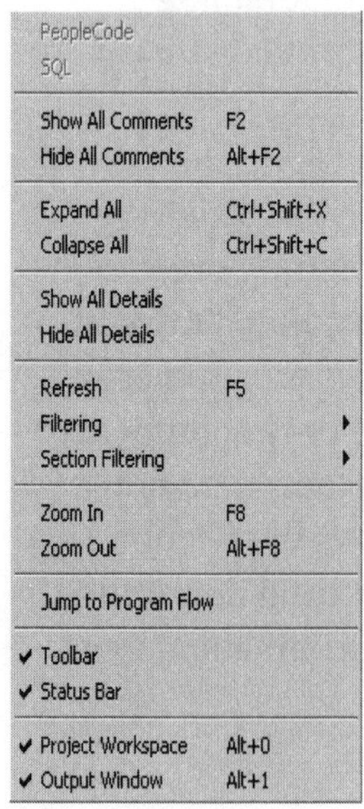

Figure 1.5 View Menu

This view menu controls not only the view of the Application Engine Section but the Application Designer itself. Each will be explained now in detail.

Command	**Explanation**
PeopleCode	This menu is active when you are on an Action that contains PeopleCode, meaning the Action type has been set to PeopleCode (you will learn later in the Action section what a type is). If you select this view command, a new window will open that contains the PeopleCode already entered for this Action.
SQL	This menu is active when you are on an Action that contains SQL. Most Actions contain SQL. This will all be fully explained in the Action section below.
Show All Comments	This menu action will open all comments for each Section, Step and Action. Each item (Section, Step and Action) allows comments to be placed so that anyone else can see the information and understand the purpose and function of the
Application Engine.	
Hide All comments	This menu action hides all comment fields showing for each Section, Step and Action.
Expand All	This menu action will expand each Section to show all the Steps and Actions within that section. The Application Designer shows the Application Engine program in a format similar to a tree structure with the Section being the root or base. The Steps are the limbs while the Actions are the leaves. You may find that a single Section contains a handful of Steps and each Step may contain a handful of Actions. There is no limit to the number of Steps and Actions that a Section can contain. This menu action allows you to expand a full Application Engine program quickly. There are other short cuts to open only a single Section that will be discussed later.
Collapse All	This menu action will collapse all Sections and Steps (you cannot collapse Actions since they have no object below them in the tree structure).
Show All Details	Here you can open all the information on each Section. The detail information is not normally shown for each Section while the Step and Action are. This will open all detail information for each Section, as well as, Step and Actions if you have previously done a Hide All Detail menu command. There is also a shortcut to open and close this set of

	information on Sections, Steps and Actions, which is discussed later.
Hide All Details	This menu action closes all detail information on all Sections, Steps and Actions.
Refresh	This command refreshes the Application Engine window. If you have a large program this is handy to get things in alphabetical Section order. Sections are stored in alphabetical order while Steps are held within the order of placement within a Section. Actions are in a predicted order explained later in this Chapter.
Filtering	This menu command has a few sub commands that allow you to restrict the Sections, Steps and Actions that will be displayed. The main commands are to show Sections, Steps and Actions that are targeted to be in an Upgrade or not. You can use this when you have a large Application Engine program to help find those places you are working on.
Section Filtering	This menu command, also like the filtering command, has some sub commands. Here you can select some parameters (via the custom command) to show only Sections with certain parameters; such as Base Language, Database platform or Effective date.
Zoom In	This zooms out (makes the data within the window larger so that you see less of it) the Application Engine window. You will need to use this when you have a large program that has a complicated flow structure. You will use this more when you are in the Program Flow tab, which you have not yet learned about.
Zoom Out	This zooms out the Application Engine window
Jump to Program Flow	This command will take you on the Section, Step or Action that was last highlighted from the Definition tab (the one you are in right now) to the Program Flow tab and place you in the flow where the highlighted Section, Step or Action is. You will learn all about the Flow tab in just a bit.
Toolbars	This is a command that concerns the whole Application Designer and turns on and off the toolbar.
Status Bar	This is also a command that affects the whole Application Designer by turning on or off the status bar at the very bottom.
Project Workspace	Another Application Designer command that turns on or off the Project window.
Output Window	The last Application Designer command that turns on or off the Message window.

Right Click Menu

The second way to change the view of this window is to use the right click of the mouse. This will open a small menu, as shown in figure 1.6.

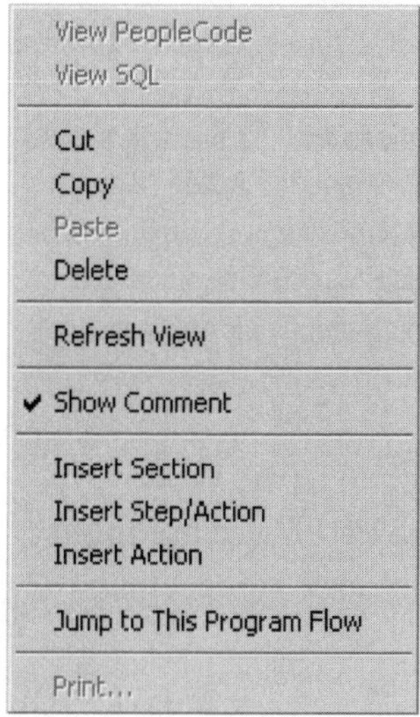

Figure 1.6 Right Click Menu

Here, you see a small subset of the menu commands you have already learned, plus a few more.

Command	**Explanation**
View PeopleCode	This is the same as the PeopleCode command as before.
View SQL	This is the same SQL command as before.
Cut, Copy, Paste	These are the standard window commands that allow you to cut, copy and Paste information quickly.
Delete	This command allows you to delete a Section, Step or Action depending on where you just right clicked. You will see that the Section, Step or Action is highlighted so that you can determine which line is going to be affected. Be sure to do this only if you really want to delete a Section, Step or Action.
Refresh View	This is the same Refresh command as before.
Show Comment	This is similar to the Show Comment on or off command but here you only have a toggle switch. You will see in the figure above the Show Comment has a checkmark next to it. This means you right clicked where a comment is

	already showing and if you select it now, it will hide the comment.
Insert Section	This is a new command that allows you to insert in a new Section. There is also a menu command as well as a button command that you will learn in Chapter 2.
Insert Step/Action	Just as you can insert a new Section, you can also insert a new Step and Action. This will be fully explained in Chapter 2.
Insert Action	Here, you can insert just a new Action. This is only active when youright click on a Step or another Action. This also will be fully explained in Chapter 2.
Jump to This Program Flow	This is the same Jump to This Program Flow as before.
Print	This is a short cut to allow you to print your Application Engine Program directly.

Now that you have learned the two ways to change the view around, there are some even easier ways to do it. There are mouse click methods to use that will accomplish the same thing, in a limited manner.

Mouse Click

To expand the sections, click on the plus symbol next to the Section, Step or Action name. If you clicked on a Section, then the Section and all the Steps and Actions within the Section will expand. Where before with the menus it was an all or nothing selection, here you can specifically select which lines to expand. Clicking on the minus symbol next to a Section (this only shows on expanded Sections) will then collapse the Section to one line. It will also collapse all the Steps and Actions within the selected Section. If you click on the minus symbol on a Step or Action, then only that one line is collapsed. You will find that you will use this method a lot since the Application Engine program shows only the Sections un-expanded when you first load a program, as is done in our example.

Before you proceed much further, you need to expand just one section. In our example, in figure 1.7, the Main Section is expanded by clicking on the plus symbol.

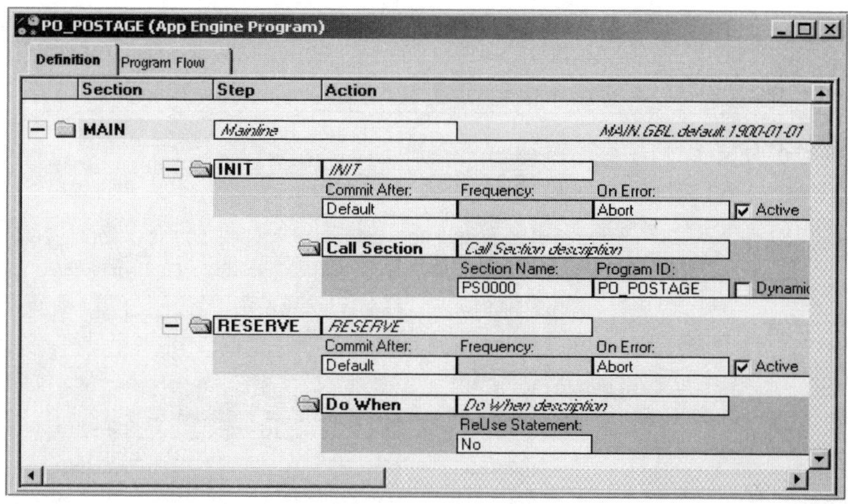

Figure 1.7 Main Section expanded.

Now you can see a fully expanded section. You will notice that each line has a folder. Some of the folders are open (INIT, RESERVE) and one is closed (MAIN). This is to inform you whether the details Sections are open or closed. If you click on the folders, the detail information for that line will open if it was closed or close if it was open. If you click on the MAIN folder you will see it open the detail information area, as shown in figure 1.8.

You can also perform mouse actions on the Action lines. If the Action line has PeopleCode or has SQL within it, you can double click on the line and it will open the PeopleCode editor or the SQL editor. This allows you to review the code easily and quickly.

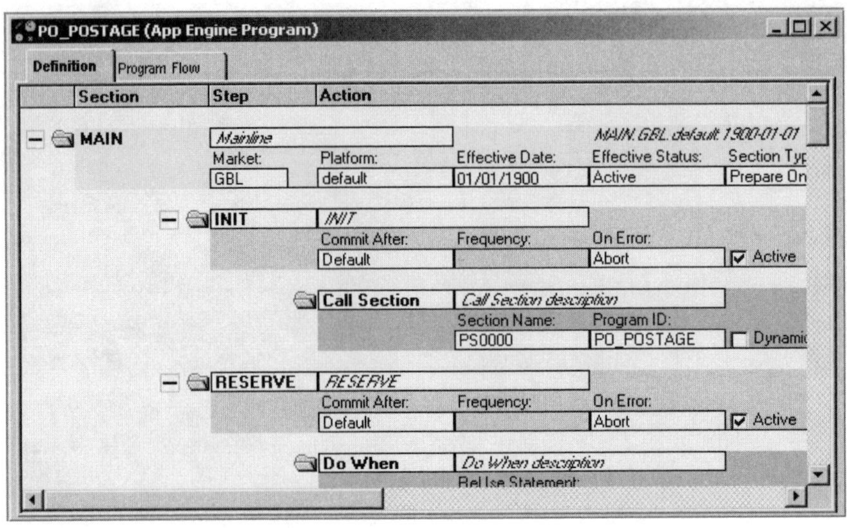

Figure 1.8 Main Section Detail Information.

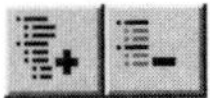

Finally, there is one last way to affect the display. There are two buttons on the toolbar of the Application Designer. If you click the button with the '+' symbol it will expand all Sections and Steps within the open Application Engine. The other button, the one with the '-' symbol, will collapse all levels to the main display. These are typically used on small Application Engine programs to open for review. These are not used for large programs as this opens too many Sections and makes it more difficult to find the one Section you need.

You now have all the information on how to move around and set the display controls. Now, its time to be a bit more specific on what Application Engine is and some of its structure, then you can continue learning about the Program Flow display.

Application Engine Structure

In this section, you will learn how Application Engine programs are structured. You will build on this knowledge to move around, read and then build your own Application Engine programs. To understand the structure you have to be fully cognizant of the three elements in the structure; Section, Step and Action.

Section

Every Application Engine Program must have at least one Section and the name must be MAIN. This is required because the system has to know the place to start when the Application Engine program is launched. Instead of having to set a flag or other indicator to show where the start is you only have to have this one Section. Of course, usually, you will add many more Sections but you must have one 'MAIN' Section.

Note: *There is one exception to this rule and that is Application Engine Library programs. A Library program is a collection of Sections that can be called by other Application Engine programs.*

The purpose of the Section element is not only to show the start place, but when you create other new Sections you can group Steps and Actions into a logical structure. You will find in the Action area below that you cannot only run SQL or PeopleCode but you can also jump to other Sections. This is why you will create other Sections because you will make decisions and decide to jump to other Sections that will perform an action. Take, for example, the process of creating a Sales Order; you want to verify the price but there is a flag stating whether the order line allows the price to be overridden or not. A typical Application Engine Program would have an Action element using PeopleCode to review this flag setting. If the flag were found to be true (meaning it could be changed), then the next Action would be set to jump to a new Section that takes the information and calculates a new price. Now if the flag were false, the next Action would be skipped so the code in the new Section would not be processed.

As you can see, you will need to break your program into Sections that process specific conditions. There are other reasons you may create a Section but this is the main reason.

Sections display in Alphabetical order in the Application Designer window. This means that Sections are not shown in the order of the program flow. There is only one exception to this rule and that applies to the Main Section. This section is always shown first no matter the order since this Section is required. There is another view of the Application Designer you have not yet covered that shows the proper program flow. All of this will be explained later in this chapter under the heading Program Flow.

Step

Every Application Engine program must have at least one Step. A Step cannot exist on it's own but must be under a Section. You will notice (review figure 1.8) that each Step is indented. This is to show you the ownership of the Step and which Section this step belongs to. You may find that a Step will exist without an Action; this is normally not done but is a leftover from the previous version of Application Engine. In the previous version, one Step was created to hold a comment about what the following Steps completed within a Section. These comments were wonderful and made it very easy to understand what a specific Section was trying to accomplish and then what each specific Step was trying to perform. With the new Application Engine, you do not need to reserve a Step just for comments. You will find in the next chapter that you can add comments to each Section, Step and Action.

The purpose of a Step is to create a logical path within your Section. They are typically used to breakup Actions into logical chunks that can be described. Usually you go from one Step to the next within a Section. You are allowed to have more than one Action per Step but you will find that mostly each Step has only one Action.

So you may see that Steps really do not do much but their structure allows you to setup various events using different Actions. As you learn more about the structure and the events you can perform this will become clearer.

Steps within a Section are displayed in the order you create them. They are not re-sorted into alphabetical order, as in the Sections. This is required since each Step is to do an Action and having the system change it all around would really mess up any program.

Action

This is the heart or core of the Application Engine. Here is where you place your program code to perform actions, check validations and do all the processing that is required. Actions cannot exist on their own for they must be under a Step. As mentioned earlier, a Step can have many Actions and each will be run in turn unless specifically directed to skip certain Actions. Actions are the lowest level within the Application Engine program and contain all the PeopleCode, SQL and other functions that can be performed within Application Engine. Each of these functions will be explained later in the next 2 chapters.

Actions are sorted in a specific order no matter the order you place them in. This re-sorting is done to place in proper order how the Action types will work. You will learn all about the types of Actions in the next chapter but you need to understand the order because you will learn later that an Action can determine if the next Action processes or not. The Action types work in the following order. This does not mean that you have to have each Action type within your Step, only if you have multiple Actions will they go in this sort order.

1. Do When
2. Do While
3. Do Select
4. PeopleCode
5. SQL
6. Call Section
7. Message Log
8. Do Until

Well, now you have completed the process to learn all about the Definition window. There is another window to learn that was mentioned, Program Flow. These two windows allow you to see the Application Engine program easily and to review, debug or modify it.

Application Engine Program – Program Flow Window

Referring back to figure 1.8, you will notice that at the top of the window there is a tab with the words Program Flow. Click on this tab to now access the Program Flow window, as shown in figure 1.9.

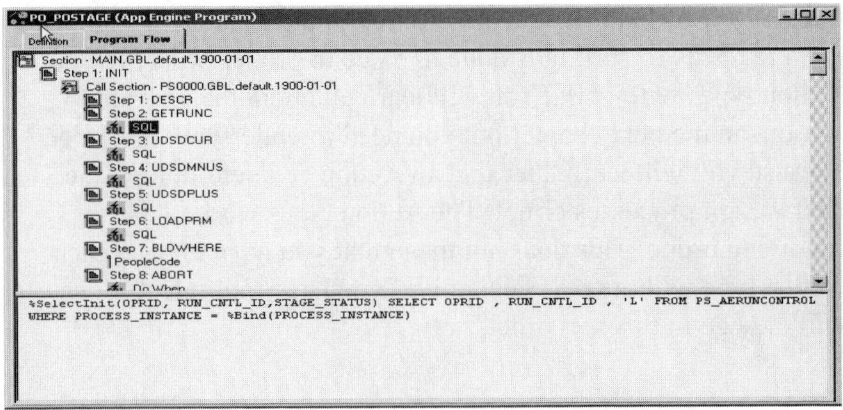

Figure 1.9 Program Flow window

This view is dramatically different from the Definition view. The purpose of this view is to show you the program in the flow of how it will work, based on your development. If you take a moment, it will be easy to understand the layout.

Starting with the Main section, you can see the next item indented (INIT) which is a Step under the Main section. On the next line (line 3), you will see a small icon showing the Action. The icon here represents a Call to a Section. On this same line to the right, you will see the Section that was called by the Action. This new Section (PS0000) has indented underneath it, it's own Steps. The first Step, DESCR, is a step without an Action that contains comments about what the further Steps are trying to do. The next Step is shown (GETRUNC) and the Actions that are going to be performed are indented underneath.

This view can be thought of as a tree with the root or base being the Main Section. A Step is the branch under the Section with the Action being the leaf. The only trick is that a leaf can call another Section. You can continue this way for as many levels as you need. This way of showing the indented program allows you to view the program in the order that Sections, Steps and Actions will be performed.

If you notice there are a series of pictures that represent specific information. This information is explained in the following table. You can use this information to help tell what an Action is trying to do by just looking at the icon, but there is text next to this icon explaining the Action specifically.

Picture	Description
SQL	SQL Actions or any Action that requires SQL such as Do When or Do Select.
	PeopleCode Action
	Calling Section Action

NOTE: *Log Messages do not show in this view. You will only see the Step without any actions.*

This Program Flow view is only for reviewing data and is not for doing development. You cannot add Sections, Steps or Actions in this view. You will have to change back to the Development view by clicking on the development tab. There is also a shortcut to move back and forth between these views. Earlier you saw in the right click menu an item called "Jump to this Program Flow". If you are in the Definition view, you can jump to the exact location where this Section or Step is being used, you cannot jump to an Action. You can also use the right click in the Program Flow window to jump back to the Development window. Here, the command is "Jump to This Definition". Again you can only jump from a Section or a Step. This command allows you to move back and forth as you read an Application Engine program, to help with understanding the flow and where a specific Step is being used.

You had in the Definition view a way to collapse and expand the various levels. In this view you do not have buttons to do this but by double clicking on a Section or Step you can get the system to collapse and then expand. The default is to show the expanded view but you can collapse if you need to, so that you can see more of your Application Engine program.

There is also a new view area that shows below in the Program Flow. This area is blank until you click on an Action of SQL or PeopleCode. Clicking once on the Action will fill this blank area with the SQL statement or PeopleCode. This view does NOT allow you to update, add or delete the SQL or PeopleCode directly. This is only a display so that you can read the PeopleCode or SQL to work through your program quickly and easily.

If you need to update the SQL or PeopleCode, you have capabilities just like you had within the Development window. You can double click on an Action that contains SQL or PeopleCode and the edit window will open. You can edit the SQL or PeopleCode in their respective edit windows. Of course, you have to save the Application Engine to make sure your changes are truly saved.

In the right click menu, as shown in figure 1.10 below, you can see the various commands that are available to you. The View SQL and View PeopleCode commands perform the same actions as double-clicking that you just learned to open up the respective editors. If you ever have a problem with the display of the Program Flow view, you can select Refresh View to have the display re-drawn. You can also show the comment by clicking on this command. This is a switch that you can flip back and forth to show the comments on a Section, Step or Action. You can also jump back to the Definition view, right to the Section or Step that you just right clicked, by selecting the Jump to this Definition command. The last command is print and this brings up a new panel. The printing capability of the Application Engine toolset is discussed in a later section entitled, "Printing".

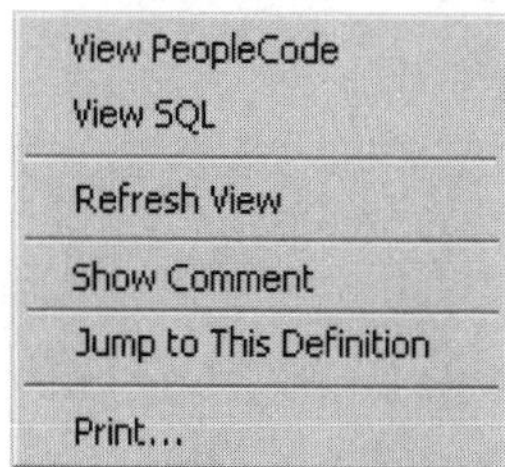

Figure 1.10 Right click menu in Program Flow window

Now that you have the development environment understood there are a few new points to learn before we move onto actual development.

Goto Section

There is a special command that helps you locate a Section within an open Application Engine program. If you happen to know the Section name but just cannot seem to find it by scrolling up and down, you can use this menu command to jump right to it. Use the menu: Edit – Goto Section. This will open a new window, as shown in figure 1.11.

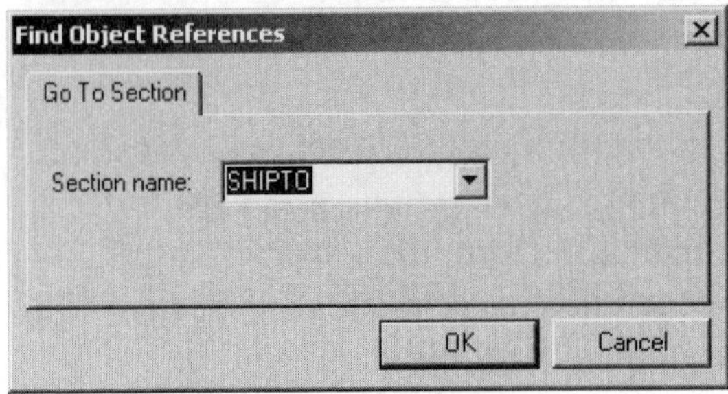

Figure 1.11 Goto Section window

You can type in the name or use the drop down to find the Section you wish to see. Then, you only have to click on the OK button and you will be taken to the Section you have chosen here in the open Application Engine program.

Another item to learn about is where an Application Engine section is used. This capability can save you valuable time finding the correct Application Engine Section.

Find Object References

Although this has not been fully discussed, you will learn later that an Application Engine Section does not only have to be in one program but you can write what is called an Application Engine Library program. An Application Engine Library program allows you to write code once and then reference and call it from the standard Application Engine program. This link is easy to see on the standard Application Engine but there may be times when you need to find everywhere this Section is used.

To use this capability, you first need to open a library Application Engine. You can open a working Application Engine program but you will only find the Sections in the program you have open. The next step is to use the menu: Edit – Find Object References. This will open the window, as shown in figure 1.12.

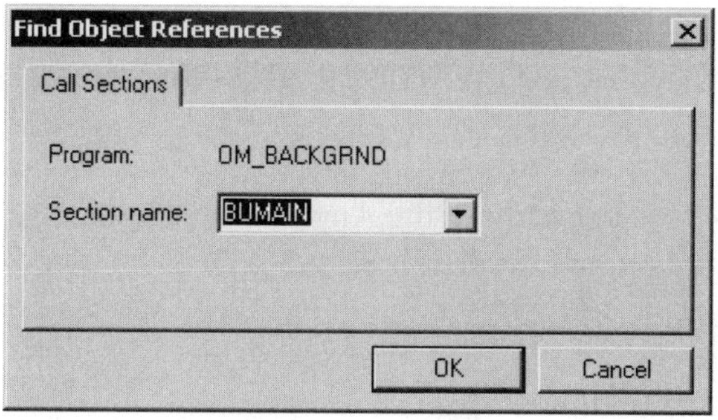

Figure 1.12

This window allows you to set the Section name you want to find. You can type in the name of the Section or use the drop down, just as you learned in the Goto Section window – they both work the same. Once you enter in the Section name and click on the OK button the Application Designer will start to process and locate all the places where this Section is used. All of this information is displayed in the Application Designer Message Area under the Find Object References tab.

The following section is an example of an output:

```
Searching for references to Program 'OM_BACKGRND2'
   Section 'BuMain2'...
Found: Program 'OM_BACKGRND2' Section 'BuMain' Step
   'BuMain2'.
Found 1 reference(s) to Program 'OM_BACKGRND' Section
   'GlpHDR'.
```

Read through this to fully understand. The first line says what the Application Designer was doing. This line shows the Application Engine program "OM_BACKGRND2" and the Section "BuMain2" was the one being searched for. The second line shows that this Section name was found in an Application Engine program. This should always happen in that the Section must be in some Application Engine Program. The third line is the special one that will show what Application Engine program is using this Section as a Library. In the example, our Library Section is being called from another Application Engine program called

OM_BACKGRND from a different Section called "GlpHDR". Here you can see that the listing in line three may be repeated multiple times so that you can see exactly where every reference of the Library Section is used.

The last item to learn is how to print out the Application Engine program. This capability is new for version 8.

Printing

There are a built in reports for Application Engine programs that allows you to review the Application Engine program in hard copy form. Sometimes it is good to have a hard copy so that you can review and scan through the program quickly and efficiently. To create a printout, you first have to open an Application Engine program. Then you use the menu: File – Print or by right clicking on any part of the Application Engine program and selecting Print from the menu offered (as you have been shown before). This will open the new Application Engine print panel, as shown in figure 1.13.

This panel is new and allows you to control what will be printed. If you had selected to print from the menu, some of the choices are not offered since it is assumed you wish the whole program to be printed. If you have right-clicked from a Step (like was done for this example) you have the option to print just the information from the Step, the Section above it or the entire program. If you look closely at figure 1.13 you will see that the check boxes in the first section – entitled Print – are only set on for the Step. This is due to the right click that was done on this Step. If this and the Section listing above it were blank with the checkbox grayed out, then you had used the menu to request a print and so the system assumes you wish to print the entire Application Engine program. These three checkboxes allow you to print just a Step, Section or the entire Program but only if you started from a Step using the right click menu.

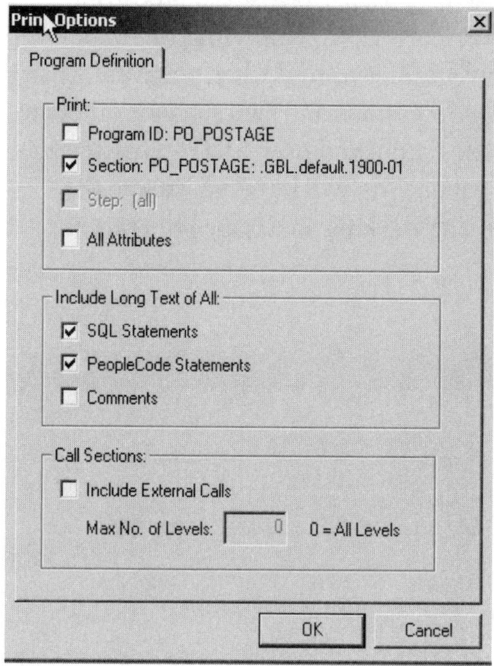

Figure 1.13 Print window.

The next section entitled, "Include Long Text of All" controls the amount of text information to be printed. Do you want to see all the PeopleCode, SQL and Comments? Select the appropriate control for your needs.

The last section – Call Sections – allows you to control how many levels down you will go if this Application Engine calls another Application Engine. This setting is to control the amount of drill down that will occur on your printout so that you can save some paper.

Once you have all your settings determined, click the OK button to have the report start printing.

You can also print to a window where you can review online but the layout is not better than what is already shown in the Application

Designer window. The purpose is to just look at how the report will print to decide on which printer to use. To perform this online print review you use the menu: File – Print Review. This will open the new Application Engine print window just like you did when you were printing the program. You can review online and then send the output to your printer. Once you review the output and/or send it to a printer you need to close the Print Review panel. You will be taken back to the Application Designer but now in the working area is the print out, as shown in figure 1.14.

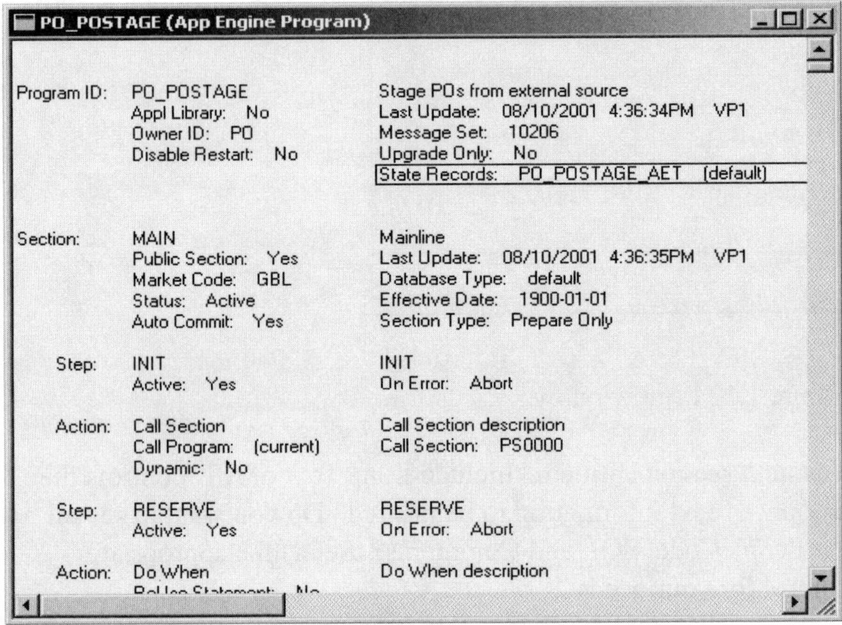

Figure 1.14 Application Engine print review window

You can see all of the information about the Application Engine program. The start of the report shows all the Header information followed by each Section. Under each Section is the Step and Action showing the SQL or PeopleCode that is within that Action. The sort order is the same that is displayed. You can review here and even save this output using the menu: File – Save As. You can open these files later using the menu: File – Report From File – View Report.

***Note**: You will get a different looking report if you print from the Program flow view. The data is the same it is just now in a different order.*

Next

Now that the first chapter is complete, you should have learned all you can to move around, view and print Application Engine programs. With this complete, you can now move onto the core of Application Engine. The next chapter teaches how to do technical work like adding Sections, Steps, Actions, SQL and PeopleCode to Application Engine programs.

Chapter 2

Using the Application Designer tool

Now that you know how to move around the Application Designer it is time to learn some specifics about how to modify Application Engine programs. You will not learn how to program in this chapter – that is for succeeding chapters – but you will learn a few more mechanics that you will need to use when you begin programming. These mechanics allow you to: add new Sections, Steps and Actions; delete Sections, Steps and Actions; Validate your Application Engine and finally work with the Projects system.

Inserting New Sections

If you start with a new Application Engine you will definitely have to insert new Sections, but you may also have to insert new Sections when you are modifying an existing Application Engine program. The process of inserting a new Section is easy and there are a few ways to accomplish this.

Note: *This assumes you are in the Definition view. If you are not, be sure to click over to the Definition Tab in the Application Engine program. All inserting and deleting of Sections, Steps and Actions are prevented in the Program Flow view.*

The easiest way to insert a new Section is through the toolbar. There is a set of buttons on the toolbar with the one on the far left looking like a scroll of paper with writing on it (see example in margin). This button, when clicked, will create a new Section immediately following the Section your cursor was last in. If you have not placed your cursor within the Application Engine program yet then the new Section will be added just after the last Section within the program.

You can also add a new Section through the menu by clicking: Insert – Section. There is also a HOT key for this – holding down the Ctrl key and type the number one (Ctrl-1), which will perform the same action.

Finally, there is the right click menu you learned how to use in Chapter 1. You can right click on any existing Section, Step or Action then select within the menu Insert Section (see Figure 1.6).

No matter which process you choose to add a new Section, the results are the same in where the Section is created. If we continue to use our example program (PO_POSTAGE) and add a new Section you get the results as shown in figure 2.1.

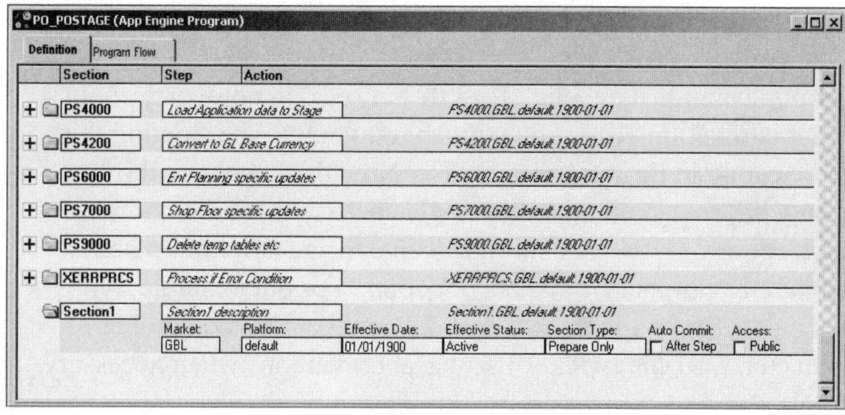

Figure 2.1 PO_POSTAGE with new Section

Section Controls

You can see our new Section was added to the end of the program. Note the defaults used on the name and description. This is not very informative so this is the first thing that you change. If you change the Section name (Section1) to APPLYFRT (the name at this point is just made up) you will be forced to save the Application Engine program. In fact, you will see a pop-up window appear that gives you this warning, as shown in figure 2.2. If you click on cancel to prevent the save then your Section name will be changed back to what it was. You have to click the OK button to commit the change.

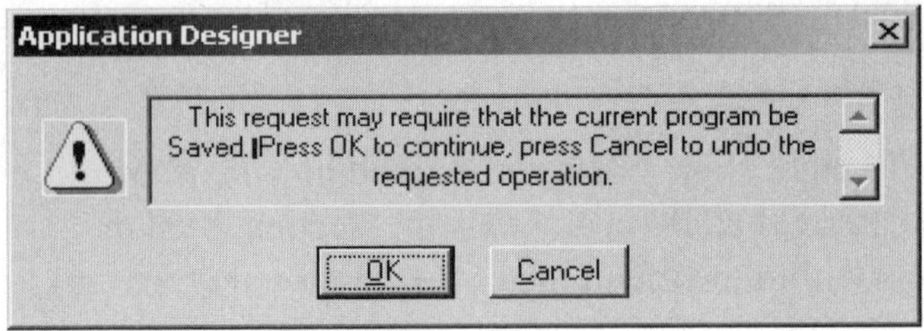

Figure 2.2 Save Warning

Warning: *If you are working on a live system do not commit this change as you may cause a program to crash. Only work within an environment where it is acceptable to be doing modification and development work.*

For our example here, click the OK button. Do not worry about this modification becoming permanent; you will be deleting this new Section in the next area below. Now that you have the name changed, you can edit the other fields here without any more interruptions. First, you should change the description to better explain the purpose of this new Section. For our example, type 'Calculate Special Freight Chg'. There are a limited number of characters you can type (30) so use abbreviations when necessary.

The next field you can change is the Market. This field represents a specific language so that if you have multi-language needs you can have specific statements for a specific language. This allows you to write one Application Engine program that may work differently depending on the location or the language being used. This is an advanced concept so only use this when you have to and under the direction of your management. For now, just leave this field as GBL, for Global. Next comes the Platform field. This field is like the language field but now we are concerned on the database that this program is going to run on. There are some quirks, or specific functions, that work in one database but not another; or there may be specific formats that need to be followed to perform a specific SQL task. This allows you to write statements that are specific for a database platform. With the old version of PeopleSoft (7.5) there used to be a problem with formatting dates for each database version but you will find in this new version the problems are almost non-existent. This is due to the addition of PeopleCode and some new Meta SQL variables that have been worked into this new version. These all will be explained in the later chapters. For now, leave this field as is – set on default (which means all databases use this Step).

Handling Effective Dates

The next two fields are Effective Date and Effective Status. These two fields, although separate, are used together to generate the necessary controls. This Effective Date Process allows you to inactivate a Section so that it is no longer used. The reason you would do this instead of just deleting the Section is so that you can see the change history. This may not seem important now but this will be when 6 months or a year later someone asks why this program was changed. You can see specifically what was done and this will help with understanding what to do in the future, including any new upgrades that need to be accomplished.

To use Effective Dates you have a few options. If you are no longer using a Section you can just go in and set the status flag to inactive but this does not really pass any information on except that this Section is no longer used. If you want to do this correctly, you would copy a Section (see the following section entitled Copying a Section) and then set the new Section Effective Date to today and the Status to inactive. This now shows that this section was used once but on this date it was turned off.

If you want to change a Section showing new logic, you just add a new Section, change the Effective Date to today, set the Status to active and change the Name to the old Section. What this shows is that on this date (today) this Section was changed to the new code line.

Now that you fully understand the use of Effective Dates and the Status we can proceed with learning the rest of the fields.

Next up is the Section Type field. This field is highly specialized for controlling processes within the Section that if not completed will cause the program or data to be out of sync. By setting this value to 'Critical Update', you are telling the system that if this Section does not complete it must be run over again in total. If the Section is not critical, you can leave this value at 'Prepare Only'. For 99% of the time you will leave this value at 'Prepare Only'.

The next field is Auto Commit. This is normally turned off when you add a new Section. If you turn this value on, then you will force the program to commit (meaning save to the database) after each Step that processes a SQL command or PeopleCode function. This should only be turned on if you understand the process of restart. This is all explained in a later section entitled Commits.

The last field, called Access, is used to set whether you want to allow this Section to be called by another Application Engine program. You will learn about this when you get down to the Adding Actions section below. You can allow outside use of this Section by clicking on the Public checkbox. The normal default is to have this value turned off.

Now you have completed all the fields within a Section but your work is not done. If you notice, you will see that you have a Section without a Step or Action. You will need to learn how to add Steps and Actions; which is covered in the next few sections below but first you need to learn how to delete a Section.

Deleting Sections

Deleting a Section is very straightforward. There are three ways to delete a Section but all require that you first click and highlight the Section that you wish to delete. Once a Section is highlighted you can use the menu: Edit – Delete, just type the delete key or right click on the Section and select Delete in the menu (this is the menu you saw back in Chapter 1). You will need to save the Application Engine program to have your delete stay, but that is all there is to it.

If you delete the Section, you have also deleted all the Steps and Actions within the Section as well. This can be looked upon as a short cut but there are a few caveats to be aware of. If you have loaded all of your objects into a project, you will need to manually remove any SQL or PeopleCode objects from the project that were contained within the deleted Section. If you do not, then you will have a minor problem when you migrate this project to another database. You will receive an error that states this SQL object or PeopleCode object within the project cannot be placed into the Application Engine Section as defined. This does not corrupt or prevent the program from working – its only an error message to the project migration and is just a nuisance.

Copying a Section

This function allows you to not only copy a Section but also all the Steps and Actions within a Section. This is normally used in combination with an Effective Date or Status change. To perform a copy of a Section, you first have to click on the Section to copy, so that it is highlighted. Once you have the Section highlighted, you then click on the menu: Edit – Copy or you can right click on the Section to get the menu and select Copy. In either case this will copy the Section including all the Steps and Actions.

***Warning**: This copy process will only work within an Application Program and not between Application Engine programs*

Now that you have the Section copied, you can click again on a Section to choose where it will be placed. If you remember, back in Chapter One, the placement of Sections do not matter as the Application Designer will re-sort the order based on the name. This sets up for where the paste will occur. To do the paste, you can use the menu: Edit – Paste or the right click menu: Paste. Once you run this command, the new Section will be added with all the Steps and Actions. The name of the Steps and Actions are the same but the name of the Section has changed slightly. The Section name is changed by adding a number to the name or removing the last character and putting a number in. In either case, this is the default that takes place. If you are trying to copy a Section to reset the Effective Date, you first need to change the Effective Date and then you can change the Section name back to exactly match the Section you copied it from. If the Effective Date and the Section names are the same, then you will not be allowed to save this Application Engine Program. Either the Section name or the Effective Date has to be different. Note figure 2.3 to show a copied Section PS0000 into PS0001.

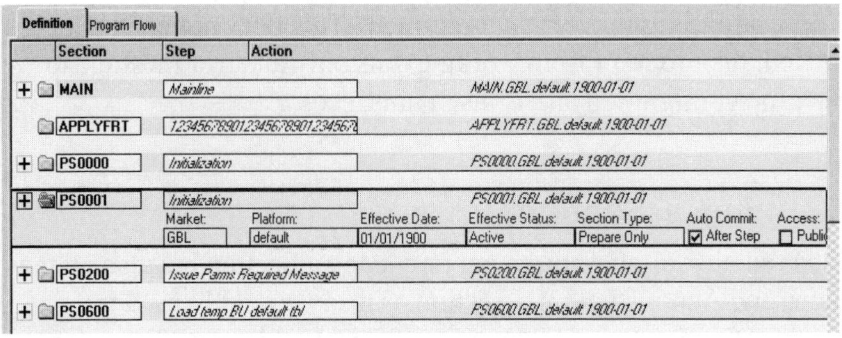

Figure 2.3 Application Engine copied Section

Once a copy is done you will likely need to change the Actions, as these are exact copies from the copied Section. You can do this at any time but just remember you must save the Application Engine program otherwise your changes will be lost.

Inserting New Steps

Once you have copied a Section or created a new one you will find that you need to add new Steps. This process is easy to do, with multiple ways to obtain your needs. Now Steps are slightly different than Sections; as the order and location of a Step is paramount to it's operation while Sections are just holders of Steps. This means you must very carefully select the location to add your new Step. You do this by clicking within a Section onto a Step where you want your new Step to follow. If you need to add a Step to be first in a Section (in front of all the other Steps), you can then highlight the Section and your new Step will be added, first.

For our example here, you are going to be adding a new step within the section PS0200 right after the step AbortMsg. To start, open the section of PS0200 by clicking on the plus symbol and then click once on the step AbortMsg to highlight it. Your screen should look just like it shows here, in figure 2.4.

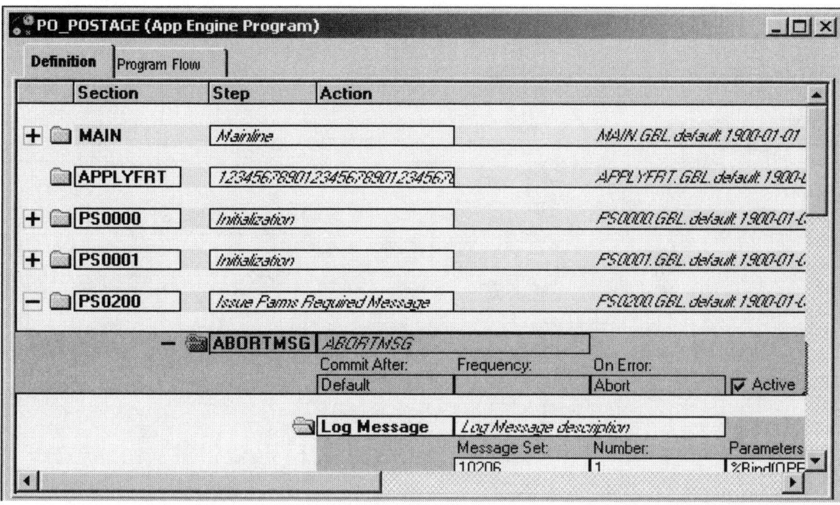

Figure 2.4 AbortMsg Step highlighted

There are three ways to now add a Step; the menu, the right click menu or the toolbar button. You can use the menu: Insert – Step/ Action. This will insert a new Step as well as a new Action. You can also right click on the Step AbortMsg to display the menu you have seen before. Then you select the Insert Step/Action menu choice to have the new Step added, as well as a new Action.

The last way is to use the button on the toolbar that is shown here. This button will perform the same action, adding a new Step and Action as you have seen from the menus.

Note: When you add a new Step a new blank Action is also added to the new Step since every Step is to have an Action. This is done as an aid to you, the developer.

Use one of the above methods to add a new Step and Action. Your Application Engine window should now look like the one here, in figure 2.5.

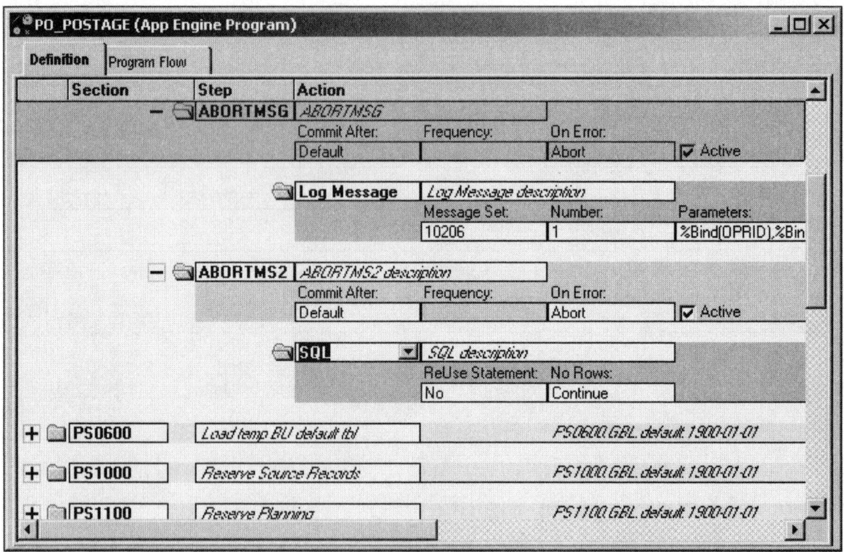

Figure 2.5 New Step and Action added.

Again, note that the Step name has been set almost the same as the Step you were just on. The difference is that the name has had a number added to the end. If we had added another Step, it would have been designated AbortMs3. You can see how this naming process works. Looking closely you will also see that a default description has been put in place; you can change this at any time. It is good practice to name the Step as well as the description with as much information as you can; to help succeeding developers in figuring out what this Step and Action are trying to perform.

Also note the Action that was added. You will learn about this in detail in the next few sections but a few words here would be helpful. The Action is set with a default Type and a default description that you will want to set later. You can change this Action, delete or add new ones as you see fit.

Step Controls

Before you move on further, you need to learn all of the controls on the Step. First is the Step name, this is just a name of the Step; you are limited to 8 characters. Normally, you would want to have this Step named something that would allow you to understand the purpose of this Step. Since you only have 8 characters you should keep it simple and rely more on the description field to fully describe the Step purpose.

The next Step property to define is the Commit After field. This field controls when the database is committed to all of the changes in the program. The default is "Default", which means the control is not set here but allows the Section control to choose. Refer to the section above, "Section Controls", if you need to go over the Section controls again. The other two choices are Later and After Step. The control, Later, forces the commit to occur later; even if the Section control was to Auto-commit. A setting here on the Step overrides the Section control unless you leave it at Default. The After Step setting is usually used when the Section Auto-commit setting was placed on None (meaning no commits within the Section) so that you can force a commit. The setting of After Step will force a database commit after all the Actions within the Step have completed.

The Frequency control only works with Actions of Do Select, Do Until or Do While. The Action types are SQL calls that are going to loop through sets of data. The frequency will force a commit, if you have set up for commits to occur, every n times of the number that you enter here. This field only takes number value entries. You should set this value in case of large SQL calls that will load the buffers of your database and potentially slow it down. Talk with your Database Administrator about setting this value if your Application Engine encounters this problem.

The on Error field controls the reaction of the Application Engine program if an error is encountered while performing SQL commands or PeopleCode. If a warning occurs, these settings are not followed. The default is Abort, which means that the Application Engine program will report an error to the log and abort (stop) the program with an error status on the Process Scheduler. The Ignore setting allows a log file error to be captured but it will not stop the program from continuing. Only use this setting if you are sure that when having an error any further processing can continue. Usually when you have an error, you want the program to stop; since later Steps depend on earlier processes being completed.

The last setting is the Active checkbox that is defaulted on. If you want to stop the Step from processing, you only have to uncheck this box and then all the code within the Step will be skipped. This simple checkbox allows you to turn on and off all the code and SQL within the Step easily. This is how you normally will cancel a Step versus deleting a Step.

Deleting Steps

Once you have a Step within an Application Engine you may have a reason later to delete it. It is not recommended you do this. You should inactivate the Step so that the Application Engine program will no longer use that Step and you can have history in the Application Engine program as to the removal of this Step. With this warning given, you can still delete a Step if you require. To delete a Step, you first have to highlight the Step that you wish to delete. Click on your newly added Step AbortMs2 to start the delete process. You have three ways to delete the Step. You can use the main menu: Edit – Delete or the right click menu: Delete. The last way is to just type the Delete key. In any case, you will receive a pop-up window asking for you to confirm your request to delete this Step, as shown in figure 2.6.

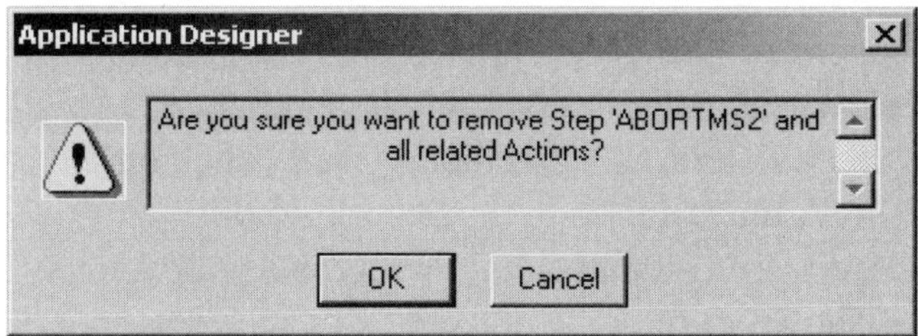
Application Designer
Are you sure you want to remove Step 'ABORTMS2' and all related Actions?
OK
Cancel

Figure 2.6 Delete Confirm.

By clicking the OK button you will confirm the delete of the Step and all of the Actions associated with this Step. If you click the Cancel button, you will abort the delete. Remember that you still need to save the Application Engine to commit the delete.

***Warning**: If you delete a Step, any Actions connected to the Step are also deleted.*

Copying Steps

You have a special capability that allows you to copy a Step. You will want to do this when you are building a fairly large program or you have similar Steps to create. This Copy and Paste process will allow you to build not only the Step but the Action(s) as well. Just like you had to highlight the Step to delete it, you also have to highlight the Step to copy it. Once you have this Step highlighted, you can copy it. You can do this by using the main menu: Edit – Copy, right click menu: Copy or the standard Copy button on the Application Designer toolbar. Once you have the Step copied you can then click on where you want the new Step to be pasted. You need to highlight the Step after which you want the new Step placed. This is the same as when you added a new Step.

You could, of course, just add new Steps but with the Copy process you not only get the Step, but you also get the Actions. You do not just get a blank Action with default information; you get the Action with all of the underlying PeopleCode or SQL. This gets you the real benefit of copying not only the Step and the Action but also the code or SQL within the Action.

To show the full benefit of this, copy the Step GETRUNC under the Section PS0001. Be sure to highlight the Step and then perform the Copy in one of the three methods. Next, click on the Step CATTYPE (this is the last Step in the Section PS0001) to paste your copied Step. You should end up with the Application Engine program as shown in figure 2.7.

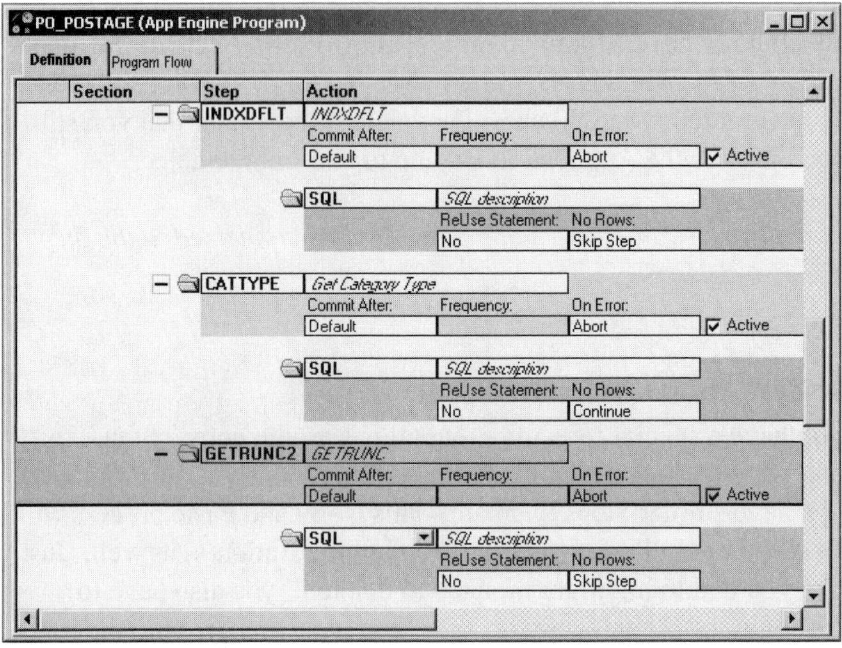

Figure 2.7 Copied Step.

You can see the new Step using the newly made Name but note that the description is an exact copy. Also, the Action Type and description are also copied exactly. Once you open the Action you will also see that this Action contains the SQL code; since our Step contained one Action that was of the SQL type. Now you can open this Action and modify the SQL code, if required. If this were an Action with PeopleCode or a Log message then those would have been copied as well. This leads right into the next section, learning all about Actions.

Adding Actions

The Action is where you put in the PeopleCode, messages and SQL that make the Application Engine program work. First, you need to learn how to add an Action and then you will learn more about the different types of Actions.

First, remember that you have already added Actions back when you added Steps. This process works just fine but you are allowed to have more than one Action per Step; there is only one limitation. You can only have one type of Action under each Step. This will be explained later, in Chapter 5, when you get to actual coding.

To add an Action, you first have to highlight the Action behind which you want the new Action placed. If you want the Action to be first in the list, then you have to highlight the Step and it will be added first. Once you have the Step or the Action highlighted, you can then add your new Action. You have three ways to do this (see a common thread here?). You can use the main menu: Insert – Action, right click menu: Insert Action or the toolbar. You can see the toolbar icon in the margin at the beginning of this paragraph.

***Note**: Even though you can define the order of the Action it will not remain this way. You learned this sort order in Chapter 1.*

Action Controls

The above process is all you have to do to add a new Action. The Action is a blank slate with a default Name and description - you can add these items any time you like. The other controls on the Actions depend on the Action type selected. Each of these types will be discussed in the next few sections. To set an Action type, you just click within the first drop down box (there is no heading on this field).

Each Type also has a description field that you should change to match the purpose of the code, SQL, message or whatever the statement is attempting to perform. This will be very helpful to any developer that reviews your program later.

SQL

This Action Type is used most since the object of a program is to manipulate data. Here, you write your SQL statements that can select, update, delete or insert data. Once you have set the type you can define the Re Use Statement.

Re Use Control

This field is used to control SQL database parameters. The values allowed are No (this is the default), Yes and Bulk Insert.

No	This tells the database that the SQL statement is to be re-compiled every time it is run; requiring some work on the database server. This setting is the default and allows the most freedom.
Yes	This tells the database that the SQL statement can be compiled once, allowing re-use. This setting may help performance but can only be done if the SQL statement does not change during a loop. This is typically used on looping select statements. A cursor is built to allow the database to process through the set of data one row at a time without re-building the SQL statement over and over. Since the SQL statement is built once you cannot have any value change within the where statement for the entire set of data. If a value needs to change then you must use the "No" setting.
Bulk Insert	This should only be used when doing an Insert. This allows specific databases to use a special process to load data that will vastly increase performance.

The decision to use which of the settings above should involve your DBA.

The next setting is the control of the No Rows. This allows you to take control if you proceed to the next Action. This setting is used when 0 rows are returned from a select statement, 0 rows are affected by an update statement or if 0 rows are inserted with an insert statement. The settings are listed below.

Setting Value	Description
Continue	This is the default value and if 0 rows are returned, by what ever means, the next Action will be performed. Basically, there is no change if 0 rows in the SQL statement is affected.
Abort	This setting states that if 0 rows are affected, this entire Program is aborted, as if an error had occurred. This will hard abort the program even if the Step had been setup to ignore errors and continue.
Skip Step	This setting says to skip any further Actions within this Step allowing you to bypass them all with a type of conditional logic.
Section Break	This setting forces not only the remaining Actions within the Step but also all of the remaining Steps within this Section to be skipped. The program then starts based on the where the call was to this Section. If this is done on the Main Section, then the program stops.

Use of NoRows

Before you move onto the next field, make sure you really understand the capability you are given here. By allowing you to skip Actions and Steps you can use these values to do some conditional logic. For example, there may be a set of data that you want to update if a specific condition exists. You could have a SQL statement select data here but if 0 rows are returned, meaning the condition does not exist, you could skip the next Action or the next Steps. You will learn better ways to do this type of Action later but this shows you how to use the No Rows control.

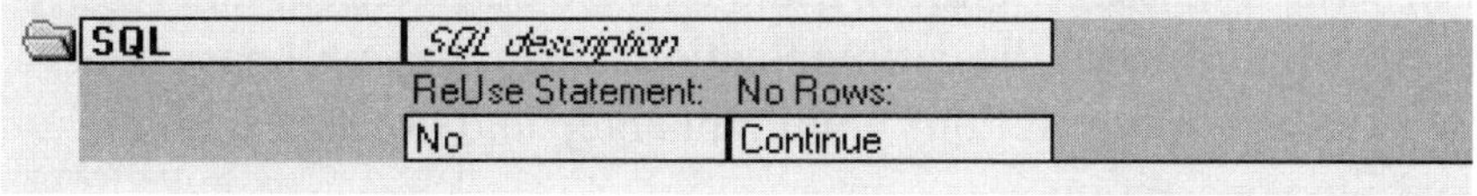

SQL	SQL description	
	ReUse Statement:	No Rows:
	No	Continue

Figure 2.8 SQL Action

PeopleCode

PeopleCode is probably the second most used Action type and the newest to the Application Engine program. This allows you to really use Application Engine since one of the hardest things, previously, was to process single rows of data and make logic decisions. There are a few restrictions on the use of which functions and methods you can use but 90% of the PeopleCode you can use in the standard Record and Page code, you can use here as well.

There is one thing that you must use the PeopleCode for: file output and input. The file output and input process allows you to take data in tables and write them out quickly, or the reverse, easily. This will be fully explained in Chapter 7 since this is important to use; and you have to coordinate Application Engine, PeopleCode, Record definitions and File Definitions.

The PeopleCode Action type only has two controls. First is the description and the second is the On Return field. You should know what to do with the description by now. The On Return field allows you to control logic flow just as was done with the SQL No Rows control. You have three allowable settings: Abort, Break and Skip Step. Each of these controls are processed by a return value from the PeopleCode Action. If you do not define a return value then it is assumed to be a True value. You can set this return value within your PeopleCode based on an action, value or process (you will learn how to do this in Chapter 3). The value is then reviewed and if False, the On Return value is processed. Abort means that the Application Engine program will write a message to the log and then end the problem in an error status. Break means the program will write a message to the log and exit the current Step and Section returning to the calling Section. Skip Step will pass over (or skip) any more Actions within this Step and proceed with the next Step or Section.

Note*: You will find that PeopleSoft has coded a lot of their delivered Application Engine programs to use this On Return process to skip SQL Action statements if conditions are correct.*

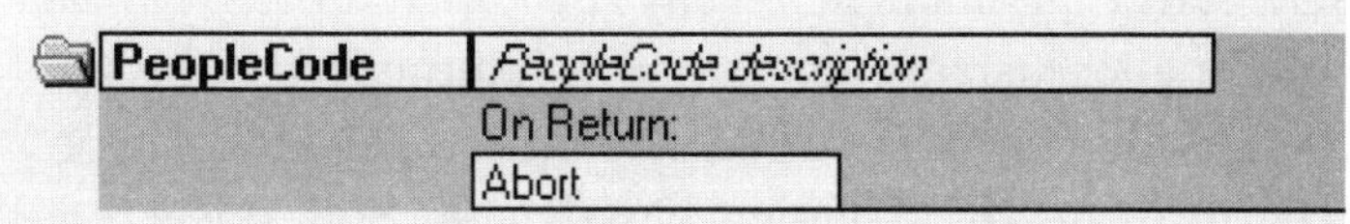

Figure 2.9 PeopleCode Action

Log Message

This Action type allows you to force a message to the Message log so that it can be reviewed after the Application Engine program is complete. You can use this to help debug Application Engine programs, as well as provide information such as outputting the number of rows processed, the Business unit used, or any type of message.

This type of Action is fairly easy to use with the controls to set the Message Set and number of the Message to apply to the Log. The parameter field also allows you to pass variables into the Message using the standard process, assuming the Message has set variables to be input. The list of variable(s) here should be a comma-separated list. You can only use Hard coded values or Bind variables. You have not learned about BIND variables yet (see Chapter 4) but you can think of them as simple variables.

A trick to use here is to create a special Message that accepts only variables so that you can then supply them in this Action type. You can then use this Message to do all kinds of debugging and information passing for any Application Engine program as you develop and test.

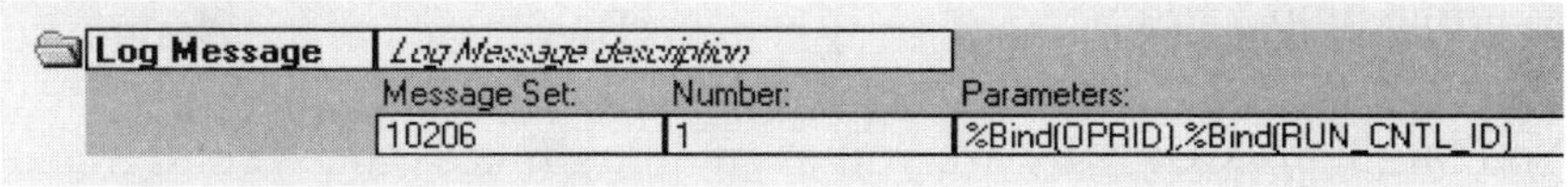

Log Message | Log Message description
Message Set: 10206 | Number: 1 | Parameters: %Bind(OPRID),%Bind(RUN_CNTL_ID)

Figure 2.10 Log Message Action

Do When

This Action is of a special type that allows you to control the flow of the Application Engine program. The process here is that you will write a SQL select statement that if any rows are returned (the data selected does not matter just that you get a row returned) then the following Actions within this Step will be performed. This Action type allows you to perform an "IF" statement based on the SQL select statement. You will find this Action type used within PeopleSoft a great deal.

Here is an example of how this can be used: First, you review the Customer outstanding AR balance and when a certain limit is reached you want to update the Customer Master record with a flag setting. To do this you would create the Do When Action type with a SQL statement, such as:

```
Select customer_id from ps_customer where ar_balance >
30000.
```

The next Action you could add to this same Step would be a SQL type where you would input an insert statement to load a reporting record.

```
Insert into ps_ss_cst_ar select setid, cust_id,
ar_balance, %Currentdateout from ps_customer where
ar_balance > 30000.
```

Note, in this example, the information or selection of the customer id is NOT passed on to the second SQL Action statement. Each statement runs on it's own without passing information to the next Action. That is why you see the same where clause in both SQL statements. If you needed to pass the customer id information to the next statement you should use a Do Select loading the customer id into a bind variable.

You might also ask why are you even doing this as the second SQL statement could be run on it's own? This is true for this simple example but you need to understand this point. By using the Do When you can determine if you need to do one Action or by using a Call Section Action type multiple Actions. This can save processing time for checking if a condition exists and to then skip if nothing is returned.

Do When | Do When description
ReUse Statement:
No

Call Section | Call Section description
Section Name: PS0200 | Program ID: PO_POSTAGE | Dynamic

Figure 2.11 Do When Action – with Call Section following

Do While

The Do While Action is similar to the Do When Action with one minor exception. You will create a SQL select statement that, if true, will run all Actions following this Action but after all the Actions within the Step are done, this Action will run again selecting data all over again. This type forces a loop condition; the same as if you had programmed a While loop in SQR. The SQL in the Do While Action is run every time through the loop until no more rows are returned so the following Actions within the Step are skipped and the program resumes on the next Step within the Section.

The Do While Action is not used a great deal since these loops really are not done all that much with the Application Engine programs. You do not really want to think in terms of loop processing but rather more in terms of set processing. If you need more help with set processing, see Chapter 8, which will explain it in more detail.

***Note**: Be sure to have some way to exit this loop or your program will never finish.*

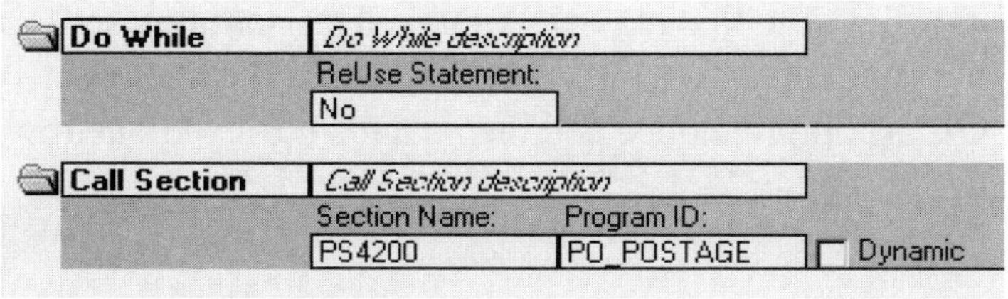

Do While | Do While description
ReUse Statement:
No

Call Section | Call Section description
Section Name: PS4200 | Program ID: PO_POSTAGE | Dynamic

Figure 2.12 Do While Action

Do Select

The Do Select Action takes a SQL select statement and will run subsequent Actions within this Step (remember the order back in chapter 1), the same number of times as to how many rows were returned from the SQL statement. Where as in the Do While Action you had an undefined looping condition, here you have a fixed number of times to run through a set of Action statements.

You can also use this Action to do row by row processing. PeopleSoft does use this Action type processing in their delivered Application Engine programs. This, and much more, will be explained in Chapter 11 on the row-by-row process, its uses and why it should only be used when necessary.

The controls here are the same as you have already learned with then Re Use statement but now there is a new control – Do Select Type.

Do Select Type

This control configures how the Do Select process runs. It also will impact on the Restart-ability of this Step. Normally, a Do Select Action will not be re-startable in the middle but will have to re-start at the beginning of the process. Review each setting to see the process and the impact to the restart.

Select/Fetch

Select/Fetch is the default setting that does not allow this Step to be re-started in the middle. This is accomplished by not allowing any commits to the database even if Sections or Steps are set to commit while still within this Do Select loop. This setting also determines that a cursor process will be used within the database so that the SQL is complied once and then data is retrieved one row at a time using this cursor.

Re-Select

Re-Select changes the SQL select process in that each time a new row is needed, the SQL is compiled and run again. Since each row is a new SQL statement, you can re-start this Action type; there is one caveat. You need to have in subsequent Actions the ability to manipulate the data in the original Action select in order to remove, update or change the data, so that the SQL select no longer finds these rows that have already been processed. If you do not do this, then you may encounter situations where you will not exit this loop since the SQL re-runs for each row selection; acting like the Do While Action type.

Re-Startable

Re-Startable works just like the Select/Fetch but you have been allowed, with a special override to re-start this Step. Now, nothing is done to allow the re-start so you have to put in all the code to do a proper re-start. This means that if the program was on row 26 of 75 rows you have to control the code to start on the proper row, otherwise it will start on row 1 as normal. You can do this by having a flag on the Record in the select statement and while in the loop you set this flag to a processed status. That way when the SQL for this Do Select re-starts, it will only see rows where the flag has not be set to processed status.

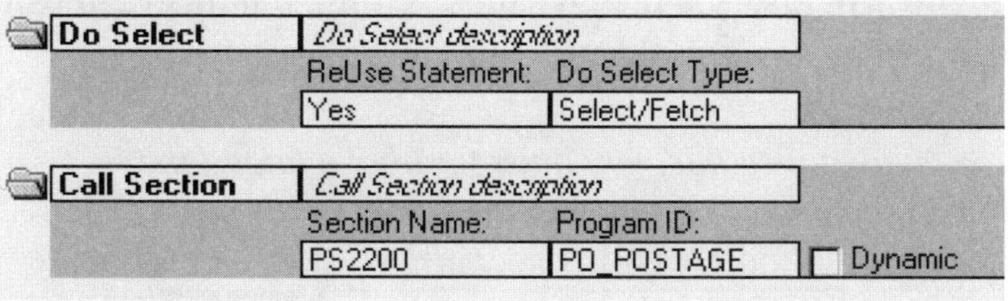

Figure 2.13 Do Select Action

Do Until

Do Until works the same as a Do While but the SQL Select of the Do Until is run AFTER all the other Actions within this Step. The main difference is that the other Actions will run no matter what and then the Do Until SQL will run seeing whether you are going to loop through the Actions again.

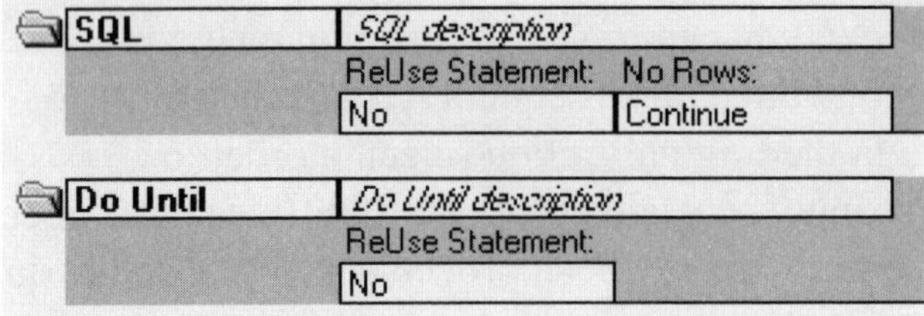

Figure 2.14 Do Until Action

Call Section

Call Section is a simple call to another Section that has already been created. The call can go to another Section within the Application Engine Program as well as be a call to another Application Engine program that has been set up as a Library.

First you will see the standard description field followed by the Section name. This is where you input the Section name – note that the Program ID is already input with the current Application Engine program name. If you want to use a Library, you first have to set the name here and then the Section name within that library. You will learn more about using and creating library functions in Chapter 4. You will also see the Dynamic setting, but this field can be ignored, as it has no control here.

Warning: *When you use this, you must first have added the Sections since they need to appear in the list.*

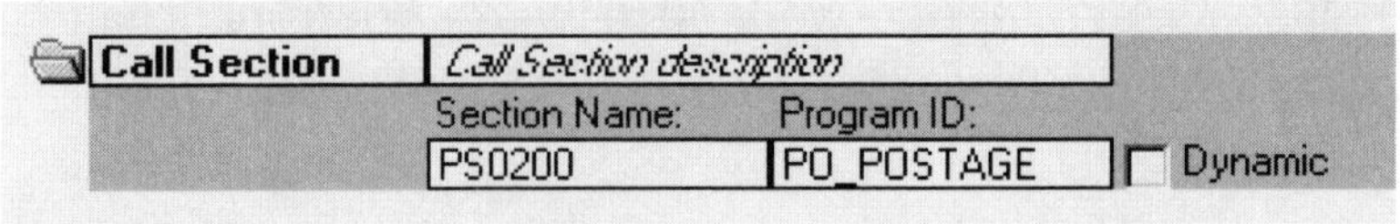

Call Section | Call Section description
Section Name: PS0200 | Program ID: PO_POSTAGE | Dynamic

Figure 2.15 Call Section Action

Deleting Actions

You will need to delete Actions in the process of the developing Application Engine programs. Normally, you should just inactivate the Step but sometimes you just need to delete. First you have to select the Action by clicking on it once. This will highlight the Action. Now, you can use one of three methods to delete the Action: Main menu – Edit - Delete, right click menu - Delete or the delete key.

Validation

The Validation process is unique to the Application Engine program. It allows you to validate that the Application Engine is built correctly, SQL is not missing or that there are empty PeopleCode objects. It is a type of process that checks to make sure all is in order and gives you a message if any problems are encountered.

To launch this process, use the main menu: Edit – Validate Program Now. This will launch the validate process and display any errors in the message area (under the validate tab) of the Application Designer window. You will see any errors or problems here if any exist.

Note*: This will not guarantee your program will work. It will just validate that all the correct objects have been created within your program.*

You can save an Application Engine program with validation errors as you will want to save your work often even when its only half done. You will even find cases where delivered PeopleSoft Application Engine program fail validation because of the old way in which comments were added in earlier versions i.e. Sections without Actions.

Once you have your program complete, you need to add it to a project to allow easy migration between the development, testing and production databases. There are also numerous other reasons to add objects to a project but those are not discussed in this book; it is assumed you already know this information. Attaching your Application Engine to a project is addressed next as there is a special condition that you need to be aware of.

Attaching the Application Engine program to a Project

The Application Engine program you have completed or modified now needs to be placed into a project. This is an easy process but you have to be careful as an Application Engine program can be made up of 3 different object types. Each type is discussed below showing why this object is there, what it includes and how to add it to a project.

Adding Application Engine to the Project

Application Engine is the main program and must be included in the project if any of the other object types are also to be included. There are only a few cases where you do not need to do this but they are few. It is recommended that you always load the Application Engine program to the project, as there are no drawbacks to doing so.

There are two ways to add Application Engine program to your project. First, and the easiest, is when you have the Application Engine program open in the Application Designer (work area). Just use the main menu: Insert – Current Object into Project of the hot key of F7. This will add the Application Engine program directly to the project. Don't forget to save the project or your changes will not be saved. The second way is to add the Application Engine program manually. First you use the main menu: Insert – Objects into Project. This opens a new window, as shown in figure 2.16.

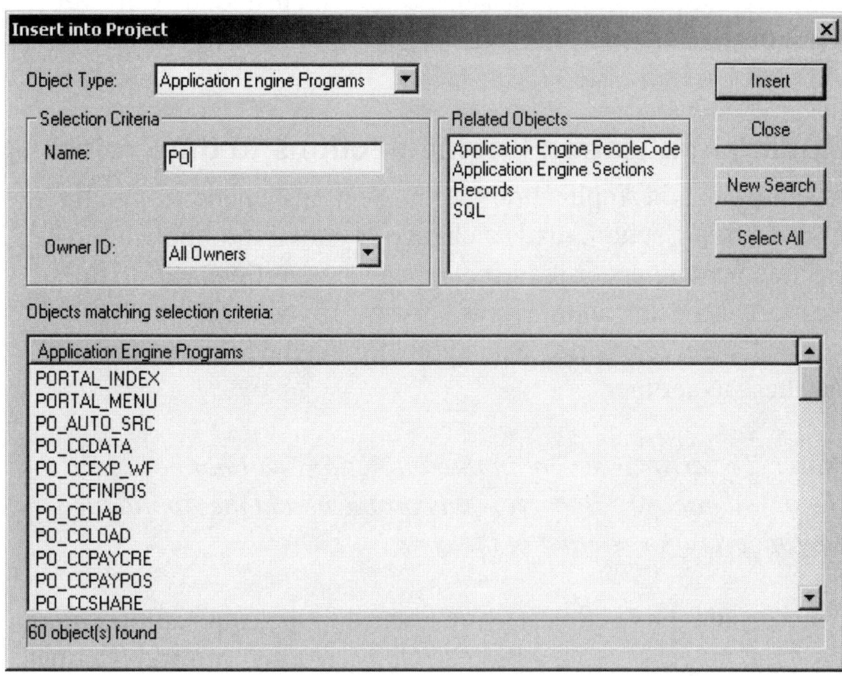

Figure 2.16 Insert into Project

This will change the window to show the related objects to the Application Engine program. In the Name field, you type in the name of the Application Engine program or just the first few characters. Click the Insert button to have the list on this Insert into Project window filled in with Application Engine programs. Scroll through this list to find the Application Engine program you wish to add. Double click on the Application Engine program name or click once on the name of the program and then click the Insert button again to add the Application Engine program to the open project.

If you look in the Related Objects area you will see all the related objects of an Application Engine program. You can also, at the same time, move these objects linked to the main Application Engine program. To do this you click on one of the Related Objects. You can select more than one by holding down the Ctrl

Key. Even though this process takes a bit longer to add an Application Engine to the project you can add the program in one stroke as well as some or all of the related objects.

Adding Application Engine Sections to the Project

You need to add Application Engine Sections whenever you have added a new Section, made a change to one of the Application Section parameters or made any changes to Actions within the Section; including adding new Actions. If you forget to do this, you will receive an error when you migrate the project from one database to another.

Note: *The error is severe in that all Actions will not be copied to the new database. To correct this problem, add the Application Engine Section specified in the error.*

You can add the Sections as you learned in the Application Engine program process (using a Related Object) or you can add Sections directly. Just as you did for Application Engine programs, use the main menu: Insert – Objects into Project. Instead of selecting "Application Engine program", select "Application Engine Sections". The panel looks very much like the one used for Application Engine programs. Enter the name of the Application Engine program and click on the Insert button to have all the Sections within the Application Engine program display. If you enter only a portion of the Application Engine name, you will then see all Sections for all of the Application Engine programs listed. Scroll through the list to find the one or many Sections you wish to add to your project. You can double click or select the Section by clicking once and then clicking the Insert Button.

You also have the ability to add the Action Related Objects for each Section as well. You first have to select the Related Object by clicking on the object name (you can select multiple objects by holding down the Ctrl key). You can see that by using this feature, Insert into Project, you can add objects to your project quickly and cover issues so that you will not get errors when you proceed to migrate the project.

Adding Action Items to the Project

Adding Action Items to the Project is a bit different. You have to understand that not all Actions can be added to a project. The Action types of Log Message and Call Section do not require being added to a project. You should, however, add the Application Engine Section and the Message to your project as independent objects. All the other Action types fall into SQL or PeopleCode category.

You can, as you have learned previously, add these Actions by marking the Related Objects. To add these objects directly you have only one process to use. You must first open the Action object in the Application Designer work area. To open an Action object you have to be in the Application Engine program - you can be in either the Definition or Program flow view. Reviewing the program (be sure you have expanded the Section where you Action is) double click in any non-field area. This will open the Action object – either SQL or PeopleCode. Once you have the object open, use the main menu: Insert – Current Object into Project of hot key of F7. This will add the Action object to your project.

Migrating the Application Engine program

Once you have all your Application Engine programs and all the related objects added to your project you then can migrate this project to another database or you can export to a file to send to another PeopleSoft system. The actual process of migration is not taught here as it is just the next step that you normally would do as a developer (it is an assumed skill) or you would contact an administrator to move this for you.

Next

Now that you have all the basic movement and functions down it is time to move into one of the new areas. With the release of version 8, you are now allowed to do PeopleCode within Application Engine. This is very exciting stuff that will allow you to code very powerful and fast programs. Having this new capability means there are new things to learn and how best to use them. This new capability makes Application Engine easy to program logic that was nearly impossible in earlier versions.

Chapter 3

Understanding PeopleCode

With the new release of PeopleTools version 8 (and above) you now have the capability of using PeopleCode within Application Engine programs. This new capability allows the Application Engine program to perform complex programs by enabling logic commands, variable assignments and other standard programming constructs. Prior to version 8 you were restricted to programming within SQL statements only. This led to programs that were difficult to read and understand because the programs were trying to simulate standard programming constructs with SQL.

With the addition of PeopleCode, PeopleSoft has given a great capability to the Application Engine program that few developers in the past liked to use due to the complexity. Now, Application Engine is a highly capable and recommended development programming system. This Chapter will teach you how to use PeopleCode within the Application Engine program. This Chapter also covers prime examples of how PeopleCode is written and used, including full explanations.

To fully learn the use of PeopleCode, you have to understand its proper use and capabilities. These are taught next, along with specific examples.

Purpose of PeopleCode

PeopleCode allows the Application Engine tool to have a full programming language that enables the developer to write complex programs easily. To best understand this you need to understand the capabilities of the Application Engine tool in earlier versions.

Prior to version 8, you only had the capability of writing SQL statements. This made it hard to do branching logic. For example, it takes at least 5 steps to write an “IF” statement in SQL, and could be more depending on the actions necessary within the “IF” statement. The first SQL takes the data in table 1 and inserts it into table 2 using some condition in the where clause. The condition in the where clause is the selection, just as it would have been in your "IF" statement.

```
Insert into PS_TABLE2
(Business_unit, Order_no, Cust_id, Carrier_id)
select a.Business_unit, a.Order_no, a.Cust_id,
       a.Carrier_id
from PS_TABLE1 a
where a.Cust_id in (select b.Cust_id from PS_CUST b
                    where b.Carrier_max_amt >1000)
```

The second SQL processes an action on table 2 – doing the changes you would have put into your "IF" statement if the condition was found to be true.

```
Update PS_TABLE2
set Carrier_id = (select a.carrier_id
                 from PS_CUST a
                  where PS_TABLE2.Cust_id = a.Cust_id)
```

The third statement removes the records from table 1. This is done so that in the fourth statement, the records, in table 2 can be written back to table 1.

```
Delete from PS_TABLE1
where exists (select 'X' from PS_TABLE2 a
              where PS_TABLE1.Business_unit =
                    a.Business_unit
              and PS_TABLE1.Order_no = a.Order_no)
```

```
Insert into PS_TABLE1
(Business_unit, Order_no, Cust_id, Carrier_id)
select a.Business_unit, a.Order_no, a.Cust_id,
       a.Carrier_id
from PS_TABLE2 a
```

Finally, table 2 is deleted of all rows of data since the "IF" statement is now complete.

```
Delete from PS_TABLE2
```

This is an overly simplistic example but it should get the point across as to how a simple "IF" statement could be so complex in previous versions of Application Engine. Now expand on this to understand the full scope of this problem. In a normal program you might have 50 such "IF" statements going on, so you can see how big the program gets. This one issue alone can make an Application Engine program complex to read since you follow the SQL in and out of Table 1 to Table 2 and back again.

The other use of PeopleCode is that you have at your disposal a full programming language that can manipulate dates, numbers, values and thousands of other things - why the possibilities are almost endless. This was a big drawback of using previous versions of Application Engine because you could not manipulate a datetime field to a date field without using platform specific SQL functions. Due to this complexity, most developers did not use Application Engine but now with the addition of PeopleCode, the future will be Application Engine!

PeopleCode Capabilities

The PeopleCode editor within the Application Engine toolset looks and works just like the editor you have used in Records, Pages and Components. Double clicking an Action in the definition view or double clicking on the word PeopleCode in the program flow view will open the standard PeopleCode editor.

The PeopleCode editor contains all the same tools as before. You can find a text string within the PeopleCode. You can perform a Search and Replace function as well. There are only a few restrictions that are placed on the PeopleCode you can use. You are allowed to use every piece of PeopleCode except those that need to interface with Page or Component objects. This is because you are not running from a Page so you cannot talk with those objects and functions that are connected to Pages and Components. You can use Record and Rowset objects since these can talk to the database directly. You cannot use Record and

Rowset objects, however, to talk about Records and Rows on a Page since you have no access to Page or Component objects.

You can also think of this as to why you load PeopleCode into an Action and not an Event, as you would do for standard Page processing. This is the reason different naming is used to help show that this is very different from an Event.

Another concern that has to be understood is the scope in which Application Engine runs. Since this program runs outside of the normal Page and Component, any variables that can be used and assigned only maintain scope within the Application Engine program itself. There is only one exception. If the Application Engine is launched via a PeopleCode function call (CallAppEngine) and global variables have been defined then the Application Engine can use and update these variables that are normally only within the Page or Component; this includes a global Rowset object. Normally, Application Engine programs are launched from Pages using the Process Scheduler; this is not the same as launching from the PeopleCode function CallAppEngine (you will learn all about this function later in this Chapter under the sections "Calling Application Engine with PeopleCode").

What to Use

PeopleCode is a great tool but there are some recommendations for increased performance. The PeopleCode interpreter has to start up, run and close each time a PeopleCode Action is called. This maintains a bit of overhead that will slow down a large program. For this reason it is recommended to have PeopleCode only do minor things within the Application Engine program. It should not be the main programming logic – leave that to SQL. You should also try to eliminate all PeopleCode within high volume transaction loops, as this can adversely affect performance. With these few basic rules given, it's time to learn how to use PeopleCode effectively.

Logic Decisions

Logic decisions are done to change program flow based on some condition. While other program languages, you can do this through functions like "IF", "WHEN" or "UNTIL" but with PeopleCode in Application Engine you have to do it a bit differently. Of course, within the PeopleCode you can use all of the functions but in order to change the direction of the program, you have to use the Exit function. Back in Chapter 2 you learned about the On Return field in the PeopleCode Action. By passing a parameter in the process of exiting the PeopleCode you can cause this action to be taken or skipped. A return value of TRUE will cause the action in the On Return field to be used. You pass a true value by using the Exit function and submitting a non-zero value.

```
Exit(1);
```

This is all you have to do but, of course, there should be some other code to see if you should use this exit condition. You can also use the Exit with a zero value to not have the On Return action taken.

Another way to use PeopleCode in a logic decision is when you would normally use a Do When on a SQL Action. A Do When is a simple SQL that if rows are returned the subsequent Actions within the Step are processed. Using a PeopleCode Action, you can replace a Do When in a simple example such as checking a bind variable, as in the following example.

```
Select 'X' from ps_installation
where %bind(cust_amt) > 1000
```

This statement can easily be replaced by a PeopleCode Action and be much more efficient.

```
If RB_IN_AET.cust_amt> 1000
   Exit(1);
End-if;
```

The reason it is more efficient is the small amount of overhead on PeopleCode is less than the overhead of doing SQL and calling the database when the PeopleCode logic is so simple.

Text, Date and Number Manipulations

This section has a bit more substance than the logic decisions since you can do so much more in this area with PeopleCode. Here, you can take information and manipulate it using many different functions. One of these is to take information in the Run Control record and build a complex where clause that you can use later within SQL statements. You can manipulate date, datetime, number and text fields to build new values or variables that you can use in other SQL statements. A case in point, is you have the user enter a date on the Run Control Page but then you need to convert this to a datetime field. You could have had the user enter in the datetime field in the first place but users do not like to have to enter in information in the specific format all the time. You can use PeopleCode to take a date value and build it into a datetime value that you can then easily use in all your SQL Action statements.

You can also use the many math functions that are in PeopleCode to manipulate, calculate and change numbers. This allows you to perform any complicated number crunching that you need to do, easily and quickly. PeopleCode can also be used to do simple math functions such as creating a sequence number for items like Voucher Number or Order number. Under previous versions you would have had to create a loop using SQL to find the maximum number but now you can use a simple counter within PeopleCode.

Another capability is to create a function in PeopleCode that you can use not only in your Pages but also in your Application Engine programs. This allows you to create one functional unit of logic and have it used in multiple places. For example, within PeopleCode there exists a function that when you pass it a date and a number, the function will return the next working day taking into account holidays and weekends based on an entered calendar. This function is used in many Pages to determine a date range and can also be used in an Application Engine program to do the same thing; taking information from the Run control record or other date information.

What NOT to Do

There are a few warnings about what NOT to do in PeopleCode. You have at your disposal all kind of functions, methods and objects but there are a few that are not recommended. Arrays and Rowsets are two objects that should not be used.

Arrays should not be used as they take a lot of memory and looping logic to use them effectively. If you need to do something like this, then you should use a Temporary or staging Record and store the information using SQL. The real purpose of Application Engine is to use SQL so that Arrays within PeopleCode would not be as efficient. To better understand this you can read Chapter 8, which talks about set processing.

Rowsets can be used; you will find some Application Engine programs that use them, but PeopleSoft does not recommend this. The reason is because using a Rowset within PeopleCode is the same as using an Array. You have a set of data that you will loop through; processing a Rowset within PeopleCode is just not as efficient as using SQL with temp tables. The performance of the database just far outpaces the capability of PeopleCode.

Now to complete your training, some examples follow to show you how specific things are done using PeopleCode.

Examples of Uses

Updating Bind Variables

```
SELECT_PARM1 = &SELECT_PARM1;
PO_POSTAGE_AET.SELECT_PARM2 = &SELECT_PARM2;
```

This example shows the two ways to store information into the State Records or what is more commonly called the Bind variables. Bind variables, their use and purpose are all taught in the next Chapter – Chapter 4. In the example above, the first line shows how to load into the default State record (this of course means you can have multiple State records for one Application Engine program). The second line shows how to load information into a non-primary State record. You can see in the second line that you have to use the Record name and then the field name whereas in the first line you only needed the Field name.

Of course you can also use Bind variables to initialize regular variables as well.

```
&SELECT_PARM2 = PO_POSTAGE_AET.SELECT_PARM2;
```

Developing Where Clauses

```
If All(&BUSINESS_UNIT_IN) Then
   &WHERE = &WHERE | "BUSINESS_UNIT_IN = '" |
      &BUSINESS_UNIT_IN | "' AND ";
End-If;

If All(PO_POSTAGE_AET.PLANNER)) Then
   &WHERE = &WHERE | "PLANNER_CD = '" | &PLANNER_CD |
      "' AND ";
End-If;

If &DATE_SEL_OPT <> "N" Then
   &WHERE = &WHERE | "RELEASE_DATE = " | "%DATEIN('" |
      &DATE_SEL_DT | "') AND ";
End-If;
```

This example is longer but the entire purpose is to load the variable &WHERE with information that will be used by SQL statements later in the process. You can see that "IF" statements are used to check to see if a variable is loaded (it is assumed these were loaded from the Run Control Record where the user would have supplied information). If there is a value in the variable then the &WHERE variable is loaded. In the second "IF" statement, you can see that instead of a variable being used, a Bind variable is reviewed from a non-primary State record to see if it has data and to then update the &WHERE variable. The last "IF" statement shows some special work with dates to have the correct format used.

***Note**: This is only a snippet of code so this may not work in your program. The last "IF" statement contains an AND at the end of the &WHERE variable, so this variable is assuming that are more statements to process.*

Defining Date and Time Values

```
IN_PURGE_AET.DT_TIMESTAMP = %Datetime;
TBIN_AET.DATE_TO = %Date;
If None(TBIN_AET.DATE_FROM) Then
   TBIN_AET.DATE_FROM = AddToDate(%Date, - 1, 0, - 1);
End-If;
TBIN_AET.DATE_FROM = AddToDate(TBIN_AET.DATE_FROM, 0,
   0, 1);
&DAY = Day(TBIN_AET.DATE_FROM);
&MONTH = Month(TBIN_AET.DATE_FROM);
&YEAR = Year(TBIN_AET.DATE_FROM);
TBIN_AET.FROM_DTTM = DateTime6(&YEAR, &MONTH, &DAY, 0,
   0, 0);
```

Here are multiple examples of code using Date and Datetime functions. The first two lines show using System variables to load some Bind variables. Lines three through five are checking to see if a date is in one of the Bind variables and if it is blank to load it with today's date (System variable) that has had one year and one day subtracted from it. Lines six thru ten take a date in a Bind variable break the date field into its components and then these components are used with some constants to create a datetime value.

Rowset Object use

```
&MST_Rowset = CreateRowset(Record.EN_REVISION);
&MST_Rowset.Fill();
For &K = 1 To &MST_Rowset.ActiveRowCount
```

```
   If
&MST_Rowset(&K).GetRecord(Record.EN_REVISION).REVISION.Value
= &Current_Rev Then
      &Prior_Date =
&MST_Rowset(&K).GetRecord(Record.EN_REVISION).DATE_IN_EFFECT.Value;
      &Prior_Rev =
&MST_Rowset(&Current_Row).GetRecord(Record.EN_REVISION).REVISION.Value;
      Break;
   End-If;
End-For;
```

This example is included but is not recommended, as you should use SQL with one of the looping Actions. This does not preclude you from using this and in fact you will find examples within PeopleSoft that use this. The main reason for this issue is that the performance of a SQL Action loop against a PeopleCode Rowset is just so much better. If you must do this, then you must understand this performance issue and be sure the number of rows within the Rowset is minimized.

The first line creates the Rowset object within the PeopleCode buffer. Then a For-Next loop is done to go through all the rows of data within this Rowset. Values are checked and updated if specific conditions exist.

Using Record Object

```
&PO_POSTAGE_AET = CreateRecord(Record.PO_POSTAGE_AET);
&ZEROSTRING = Rept("0", 10);
&PO_ID_LAST_USED = PO_POSTAGE_AET.LAST_PO_STG_ID;
&TEMPSTRING = String(&PO_ID_LAST_USED);
&PO_POSTAGE_AET.PROCESS_INSTANCE.Value =
PO_POSTAGE_AET.PROCESS_INSTANCE;
&PO_POSTAGE_AET.PO_STG_ID.Value = Substring(&ZEROSTRING, 1,
   10 - Len(&TEMPSTRING)) | &TEMPSTRING;
&PO_POSTAGE_AET.Update();
```

This example shows how to create a Record object where variables are loaded with values and then used to update into the Record object. The last statement then forces the update to the Record. Even though you may think this should not be done, as was warned for the Rowset, you will find this done within Peoplesoft delivered programs. As you can see from this example, you may have to do a lot of work to get just one value updated. The use of PeopleCode is not as efficient as SQL statements but the overhead to do all the variable assignment is almost impossible – well at least very difficult – and so using the PeopleCode Record object is allowed.

Decision Logic

```
Exit (AP_PREPAID_AET.MULTI_PREPAY_SW <> "Y");
Exit(1);
```

These examples are really simple with the use of the Exit function. The only thing you have to supply is the True or False statement. Remember that a True statement will cause the On Return value to be run.

File Object Use

```
&file_ldif = GetFile(&ORGID | "*.ldif", "N");
If &file_ldif.IsOpen Then
   &file_ldif.WriteLine("dn: o=" | &ORGSUFFIX);
   &file_ldif.WriteLine("objectClass: top");
   &file_ldif.WriteLine("objectClass: organization");
   &file_ldif.Close();
Else;
   Error "**Error** Could not create file";
End-If;
```

Here is a compressed snippet of code showing a creation of a File object and a logic check to see if the file is open. If it is open, information is loaded into the File object and then closed. If the File object is not open, then an error statement is processed. In Chapters 7 and 12 you will learn all about the File object and its use within the Application Engine toolset.

Well, the short run of examples are complete but there are some other items that you will look at involving PeopleCode. Not only is there PeopleCode within Application Engine but there are times you will be in a Page, when you want to launch an Application Engine directly via a push of a button rather than through the

Process Scheduler. There are also other things to learn about a new PeopleCode object called AESection, as well as special functions that you can use to call other programs like COBOL programs. All these topics are explained in the next few sections.

Calling Application Engine through PeopleCode

This PeopleCode function allows you to launch Application Engine programs without having to use the standard Run control Page, Record and Process Definition. The purpose is so that you can run an Application Engine program while you are still within a Page, have a process complete in the background and then return to the Page when all is complete.

For an example, you have a Page where you are entering in data about a user and you want this to expand and update hundreds of different records. You could load into the Page each and every record but this would overload the Page processing and initialization. You could try to do this through SQLExec or ScrollSelect functions but this is not efficient for heavy load processing. So your only recourse is to use the process CallAppEngine function to launch this program that will do all this SQL work for you quickly and easily - so easily that the user never knows what happened.

Events

There are a few considerations in working with this process in that the results depend on from which Event you launched this function. Since the only reason to launch an Application Engine program is to perform SQL updates, deletes or inserts, you need to restrict the use of this function to the following Events.

- FieldChange
- SavePreChange
- SavePostChange
- Workflow

If you launch the function from the FieldChange Event, you have to understand that the Application Engine program will run and complete, coming back to the Page but nothing will commit until after the FieldChange PeopleCode has completed.

There are two issues here that you have to understand. One, the user is now waiting on the Application Engine program to run and complete. They are not allowed to process further in the Page until the program comes back and continues processing through the rest of the FieldChange PeopleCode. The user will not want to wait long so you should have your Application Engine program optimized to process quickly. Two, the Application Engine may make updates or inserts into tables that will not commit to the database until after all of the FieldChange code has run. This means locks on Records within the database will exist for some time longer than the program is processing. This is not a problem unless you have programs that take some time or have multiple users using the same Page. Be aware of the lock condition so that performance is not adversely affected.

There are also two other requirements by PeopleSoft in using this function within a FieldChange Event. You must run this process in Three Tier or Internet client only. This is a requirement due to performance reasons. Also, you cannot contain a DoSave or DoSaveNow function within the same FieldChange code that contains the function CallAppEngine.

Standard practice is to use the Save Events since the user is normally used to waiting for the process to finish. Again, the Page will wait while the Application Engine program processes and will hold all database updates until after all Save processes are complete. This means that if you call an Application Engine within the SavePreChange Event you will have to wait until all the save processing is complete (all way through SavePostChange) to have the database committed with your updates. This is not a problem unless your Application Engine program is long in processing or you have multiple users. You should then code your program and Page accordingly to avoid these issues.

Run Control Parameters

With the use of the function CallAppEngine, you have some problems to be aware of that you would not normally have to deal with. Normally, when you launch your program you have the Run Control Record to retrieve parameters from as well as a unique ID called Process Instance when you use CallAppEngine you have neither of these. Now you will learn how to deal with these issues.

Process Instance

Many times within programs you use the Process Instance to control data being inserted into tables or being updated where the program could be running with multiple instances. Sometimes Process Instance is used as a unique key ID or key value for data processing. If you have an Application Program that is going to be launched with the function CallAppEngine then you will have to make some adjustments. When an Application Engine is launched via the CallAppEngine function you do not get assigned a Process Instance. Since you cannot control when a user will launch this program via the function call, you have to make sure your program will handle having multiple instances running by using some method other than using Process Instance.

***Note**: One possible solution is to use the Temporary Record process so that each instance would be using a unique Record.*

Run Control ID

When you start programs, the first thing that is usually done is to gather the parameters for the program from the Run Control Record. This is keyed by the Operator who launched the program and the Run Control ID value the user input. These two key fields allow you to retrieve all the run parameters. When you launch an Application Engine program from the function CallAppEngine, you do not have a Run Control ID. This would seem to block you from passing any information from your Page but there is a way around this problem.

Passing Run Parameters

Before you call the function CallAppEngine, you need to perform some actions as shown in the example below.

```
Local Record &lclrecord;
&lclrecord = CreateRecord(RECORD.PO_POSTAGE_AET);
&lclrecord.BUSINESS_UNIT.Value = &BUIN
CallAppEngine("MYAPPID", &lclrecord);
```

The first line substantiates a Record object variable. The second line creates the Record object. This line should have defined as the Record name the State Record that is to be passed with the CallAppEngine function. There is just one value being updated here, as shown on line three but this could be as many or as few as you need. Line four shows the actual call where you can then supply a Record object which acts just like a State Record. You can also pass values into multiple State Records and have each of them within the CallAppEngine function.

***Note**: It is assumed that you have added all the necessary State Records to the Application Engine program in the PeopleCode function CallAppEngine.*

Then within the Application Engine program you can retrieve these values through standard means using the SQL Bind variables or through PeopleCode. Now with all of the warnings out of the way, you can get on with learning the function parameters.

CallAppEngine

```
CallAppEngine("MYAPPID", &strecord1, &strecord2);
```

This is the structure of the function call. First there is the hard coded value CallAppEngine followed by a parameter list, within parenthesis. The parameter list is made up of first, the Application

Engine name. Here, in the example, it is a text string but you could have used a variable as well. Next comes a list of the State records to be used. The list should be made up of Record objects. You can supply no State Records, one State Record or a list of them. You only need to supply the correct number of State Records as you have added to the Application Engine program. If you supply more, then the extra State Records in the function call are ignored. If you do not supply enough State Records, then your program may error or have unexpected results. It is up to you, the developer, to pass the right number of parameters.

***Note**: You can also pass the State Record using the RECORD.*`PO_POSTAGE_AET` *nomenclature.*

There are also some warnings that should be discussed. You should be able to use all capabilities within the Application Engine but when you use the CallAppEngine function you should not use %TruncateTable or %Execute meta SQL. This is due to some database platforms that will try to force a commit, which should not be done, as the commit should come at the end of the program. You should also not use any CallAppEngine functions within the PeopleCode of the Application Engine that is being run by the original CallAppEngine. If you must call another Application Engine program from the original Application Engine program, you should use the function CallSection in PeopleCode within a PeopleCode Action.

Page Controls

After your Application Engine program has completed you may need to refresh your Page since data may have been updated or inserted into the row buffers now displayed on your screen. This process is not automatic. If you require this, then the best solution is to issue the Refresh method of the RowSet object.

```
GetLevel0().Refresh()
```

The example above will refresh all buffer rows of the Page. If you only need to refresh a single buffer then you can issue the refresh command for that RowSet that is connected to the row buffer. Normally you will want to refresh the entire Page as this saves time, unless you have a Page with many row buffers and just one needs to be updated.

You also have to know how the process will return if the Application Engine encounters a problem and has to abort. The Application Engine will return a failure code to the calling function and this will result in an error within the PeopleCode just as if you had coded wrong. The entire Page and Component will fail and all the user input will rollback to the last save. Be sure to thoroughly test your Application Engine program to minimize this issue to the user.

AESection Object

This is an Object that allows you to dynamically change the SQL within an existing Application Engine. You can use this PeopleCode object prior to a CallAppEngine function changing the SQL within the Application Engine program so that you have one program that can dynamically change based on some set of criteria.

***Warning**: In previous versions you could update the Application Engine Tool Records directly to change the SQL but this should no longer be done. The SQL is now "cached" so updating the Tools Records may not really update the SQL.*

First you have to initiate the object, as shown in the example below.

```
Local AESection &POStageC;
```

Once you have the object defined, you can then apply the functions, methods and properties taught below.

AESection Object Built-in Functions

There is only one function for AESection – GetAESection.

GetAESection

This function creates the AESection object. You must create the object before you can use it. Here are two examples of the function call.

```
&POStageC = GetAESection(&AEName, &AESection)
&POStageC = GetAESection("PO_POSTAGE", "CUSTOM",
%Date)
```

The purpose of the function is to set the value of a variable that you have defined as a AESection object using the GetAESection function call. The GetAESection function call is made up of two or three variables. The first variable (first example) or hard code value (second example) is the name of the Application Engine that you are going to be modifying. The second variable or hard code value is the name of the Section within the Application Engine that you are going to modify. The third value in the function, which can be a variable, system variable (shown in the second example) or hard code value is the effective date. This third value is not required unless you want to use the effective dating process.

***Note**: Under normal circumstances you would use the effective date process so that you could see your changes over time but if the program is running multiple times a day or the changes are not required to be logged then do not use the effective dating process.*

To use the function GetAESection properly, there are a few things you need to know. The Section name supplied in the function parameter does not have to first exist within the Application Engine program. If the Section is not already in the Application Engine program it is then created with the effective date if supplied, otherwise 01-01-1900 is used. If the Section does already exist, then any Steps and Actions within that Section are deleted if they match the supplied effective date. If you do not use the effective date, then all Steps and Actions of all effective dates are removed. This means that you cannot just add a Step and Action to an existing Section, which has multiple Steps and Actions – you will have to create all the Steps and Actions within a Section. You will need to code your Application Engine program accordingly so that if you have Steps and Actions that must be dynamically changed, they are in separate Sections from the Steps and Actions that are to remain constant.

Note: *The Market (the language control) is also used in seeing if a Section exists in the defined Application Engine program. The market value is derived from the calling Component. If no market is defined, then the default of GBL (Global) is used.*

After having defined the Section, you can then apply the Methods.

AESection Object Methods

The available methods are AddStep, Close, Open, Save, SetSQL and SetTemplate. These methods are used to copy Steps and Actions as well as update Actions.

SetTemplate

This is the required method that must be run first. This connects the Application Engine Section you are about to modify with a different Section (same or different Application Engine program). Once you define the template to be used you can then copy Steps and Actions from the template into the Section you have defined to modify back in the GetAESection function.

This method defines how you will have to create your Application Engine programs. You will have to create the Application Engine program that you are going to change and you will have to create another Application Engine program that stores the template Section, Steps and Actions.

***Warning**: You can create all the Sections, both the one to be modified and the template section, in one Application Engine program but this is strongly discouraged.*

The reason you have to define a template is due to the fact that you can only update SQL Actions steps. By having a template to copy from, you can copy other Action types like PeopleCode or Log Messages. You can even have in the template Section hundreds of Steps and Actions but you can selectively choose which Steps and Actions you want to bring into the Application Engine program.

Here are some examples.

```
&POStageC.SetTemplate(&AENameC, &AESectionC);
&POStageC.SetTemplate("PO_CUSTOM", "ROLE1");
```

These two examples show how you use this method. You have to use this method as part of the AESection object you created earlier following the dot notation. Using only two parameters you then define the Application Engine name (first value) and the Section (second value). As you can see, the parameters may be hard code values or variables.

This is very similar to the GetAESection function but you will notice that the date parameter is missing. This is because this method assumes the effective date of 01-01-1900. You are not allowed to change this so you will have to code your template Application Engine in this manner. The Market is hard coded from the calling Component just as was done in the GetAESection.

AddStep

This method copies a Step and then all the Actions under that Step from the template Application Engine program to the defined Application Engine Section object. This method can be used multiple times but you must understand that the order in which you add each Step is the order in which the Steps are placed into the Application Engine program. You cannot override the order at any time unless you close the object and re-open thereby deleting all Steps and Actions within the Section.

Here are a few examples of using this method.

```
&POStageC.AddStep(&AESStepC);
&POStageC.AddStep("STEP1", "PROC1");
```

This method requires using the object defined in the GetAESection with one or two parameters. The first parameter is the Step Name within the Template Application Engine Section. This must always be used and must match a name of a Step that exists within the defined template Section. The second parameter, which is not required, will become the new name within the Application Engine program object. The second parameter allows you to define the name differently than the template Step name.

***Warning**: If the name you defined for the template Application Engine (first parameter) does not exists the PeopleCode will error out causing the program to abort.*

This process will copy the Step and all of the Actions within the Step including all parameters and comments. The Actions will copy as they are input and cannot be changed except for the SQL within each Action. See the next section on SetSQL to see on how to modify the SQL.

SetSQL

This method allows you to modify (by inputting a new SQL string) SQL commands within the defined Application Engine object. You can only modify a SQL Action that has been placed into the defined Application Engine object via the AddStep method. You must also modify the SQL of Actions within a Step prior to adding more Steps since this method only works on the most recently added Step within the defined Application Engine object. You cannot go back to a previous Step to modify SQL within an Action.

Here are some examples:

```
&POStageC.SetSQL("SQL", &SQL1);
&POStageC.SetSQL("DO_WHILE", "%SelectInit(TEMP_FLD)
   SELECT 'X' FROM PS_INSTALLATION_PO  WHERE
   %Bind(ABORT_FLAG) <> 'N'");
```

This method requires the use of the Application Engine object in the dot notation using two parameters. The first parameter must be a string that stores the name of the Action TYPE not the Action name. Here is a list of the allowed Action Types.

- Do_Select
- Do_Until
- Do_When
- Do_While
- SQL

Warning: *If the Action type does not exist within the Step defined on the Application Engine object the PeopleCode will have a runtime error.*

This method will then place the SQL into the Action Type as defined in the string or the variable. It will not append but will override anything that existed there from the AddStep process or a previous SetSQL method call.

Save

This method will save all the information into the database including the "cache" storage so that the new SQL can be used. The defined Application Engine Section object however still remains open for use. You normally use this function to Save changes at an interval to prevent too many locks on the database.

Here is the syntax.

```
&POStageC.Save();
```

This requires the Application Engine Section object but no parameters.

***Warning**: You must do the Save prior to closing the object otherwise your changes will be lost.*

Close

This method will close the Application Engine Section object. If you have not saved any changes, all changes will be lost. You will not receive any error message or warnings if you have not yet saved your changes.

Here is the syntax.

```
&POStageC.Close();
```

This requires the Application Engine Section object but no parameters.

Open

This method is very similar to the GetAESection function. The difference is that the object has already been created and you just need to connect the Application Engine Section to the object. The purpose of this method is to allow you to reuse one Application Engine Section object over and over without having to create new objects by using the GetAESection function. Either process will work fine.

Here are some examples.

```
&POStageC.Open(&AEName, &AESection)
&POStageC.Open("PO_POSTAGE", "CUSTOM", %Date)
```

The use of this method requires a created Application Engine Section object. The parameter list is just like the one used in the GetAESection function. The first parameter is the Application Engine name in either variable or hard coded value. The second parameter is the name of the Section being created, which can be supplied in either variable or hard value. The third parameter is optional and is the effective date to be created. Again if this third parameter is not supplied, the default of 01-01-1900 is used.

All of the same concerns and rules apply as was already discussed in the GetAESection function above. This method will open a new Section within the defined Application Engine name and eliminate all Step and Actions within that Section. See the GetAESection for further details.

***Note**: If the Open method is used on an Application Engine Section object that has not been closed or saved, then all the previous changes to the first Application Engine Section object is lost and not saved to the database.*

AESection Object Properties

There is only one property for the AESection object – IsOpen.

IsOpen

This property returns a value that will define whether the AESection object is already open or not. You can use this property to ascertain whether you have already closed the AESection or not, to know if you should open the next Section.

Here are some examples of the property in use.

```
If Not(&POStageC.IsOpen) Then
Evaluate & POStageC.IsOpen
```

This property returns a True if the AESection is open or a False if the AESection is not open.

Complete Program

Here is a short example of an entire program using all the functions, methods and properties.

```
Local AESection &POStageC;

&POStageC = GetAESection("PO_POSTAGE", "CUSTOM",
   %Date)
&POStageC.SetTemplate("PO_CUSTOM", "ROLE1");
&POStageC.AddStep("STEP1", "PROC1");
&POStageC.SetSQL("SQL", &SQL1);
&POStageC.Save();

If &POStageC.IsOpen Then
   &POStageC.Close();
Else;
   &POStageC.Open(&AEName, &AESection)
   &POStageC.AddStep("STEP2");
   &POStageC.SetSQL("SQL", &SQL2);
   &POStageC.Save();
   &POStageC.Close();
End-if;
```

CommitWork

This is a PeopleCode function that is only allowed to be used in PeopleCode within an Application Engine program. The purpose of this function is to save or commit all the changes, deletes and inserts to Records that have occurred so far. This function ONLY works in those Application Engines that are running in batch mode – meaning that the Application Engine was not run from the CallAppEngine function. If it is called online, then this function is ignored by the database and commits will NOT be done. This function also only works where the Restart capability has been disabled. This means a developer has purposefully determined that this program is of such critical nature that it is unable to restart and complete a process once begun.

So with these limitations, you may never use this function but it does exist. In fact the best place to use this function is on row-by-row processing that is so critical that you need to commit after processing every row.

The function is used as shown below.

```
CommitWork();
```

This function also returns a value of True if the commit was successful or False if not.

Remember that this function is highly specialized in that you are going to override two of the main recommendations for programming with Application Engine. First is the need to not restart (restart is disabled) and second is to do row by row processing within PeopleCode. These two things are not normally done but if they are required and you need to commit to the database here is the function to use.

***Warning**: If you use this function, you will have to develop a plan in how to handle if your program aborts and may have data half committed.*

Calling COBOL program

In previous versions, Application Engine was a COBOL program itself but now it has been fully re-written into the "C" programming language. This makes it a bit more difficult to launch COBOL programs from within the Application Engine program. If you are writing a new program, then it is recommended that you not use this process but create all your code in SQL, using the standard SQL object within the Application Engine program. The performance of earlier versions of Application Engine was slow at best and that is why some developers used COBOL to do the heavy processing. With this new and fast version, this is no longer necessary as Application Engine SQL processing will easily rival the performance of the COBOL programs. So why cover this topic? You may have old programs that you have already written in COBOL and still need to use, so this capability is there for those who need to use COBOL programs within Application Engine.

To call a COBOL program you will use the Remote function call within PeopleCode. Here are a few examples.

```
RemoteCall ("PSRCCBL", "PSCOBOLPROG", "PTPECOBL",
   "AECOBOLPROG", "COBOLMODULE", "STATERECORD",
   "AETRECORD", "PRCSINST",
   AETRECORD.PROCESS_INSTANCE);
RemoteCall ("PSRCCBL", "PSCOBOLPROG", "PTPECOBL",
   "AECOBOLPROG", "COBOLMODULE", "STATERECORD",
   "AETRECORD", "PRCSINST",
   AETRECORD.PROCESS_INSTANCE, "RETCODE", &RetCode,
   "ERRMSG", &ErrorCD);
RemoteCall ("PSRCCBL", "PSCOBOLPROG", "PTPECOBL",
   "AECOBOLPROG", "COBOLMODULE", "STATERECORD",
   "AETRECORD", "PRCSINST",
   AETRECORD.PROCESS_INSTANCE, "RETCODE", &RetCode,
   "ERRMSG", &ErrorCD, "PO_ID", AETRECORD.ORDER_NO);
```

The first example shows the minimum amount of information, the second with return and error variables included and the third with all the necessary information. To fully review, use the third example.

The function call is initiated with the value of RemoteCall followed by a string list of parameters.

The first parameter, `"PSRCCBL"`, is hard coded to specify the RemoteCall
"dispatcher".

The second and third parameters are a pair of values. The second parameter is hard coded with "PSCOBOLPROG" to signify the name of the COBOL program, which is the third parameter and should be set to "PTPECOBL".

***Note**: Because the parameter is PTPECOBOL the following parameters are specific to this call for COBOL program launch versus standard use of the RemoteCall function.*

The fourth and fifth parameters are a pair of values. The fourth parameter is hard coded with "AECOBOLPROG" to signify the name of the Cobol Module, which is the fourth parameter. This fourth parameter is required and you can change it to anything you wish as long as this module has been created and placed within the standard COBOL directories.

The sixth and seventh parameters are a pair of values. The sixth parameter is hard coded with "STATERECORD" to signify the name of the State record that has preloaded values in it. The seventh parameter is the State Record name. Note that you do not put in the leading PS_ on the Record names as you can use the PeopleTools naming convention. Even if you do not have any values within a State Record to pass you must set these parameters. The purpose of these parameters is to pass values and allowing the COBOL program to create memory space for all the field values within the State Record automatically.

The eighth and ninth parameters are a pair of values. The eighth is hard coded with "PRCSINST" to signify the process instance number to use. The process instance should be loaded into a field within the State Record and that is what is then shown in the ninth parameter.

The tenth and eleventh parameters are a pair of values. These values are not required. They allow you to pass back from the COBOL program a return code. You can then check this return code for a value to show if the program passed, failed or some specific condition was found. The eleventh variable must be a variable that will be filled in by the returning COBOL program.

The twelfth and thirteenth parameters are a pair of values. These values are not required. They are like the return code but now you have a place to put an error code. You can use these two parameters (return and error) to pass back information into the PeopleCode program to decide on further action or direction within the program.

The fourteenth and fifteenth are a pair of values. The fourteenth is a Field name within the State Record supplied. The name must exist in the State record. The fifteenth then contains the value that is to be initialized into the variables. The State record is NOT initialized with any values; you must pass all initial values in the string this way. To include more you just add more pairs of values; first the field name followed by the field value. The field value (fifteenth parameter) can be a hard coded value, variables or even Record.Field nomenclature.

***Note**: Within the COBOL program you can use the PTPECACH module to retrieve and update values within the State record.*

COBOL Concerns

With the use of this function, there are a few things to understand and be aware of. First, there is the understanding of when the COBOL program being launched is running not as part of the Application Engine but on it own. This means that you have to commit all work prior in your Application Engine to the database otherwise your COBOL program will see data in the database before any updates or inserts were committed. The recommendation by PeopleSoft is to commit in the Step Prior and then within the PeopleCode Action that launched the COBOL program, to be absolutely certain that all database updates are committed.

Because the COBOL program is running on its own, you also have to be certain to commit any work done by the COBOL program before returning to the Application Engine program. The COBOL interface program will not automatically commit any work so you have to be sure you do it prior to the return. If you do not, the database will ROLLBACK (uncommit) all the database work that it did.

Now that you know what could happen, you also have to code all your programs, both Application Engine and COBOL, to be able to handle conditions where the program fails or the database has a problem. In other words you need to be able to restart the program and have it handle rows of data that may be halfway committed.

Finally there is one last thing to understand about problems with the State Records. You can only interface and talk with one State Record even though Application Engine can process multiple State Records. You will have to funnel all your variables into one State Record to work with the COBOL program. There is also an issue with the one State Record in that the State Record cannot contain any Sub-Records nor can it contain any long character Fields.

Next

This completes all the special learning for PeopleCode and any special functions involving PeopleCode and Application Engine. In the following Chapters there are more specific things to learn including more examples of PeopleCode. So don't miss anything as you start learning all about State Records within Application Engine.

Chapter 4

Understanding State Records

State Records are used in Application Engine programs to store temporary data while an Application Engine program is running. State Record data values are then used as variables within SQL statements. Of course, you could use an actual Record to hold these data values but then you would have to join this Record into each SQL statement. This join would complicate the SQL statement so State Records are so much easier to use. This chapter will teach you about State Records; how to create, use and associate them to Application Engine programs and SQL statments.

How State Records Work

When you create your Application Engine program, you can define the State Record(s) to use. This connects the Application Engine to a Record you have defined and allows the Application Engine to communicate and write values into all the fields of the State Record. When your Application Engine program starts, it will create the database connections to select and update the field values as you use them within your Application Engine program. This happens automatically for you and the fields are initalized in a blank state.

What takes place is a new row is inserted into each State Record using the field of Process Instance (you will learn about how to create a State Record in the next section). The Process Instance is used as a unique identifier for every run so that the Application Engine program can run in multiple instances. This is the reason that Process Instance is a requirement for each State Record.

Once the row is created in the database, the fields can be used just like variables within your Application Engine. However, the data is not saved to the database unless a commit is performed sometime within the Application Engine program. This means that you cannot use SQL to select the state of the variables within the database unless you force a commit. This also means that the information in the database is only current to the last commit performed. You must understand this when considering the value of the information within the database.

The State Record is not saved after the Application Engine program completes. In fact it is deleted. This is done so that the State Records do not become overfilled with data from old runs. If you need to see and read the State Records after the program has completed, you will need to write this information into the message log so that it is saved permanently or copy to a staging Record.

State Record Scope

State Records defined to an Application Engine program can be used in any Section, Step or Action of the program. The State Records can even be used in other Application Engine programs when they are called from the Application Engine program where the State Records are defined.

More than one Application Engine program can have the same State Record defined within it but they cannot pass values through the State Record. It is only when a Single Application Engine program calls another Application Engine that both can see and use the same State Record. The *called* Application Engine program can also have State Records defined – these are initialized at the time the new program Section is started. The called Application Engine program can then utilize these fields for variables. The called Application Engine's State Record can only be used for the time that the *called* program is active; when the called program ends, the State Records are closed out and removed from the database.

Be sure you are aware that if an Application Engine program calls another Application Engine program and they share a State Record that upon completion of the *called* program the values changed by that program will remain. This can be helpful to pass information back and forth between the Application Engine programs. This could also cause issues if you do not account for these values being changed.

Building State Records

To build the State Record, you have only two requirements. First, you must have the PROCESS_INSTANCE as the first and *only* key field. There can exist no other key fields on this Record. The Process Instance is a number that is determined by the Process Scheduler upon launch. Each process, launched in batch mode, is assigned a unique Process Instance number. As was mentioned before, this is how you can control each run of the same program, uniquely.

There is only one exception to this rule; State Records that will only be used for Application Engine programs that are always launched from online using the PeopleCode function CallAppEngine. These do not require the use of the key process instance nor any key fields since these values will only be held in memory and not stored to the database directly.

The second requirement is that the name of the State Record must end in "_AET". You have no other limit on the name except that this suffix is used. This is done so that special processing can be done on these Records and it is also far easier when searching to find these types of Records.

Warning: *If you build a Record using the "_AET" suffix but do not make the PROCESS_INSTANCE field the only key, you may cause a problem in that you will be able to assign this Record to an Application Engine as if it were a valid State Record. This will cause a run time error in the Application Engine program since the Record does not contain the PROCESS_INSTANCE field. Only use this suffix if this is a valid State Record.*

With this known requirement, you can build a Record definition just as you have done many times before. You can place any type of field as well as any number of fields. Your State Record may be only two fields long (the PROCESS_INSTANCE field being one of them) or two hundred fields long. The purpose is to add fields to this State Record that you will want to use as variables in your program.

Typical variables are for storing SETID values of different records such as the Item, Customer, Book or other Setid controlled Record. This way you can make one call to retrieve the Setid value using the variable to make your heavy processing SQL more efficient by not having to use multiple joins to retrieve the Setid. Other variables can be used to store temporary information like counters or flag settings. You can also use State Records to hold data such as SQL where clause strings. These strings are powerful in that you can use PeopleCode to build up a Where clause and then store it in a variable to use in one or more later SQL statements.

Note: *In building your State Records you have to follow all the other rules of building records such as having only one Long field type per Record.*

Type of State Records

You can create State Records that are of type Record, View or Derived. Record type is normally used and View type can be done but it is not recommended since you have to create a Record to create a View why not just use the Record directly? This is why you will not see any View type State Records used. Derived type Records can be used but there are some caveats to their use.

Since Derived Record types are not stored into the database, the values cannot be saved or committed. This requires you to make sure that the use of Derived State Records takes into account when your Application Engine program restarts, to reset or re-initialize these values from the start or last commit. It should be noted; when forcing a commit, the Derived State Record values will also be reset blank or put back in their initial state. Your program may now fail or produce bad results.

Derived State Records also have the requirement that these values are re-initialized when you force a commit. Just as if the Application Engine program had started – these Derived State Records are wiped clean and set to blank values. This can be a benefit, if this is what you need your program to do, or can cause you many hours of debugging to find the problem. This may seem like a drawback but you have to understand the main use of Derived State Records. This type of State Record is used for storing temporary values that are determined and then used immediately since a commit will refresh them. They are also used to store information for use within an Application Engine program where you do not want to take the hit of the database time to store information into the database. Having these Derived State Records will allow a program to work faster without having to go to the database too many times.

Note: *Be sure to build your State Records just as you would normally for any Record type.*

Associating State Records to Application Engine

Once you have your State Records created and built, you can move onto the next step in where you connect or associate the State Record to your Application Engine. To do this, you need to have your Application Engine program open in the working area of the Application Designer. Then using either the menu: File- Object Properties or clicking on the Properties button on the toolbar. This will open the Application Engine Properties panel as shown in figure 4.1

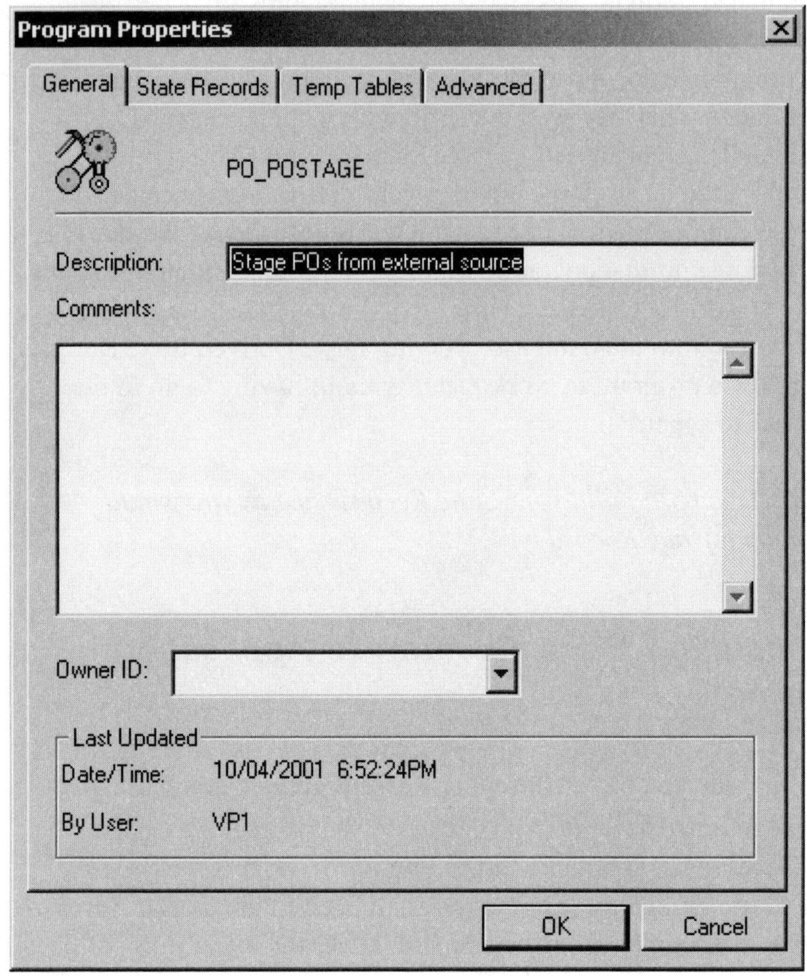

Figure 4.1 Application Engine Properties

You can enter in the text about your Application Engine here but to enter in the State Record information you need to click on the State Record tab. This new panel is shown in figure 4.2.

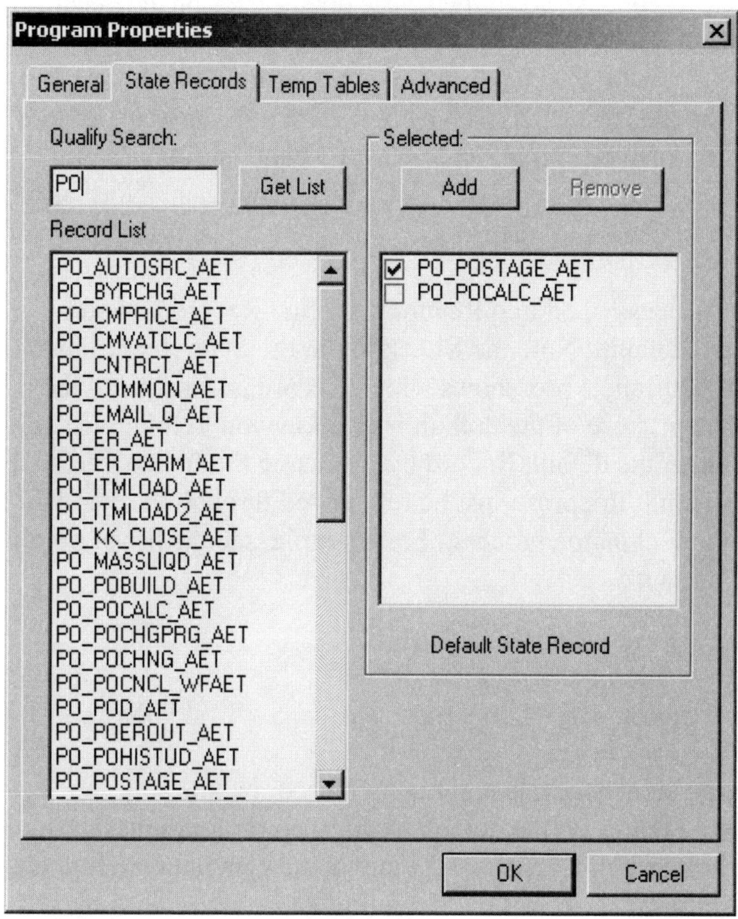

Figure 4.2 Application Engine Properties – State Records tab

This shows you the panel where you can add or delete State Records from the open Application Engine program. On this panel you find the Qualify Search field. This field is used to find all the State Records. You can enter in the full name or just a portion (shown as PO in figure 4.2). Then you have to click on the Get List button to have the Record list displayed just below the button. Remember a State Record has to end in "_AET". Here is one of the reasons why since it only brings up valid and working State

Records. You can then scroll up and down through the Record list to review it. Once you determine a Record to add to the Application Engine State Record list, you only have to double click on the Record name to add it.

This will add the Record you have clicked on into the State Record list. You can keep on filling the Record List and adding more Records to the State Record list – as many as you wish. Normally, you only need one State Record.

During the process of adding Records, the first Record you add becomes the default. Note the Checkbox in the State Record list in figure 4.2. This checkbox shows which Record is considered the default. The purpose of the default is to allow you to reference any of the fields on the default Record by just using the field name. All other non-default Records must be referenced through the standard Recordname.Fieldname process. For example, see the list of bind variables below.

```
%bind(VENDOR_ID)
%bind(PO_STAGE_AET.BUYER_ID)
%bind(PO_COMMON_AET.TEMP_FLD)
```

Example one shows the use without any Record name so it is assumed the Field is on the default State Record. Examples two and three both use the Record and Field name convention but you cannot assume these are not the default State Record. With the default State Record you are not required to use the Record name but you still can. In fact, example two is a case where the Record name is the default while example three is not.

Warning: *If your Application Engine program calls another Application Engine Section, the defined default State Record within that Section takes precedent over the calling program default State Record. Be sure to use the correct default within each Section.*

Updating Bind Variables

Now that you have defined the State Records to use, you need to learn how to set values within these Records. You have already learned in Chapter 3 how to do this with PeopleCode but you can also do this through SQL statements. This allows the program to retrieve data from the database and store it in these State Records. When you update a State Record field value it is referred to as updating your Bind Variables. This nomenclature is taken from how you use the field values by the use of the %bind Meta SQL command.

To use this process you, of course, have to be using a SQL type Action. The Action type list includes: Do When; Do While; Do Until; Do Select and SQL. When you create the SQL statement you have to use a Meta SQL command. You will learn all about these in Chapter 6, but you will need to learn this one here so that you can understand how to update Bind Variables in State Records. Here is an example of a valid SQL statement that can be used in Application Engine.

```
%Select(OPRID, RUN_CNTL_ID,PO_COMMON_AET.STAGE_STATUS)
 SELECT OPRID, RUN_CNTL_ID, 'L'
 FROM PS_AERUNCONTROL
 WHERE PROCESS_INSTANCE = %Bind(PROCESS_INSTANCE)
```

On the first line, you will notice that the %Select Meta SQL command is followed by Field names within parenthesis. This list of Field names is the Fields to be updated by the following SQL select statement. The list of names here must exist within the defined State Records for this Application Engine program. The first two Field names are within the default State Record, while the third Field name is within a different State Record. You must have at least one Field name in the list but there is no maximum number of Fields.

Following the definition of the Bind Variables to be updated, you will find a SQL select statement. This is a standard select statement that queries data from the database. The example you see here is very typical for the first SQL as it captures the Operator and the Run Control ID. These values are then typically used to grab the Run Control parameters from the Run Control Record.

You need to make sure that the SQL statement has the exact same number of fields being selected as was listed in the %Select command. If you do not, you will receive a run time error. As you can see from the example in the SQL Select statement, a hard coded value is used to make up the third variable. This is perfectly acceptable.

A special item to note is that this SQL select statement has within it a Bind Variable in the where clause. This is noted because the Process Instance is not required to be initialized by you as this is done automatically once the program is launched. Remember when you learned that once the Application Engine program starts, a row of data is created in your State Records and as shown here, the Bind Variable – PROCESS_INSTANCE – is captured and initialized and why it is required to have this field as key on your State Record.

***Note**: If your SQL select statement does not return any values, then none of the Bind Variables are updated – they are left with the information they had before this command was run.*

***Note**: There is also another similar command that can be run, %SelectInit. This Meta SQL command format is the same as listed above but has some different features. See Chapter 6 for more information.*

Using Bind Variables

Now that you can update values into your Bind Variables you need to know how to use them. As you learned in Chapter 3 – how to use Bind Variables within PeopleCode – there is a way to use Bind Variables within SQL statements. The same rule applies; the Bind Variable must be used within a SQL Action type statement (see section above, Updating Bind Variables, for the list).

To use a Bind Variable, you have to use the Meta SQL command of %bind, as shown in the examples below.

```
%bind(VENDOR_ID)
%bind(PO_STAGE_AET.BUYER_ID)
%bind(PO_COMMON_AET.TEMP_FLD)
```

You can see that only one variable is allowed – there is no listing of variables. The command is followed by the Bind Variable Record and Field name (using the record.field naming) within the parenthesis.

Once you have the Bind Variable command understood, you can use this as you would any hard coded value within a SQL statement. Just take a look at how this can be used.

```
%Select(OPRID, RUN_CNTL_ID,
PO_COMMON_AET.STAGE_STATUS)
 SELECT PO_DT, PO_REF FROM PS_PO_HDR
 WHERE PRICE_VENDOR = %bind(VENDOR_ID)

Update PS_PO_HDR set BUYER_ID =
%bind(PO_STAGE_AET.BUYER_ID)
 WHERE PRICE_VENDOR = %bind(VENDOR_ID)

Insert PS_PO_TEMP1
 Select BUSINESS_UNIT, PO_ID, %bind(VENDOR_ID) from
 PS_PO_TEMP
 Where PROCESS_INSTANCE = %bind(PROCESS_INNSTANCE)
```

As you can see from these three examples, you can use Bind Variables just about any place you choose. You can use them just as you would any variable within a valid SQL statement.

Next

This completes your learning on the State Records and Bind Variables. PeopleSoft has also added a new feature in what are called Temporary Records. These are used only within Application Engine programs so you will need to learn how to read, use and write these into your program.

Chapter 5

Temporary Tables

One of the purposes of Application Engine programs is to update Records or insert new rows of data into Records. This is usually accomplished through processing data from a set of initial Records, potentially through some midstage Records and into the final Records. You will create the Records as necessary for all the processing but some problems may eventually occur. These "problems" are due to time limits or database contention problems. Temporary Tables were created to solve these "problems".

Time Limits

The problem of time limits is due to the fact that you have a process that is handling 500,000 records and needs to complete within 2 hours. The processing may be complicated and the program takes 4 hours to complete; even after you have done all the tuning you can to make the process as efficient as possible. Temporary Tables are used here so that you can duplicate the program but each new program instance will handle only a portion of the data.

To get a better understanding, think of where you have to process 500,000 employee records to calculate some value. Since the one Application Engine program takes 4 hours, but you only have 2 hours in which to process, you need to duplicate the program so that each program can process 125,000 records in about an hour. By using Temporary Tables you can duplicate your program to have each one process through a set of midstaged Records that are all the same so that you do not have to create unique Records for each duplicated Application Engine program.

What you will need to do is to duplicate your Application Engine program three times and then install a where clause on the initial select to pull Last names from A-G in the first program, H-L in the second program, M-P in the third and Q-Z in the fourth program.

This way you have 4 programs but each one works on a different set of data. The mid stage Records would then be created as Temporary Tables so that the system will automatically create multiple Records from the same definition and use them individually on each Application Engine program run. By using Temporary Tables you only have to create one Record definition to cover all your duplicated programs. Do not worry about all the details yet – you will learn all this throughout this Chapter.

Database Contention

The problem of database contention is due to having the same program running multiple times within the same time frame. This problem may not be an issue but in certain cases the database can just lock up or become very slow to process all these concurrent programs. You should be using Process Instance in all your midstage Records to load, update and retrieve data in order to keep each program separate but when performance is degraded or the needs of security require that the data be separate, you can use Temporary Tables.

To solve this issue, you still only need the one Application Engine program but by changing the midstage Records to Temporary Tables you can guarantee that each run will be in its own Record. Of course this is the simple solution, there is a bit more to it, but now you should understand the reasons for Temporary Tables. You will find some Application Engine programs within PeopleSoft do not use Temporary Tables, as their process is quick and efficient and do not have any time restrictions yet. When you run your PeopleSoft system and apply it to your business, you may then find delivered or your custom Application Engine programs in one of the two problems listed.

To start learning, you have to understand the order in which to develop using Temporary Tables within Application Engine. First, you have to set some special options if your Application Engine program can be run from an online process. This is done in the PeopleTools option global system wide setting. This setting is normally assigned once, at the time you set up your system, and then never changed. Second, is to create your Temporary Tables. This is assuming you are building a new Application Engine program. You could create your Temporary Tables after you have built your Application Engine programs but then you would have to go back into the Application Engine program and connect the Temporary Tables to it. There are a few new items that involve using some special Meta SQL and that will be discussed here as well.

Setting PeopleTools Options for Temporary Tables

This is a PeopleTools options system wide setting where you define processing for Application Engine Temporary Tables. This is a system wide value to give the most likely number of an Application Engine program that will be running at the same time. There is a caveat to just making this a very large number. This does take up Database space in creating large number of files; you are also limited to a maximum of 99. Just because you can set a large value here does not mean you should. Set this value to a reasonable, expected number.

To fill in this value – use the Internet client menu: PeopleTools – Utilities – PeopleTools Options. This will open a page, as shown in figure 5.1.

Input in the value of the number of instances for online process in the Temp Table Instances (Total) field. Once you input this number you will receive a warning that you will need to update all Temporary Tables. This value you just entered does affect ALL Temporary Tables so only change this if you have to. A change here could cause a lot of work to be done to make sure the necessary number of Temporary Tables is created. Once this value is set, you typically do not have to ever change it again.

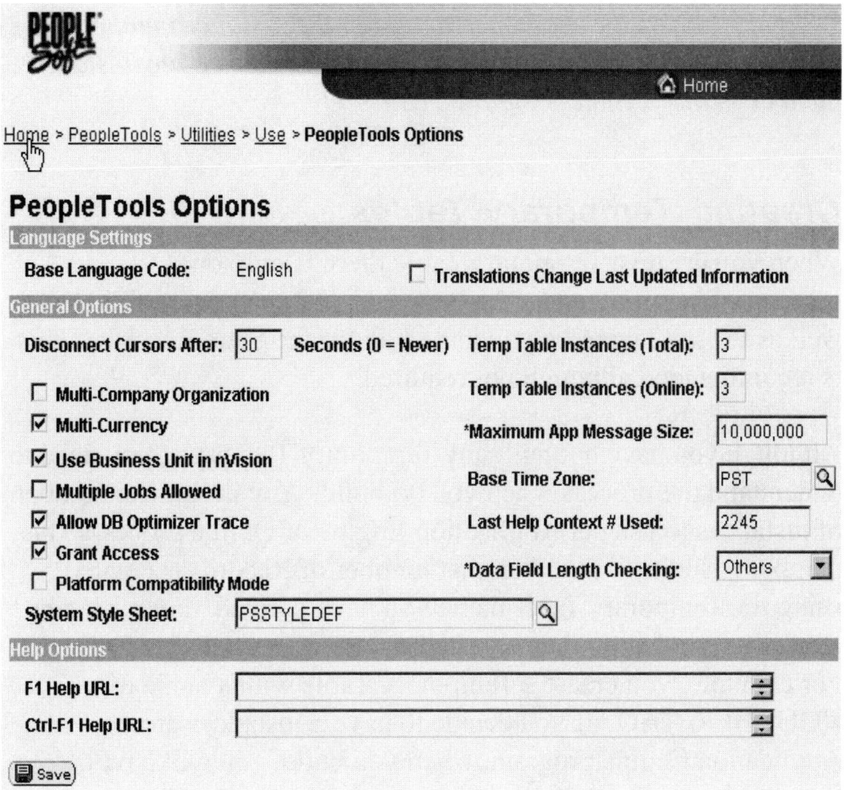

Figure 5.1 PeopleTools Options

The input of the (Total) field will change the value within the Temp Table Instances (Online). It is really this field (Online) that controls the number of instances to be created and allowed to run but this field is controlled by the (Total) field. The (Online) field cannot exceed the (Total) field but it can be less. It is recommended to leave these two fields the same, changing them when recommended by your System Administrator and only in specific conditions.

***Note**: The (Online) field should be set with a value for compatibility with earlier versions of PeopleTools. Meta SQL - %Table – allows the developer to assign the instance number. The number input here in this field must equal or exceed any instance number in the %Table Meta SQL call.*

Creating Temporary Tables

When you create a Temporary Table there is only one recommendation, to make the Process Instance the first field as well as the key; just like you had to do for the State Records. This is recommended although not required.

Although you have not built any Temporary Tables yet, you need to understand the process when you do build. You define the number of instances to use per Application Engine or Online process. This number is summed and then that number of Records is created using the Temporary Table name you have defined. For each new Record created a number is suffixed onto the base Record name. For example, you create a Temporary Table with a name of VOUCHER_TAO. If you decide to have 3 instances on an Application Engine program, when you build, you will have created the one Base Record with the name as you defined and 3 more Records with the names of VOUCHER_TAO0, VOUCHER_TAO1, VOUCHER_TAO2.

When the Application Engine program runs, PeopleSoft will keep in the background a table updated with the Process Instance and the name of the Temporary Table – such as VOUCHER_TAO2. This table tells the system that this Temporary Table is busy with which process instance. So you can see you do not have to have Process Instance in the field since a Record is linked to a specific Process Instance run. There is, however, one condition where this can be a problem.

This condition exists when you have defined for an Application Engine the number of Temporary Instances to have but that number has been exceeded when users launch the Application Engine program many times concurrently. What happens then is the Base Temporary Table (VOUCHER_TAO) will have added to it a row of data using the process instance to keep the data unique. This is a safeguard to keep the program running although you lose all efficiency by having separate Records. This condition is allowed by a control on the Application Engine runtime value. (You will learn this in the next section when you connect your Application Engine to Temporary Tables). The normal default is Continue – meaning to allow programs to continue if the number of instances has been exceeded. The other allowed setting is Abort, you will learn all about this in the next section.

***Note**: If you decide to use the setting of Continue, you must then have Process Instance in the key structure of your Temporary Tables.*

At this point, you decide whether to add Process Instance as a key and then you can continue to add Fields to your Temporary Table definition, just as you would any Record definition. You can add any Field you wish with any type that you will need in the processing of your program. Once you have your Temporary Tables created in Application Designer, be sure to go to the Record Type and select Temporary Table, as shown in figure 5.2.

The name you give your Temporary Table is not constrained by any rules but if you follow PeopleSoft's recommendation you will see that all Temporary Tables end in "_TAO". This is done so that it is easy to see a Temporary Table, not only for the base Record but all the instances that are built.

Determine your name and save your Temporary Table continuing on with the process by connecting this Temporary Table to your Application Engine program.

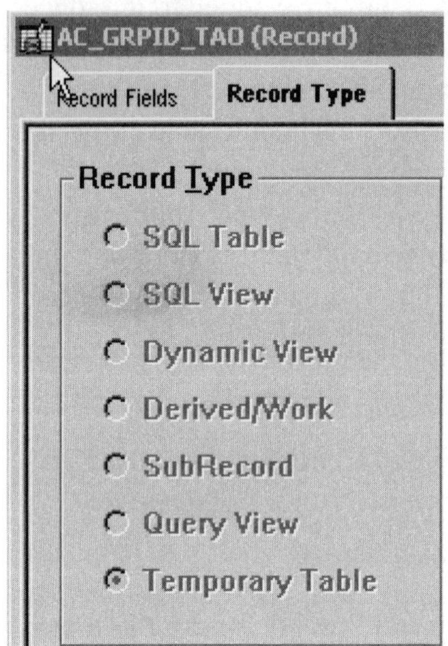

Figure 5.2 Record Definition – Record Type tab.

***Note**: Special attention may need to be given to proper indexes. Handling large amounts of data or special ways in which you will use the Temporary Table may require you to use system or non-system indexes. Work with your database administrator for proper indexing as to how you have decided to use your Temporary Table.*

Connecting Application Engine to Temporary Tables

You do not have to have the whole Application Engine program written to perform this set up as you can do it when you first create the program. You can also add Temporary Tables later as you determine your program flow. The way to associate the Temporary Table to an Application Engine is to have the program open in the Application Designer work area.

Once your program is open, click on the Properties button, or use the menu: File – Object Properties. This will open the Application Engine Properties panel, as you have seen before in Chapter 4 on State Records, except this time click on the Temp Table tab, as shown in figure 5.3.

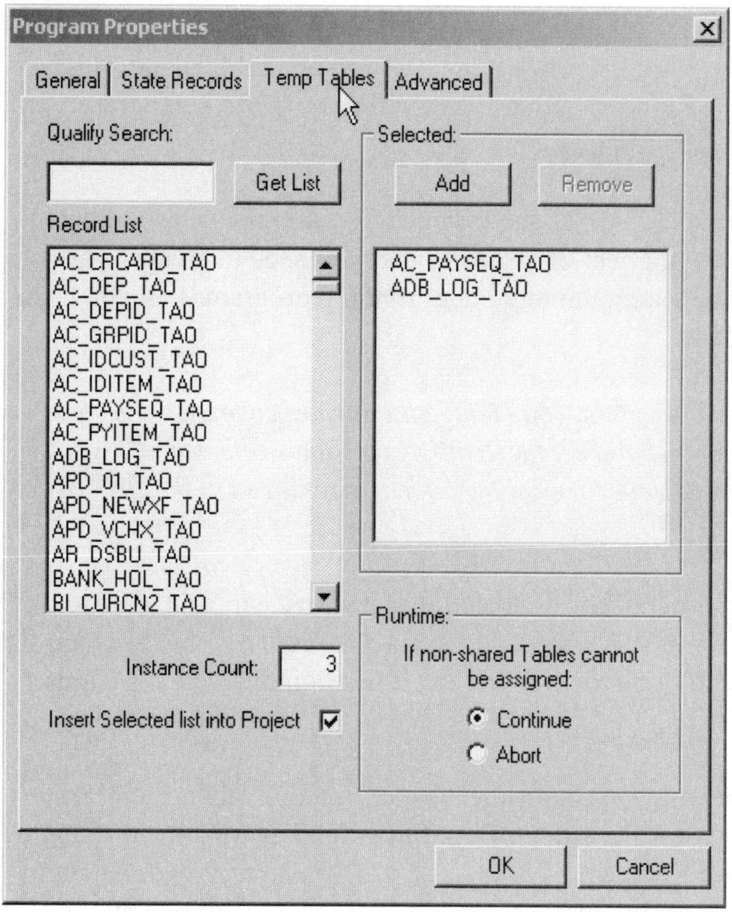

Figure 5.3 Application Engine Properties – Temp Table tab.

This looks and acts very similarly to the State Record tab. You have the Qualify Search field where you can enter in a partial name or just leave blank. Then, click on the Get List button to have the Record list area fill in. You can then scroll up and down the list to find the exact Temporary Table that you wish to connect to this Application Engine program. Once you find the Temporary Table you want to use, double click on it to have it appear in the Selected list. You can also click once on the Temporary Table name in the Record list and then click the Add button to also have it added to the Selected list.

If you need to remove a Temporary Table from an Application Engine program; first click on the Temporary Table name and then click on the Remove button. This will remove the Temporary Table from the Application Engine.

Next you move lower to the Instance Count Field. This is where you enter the number of instances that you need to create. This is typically the maximum number of running programs that you have or will allow.

***Warning**: Every time you change the Instance Count values you will have to re-build all the Temporary Tables affected. This includes the Temporary Tables added or removed in the Record list.*

Next you see a check box that allows you to easily add all of your Selected Temporary Tables to the current project. This is a nice aid to easily add these to your project; it is recommended to use this feature.

The last setting you can change is the Runtime value. Here, you can see the default setting of Continue. This is what most Application Engine programs use but if you have a requirement to control the number of running programs that are defined by your Instance count, you can then force any additional attempts to run this Application Engine program to automatically abort by selecting the setting to Abort.

Once these settings are in place you are ready to build the Temporary Tables.

Building Temporary Tables

Before you actually get to building you need to understand the number of tables to be built and the limitations there. The number of tables to be built cannot exceed 100 (0 through 99). This number is calculated from the PeopleTools Option field, plus taking every Application Engine program the Temporary Table is used in, plus the Instance count within the Application Engine properties field. To understand better, note the following information:

- PeopleTools Option – (Total) field set to 3
- App Engine 1 using Temp Record PS_TMP1_TAO with Instance of 4
- App Engine 2 using Temp Record PS_TMP1_TAO with Instance of 2
- App Engine 2 using Temp Record PS_FLR1_TAO with Instance of 2
- App Engine 3 using Temp Record PS_TMP1_TAO with Instance of 3

This would create Temporary Tables PS_TMP1_TAO with 12 instances (3 + 4 + 2 + 3) and PS_FLR1_TAO with 5 instances (3 + 2).

From this you can see that if your Temporary Table is used in many programs the count can be built up fast. The numbering convention starts with 0 and goes up through the maximum of 99. A specific number is NOT assigned to the Application Engine or Online process at this point. Only the number of Records is created and available for use.

When you build these Temporary Tables you should not just build online; the recommendation is to use the SQL script. This is done so that you can take the information in the script and modify it.

The reason for modifying the script is that you may want, and it is recommended, to move different Temporary Tables into different table spaces within your database. This is done to keep up the efficiency of the database and distribute the load among many table spaces. You should work this issue through with your database administrator.

Once you complete your building of the script you are complete with the process of building Temporary Tables.

Understanding Temporary Tables

There are three ways the Application Engine programs can run. First, and most likely, is running through the Process Scheduler. Secondly, is running an Application Engine program that is called from within another Application Engine program. Last, is the process of launching from PeopleCode. Each of these methods has some specific ways of processing which affect how the program is written and used for Temporary Tables. Each of these is discussed in the next sections.

Standard Application Engine using Temporary Tables

When you run an Application Engine program that has Temporary Tables, the PeopleSoft system assigns a number to each Temporary Table Instance. This number may be different for each Temporary Table. To make this clear, review the example of multiple Application Engine programs.

- App Engine 1 using Temp Record PS_TMP1_TAO with Instance of 4
- App Engine 2 using Temp Record PS_TMP1_TAO with Instance of 2
- App Engine 2 using Temp Record PS_FLR1_TAO with Instance of 2
- App Engine 3 using Temp Record PS_TMP1_TAO with Instance of 3

When App Engine Program one runs, it is assigned the Temporary Table of PS_TMP1_TAO0. Then, when App Engine 2 is started, it receives the Temporary Tables of PS_TMP1_TAO1 and PS_FLR1_TAO0. You can see with the second program Record one is referenced with a '1' while the second record (PS_FLR1_TAO0) is referenced with a '0'. This shows you the process is just allocated with the first available Record reference starting from 0 and continuing on up until the maximum number is reached.

Once a Temporary Table is assigned, the first action automatically done is that the Record is truncated – this means the entire Record is deleted of all data. This is so you can start with a clean slate so that no previous data clutters up your process. If you need to pass information between Application Engine programs, you should use a standard Record definition and not a Temporary Table. If the Application Engine program has exceeded the number of instances and you have allowed the program to run by having the Runtime value of Continue, the PeopleSoft system will first delete data from the base Temporary Table using the Process Instance of the starting program, then the system will insert a row of data using the Process Instance. A truncate cannot be done here, as that would remove all rows when only the one process instance needs to be deleted.

There is a Control Record within PeopleSoft (not the Base Temporary Table - PS_AEONLINEINST) that is monitoring which Application Engine process has control of which Temporary Tables, so that all is kept in control. Once a Temporary Table is assigned, it is "locked" to the running Application Engine and is not released until the Application Engine program is finished or cancelled by the user through the Process Monitor page.

You will note that an error status was not mentioned about when the Temporary Table is released. This is because there are special conditions for when an error occurs. If the Application Engine program can restart, the Temporary Tables are locked and remain locked until either the program completes normally or is cancelled. If restart has been turned off in the Application Engine program, the Temporary Tables are released if the abort was a controlled abort – meaning an error existed to cause an abort function like a database or PeopleCode error. If this same non-restart program "crashes" – meaning that a major problem was encountered like a system crash or database failure – the Temporary Tables remained locked and are unable to be used by this or any other Application Engine program. The only way to fix them is to use the Process Monitor page process to cancel the Process Instance.

If you happen to use an outside process, command line or 3rd party system to launch Application Engine programs you may have an issue. If your program goes into an error status, the Temporary Tables are locked and you have to use the Manage Abends page to release the Temporary Tables.

Using the Manage Abends Page

If an Application Engine program has gone to an error status, you can manually release the Temporary Tables by using a page called Manage Abends. This is not recommended unless you are certain of what you are doing. The only specific case where this may need to be done is with the command line or 3rd party process launching systems.

Use the Internet client to access this Page. Follow the menu: PeopleTools – Application Engine – Use – Manage Abends. This will open the page as shown in figure 5.4.

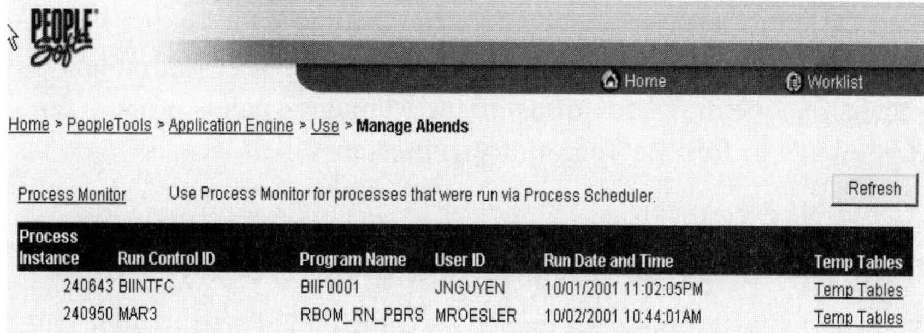

Home > PeopleTools > Application Engine > Use > **Manage Abends**

Process Monitor — Use Process Monitor for processes that were run via Process Scheduler. [Refresh]

Process Instance	Run Control ID	Program Name	User ID	Run Date and Time	Temp Tables
240643	BIINTFC	BIIF0001	JNGUYEN	10/01/2001 11:02:05PM	Temp Tables
240950	MAR3	RBOM_RN_PBRS	MROESLER	10/02/2001 10:44:01AM	Temp Tables

Figure 5.4 Mange Abends Page

Once you see the program from which you wish to release the Temporary Tables, click on the hyperlink on the far right called Temp Tables. This will open the Page, as shown in figure 5.5

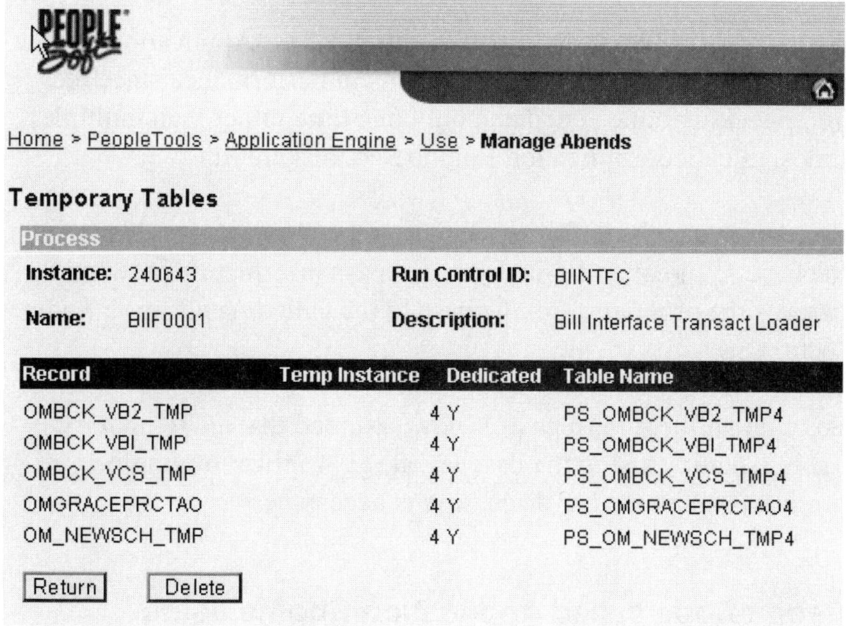

Home > PeopleTools > Application Engine > Use > **Manage Abends**

Temporary Tables

Process

Instance: 240643 **Run Control ID:** BIINTFC

Name: BIIF0001 **Description:** Bill Interface Transact Loader

Record	Temp Instance	Dedicated	Table Name
OMBCK_VB2_TMP	4	Y	PS_OMBCK_VB2_TMP4
OMBCK_VBI_TMP	4	Y	PS_OMBCK_VBI_TMP4
OMBCK_VCS_TMP	4	Y	PS_OMBCK_VCS_TMP4
OMGRACEPRCTAO	4	Y	PS_OMGRACEPRCTAO4
OM_NEWSCH_TMP	4	Y	PS_OM_NEWSCH_TMP4

[Return] [Delete]

Figure 5.5 Temporary Tables.

You can see the full list of Temporary Tables here and the information about them. If you wish to release these Records, you click on the Delete button. This will release the hold on all of the Temporary Tables. You will get a warning that by releasing these Temporary Tables the Process Instance will not be re-startable. This is the one drawback of using the Manage Abends process but if you have to free the Temporary Tables, this is the means to do so.

Called Application Engine using Temporary Tables

You can have Temporary Tables within the called Application Engine program but this is not recommended. The issue is that the Temporary Table is not assigned to the running Application Engine program until it is called and the number of instances may be exceeded causing the base Application Engine program to abort. If this is needed, it is better to supply the Temporary Table within the base or calling Application Engine program so that a Record is locked for its use.

By having the Temporary Table within the base Application Engine program there are some improvements in performance since the Temp locking table is updated only one time rather than multiple times, as called Application Engine Sections are run.

Another reason is that by having all of the Temporary Tables within the base Application Engine you can pass information between all parts of the program from the base to the called Application Engine section.

So, with all these reasons, it is now assumed that all Temporary Tables should exist in the base or calling Application Engine program and no further discussion is necessary.

PeopleCode called Application Engine using Temporary Tables

When you use the CallAppEngine PeopleCode function and you are going to be using Temporary Tables; the called Application Engine program must contain at least one Temporary Table. This is a requirement because the PeopleSoft system needs to determine and lock a process instance. Normally, a process instance is not assigned to a PeopleCode called Application Engine program but the requirement for Temporary Tables means one will be assigned.

A process instance is assigned via a random selection process. This process instance is then locked and cannot be used by any other program. If during processing, another Application Engine program is launched online and is defined with the same process instance, this second Application Engine program will wait until the first called Application Engine program is complete or errors out.

The random number is defined as the PeopleTools Option (Online) field – see Setting PeopleTools Options for Temporary Tables section above for more information. This field defines the set of numbers beginning with 0 to the number entered in this field. The larger the number here, the less likely that you will have a conflict on one process holding up another.

If your Application Engine program does not use Temporary Tables then this requirement to have a Temporary Table does not need to be met. If you have this issue and forget to place a Temporary Table within the Application Engine, you will receive a run time error where the message will be "Invalid attempt to process Temporary Table".

Inquiry Information on Temporary Tables

Within the PeopleTools Application Engine Inquire menu there is a page to use that can show you where a Temporary Table is used. You can use this to help in debugging or find what impact you will have when making a change to this Temporary Table. This is a very useful page to an Application Engine Developer. To locate this Page, use the Internet client and follow the menu: PeopleTools – Application Engine – Inquire – Temporary Table Usage. This will open a Page, as shown in figure 5.6.

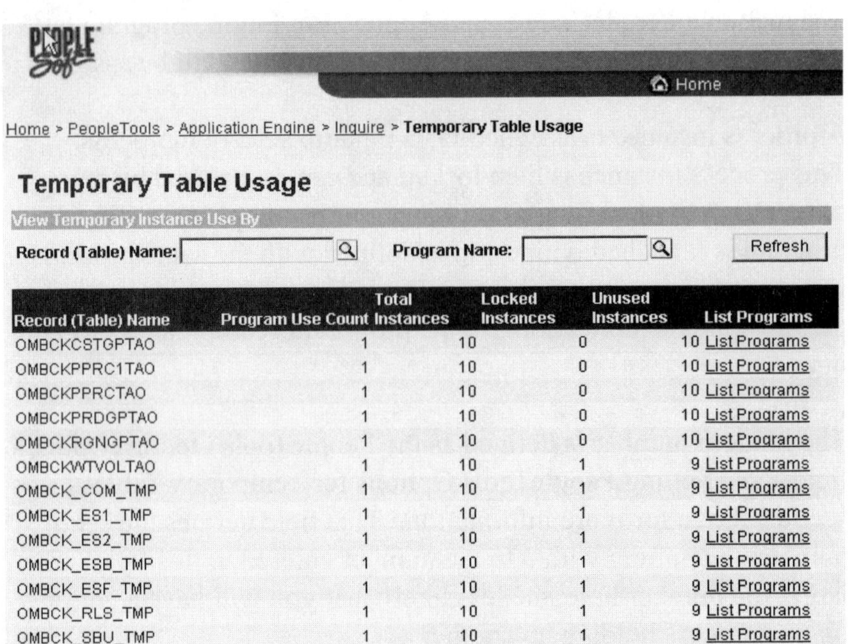

Record (Table) Name	Program Use Count	Total Instances	Locked Instances	Unused Instances	List Programs
OMBCKCSTGPTAO	1	10	0	10	List Programs
OMBCKPPRC1TAO	1	10	0	10	List Programs
OMBCKPPRCTAO	1	10	0	10	List Programs
OMBCKPRDGPTAO	1	10	0	10	List Programs
OMBCKRGNGPTAO	1	10	0	10	List Programs
OMBCKWTVOLTAO	1	10	1	9	List Programs
OMBCK_COM_TMP	1	10	1	9	List Programs
OMBCK_ES1_TMP	1	10	1	9	List Programs
OMBCK_ES2_TMP	1	10	1	9	List Programs
OMBCK_ESB_TMP	1	10	1	9	List Programs
OMBCK_ESF_TMP	1	10	1	9	List Programs
OMBCK_RLS_TMP	1	10	1	9	List Programs
OMBCK_SBU_TMP	1	10	1	9	List Programs

Figure 5.6 Temporary Table Usage Page

You can see here a full list of Temporary Tables that have been assigned to an Application Engine program. If you know of a Temporary Table and you do not see it in the list, that is because the Record is not connected to any Application Engine programs. You can also use the Record name field to find a specific Temporary Table name and then click the Refresh button to have it show the information. You can also input the Application Engine program name in the Program Name field to have it show all the Temporary Tables connected to just that one program.

The Program Use Count displays the number of instances that could be assigned to the program. Total Instances displays the total number of instances of each Record name. Locked Instances displays the number of instances that have been locked for the Record name. Unused Instances are the number of free or available instances for the Record Name. The hyperlink of List Programs on the far right of each Temporary Table will take you to a new Page that shows all of the Programs that use that selected Temporary Table, as shown in figure 5.7.

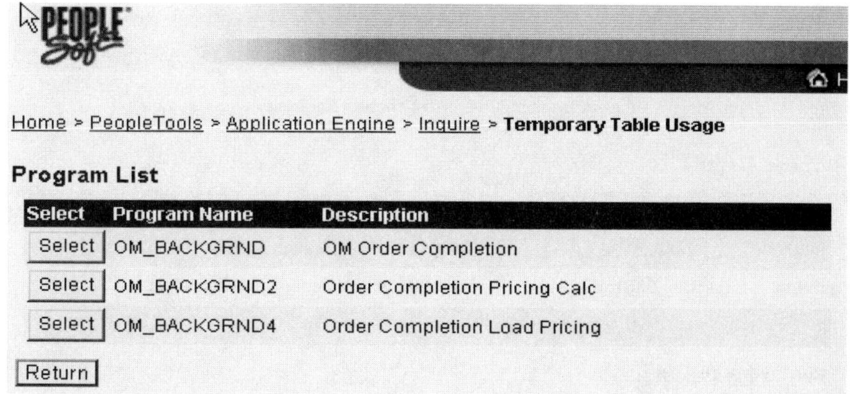

Figure 5.7 Temporary Table Usage Page – List Programs

Process Monitor

With Process Monitor itself, you can see a few things about an Application Engine. If the program goes into error or no success, you can see which Temporary Table is locked by clicking on the Process Instance. This takes you to the Process Detail Page, as shown in figure 5.8.

You can see here a Hyperlink in the bottom right corner called Temp Tables. By clicking this link you will be taken to the Temporary Tables page. Here, you can see the Base Temporary Table name, the Instance number used and the full Record name, as shown in figure 5.9.

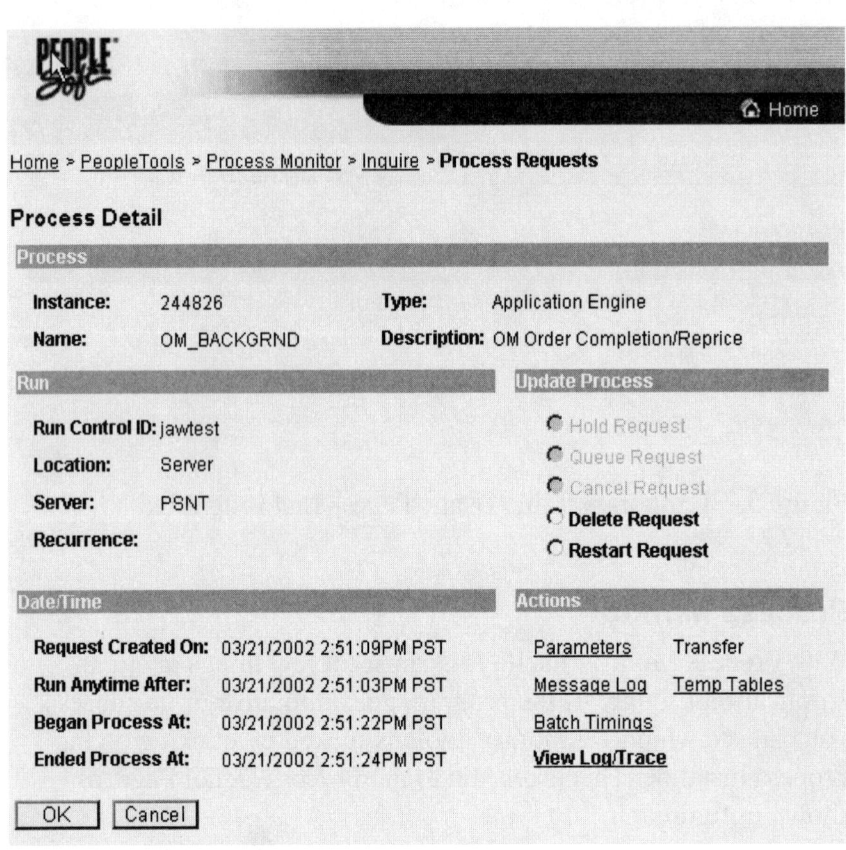

Figure 5.8 Process Detail in Process Monitor

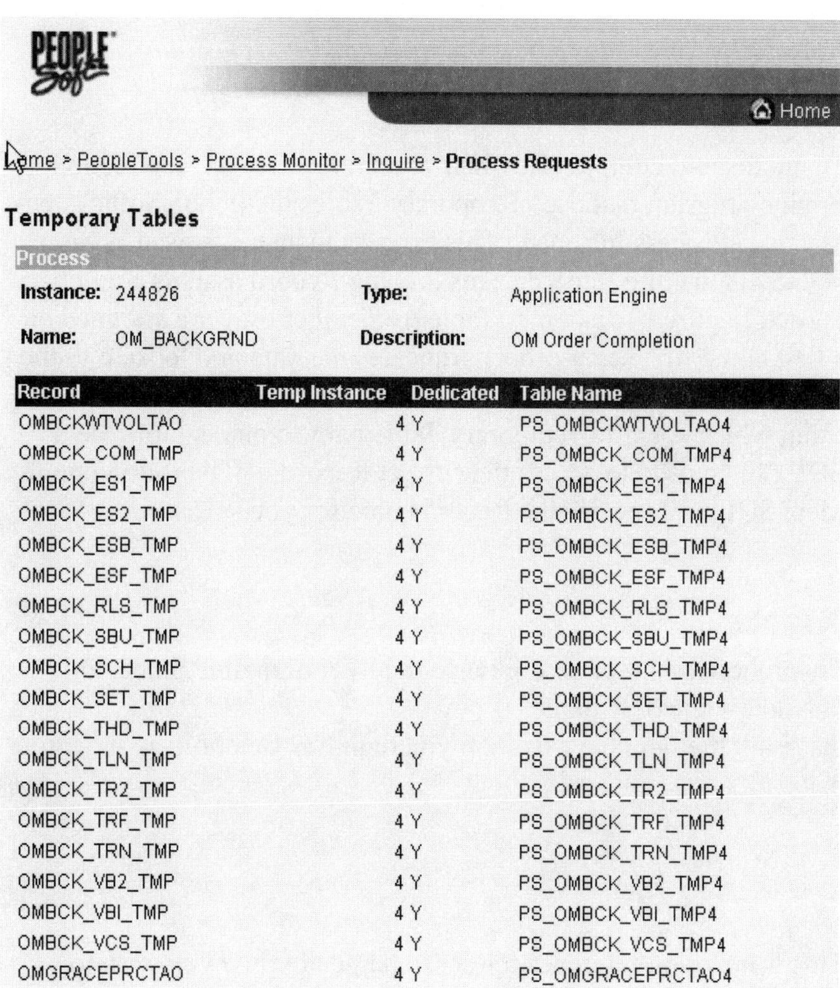

Record	Temp Instance	Dedicated	Table Name
OMBCKWTVOLTAO	4	Y	PS_OMBCKWTVOLTAO4
OMBCK_COM_TMP	4	Y	PS_OMBCK_COM_TMP4
OMBCK_ES1_TMP	4	Y	PS_OMBCK_ES1_TMP4
OMBCK_ES2_TMP	4	Y	PS_OMBCK_ES2_TMP4
OMBCK_ESB_TMP	4	Y	PS_OMBCK_ESB_TMP4
OMBCK_ESF_TMP	4	Y	PS_OMBCK_ESF_TMP4
OMBCK_RLS_TMP	4	Y	PS_OMBCK_RLS_TMP4
OMBCK_SBU_TMP	4	Y	PS_OMBCK_SBU_TMP4
OMBCK_SCH_TMP	4	Y	PS_OMBCK_SCH_TMP4
OMBCK_SET_TMP	4	Y	PS_OMBCK_SET_TMP4
OMBCK_THD_TMP	4	Y	PS_OMBCK_THD_TMP4
OMBCK_TLN_TMP	4	Y	PS_OMBCK_TLN_TMP4
OMBCK_TR2_TMP	4	Y	PS_OMBCK_TR2_TMP4
OMBCK_TRF_TMP	4	Y	PS_OMBCK_TRF_TMP4
OMBCK_TRN_TMP	4	Y	PS_OMBCK_TRN_TMP4
OMBCK_VB2_TMP	4	Y	PS_OMBCK_VB2_TMP4
OMBCK_VBI_TMP	4	Y	PS_OMBCK_VBI_TMP4
OMBCK_VCS_TMP	4	Y	PS_OMBCK_VCS_TMP4
OMGRACEPRCTAO	4	Y	PS_OMGRACEPRCTAO4

Figure 5.9 Temporary Tables page in Process Monitor

Using Meta SQL for Temporary Tables

The purpose of Meta SQL for Temporary Tables is how do you write your Application Engine code to use the correct instance since you do not, at the time of writing, know which instance may be assigned? They are used to help the system understand which

Temporary Table to use, without having the developer write in lots of code.

Note*: All of the Meta SQL is not included in this section, just those functions used specifically for Temporary Tables.*

To understand completely, when you first launch an Application Engine program that uses Temporary Tables the PeopleSoft system assigns a Process Instance. This Process Instance is used as the key to the locking Record. This locking Record assigns a number to each required Temporary Table (remember they are assigned on a first come first serve order), truncates the data and locks it to the program. Now that the program knows which Process Instance is using which specific Temporary Table name, some simple Meta SQL can be used to access the correct Records. The following Meta SQL will specify the Record name for you.

%Table

This function is used to reference the Record name. Since you only know the base name,
that is all that you have to supply here in this function, as shown below.

```
%Table(TMP1_TAO)
%Table(FLR1_TAO)
```

This is how you reference a Record name anytime you wish to access a Temporary Table. The first example assumes you have a record name of PS_TMP1_TAO, the second example is for the Record of PS_FLR1_TAO. This function can be used in a Select, Insert or Update SQL statement. Check out the examples below.

```
%Select(PO_ID, VENDOR_ID)
select distinct PO_ID, VENDOR_ID from %Table(TMP1_TAO)
where exists (select 'X' from PS_VENDOR A
         where %Table(TMP1_TAO).SETID = A.SETID
         and %Table(TMP1_TAO).VENDOR_ID = A.VENDOR_ID
        and A.VENDOR_CLASS = 'A')
```

```
Update %Table(FLR1_TAO) set STATUS = 'C'

Insert %Table(FLR1_TAO)
select BUSINESS_UNIT, VOUCHER_ID
from PS_VOUCHER
where ORIGIN = 'ACX'
```

You can see here the way to write various SQL commands using the %Table Meta SQL function. You can use this just as if you had to write the Record name.

There is just one issue that needs to be noted here. It was not shown in the examples above but if you have set your Application Engine to allow it to continue when the number of instances is exceeded, you MUST have in all where clauses the Process Instance included where you use a Temporary Table. This is because you may not be using a specific instance of a Temporary Table but may be using the base Temporary Table and this may have multiple instances running at the same time. If you do not include the Process Instance in the where clause, you may be affecting data not only in your specific run of this program but others as well.

%TruncateTable

There may come a time within your Application Engine program that you wish to remove all the data in a Record. You could do this through a delete command and use of the %Table Meta SQL command but PeopleSoft offers a much better and more efficient way of handling this issue. When your Application Engine program starts, all of the Temporary Tables are deleted using a Truncate SQL command. If your program requires, you can truncate the tables again using the %TruncateTable function.

***Note**: PeopleSoft recommends using the %TruncateTable function as this is much more efficient SQL on database engines when performing an all encompassing delete of data from a Record.*

Once you need to delete all data from a Temporary Table you can use the following function.

```
%TruncateTable(TMP1_TAO2)
%TruncateTable(%Table(FLR1_TAO))
```

Here, you can see two examples. The first example can be done but is NOT recommended. You can see that the function call uses the Record name exactly. This is allowed but how do you know that your Application Engine program is using the 3rd instance. It is not recommended to use this way to call the function. Instead, it is recommended to use the second example. Here, you have to use not only the %TruncateTable function but in the Record name area you use the %Table function as well. You can see that using the %Table function precludes you from having to use the hard coded Record name. By using this process the Application Engine will convert to the correct instance and remove the information correctly.

Just as in the %Table function, there are the rules about using Process Instance if you have set your Application Engine to continue and the number of instances is exceeded. This is due to the fact that the %TruncateTable function will not truncate the full table if you have exceeded the number of instances and you are using the base Temporary Table. In this case, this function knows that and converts itself into a Delete SQL command to remove only those rows of data in the base Temporary Table that match the process instance.

Next

This completes the information on the Temporary Table but there are new things still to learn about the Application Engine program. The next chapter deals with the functions of Meta SQL. You have learned some here already and in Chapter 4, but there are many more to use that can make your program much more powerful and easier to write as well.

Chapter 6

Application Engine Meta SQL and Variables

This chapter covers all of the Meta SQL and Variables that can be used within Application Engine. You have also been exposed to some of the commands in the earlier chapters but this chapter will cover them completely. You may have learned the basics of the command but it would be good to review here as all of the parameters for the command are listed in this chapter. First, you will learn all the Meta-SQL commands and then the system variables.

Application Engine Meta SQL

The following Meta-SQL commands can be used in Application Engine processing. These can be used not only for Application Engine but regular Record PeopleCode, COBOL or other processes as well. Since you are only learning about Application Engine, it is not noted as to where else these commands may be used. For that type of information, see Developing PeopleSoft Applications with PeopleTools 8.1.

%Abs

This command takes a number value and returns the absolute value. You can use a single variable, field or expression in this command.

```
%Select (PO_ID)
Select PO_ID from PS_TEMP1 where %ABS(PRICE * QTY)
>100
```

%Bind

This command allows you to retrieve information from your State Records and use it just like a variable. You are allowed to use the %Bind command just as if you were typing in a hard coded value within an SQL statement. This means you can place the %Bind command in just about any place within a SQL statement, as shown in the example below.

```
Select %bind(value1), EMPLOYEE_ID, USER1
from PS_EMP_TEMP2
where PROCESS_INSTANCE = %bind(process_instance)
```

As you can see, you can use the %Bind in the field list and the where clause. The %Bind can also be in sub selects, insert statements and update statements.

The only required parameter in using the bind command is knowing the field name, as shown in the following example. This also assumes that the field listed here is in the default State Record. If you need to access a field that is not in the default State Record, you need to include the State Record name in the command, as is shown in the following example.

```
Select %bind(emp2_aet.value1), EMPLOYEE_ID, USER1
from PS_EMP_TEMP2
where PROCESS_INSTANCE =
  %bind(emp1.aetprocess_instance)
```

The same SQL statement is shown here as before but shows now with the State Record names defined. You can use any number of State Records since you are only requesting the value be taken from the State Record and replaced here. You are not required to list the default State Record but you can if you desire.

***Note**: If you call another Application Engine section – the called Application Engine program may have a different default State Record. You must be aware of this when running Application Engine programs.*

It is assumed that when you use a %Bind command that the field type you are using matches the field type within the SQL statement. This means, if you have a character field in the %Bind command that you use this %Bind command where a character is to be used and not against a number field. If you use a wrong type, you will receive a run time error within your SQL.

That is the basic use of this command and what you will use most of the time but the %Bind command does have a few more parameters to use.

- NOQUOTES
- NOWRAP
- STATIC

NOQUOTES

This parameter forces the use of the %Bind command to not automatically wrap character based fields with quotes. Normally, you would not ever want to do this, as it would cause the SQL statement to fail and give you a run time error; but you have not learned the real power of the %Bind command yet. So far you have only learned that you can use the %Bind as a variable within a SQL statement but you can do more, as shown in the examples below.

```
Select voucher_id, vendor_id, journal_id
from %bind(empl_aet.table_name, NOQUTES)
where date < %Date

Select %bind(field_list, NOQUOTES)
from %bind(table_name, NOQUOTES)
where %bind(where_text, NOQUOTES)
```

If you look at the first example, you see that the record name is missing from the SQL statement and has been replaced with a %Bind command. You can have the Record dynamically defined here. Of course, this assumes prior to this SQL statement, you have defined this variable with the full Record name (PS_xxxxx). Normally, the %Bind statement would have put quotes around the record name but then this would then not have resolved to a correct SQL statement as shown in the following example.

WRONG

```
Select voucher_id, vendor_id, journal_id
from 'PS_EMPTEMP1'
where date < %Date
```

CORRECT

```
Select voucher_id, vendor_id, journal_id
from PS_EMPTEMP1
where date < %Date
```

The first example shows what happens without the NOQUOTES parameter. This is an invalid SQL statement and will fail, whereas the second SQL statement is accurate and will work just as planned.

In the second example of NOQUOTES there were three %Bind commands used. This just shows to the level of what you can do. You can replace all of a SQL statement if you wish by using just one %Bind command, if that field has been loaded with the text of the SQL Statement. Combining this parameter with PeopleCode, you can first have PeopleCode make some logic decisions and build the SQL statement string, then you can use the %Bind command to issue the SQL statement. Very powerful stuff!

NOWRAP

This parameter is used specifically for date, datetime and time fields. Normally, when a %Bind command is used with date, datetime or time field, the PeopleSoft processor modifies the %Bind command behind the scenes to use the %datein or %dateout Meta-SQL commands. This makes the date, datetime or time field work correctly for the specific database platform. You can, however, turn this process off by using the NOWRAP command.

```
Select voucher_id, vendor_id, journal_id
from PS_EMPTEMP1
where DATE < %Bind(date_early, NOWRAP)
```

This example shows the use of the parameter. The only reason that you should do this is when you are sure the date, datetime or time field is perfectly in the format for the database you are using.

Now, should you go through all your code to find where your date is formatted in the database? Do not waste your time – only use this parameter when your program has a need to override the database specific format for some reason.

STATIC

This parameter is only used when your SQL statement is using a BIND variable and it has been set with the ReUse statement to Yes. What this says is that the variable using this parameter is NOT changing in the following SQL code so that the database can optimize the code properly; otherwise the database will assume this variable is changing. This helps a great deal when you have to optimize your code. The proper use of the parameter is as follows.

```
Select voucher_id, vendor_id, journal_id
from PS_EMPTEMP1
where vendor_id = %Bind(vendor_id, STATIC)
```

%ClearCursor

This Meta SQL recompiles a SQL statement or many SQL statements, if allowed to be recompiled, depending on the use of this command. It also resets any static bind variables used within the re-compiled SQL statements. This would normally be used when a section is used once and then is going to be used again. This helps the database run optimally.

There are two ways to use this command. First, is the All method, as shown in the following example. This example will re-compile all SQL statements within the Application Engine program where it is used.

```
%ClearCursor(ALL)
```

The second way to use this command is to specify the exact SQL statement to be re-compiled. In this command you have to supply the program name, Section name, Step name and Action type (of course the Action type must contain a SQL statement).

```
%ClearCursor(PO_POSTAGE, PS0600, GETBU, S)
```

The example shows how to re-compile the SQL statement in the program PO_POSTAGE, section PS0600, Step PS0600, Action SQL. See the list below for all of the Action types and special codes to use.

Action Type	**Code**
Do Select	D
Do When	H
Do While	W
Do Until	N
SQL	S

%Concat

This command concatenates two character string fields together into one field. This is sometimes used to combine key fields together into one string.

```
%Select(KEYVALUE)
Select BUSINESS_UNIT %Concat PO_ID %Concat LINE_NBR
from PS_TMP1_VW
```

***Note**: Some databases will not allow you to concatenate number fields with string fields or other combinations. This is specific to each database so it is only recommended to use this command in character type fields.*

%DateAdd

This returns a date value when you supply the start date and the number of days to add or subtract. If you use a negative number, then the process will do subtraction, versus a positive number that adds. This Meta-SQL function is typically used within PeopleCode (Record, Page, Component or Application Engine) but can be used within the Application Engine SQL.

```
%Select(Due_date)
Select %DateAdd (%CurrentDateOut, %Bind(BU_Leadtime))
from PS_INSTALLATION
```

%DateDiff

This returns an integer number representing the number of days that is the difference between two dates supplied to the command. Again, this is normally used in PeopleCode but can be used within Application Engine SQL.

```
%Select (Track_Nbr)
Select Track_Num from PS_TEMP1
where %DateDiff(%CurrentDateIn, %Bind(BU_Date)) > 10
```

%DateIn

This expands to a database specific SQL string representing the date supplied in the parameter list. This is normally used in the where clause of a SQL select statement or update statement. This can also be used to update or insert a date to a date type field. The key is that you are loading the date into a field within a database Record.

```
Update %Table(FLR_TAO)
set RUN_DATE = %DateIn(%Bind(Process_date))

Update %Table(FLR_TAO)
set RUN_DATE = %DateIn('2002-04-27')
```

The command assumes the value in the parameter list is either a date field or is in the character format of YYYY-MM-DD.

%DateOut

This expands to a database specific SQL string representing the date supplied in the parameter list. This is used for dates within the select clause of an SQL query. This select statement can be used to load Bind variables or to be part of an insert statement where this is used within the select portion only.

```
%Select (run_date)
select %DateOut(DATE_TO)
from PS_RUN_CNTRL_IN
where PROCESS_INSTANCE = %ProcessInstance
```

***Note**: A special point to understand in the "%Date" Meta SQL is that IN means into the database and OUT means out from the database. This simple understanding will help you understand when to use each type.*

%DateTimeDiff

This command is similar to the %DateDiff but now the comparison is between two datetime fields and the results are the number of minutes.

```
%Select (Track_Nbr)
Select Track_Num
from PS_TEMP1
where %DateTimeDiff(%CurrentDateTimeIn,
   %Bind(MAX_DTTM)) > 10
```

%DateTimeIn

This expands to a database specific SQL string representing the date and time supplied in the parameter list. This is normally used in the where clause of a SQL select statement or update statement. This can also be used to update or insert a datetime value to a datetime type field.

```
Update %Table(FLR_TAO)
set PROCESS_DTTM = %DateTimeIn(%Bind(Process_dttm))

Update %Table(FLR_TAO)
set PROCESS_DTTM =
   %DateTimeIn('2002-04-27-06.15.01.000000')
```

The command assumes the value in the parameter list is either a datetime field or is in the character format of YYYY-MM-DD-hh.mm.ss.ssssss.

%DateTimeOut

This expands to a database specific SQL string representing the datetime supplied in the parameter list. This is used for datetime in the select clause of an SQL query. This select statement can be used to load Bind variables or to be part of an insert statement where this is used within the select portion only.

```
%Select (run_dttm)
select %DateTimeOut(PROCESS_DTTM)
from PS_RUN_CNTRL_IN
where PROCESS_INSTANCE = %ProcessInstance
```

%DecDiv

This returns a number value where the first parameter is divided by the second parameter. The parameters must be number values. A parameter is also allowed to be an expression where the results are a number value.

```
%Select (VOCUHER_ID)
select VOUCHER_ID
from %Table(FLR1_TAO)
where %DecDiv(%Bind(OPRAND), %Bind(DECIMAL)) > 100
```

%DecMult

This returns a number value where the first parameter is multiplied by the second parameter. The parameters must be number values. A parameter is also allowed to be an expression where the results are a number value.

```
%Select (VOUCHER_ID)
select VOUCHER_ID
from %Table(FLR1_TAO)
where %DecMult(%Bind(OPRAND), %Bind(DECIMAL)) < 100
```

%DTTM

This command takes a date parameter and a time parameter and creates a datetime value. The first parameter is a date while the second is the time value.

```
%Select (VOUCHER_ID)
select VOUCHER_ID
from %Table(FLR1_TAO)
where LAST_EDIT_DTTM = %DTTM(DATE, %Bind(TIME))
```

%EffDtCheck

This command takes parameters and creates an effective dates sub query to be used within a where clause. This is used to make it easier to write valid SQL statements with effective dates Records.

```
%Select (status)
Select A.eff_status
from PS_CURRENCY_CD_TBL A
where A.currency_cd = %Bind(Currency_cd)
and %EffDtCheck(CURRENCY_CD_TBL, A, %CurrentDateIn)

%Select (status)
Select A.eff_status
from PS_CURRENCY_CD_TBL A, PS_ORD_HEADER B
where A.currency_cd = B.currency_cd
and %EffDtCheck(CURRENCY_CD_TBL C, A, %Bind(Order_dt))
```

These two examples show how to use this command. The first example shows the basic structure with the Record name (string variables are not allowed here) to be used for the sub select, the Alias to use for the subselect Record and then the date parameter. The date parameter will be automatically wrapped with the %DateIn command unless you input this yourself. The first example would have expanded into the following SQL select statement.

```
Select A.eff_status
from PS_CURRENCY_CD_TBL A
where A.currency_cd = %Bind(Currency_cd)
and A.effdt = (select max(effdt)
               from PS_CURRENCY_CD_TBL
               where A.setid = setid
               and A.currency_cd = currency_cd
               and effdt <= %CurrentDateIn)
```

You can see how the SQL is built up from the command using the Records key fields that match between the first Record and the Record within the command. The application of the effdt to the date supplied is then used so that you get a proper sub select statement for an effective dated row.

The second example above shows one more parameter that is allowed. If you look just after the Record name you will see an alias listed (prior to the comma). This tells the %EffDtCheck command that the sub select table should use this as the alias. This is done so that you know which alias to use if you have to add more where clause information (see Note following). This way you can add more where clause information on the sub select record. This is not required but is highly recommended. This second example would expand into the following SQL code.

```
Select A.eff_status
from PS_CURRENCY_CD_TBL A, PS_ORD_HEADER B
where A.currency_cd = B.currency_cd
and A.effdt = (select max(C.effdt)
               from PS_CURRENCY_CD_TBL C
               where A.setid = C.setid
               and A.currency_cd = C.currency_cd
               and C.effdt <= %CurrentDateIn)
```

***Note**: This command does not take into account EFF_STATUS values or the correct EFFSEQ values. If this is required, you will need to add these fields to the where clause manually.*

%Execute

This command allows you to issue SQL commands that are specific to the database engine you are using. There may be times when you need to run a specific command using some specific syntax for an Oracle database or SQL Server database.

Note: *Even though you can, it is not recommended to use this macro for select, update or insert statements.*

This macro is mainly used to allow you to write PL-SQL (in Oracle databases) or Transact-SQL (in SQL Server databases) programs. If your database has a special programming language, then you can use it here. The Oracle and SQL Server are just examples of special database specific languages.

This macro can contain one statement or multiple statements. The requirement is that the semi-colon character (;) is used to show the break between one statement and the next. In some database languages, you may need to use the semi-colon within the statement not meaning the end of a command. This macro allows you to override the normal command break character. Review the two examples below showing different uses in different database languages.

SQL Server example using one command.

```
%Execute
While (select avg(COST) from PS_PO_TMP1 where
  IN_PROCESS_FLG = 'Y') > 3000
Begin
   update PS_PO_TMP1 set COST = COST / 10
   if (select max(COST) from PS_PO_TMP1) > 1000
      Break
   Else
      Continue
End
```

Oracle example using multiple commands and override of the break character.

```
%Execute (/)
DECLARE
   CURSOR dept_cur IS
   SELECT DEPT_ID FROM PS_DEPT_TBL ORDER BY DEPT_ID;
   CURSOR emp_cur (v_dept_no DEPT.DEPTNO%TYPE) IS
   SELECT NAME FROM PS_EMPLOYEE;
BEGIN
   FOR dept_rec IN dept_cur LOOP
      dbms_output.put_line('Employees in Department
  '||TO_CHAR(dept_rec.deptno));
      FOR emp_rec in emp_cur(dept_rec.deptno) LOOP
         dbms_output.put_line('...Employee is
  '||emp_rec.ename);
      END LOOP;
  END LOOP;
END;
/
COMMIT;
/
```

As you can see from the Oracle example, the override character is listed right after the use of the %Execute command within parenthesis. This allows the change as is needed for Oracle since you have to end some of the lines with a semi-colon.

You should also see that the %Execute command is listed first and then is followed by the database statements. This is a requirement. There is also a requirement that the Action type is only allowed to be SQL. This is done to prevent possible conflicts with the programs in how Application Engine will work with them, since you can write just about anything you can think of here.

%ExecuteEdits

The command %ExecuteEdits is a complicated function in that it requires upfront knowledge of the structure and edits that are on the Record definition. This command returns only a true or false value in its use so it is only used within SQL statement where clauses. It is typically used to find rows in a Record where the edit conditions in a different Record do not pass on to the first Record. To better understand this, review the following example.

Assume you have a Record called SALES_ORDER_TMP, which holds values that you have loaded from your Application Engine program. You want to verify that the values in this temp Record are accurate to the normal Sales Order Header Record (called ORD_HEADER). You want to verify the data since you are not going through the Order Entry Pages to load information. By not going through the Pages, the standard edits that are in the Record definition are not taken into effect. This means you could be loading information into the Record that is not fully edited and it may cause the Page to crash when some user just does an inquiry, let alone a process. To cause this edit check you have to use the following SQL statement.

```
UPDATE PS_SALES_ORDER_TMP
SET ERROR_FLAG = 'Y'
WHERE %EXECUTEEDITS(%Edit_Required + %Edit_YesNo +
  %Edit_DateRange + %Edit_PromptTable +
  %Edit_TranslateTable, ORD_HEADER)
```

This SQL Statement will update the field ERROR_FLAG with a value of 'Y' if the following condition is true. A return of True means that one of the validations has failed. This may seem backward since a true means a problem; but you have to understand the purpose of the function is to find an error and so a true result when an error occurs is logically correct.

Dissecting the %ExecuteEdits command you first see that it is used in the where clause to return a true or false logic value. The command is not used in logical comparison – such as =, < or >. Then, you will see that the command has many parameters. The first is actually a set, which you can see is put together with the plus (+) symbol. This first parameter is actually a list of the types of validation that you want to perform. Below is a list of all of the types of validation that you can perform with information on the type of validation.

Type	Validation process
%Edit_Required	This validates that a field is filled in with some value other than 0 or ' ' if the required setting is set to 'Y'.
%Edit_YesNo	This validates that all values in the field are either a 'Y' or 'N' if the prompt is set to be for Yes/No.
%Edit_DateRange	This validates if the date entered in the field is set within the reasonable range from today's date (system default is 30 days) if the reasonable date check box is set to 'Y'.
%Edit_PromptTable	This validates all values in this field match to a value within the Record that is defined in the prompt field.
%Edit_TranslateTable	This validates all values in the field match to one of the fields translate values (Xlat values).

The %ExecuteEdit command must have atleast one type of validation – it cannot be blank. You can mix or match in any way you wish as long as you use the plus symbol to join the differing validations. There is no specific order of the types that you have to use.

The second parameter is the Record definition that contains the validation routines to perform on the original Record within the SQL call. In the example, the Record definition for ORD_HEADER is gathered and applied to the Record SALES_ORDER_TMP. You may have thought here how does the system know which fields to validate. This is all based on the field name. If the field name in ORD_HEADER matches a field exactly like one in SALES_ORDER_TMP then the validation is performed using the information from ORD_HEADER on the data within the SALES_ORDER_TMP Record.

Using our example and the field BILL_TO_CUST_ID, assuming this field is on both Records, the validation would check the prompt Record since this field on the ORD_HEADER Record has the prompt table of CUST_SLDBLL_VW. The system would then use this view (CUST_SLDBLL_VW) to verify the field BILL_TO_CUST_ID on the Record SALES_ORDER_TMP that all values in this field match a value within any of the rows of data within the view CUST_SLDBLL_VW. This is just how the prompt edit would work to show how settings in one Record affect the other Record when using this %ExecuteEdits command.

Note: *The prompt edit does not have to use a view as it could use a Record.*

This is the basic use of the %ExecuteEdits command but there is more to learn here. There are additional parameters that can be applied. First, there is the possibility to use this command within an Insert SQL statement. The insert would contain a select statement where data is captured and could contain an alias on the Record name. If this is the case, you need to supply the alias name within the %ExecuteEdits as follows.

```
Insert into PS_SALES_ERROR
select A.BUSINESS_UNIT, A.ORDER_NO, A.CUST_ID
from PS_SALES_ORDER_TMP A
where A.PROCESS_INSTANCE = %Bind(PROCESS_INSTANCE)
and %ExecuteEdits(%Edit_PromptTable, ORD_HEADER A)
```

You can see here that the only thing added to the command was the addition of the letter 'A' just behind the Record name of ORD_HEADER. This is the alias that needs to be specified since the Record name within the SQL select statements has been aliased. This is required since what is really happening here is that the command is modifying the SQL statement behind the scenes to include sub queries to validate for the additional checks.

The last parameter that can be done is a list of fields that you wish to validate. In this way you do not have to validate every field but you can control the validation to occur on certain fields. Of course the name has to be the same between both tables but if you only want to validate the Order Number and the Order date you only have to process those fields, as is shown in the example below.

```
Insert into PS_SALES_ERROR
select A.BUSINESS_UNIT, A.ORDER_NO, A.CUST_ID
from PS_SALES_ORDER_TMP A
where A.PROCESS_INSTANCE = %Bind(PROCESS_INSTANCE)
and %ExecuteEdits(%Edit_PromptTable + %Edit_DateRange,
  ORD_HEADER A, ORDER_NO, ORDER_DATE)
```

Here you can see the addition of the fields behind the alias. This is just a comma-separated list of fields to validate. In the example above, even if both Records had the field BUSINESS_UNIT it would not be validated in any way. Only the fields ORDER_NO and ORDER_DATE would be validated if both of them existed on both of the listed Records.

Now that you understand the power of this command you need to understand it's limitations. This command is very SQL intensive and may have performance issues since it uses sub queries to perform the validations. It is highly recommended to use a specific where clause to reduce the number of rows that have to be processed. A high row count can seriously impact performance. It is also recommended that only the specific validations that need to be done on the specific fields be used. This just reduces the SQL complexity and hence the impact on performance.

There is also one key on the %Edit_Prompt type that must be discussed. If you review the example that was used earlier you would see that the command is doing a prompt Record validation, as shown following.

```
Insert into PS_SALES_ERROR
select A.BUSINESS_UNIT, A.ORDER_NO, A.CUST_ID
from PS_SALES_ORDER_TMP A
where A.PROCESS_INSTANCE = %Bind(PROCESS_INSTANCE)
and %ExecuteEdits(%Edit_PromptTable, ORD_HEADER A)
```

This validation will do the prompt Record on all fields that match within the two Records. If you review the field

BILL_TO_CUST_ID it uses a prompt table of CUST_SLDBLL_VW. This view has as its Key structure not only the value for the BILL_TO_CUST_ID but also the field SOLD_TO_CUST_ID. This is done so that once you set the SOLD_TO_CUST_ID value, you can then see a prompt of only the valid BILL_TO_CUST_ID for that SOLD_TO_CUST_ID. The validation that will take place on this field is to validate the BILL_TO_CUST_ID field assuming that the SOLD_TO_CUST_ID field is on the Record as well. You have to be very aware of the validations that are done on each field so that you do not get errors because the validation requires more than one field. Your only choice in this case is to either not use the %ExecuteEdits command and write your own validation or include the SOLD_TO_CUST_ID field on the SALES_ORDER_TMP Record so that the validations can be performed correctly.

Note: *All key fields are used to work the validation on prompt tables except the field EFFDT.*

%FirstRows

This command allows you to control the number of rows to be returned within the SQL statement. This is to be used on Select statements only and not within any sub select, where clause, or any part of an update or insert statement. This command also must not be used if there is any possibility that you will request x number of rows to be returned and the SQL returns any number less than anticipated. This may cause the program to abort or the database to extremely slow down. The last caveat is that you cannot use this command with the DISTINCT clause in the SQL statement, as this will cause failure in some database platforms.

```
%Select (Business_unit, Order_no)
Select %FirstRows(1) Business_unit, Order_no
from PS_ORD_HEADER
where USER9 = 'T'
```

The example here shows how this command is used within the SQL select statement. The command is listed after the select command and before any fields listed in the select clause. The example will then select and display only the first record found. If order is important you can include an order by clause. The number you use as a parameter can be any number you wish but normally within Application Engine you only use one, since retrieving more rows will only place the last selected row of data into the Bind variables. This is typically used in conjunction with the No Rows control on the Action. If no rows are found then skip the next Action or jump to the next Section. There is no reason to show all rows if one row is enough to run the next Actions. By using this command, you are saving database processing time to make your program much faster.

Warning*: This command will not work on the Sybase database platform.*

%InsertSelect

The purpose of this command is to build an insert SQL statement utilizing a select SQL statement to load data. This command allows you, with a few parameters, to write a command that will then expand into a full SQL statement. This is designed to save time in building large insert statements on Records with hundreds of fields. It is also used as a shortcut on small Records, just because it is easier to write.

The command will only build the Insert field list and the Select field list. It will NOT build the from or where clause portion of the SQL statement. To understand its use, review the following simple example.

```
%InsertSelect(TMP1, TMP2) from PS_TMP3;
```

This is the most basic usage of this command. The first parameter is the Record name of the table to have data loaded into. The second parameter is the Record name of the table to extract data from. You can also see that the FROM statement is included in using this command since this is not resolved by the command. This simple command would resolve into the following SQL.

```
Insert into PS_TMP1 (field1, field2, field3, field4)
select field1, field2, field3, field4 from PS_TMP3
```

***Note**: If the Record names listed here are Temporary Records, they will automatically resolve into the correct Record names as if you had used the %Table Meta-SQL command.*

There are a few things to learn here as to how the command is used. The first parameter is the Insert Record. The Record name is used as well as all the fields on the Record in the insert field list of the SQL statement. The second parameter is only there to get the fields for the select list. Notice that the second parameter is not the same name as the From Record name. This is shown on purpose to show that these do not have to match. The second parameter is there only to get a list of fields to use. Of course these fields must be on the Record in the From portion but the From Record could have many more fields. You normally have the second parameter the same as the From Record but this is not required.

Now with the basics down, review this command using all of the available parameters.

```
%InsertSelect (DISTINCT, TMP1, TMP2, A, TMP3, B,
  Field3 = 'X', Field5 = 'Y')
from PS_TMP2 B, PS_TMP3 A
where A.SETID= B1.SETID, A.FIELD1 = B.FIELD1
```

The first parameter is the distinct command. This is not required unless you want the select portion to contain the DISTINCT clause. Next, is the name of the Record to be inserted. This was shown before in the previous example. Then, is the Record name to use for the select field list. This time it is followed by an alias. This will allow you to input a select field list with an automatic alias. This requires that you have a Record in the From clause that uses this alias, otherwise when the SQL statement is created you will get an error. The next parameter is another Record name followed by an alias. You can now see that you can enter in more than one Record to build up the full field list in the select statement. There is some logic in how the select field list is built so you need to learn it now.

The select field list is built in a series of actions. First, the select field list is built from the insert field list. This process does NOT load the field names but loads the default values based on the insert Record definition. If no default value is specified or one cannot be determined (being that the default specifies a Record.Field for a default value) then the database default is used (0 for number type Fields and a space for character based Fields). If no default is specified and the Field on the Record is allowed to be NULL then the NULL value is placed into the select list.

Insert Record	**Default**	**Select List to be used**
Char1	none	' '
Char2	%OPRID	'JOEW'
Char3	PO_HEADER.PO_ID	' '
Num1	none	0
Num2	35	35
Date	%Date	'2002-07-02'
Datetime	none	NULL

Next, the process checks all of the Record names you have defined in the select Records. The process starts with the first Record in the parameter list of the command so there is an order it follows. If a Field is found in one of the select Record definitions, the hard coded value is removed and replaced with the Field name including the alias. If a field is found more than once, meaning that a field is listed on two or more select Record definitions, after the first select Record has been found, the Field name is protected and will not be replaced by any further select Record definitions.

Insert Record	Select List Old	Record A	Record B	Select List
Char1	' '	Char1		A.Char1
Char2	'JOEW'		Char2	B.Char1
Char3	' '	Char3	Char3	A.Char3
Num1	0			0
Num2	35	Num2		A.Num2
Date	'2002-07-02'		Date	B.Date
Datetime	NULL			NULL

Finally, the last two parameters are new but not required. If you have a need to set an override on the select statement, then you can input the specific field to override and the value to use. You can see there is a field, equal sign and a value in the parameter list that makes up one override parameter. You can have as many overrides as you need here, just separated by a comma. Note that the equal sign is a required parameter.

Insert Record	Select List Old	Overrides	Select List
Char1	A.Char1		A.Char1
Char2	B.Char1	Char2 = 'BOB'	'BOB'
Char3	A.Char3		A.Char3
Num1	0	Num1 = 99	99
Num2	A.Num2		A.Num2
Date	B.Date		B.Date
Datetime	NULL		NULL

The override does not have to take into account the alias being used as it is really matched against the insert Record definition name. If a match is found, the value is then placed into the select list. You now have a completed select list that will be used to create the new insert rows of data. If you fully understand this process, you can build insert SQL statements now in record time without having to list hundreds of fields manually.

***Warning**: All long character and image fields will not be placed into the Insert or Select field list due to database restrictions.*

The override capability also is used for one more item that can really be an aid. If you have to build a select statement that is to use an aggregate function (Sum, Min, Max, Avg, etc…) you cannot put this in directly but you can do so by using the override parameter. Since you are not putting in a value but an aggregate function, you would use the command, as in the example below.

```
%InsertSelect (DISTINCT, TMP1, TMP2, A, TMP3, B,
  Field3 = sum(B.Field3)
from PS_TMP2 B, PS_TMP3 A
where A.SETID= B.SETID, A.FIELD1 = B.FIELD1
group by A.FIELD1, B.FIELD2
```

You can see that the Field name is listed including the alias to be used. Since this replacement of the Field name will use everything you type after the equals sign, you have to input the alias and the Field name. Plus, do not forget to input the Group By clause, if required, since without this you may receive a run time SQL error.

%Join

This command is most commonly used with the %InsertSelect command. The reason is that this command, %Join, builds a where clause. This does not preclude you from using it in other places, and is in fact recommended that you do so, but you will see this command used a great deal by PeopleSoft developers in this way.

The command is used to build a where clause between two Records. With parameter settings you can define to join on Keys or you can join on all Fields named the same. As always, there is also an override command. Now, review the code samples below to understand the structure and use of this command.

```
…%Join(COMMON_KEYS, TMP1, TMP2)
…%Join(COMMON_FIELDS, TMP1 A, TMP2 B, FIELD4, FIELD7)
```

These are not full SQL statements but just show the use of the %Join command. The first example shows the use of the parameter COMMON_KEYS while the second shows COMMON_FIELDS.

The first parameter must be one of these values. This parameter tells the process how to join the two Records together.

COMMON_KEYS will find all the Fields named the same in both Records where the Field is listed as a key in both Records. If a Field is listed as a key in only one Record or is listed as an alternate key, then it will not be used.

COMMON_FIELDS will find all Fields named the same in both Records. There is no restriction on the Fields here except that they are named the same no matter if they are a key or not. This can find more fields than before and since they are not required to be a key you may have to be concerned about proper indexing. Large amounts of data joined together without proper indexes may lead to slow performance of the SQL. Be sure of the consequences of using this parameter or contact your DBA for assistance.

The next two parameters in both examples list the database Records to use. You must input two Records to use this command. The Record name can be as shown here or as a Bind variable. You cannot use hard coded text to input the Record name. Example two also shows the use of alias. Remember that if you use an alias, then your field list must also have the alias; otherwise you may receive a run time SQL error.

Example two also contains two more parameters and this is the override. The override parameters can be none (as in example one) or many. They only need to be separated by a comma. The process normally joins the two Records together based on the parameter you have input but there may be cases, particularly with the COMMON_FIELD parameter, when you do not want to use all the fields but a smaller list. This is what the override parameters are for. Here, you list the Fields that you DO NOT want to have used in the join list.

To show a full use of a %Join command, review the SQL statement below. You can compare this to the original SQL statement back in the %InsertSelect area above.

```
%InsertSelect (DISTINCT, TMP1, TMP1, A, TMP2, B,
 Field3 = sum(B.Field3)
%Join(COMMON_KEYS, PS_TMP2 B, PS_TMP3 A)
group by A.FIELD1, B.FIELD2
```

This small example may not be able to show the full power but if you think of a Record with 8 keys, building the where clause can take time. This %Join command is very helpful in making it easier to build SQL statements; quicker and more accurate.

%List

This command works somewhat like the %InsertSelect but only gives you a list of field names from one Record. This command is made up of two parameters with varying options. The first parameter sets the fields within the defined Record that are to be made into a comma-separated list. For the second parameter, there are four different options but you can only select one of them.

Value	**Action**
KEY_FIELDS	Build using only Fields set as Key. Alternate Key does not build.
FIELD_LIST	Build using all Fields
FIELD_LIST_NOLONGS	Build using all Field except fields with LONG character type.
ORDER_BY	Build using all Fields and add 'DESC' behind all fields where the order has been set to descending in the Record Definition. This option is used when this command is to build a field list within the Order By clause of a SQL statement

The second parameter is the Record name. This can just be the name or a bind variable, but not a string of characters. This parameter can also have an alias included as well, if the field list being built needs one.

Review the following example.

```
Insert into PS_TMP2 %List(FIELD_LIST, TMP2)
Select %List(KEY_FIELDS, TMPMST A)
from PS_TMP1 A
```

The first line of the example shows that you can use the Record itself to build a full field list. The field list is built following the order of the Fields as defined on the Record definition. The first command uses all the Fields but does not use the alias condition as shown in line 2. Here, a select statement field list is created and is aliased with the value of 'A'.

***Note**: The field list generated must match field types within a SQL statement so that if you are using an insert / select type statement, the select field types must line up with the insert field types; otherwise you will receive a run time SQL error.*

You can use this command more than once in a SQL statement. For an insert SQL statement, you can have one build the insert field list, a second build the select field list and a third the Order By clause. You can even have two or more of these commands build one select field list. There is no limit on the number of times within one SQL statement that you can use this command.

There are some issues to be careful of when using this %List command. The Field order is based on the Record Definition so if anyone changes this, you have just changed all of your underlying SQL statements. You need to be aware of this condition and take into account when you are modifying Record definitions. PeopleSoft recommends that if you create a statement, like in the example, you should create it as follows.

```
Insert into PS_TMP2 %List(KEY_FIELDS, TMPMST)
Select %List(KEY_FIELDS, TMPMST A)
from PS_TMP1 A
```

The command uses the same Record to build not only the insert field list but the select field list. This way when you change the PS_TMPMST Record, you effectively change this SQL as well, and it should stay in sync. This is true but note that the Record being loaded, PS_TMP2, is a different Record than the Record in the %List command. PS_TMP2 will have to be updated as well since you cannot have a Field in the insert list that does not exist on the insert Record.

%ListBind

This command is similar to %List but instead of a list of field names this is a list of Bind variables using the field names separated by commas. The parameters are the same as %List but the options have changed slightly.

Value	Action
KEY_FIELDS	Build using only Fields set as Key. Alternate Key does not build.
FIELD_LIST	Build using all Fields
FIELD_LIST_NOLONGS	Build using all Fields except Fields with LONG character type.

The first parameter is the same except you no longer have the ORDER_BY option. The second parameter is again the Record name with an optional alias. This command takes the Record definition and using the first parameter builds a list of %Bind variables of Field names. The purpose here is that if you have loaded a great deal of information into the Bind variables you can easily build statements selecting that data.

```
Insert into PS_TMP2 %List(FIELD_LIST, TMP2)
values (%Bind(KEY1), %ListBind(FIELD_LIST, TMPBIND),
  %bind(DESCR) )
```

As you can see from the example, this is normally a value list but could be within a select statement as well.

%ListEqual

This command is special in that it does not just build a field list but it builds a list of fields with an equal to a Bind variable. This command is used in set or where clauses of a SQL statement. Normally, the %List family of commands has just been creating different sets of field lists or bind lists. This command combines the field list and bind list to make a logic statement. The first parameter sets whether all Fields are to be used or just the key Fields. Next, comes the Record name with optional alias that will be the list of Field names to use. Then, the Record name that contains the list of Field names will be used to generate the Bind variables. The last optional parameter – but recommended to use – is the separator statement that will be between the multiple Field names, if multiples are returned.

```
Update PS_TMP2
set %ListEqual(ALL, TMP1_VW, TMP_BIND_VW, AND)

%Select(ORDER_NO)
Select A.ORDER_NO
from PS_TMP2 A
where %ListEqual(KEY, TMP1_VW A, TMP_BIND_VW, OR)
```

The first example would be a list of all fields from the Record definition of PS_TMP1_VW. The ALL parameter sets to use all fields. If you look at the second example you will see the other allowed parameter, which is KEY. This only builds a field list of the key Fields – not all Fields. The second parameter is the Record name to use and in the second example you see the use of the alias option. The third parameter, in both examples, is the Record definition that is used to build the Bind Variable list. The last parameter is the showing the separator string that will be placed between the multiple rows. Now, based on the following Record definitions, review the output of the SQL for each example.

TMP1_VW	**TMPBIND_VW**
FIELD1	PO_ID
FIELD2	ORDER_CODE
NUM1	COST
NUM2	PRICE

```
Update PS_TMP2
set FIELD1 = %Bind(PO_ID)
AND FIELD2 = %Bind(ORDER_CODE)
and NUM1 = %Bind(COST)
and NUM2 = %Bind(PRICE)

%Select(ORDER_NO)
Select A.ORDER_NO
from PS_TMP2 A
where FIELD1 = %Bind(PO_ID)
OR FIELD2 = %Bind(ORDER_CODE)
```

The Bind variables shown here are assumed to be on the Default State Record, if not you will receive a run time error.

***Note**: The number of fields and the type of fields must match up exactly for this command to process correctly.*

%Next

This macro is used within SQL statements to give a running sequence number. The %Next macro listed here is for adding a number starting, say, with 1 and going to 2, then 3, then 4 and so on. The macro is used just as you would do a %Bind variable but for this macro (%Next) to work correctly, you have to use it with some specific Actions.

First, you have to set up the field that you will be using into one of the State Records on the Application Engine program. The reason for this is that you need to initialize the number value that you will be sequencing. This way you can start at one or start at 9,567 if you need too.

Then, when you get to programming your Application Engine program, you will have to create 2 steps and 3 actions, at a minimum. First, you will have a Step and Action with the type of SQL. This first Action is to be the SQL that will initialize the Bind variable that you will be using as a sequence number. Here are a couple of examples to initialize to 1 or to a beginning number.

```
%Select(Counter)
Select 1 from PS_INSTALLATION

%Select(Counter)
Select max(VOUCHER_LINE_NUM)+1
from PS_VOUCHER_LINE
```

The first example shows selecting from any Record you feel like to get the hard coded value of 1 into the bind variable. The Record used here is used like this a lot since this Record only has one row of data; so that you do not have to process through hundreds of records to just set the one value. The second example sets the Bind variable with the maximum value of a Field, plus one. The plus one is needed so that you do not duplicate the line number that is already in the database Record.

With the Bind variable initialized, you need to have another Step and Action created. You can use these within the same Section or they can be in different Sections – it does not matter. The important part is that you initialize the Bind variable before you use it, otherwise you may get false results. This second Action sets up a looping process. You need to use a type of Do Select, Do While or Do Until. This is done because you need to perform a loop that will be doing a sequence number. The Do Select type is also special, in that to perform the loop correctly you will need to set the Re-Use Statement to No and the Do Select type to Reselect; so that every time the SQL is encountered it will re-run the SQL and allow the %Next to be incremented. The Do While and Do Until types do not require this setting as they are re-run every time they process. Now that the type is set, you have to input the SQL statement. The statement here is a selection of data that drives the sequential process. To better understand this point, review a couple of the following examples.

Example 1 – Needing to insert new records where the line number needs to increment, such as in the case of a voucher line number.

```
%Select(Business_unit, Voucher)
Select BUSINESS_UNIT_AP, VOUCHER_ID
from %Table(TMP_TAO)
```

Example 2 – Needing to update a value to show salary rank from all employees

```
%Select(Employee_id)
Select Employee_id
from PS_EMPLOYEE
where PROCESS_INSTANCE = %Bind(process_instance)
Order by Salary
```

If you look closely at the two examples you will not see that much difference. The point here is that these SQL select statements need to be loading information into the Bind Variables that will be used in the next SQL statement to update or insert the correct values. The whole idea is to load into the Bind variables the key Fields of the records to be processed.

***Note**: If the looping SQL does not return any rows then nothing is updated or inserted.*

This sets up the next Action. This SQL should be within the same Step unless you happen to code in a call Section where this is the next SQL to run. In any case, this SQL should be the next to follow so that it loops within the previous Action.

This new Action should be of a SQL type because it will be performing an Update or Insert, as in your examples. Continuing the two examples, review the following code for the third SQL Action.

Example 1.

```
Insert into PS_VOUCHER_LINE
Select %Bind(Business_unit), %Bind(Voucher),
  %Next(Counter), 'BTCH', B.VENDOR_ID
from PS_TEMP1_VW B
where B.PROCESS_INSTANCE = %Bind(Process_instance)
and B.BUSINESS_UNIT = %Bind(Business_unit)
and B.VOUCHER_ID = %Bind(Voucher)
```

Example 2.

```
Update PS_EMPLOYEE
set RANK = %Next(Counter)
where EMPLOYEE_ID = %Bind(Employee_id)
```

These examples show you how the %Next is used. All you have to do is input the Bind variable name that is a number field that has already been initialized. What happens then is that every time the SQL is processed, the Counter field is incremented by one. In the first example, the insert may load more than just one record. This is ok but the %Next will not increment on every row being inserted. The %Next is set only one upon each run of the SQL statement. If the %Next is needed for part of the Key structure and multiple rows are being inserted, your SQL will fail with a duplicate key error.

The Update statement shown here may only update one row at a time but it could be updating multiple rows, and will assign the same number to each individual row. Again the key structure needs to be reviewed for multiple rows of data. To control this issue, you need to control where statement.

%Previous

This macro works exactly like the %Next macro except now the Counter is reduced by one. Other than that, the process is exactly the same with the same rules and issues.

See %Next for the full explanation.

%Round

This command allows you to round a number to a defined number of decimals. The command is used within SQL statements and has only two parameters. The first defines the number to be used while the second parameter is the number of decimals to round to. Review the examples below.

```
%Round(56.7893, 2)
%Round(A.NUM2, %Bind(PRECISION))
```

The first example would return a value of 56.79 – in order to round to the second decimal you review the third decimal place. If the third decimal is greater than or equal to 5 you round up, otherwise you truncate. The second example shows that you can use Fields as the first parameter and Bind variables as the second parameter. The second parameter is only allowed to be hard coded values, Bind variables or PeopleCode variables.

This command if used in a full SQL statement, could appear as follows.

```
%Select(ORDER_NO)
Select DISTINCT ORDER_NO
from PS_ORD_LINE
where %Round(PRICE/100, 2) >.55
```

The allowed rounding (second parameter) has a restriction in that it cannot exceed 31. Due to database limitations, you cannot round any lower than that since that number of decimals are not stored in the system.

Note*: See Truncate command for non-rounding of number fields.*

%RoundCurrency

This macro works just like the %Round Meta-SQL function except you do not define the number of decimals to use but supply a Field name. The Field name is to be the Field of the Record being updated or selected that is holding the Currency code to use. The process will read the value within this Field and select the proper decimal precision (number of decimals) from the PS_CURRENCY_CD_TBL. This way you do not have to hard code or figure out the number of decimals to round to, you can let the currency control property do it for you. This, of course, assumes you are using the Multi Currency processes within PeopleSoft – Multi-Currency option is turned on within the PeopleTools Options panel.

The Currency_cd_tbl is also an effective dated table and so it requires the use of a date. The %AsOfDate Meta-SQL function is used to gather the date to be used for the selection of the decimal precision.

```
UPDATE %Table(FLR1_TAO)
SET MONETARY_AMOUNT = %RoundCurrency( COST * QTY_TMP1,
  CURRENCY_CD)
WHERE PROCESS_INSTANCE = %Bind(PROCESS_INSTANCE)
```

The macro is shown with the first parameter being an expression, hard coded value or Record.Field value. Normally, an expression is used since by calculating a new value you need to re-round to the correct currency. The second parameter is listed following a comma with the Field name that contains the currency code value. If the value cannot resolve to a valid currency code with an effective date of today, the field being loaded (MONETARY_AMOUNT in our example) is used to set the number of decimals.

Note: *If you use this macro and Multi-Currency is not in effect, then the decimal precision will be set to the field being updated or selected. This field is normally an amount type field with decimal precision of 2 or 3.*

%Select

Where you used the %Bind command to use the State Record values, you use the %Select command to load the State Records from within Application Engine SQL code. You do not have to use this command when doing this from within Application Engine PeopleCode. You will typically use the %Select command first in loading values from your Run Control Records into the State Record so that you can use them in the where clause, such as in the example below.

```
%Select(OPRID, RUN_CNTL_ID)
Select OPRID, RUN_CNTL_ID
from PS_AERUNCONTROL
where PROCESS_INSTANCE = %Bind(PROCESS_INSTANCE)
```

This SQL statement pulls data from the Application Engine system Record and stores the operator and run control id that you can use later to pull information from the Run Control Record. You can see from the example, the only parameter is a comma separated list of fields. This list of fields should contain the State Record name, as well as the field name using the Record name.Field name convention. If the default State Record is to be loaded, then it is not required to use the Record name just as in the use of the %Bind command.

The SQL statement that follows the %Select command must have the same number and type of fields as called within the %Select command. There are also a few rules to use when selecting date, datetime and time fields. You should use the %Dateout, %Datetimeout and %Timeout Meta – SQL commands when selecting data from Records into State Records. This just assures that all the date, datetime and time information is in database compatible format.

***Note**: If the SQL statement does not return any rows of information, then the State Record Fields are left with the values they had before the SQL statement was processed.*

%SelectInit

This command is just like the %Select command with only one difference. The way the command is used and the syntax is exactly the same but the results of the command are different. Where the %Select command leaves the values unchanged because no rows are returned in the SQL select statement, this command will refresh the values to any initial values as if the Application Engine program had just started.

***Note**: It is not recommended to use this command unless absolutely necessary as the performance of this command is suspect.*

%SQL

This Meta-SQL command allows you to use a SQL object that you have created with the Application Designer. Depending on how you are going to use the SQL object you may need to be careful in how you write it. You see, the SQL object can be used within Application Engine or PeopleCode and the syntax can be exclusive to each program; or you can learn to write it in a more generic syntax.

You could write your SQL object using %Bind commands in them directly and they would work just as if you had typed them directly into Application Engine programs; but this would make them unusable to PeopleCode. This is why you need to learn to write in a generic way, as shown in the following example.

```
UPDATE PS_SALES_ORDER_TMP
SET INPROCESS_FLAG = 'Y'
WHERE PROCESS_INSTANCE = %P(1)
and BUSINESS_UNIT = %P(2)
```

By using this syntax to show the parameters, you can use the SQL object within both PeopleCode and Application Engine. To use this SQL object, you would use the following Application Engine %SQL command.

```
%SQL(SQL_ID1, %Bind(PROCESS_INSTANCE),
Bind(TEMP2_AET.BUSINESS_UNIT_GL)
```

The %SQL command is used by listing the SQL object name as the first parameter within the parenthesis. This is the only required parameter for this command. Then, following the SQL object name is a list of parameters. These can be hard coded values or bind variables (as shown here). You can list here as many parameters as you wish but only those that are in the SQL statement will be linked and built into the statement. The order of the parameters is very important, as the way the SQL is built is to place the first parameter into the %P(1) syntax, the second into %P(2) and so on until all parameters have been placed.

%Substring

This command allows you to take a character string and pull a piece out of it – substring it. This command is made up of three parameters: the character string, where to start and the number of characters to grab. Review the following code.

```
%Substring('ABCDEFGHIJKL', 6, 3)
%Substring(A.FIELD3, 1, 4)
%Substring(%Bind(ORDER_GROUP), 4, 2)
```

The first example would return the results of 'FGH'. This is because the second parameter says to start on the 6th character. The third parameter says to take the next 3 characters and return the value - hence the 'FGH'. The second example shows that you can use a Field with an alias reference while the third example shows the use of a Bind variable. These examples are not full SQL statements but you can use these snippets to build into SQL statements, as shown below.

```
%Select(DESCR)
Select DESCR15
from PS_ORDER_GROUP
where %Substring(%Bind(ORDER_GROUP), 4, 2)=
  %Bind(TEMP_VALUE)
```

%Table

You have already seen this function in Chapter 5 - Temporary Records. There is nothing new to add to the syntax structure you have already seen. Use this command as a replacement for a Record name within a SQL statement by applying a hard coded value or variable, as in the examples below.

```
Select employee_id from %Table(EMPLOYEE)
Select business_unit
from %Table(%Bind(Table_Name))
```

If you have Temporary Records you must use this Meta SQL command to allow the automatic reference of the instance to the correct table name, as explained in Chapter 5.

%TextIn

This command is specifically written to load Long Character type Fields, either through insert or update SQL statements. This command allows only one parameter and it must be a Bind variable.

```
Update PS_PO_LINE
set DESCR_LONG = %TextIn(%Bind(DESCR256))
```

%TimeAdd

This command allows you to add time in minutes to a datetime value. Some databases allow the use of just a time value instead of datetime but there are issues with each specific database; so it is recommended to always use datetime values. The first parameter is the datetime value and the second parameter is the number of minutes, as shown in the following examples.

```
Update PS_TMP2
set SCHED_ARRV_DTTM  = %TimeAdd(SCHED_ARRV_DTTM  , 10)
```

The datetime value can be a field, as shown here, a variable or even a string of characters in the correct datetime format. The second parameter can be a field, variable or number (as shown here).

%TimeIn

This command takes a string value or Bind variable and creates the correct database time format. If a string is used, the format must be – hh.mm.ss.ssssss. This command is used to load time information into the database as opposed to being in the select field list (getting data out).

```
Update PS_SHIP_TMP
set SHIP_TIME = %TimeIn(%Bind(time_set))
```

%TimeOut

This command is for selecting time and putting it into a string of hh.mm.ss.ssssss. This allows you to transfer from the specific database format to the standard PeopleSoft time format.

```
%Select(Ship_time)
Select %TimeOut(SHIP_TIME)
from PS_SHIP_TMP
where PROCESS_INSTANCE = %ProcessInstance
```

%TrimSubstr

This command is exactly like the %SubString command except this command removes any trailing blanks or spaces. This can help when spaces have been added to fields to have them removed automatically, so that when you use the variable you can expect exact matches.

```
%Select(DESCR_VIEW)
Select DESCR
from PS_ORDER_GROUP
where %TrimSubstr(%Bind(ORDER_GROUP), 4, 2)=
  %Bind(TEMP_VALUE)
```

Blanks and spaces may show up based on how the data was loaded into a Record. Take for example, if a data Record has a field with the value of 'Sr. Johnson II   ' and you select using %Substring(value, 5, 15), this would return - 'Johnson II   '. This may then cause issues if you use this variable string to select data from a different Record using a different Field where the extra spaces may cause you an issue. If you had used the %TrimSubstr with the same parameters, you would have gotten - 'Johnson II'.

%Truncate

This command truncates a number to a defined number of decimals. The number is just cut off without any rounding.

***Note**: See %Round for full Rounding number capability.*

The command has two parameters. The first is the number, variable, bind variable or Field to be truncated. The second is a number that must be less than or equal to 31 and is the number of decimals to leave.

Given the following examples, see the result of using the %Truncate command.

```
%Truncate(5.34567324, 3)       Results 5.345
%Truncate(5.34567324, 6)       Results 5.345673
```

The second parameter can be a hard coded number, variable or Bind variable.

%TruncateTable

This command was also discussed in Chapter 5 - Temporary Records. If you require a Record to have all of its data removed, then this command can help you out as it is designed to perform just that function. You can use a delete SQL statement but this command is much more efficient.

```
%TruncateTable(TMP1_TAO2)
%TruncateTable(%Table(FLR1_TAO))
```

The syntax is to have the command followed by the Record name or, better, by using the %Table command - this is especially important if you are using Temporary Records.

Note: *To use this %TruncateTable effectively your Application Engine program needs to be able to complete a commit transaction.*

%UpdateStats

This command is designed for when you add or delete tens of thousands of rows of data from a Record. This amount of data change (add or delete) can affect how the database system will access this Record in future SQL statements. This command allows the database to rebuild its statistics on the Record so that the proper optimization plan can be done to access the Record. Basically, this command performs the update statistic command for the database. This command will perform the necessary database command (update statistics) that is specific for the database platform you are using. This way you do not need to know the specifics for the command for each database.

To use this command you only have to have the name of the Record, as shown in the example below.

```
%UpdateStats(TMP1_TAO2)
%UpdateStats(%Table(FLR1_TAO))
```

You can see that you can use the Record name as in example one, or use the %Table Meta SQL to handle any Temporary Records.

There is a requirement for the use of this command in that the Application Engine program must be allowed to perform commits. In fact, a commit will be done prior to and after this command so that the database statistics are updated correctly. If you have set your Application Engine program to not commit, then this command, when encountered, will just be skipped. You must take into account when you write your Application Engine program and use this command, that commits will be done in case of re-starts.

Note: *If you use PeopleCode to launch the Application Engine program then this command will be skipped since commits are not allowed until after the entire program is complete.*

Note: *If you use this command within a loop process, the command will be skipped since you cannot perform a commit.*

There is one more point to be aware of. This is that the database will be heavily loaded to perform this command. This should only be done with the approval and recommendation of the database administrator. You have to understand when this will run, what the database load will be and the expected results. This should be carefully studied and only used when necessary. You will find this command used within some delivered Application Engine programs and it is recommended to turn them off until you have had time to review and analyze the results. PeopleSoft may have thought the program was to load thousands of rows of data but your process may not be that heavily loaded. There are a few things you can do to prevent the use of this command by errant developers or even delivered PeopleSoft programs.

First you can set a value called Disable DB Stats in the Configuration Manager. To do this you need to launch the Configuration Manager, then you need to click over to the Profile tab, as you see in Figure 6.1.

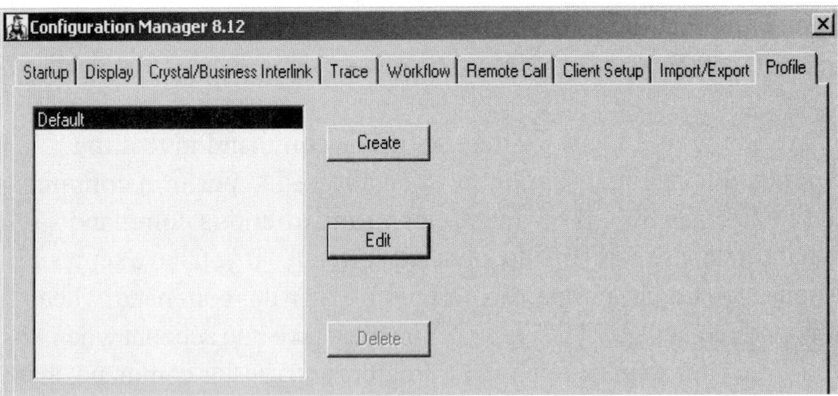

Figure 6.1 Configuration Manager – Profile tab.

You can see a list of profiles that can be used but usually there will only be one listed as the default. If you need to change each profile you will need to do the following instructions for each profile. Now, click on the Edit button, right in the middle of the panel. This will open the profile panel. Click over to the Process Scheduler tab, as shown in figure 6.2.

You can see here a lot of fields to fill in but look at the upper right corner; you can see some settings for Application Engine. The one you are interested in right now is the Disable DB Stats checkbox. In figure 6.2, the checkbox is not set so this allows the use of the %UpdateStats command. If you want to prevent this, make sure the checkbox is selected. Once you do this do not forget to click the OK button to save your changes for both panels you have opened already.

***Note**: This will only prevent the client (2-Tier) from running Application Engine programs with this %UpdateStats command but not on the Application Server.*

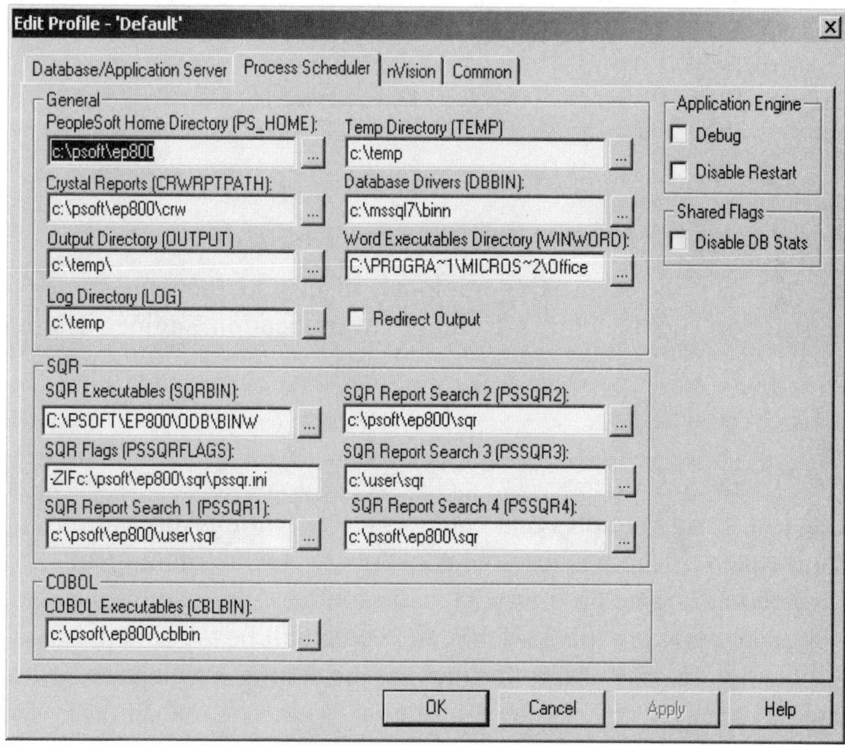

Figure 6.2 Profile Panel – Process Scheduler tab.

To disable the command on the Application Server, you have to change a setting within the Process Scheduler. Within the configuration file of the Process Scheduler there is a setting for Dbflags. Normally, it is set to 0 to allow the use of the %UpdateStats command but you can change this to 1 to prevent the process. Once you change the configuration file, you will have to stop and restart the process scheduler for your changes to take affect.

%Upper

This command converts all the character information from lower case to upper case. This command uses only one parameter and that is the string to convert. This string can be a hard coded value, variable, Bind variable or Field name.

```
%Select(Name, Descr)
Select %Upper(name), %Upper(%Bind(value))
from %Table(FLR_TAO)
```

Application Engine System Variables

In addition to the Meta SQL previously discussed, there are some substitution variables that are unique to Application Engine. These are all discussed below.

%AeProgram

This is a string in quotes that contains the executing Application Engine name. There is just one concern. If you are running an Application Engine program that calls another Application Engine section and you use this variable, the value will be the called Application Engine program name not the calling Application Engine name.

%AeSection

This is a string in quotes that contains the executing Application Engine Section name.

%AeStep

This is a string in quotes containing the currently executing Application Engine Step name.

%Comma

This is a substitution for the comma character(,). This is used when you need to pass in the comma as part of your SQL string or other needs you have where the rules do not allow you to input in a comma character.

%CurrentDateIn

This expands to a database specific SQL string representing the current date. This is normally used in the where clause of a SQL select or update statement. This can also be used to update or insert the current date to a date type field. The key is that you are loading the date into a Field within a database Record.

```
Update %Table(FLR_TAO)
set RUN_DATE = %CurrentDateIn
```

%CurrentDateOut

This expands to a database specific SQL string representing the current date in the select clause of an SQL query. This select statement can be to load Bind variables or to be part of an insert statement where this is used within the select portion only.

```
%Select (run_date)
select %CurrentDateOut
from PS_INSTALLATION
```

%CurrentDateTimeIn

This expands to a database specific SQL string representing the current datetime and is used with the same rules as %CurrentDateIn.

```
%Select(Business_unit, Voucher)
Select Business_unit, Voucher_id
from PS_VOUCHER
where ENTER_DTTM <= %CurrentDateTimeIn
```

%CurrentDateTimeOut

This expands to a database specific SQL string representing the current datetime and is used with the same rules as %CurrentDateOut.

```
%Select (run_dttm)
select %CurrentDateTimeOut
from PS_INSTALLATION
```

%CurrentTimeIn

This expands to a database specific SQL string representing the current time and is used with the same rules as %CurrentDateIn.

```
%Select(Business_unit, Order_no)
Select Business_unit, Order_no
from PS_SHIP_INF_INV
where SHIP_TIME <= %CurrentTimeIn
```

%CurrentTimeOut

This expands to a database specific SQL string representing the current time and is used with the same rules as %CurrentDateOut.

```
%Select (run_time)
select %CurrentTimeOut
from PS_INSTALLATION
```

%JobInstance

This is the Process Scheduler Job Instance as a number. This will return the Process Instance value if the Application Engine was not launched as part of a Job stream.

```
%Select (JobInstance)
Select %JobInstance
from PS_INSTALLATION_INV
```

%LeftParen

This is a substitution for the Left Parenthesis '(' and is used for issues similar to the %Comma variable.

%OperatorID

This is the Operator ID of the user who is launched the Application Engine program.

```
%Select(BUSINESS_UNIT)
SELECT BUSINESS_UNIT
FROM PS_RUN_CNTL_IN
WHERE OPRID = %OperatorId
AND RUN_CNTL_ID = %RunControl
```

%ProcessInstance

This is the Process Instance as a number. Remember if you launch using PeopleCode CallAppEngine you will not have a Process Instance.

```
%Select(Business_unit)
Select PS_PO_HDR
where PROCESS_INSTANCE = %ProcessInstance
```

%ReturnCode

This is the numeric return code of the last SQL operation performed.

%RightParen

Is a substitution for the Right Parenthesis ')' and is used for issues similar to the %Comma variable.

%RunControl

This is a string in quotes that contains the Run Control ID.

%Space

This is a substitution for a space ' '. Use for issues similar to the %Comma variable.

%SQLRows

This is a number that represents the quantity of rows affected by the last SQL statement. This could be the number of rows inserted or updated. For select statements the value returned is 0 for no rows found or 1 for some number of rows found.

Next

The next chapter covers another new concept with version 8 Application Engine. This is the new File object. With earlier versions of Application Engine you could not create flat files and were forced to build them with SQR programs. Now you can create flat file output for interface programs using Application Engine and you get the benefit of high performance. This is truly a great capability of Application Engine and one you will probably use a lot.

Chapter 7

Learning the File Layout object

The File Layout object is a new concept for version 8 PeopleTools and one that is used primarily with Application Engine programs. This object is used to read and/or write files in different formats using PeopleCode. This could be done from within a Page but mostly you will see this used in Application Engine. In prior years, interface programs utilizing flat file formats were always written in the SQR tool. Now, with this object and the more powerful Application Engine program, you can and should build all these types of interface programs within Application Engine. There are also the powerful Component Interface and Business Interlink processes that utilize the File Layout object and Application Engine to build the XML datafiles. Some reference will be made to these new processes but this chapter is focused on Application Engine. See PeopleBooks for more information on these new processes.

You can now process any flat file with ease and in fact with great speed. PeopleSoft does recommend that you now drop the use of SQR programming for future flat file processing and use the new Application Engine. You will want to follow this recommendation, even though in the past Application Engine did have some performance issues, for today Application Engine is an efficient and powerful program that VASTLY outperforms SQR programs.

This Chapter covers not only creating the File object but then how to use the object within PeopleCode. First, you have to create the File object so learning about the File object is where you should start.

Creating the File Layout Object.

A File Layout object is created based on a set of Field names, types and length. The File Layout object is not required to create flat file outputs, as you can do it manually within PeopleCode, but this is not the recommended way. You will find that most often you want to write out a set of Fields from a data Record. By utilizing the same Field names in your File Layout object as in your Record, you have just made it very easy to process the Flat file output. Read through the whole chapter to fully understand this process and you will see that spending a few minutes to build the File object will save you hours of coding and testing later.

To create a File Layout object you have to be using the Application Designer. Once the Application Designer is open, click on the new button or use the menu: File – New. Once the new panel opens, select File layout. This will open a new File Layout object, as shown in figure 7.1.

Figure 7.1 New File Layout Object

First you need to define the type of File object this will be. There are only 3 types allowed; FIXED, CSV and XML.

FIXED Each Field within the File object is set to a specific length and has a specific starting point within each row of data.
CSV Each Field is variable in length but is wrapped by a specific character, usually a double quote ("), and is separated by a specific character, usually a comma (,). The order is still specified by the File object but not the length of each field.
XML This is similar to CSV in that all fields can be variable but the wrapping character and separator are different in that this definition uses tags instead of single characters. This is required by XML definition. See a good XML book for more information on XML tags.

Once you determine the type you wish to set, click on the properties button to get the properties panel to open. Then click over to the Use tab, as shown in figure 7.2.

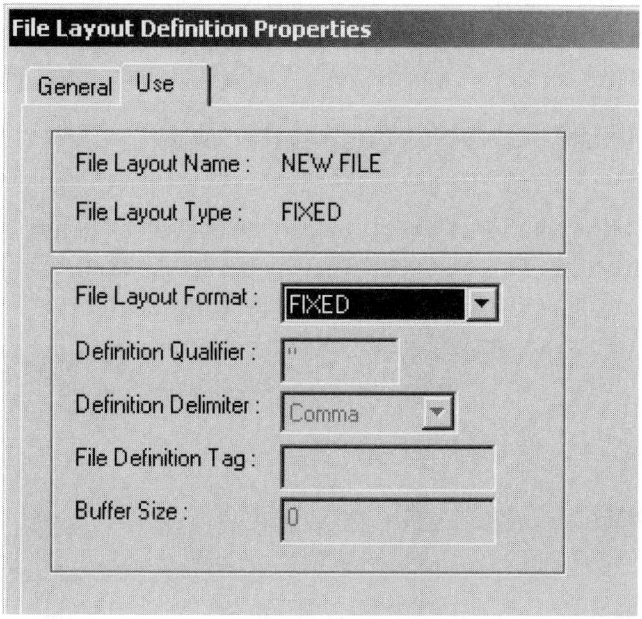

Figure 7.2 File object properties panel Use tab

Here is the field, File Layout Format, which is where you set the type for this File object. You can use the drop down list to set the type. Depending on the type you select, specific fields will open for use.

FIXED, this format does not require any further input.

CSV, here the Definition Qualifier and the Definition Delimiter need to be input. The definition qualifier is the character to be used to wrap every field. The default is a double quote ("). The definition delimiter is the character that will separate every field. The defaults is a comma (,) .

XML, the only field here is the Buffer Size. Here you enter in the maximum input buffer size to use if you want to pre-allocate an input buffer. This field is not required.

Now with the File Laout object type set, you can go about building the File Layout definition. There are two ways to build the File object and both of these will be discussed. First, the easiest and recommended way, is to use the Record definition. You can also create a File object manually and that will be shown second.

Creating the File Layout Object using Record definitions.

Assuming you still have your File Layout object open and selected, use the menu: Insert – Record. This will open a new panel, as shown in figure 7.3. You can also insert a Record definition by using the right click menu. If you right click on the File Layout object name you will get a menu where you can select Insert Record to accomplish the same thing.

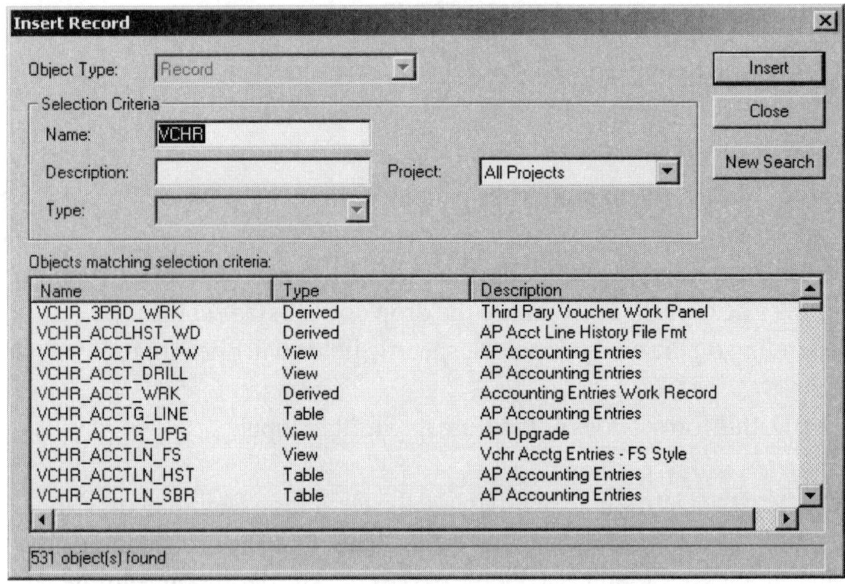

Figure 7.3 Insert Record panel

This is where you can input a Record name or portion of a Record name to find the Record you wish to insert. As in the example, a portion "VCHR" was entered into the Name field, then the Insert button was clicked to fill in all of the information in the list area. You can scroll up and down here to find the correct Record. Once you find the correct Record, either double-click on the Record name or click once on the Record name and then click the Insert button again. This will load the Record definition into the File object. Assuming you clicked on the Record VCHR_DIST_EDT your File object would now look like figure 7.4.

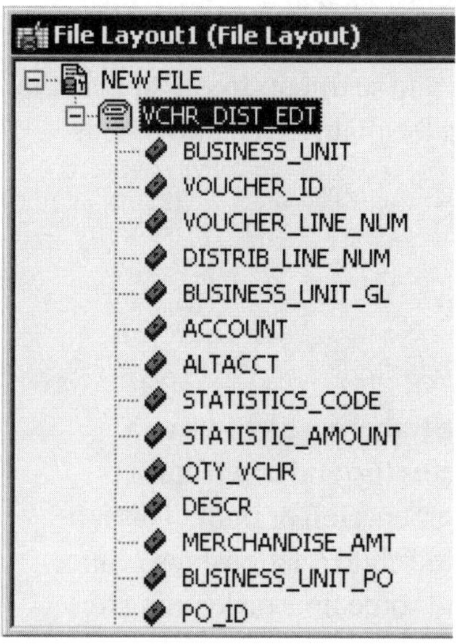

Figure 7.4 File object with Record loaded

Now, a lot has happened here but it is not as tough to understand as you might think. What you now see loaded into your File object is a list of fields from the Record definition. The File object looks like a tree structure and that is exactly what it is. The first branch under the tree shows an icon looking like a rounded rectangular box with a list inside it (this box is yellow which you cannot see from the figure). This first branch is called a segment. The segment also contains the Record name to show you where the segment came from.

Segments

A segment is just a grouping of fields that have something in common. You may end up with multiple segments or just one segment in a File object. There is no limit to the number of segments you can add.

Segments are typically used to show hierarchy; such as in the case of header, line or schedule information. A Segment will also typically relate to a single Record definition.

To add additional segments, just use the same process again - either the main menu or the right-click menu from the File object name. As you add more segments, you will see them added to the end of the File object. Remember that in CSV and XML type File objects, order is very important. If you need to move around segments to get them in the proper order, you have some buttons on the main tool bar to use, as shown in figure 7.5.

Figure 7.5 Segment control buttons

These buttons allow you to move a node (otherwise known as a segment) up or down in the list of segments (up and down buttons respectively). You can also move the segments left or right. This left and right movement is based on parent and child relationships. Since this is used a great deal, you should spend some time on learning this process.

Child Segments

When you create a file output, you write one row of data at a time. There is no header, line or schedule type of hierarchy. The file output is considered flat or only one level. Now, the data stored in PeopleSoft is not that way at all - you are allowed to have hierarchy information. By using child segments, you can represent that data in the hierarchy format, so that when you process the file you will get the correct rows of data in the proper format. To best explain this concept and how it is used, assume the following data.

Header Record	**Key**	**Line Record**	**Key**	**Schedule Record**	**Key**
Field 1	Key	Field 1	Key	Field 1	Key
Field 2		Field 4	Key	Field 4	Key
Field 3		Field 5		Field 6	Key
				Field 7	

If you need to output the data in this set of Records and Fields into a flat file, you must create a File object showing this hierarchy format. First, you create the File object and add the Header Record, as you have learned. Then, you need to add a child segment under the Header Record. To do this you can click on the Header Record and select from the menu: Insert – Child Segment, or you can right click on the Header Record name and select from the right-click menu the Insert ChildSegment command. In either case, this opens the Insert Record panel that you have already used and it works just the same as before. Enter the name and search, then double click to add your new child segment. Once you have added the line record you then need to add a child segment to it as well. Follow the same process and you should have a record that looks like figure 7.6. (Warning this is fake data to show the concept, as you will not find Record or Field names as listed in this example.)

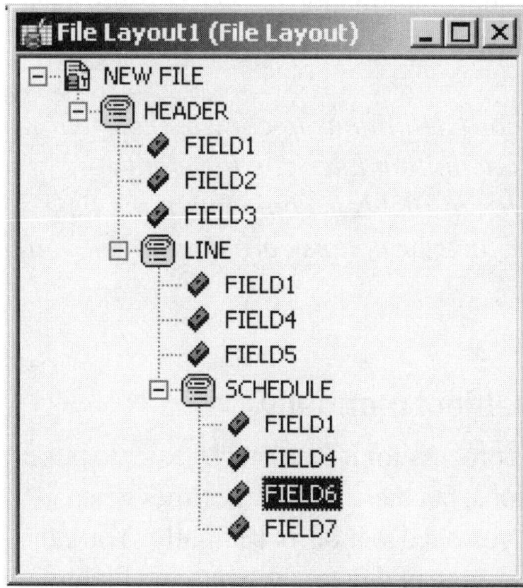

Figure 7.6 Fake Record File Object

The nice part is that PeopleSoft shows you the hierarchy using the tree format – you can see each child indented under its parent. The whole purpose of this is to make it easier to write the PeopleCode that will be outputting data using this File object. You will learn all about this in the next major section – Using PeopleCode to generate the file output.

There is one last thing to learn on creating a File object with the Record definition. You can also use the drag and drop process to add Records to your open File object. If you have a File object open in the Application Designer, you can drag a Record definition from your project list into the File object. Just click and hold over the Record definition, then drag the icon over to the File object and let go. The Record definition will be added where you drop the Record. This way when you are working on a project you can build your File objects quickly.

There is only one issue with using Record objects. If your Record object contains a LONG type field (the last Field in the Record), this will automatically be set with a FileField format of 0 length. You have not learned about FileField properties yet (see Adding Fields below) but if you wish this Field to have some information loaded, you will have to change this manually.

Warning: *If you are using Record definitions to copy in the Field list and you modify the Record definition later you have not modified the File Object. The list of Fields is copied in at the time of creation and then no further links or updates are done when you modify the Record definition.*

Creating the File Layout Object manually

Normally, you would not do this process for it is so much easier to build File objects with Record definitions; but there may come times when you can build with a Record but you need to modify it slightly. You can use this manual process to add, change or delete segments and Fields from the File object.

Adding Segments (and Child segments)

To add more Segments, you first have to decide where this new segment will go. You can do this upfront or later by using the Node buttons (as you learned earlier); it is recommended to do this upfront. To set the place for where the new segment is to be loaded, you first have to click an existing segment after which you want the new segment to go. If you want this new segment first, then you should be sure to click on the File object name instead. Once you have this done you follow the same process you have learned before: use the drag and drop method, main menu or right-click menu.

But what if you need to add a segment that is not part of a Record definition? You can also do this manually when you add the segment you select from the main menu: Insert – Segment. You can also do this from the right click menu selecting Insert Segment. This will open the panel, as shown in figure 7.7.

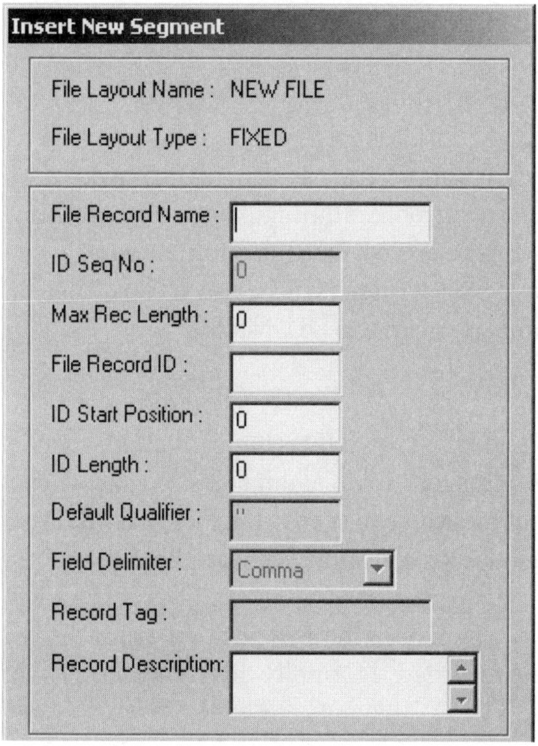

Insert New Segment

File Layout Name : NEW FILE

File Layout Type : FIXED

File Record Name :

ID Seq No : 0

Max Rec Length : 0

File Record ID :

ID Start Position : 0

ID Length : 0

Default Qualifier : ''

Field Delimiter : Comma

Record Tag :

Record Description:

Figure 7.7 Insert Segment Panel

This panel will change slightly due to the type of File object you are working on. This is why it is important that you define the type of the File object first. The name and type of File object are shown as general reference and you cannot change them. The other fields are the ones you are interested in. All the fields in the panel are listed below with the File object type that uses them and a full explanation. The Use is abbreviated for F = FIXED, C = CSV and X = XML.

Field Name	**Use**	**Description**

File Record Name — F, C, X — This is the name of the Record that created this segment if you used the insert Record process. If you are doing this manually, then you need to input a name that is unique for this File object. Maximum length is 15 characters.

ID Seq No — C — This is the sequence number of the field that contains the file record id. If it is the 3rd field, this value would be 3. Normally this is 1.

Max Record Length — F, C, X — This is the maximum number of characters in one row of data. This field is not system maintained, meaning if you add more fields with more information you may need to extend this value. If this value is exceeded, then the information is truncated even if it could have been written. It is best to set this value to a large number but not one that is so large to be wasteful.

File Record ID — F, C — This is a set of characters to represent this File Record. The File Record ID is typically used when you have multiple segments within one File Layout object, so that when you write out a row to the flat file, you can see via the File Record ID which segment this corresponds too. This field is not required.

ID Start Position — F — This is the start position within the row of data that holds the file record id. Normally this is one but can be 0 if there is no field record id.

ID Length — F, C — This is how long the record id is in number of characters.

Default Qualifier C Here, you can override the default qualifier you set for the File object itself. This allows you to change, per segment, the qualifier character.

Field Delimiter C Just like the Default Qualifier, you can override the character used to separate the fields for this segment.

Record Tag X This is the record tag used for XML files to show the file record id.

Record Description F, C, X This field is free form text where you can describe the record purpose and use. It is a good idea to always fill this out so that other developers can easily follow your development.

Once you have these input you can click the OK button. This will store the segment to the File object but you will notice that no Fields are added. Once you add Fields you may need to come back here and update parameters, such as Maximum Record Length.

Deleting Segments (and Child segments)

Deleting a segment is easy; you first have to select the segment to delete by clicking on it once so that is highlighted. Then, you can just type the delete key or right click to bring up the right-click menu, and select delete from there. In both cases you will get a warning message to ask whether you are sure if you want to delete a segment. If you answer yes, the segment will be deleted including all of the child segments and all of the associated field names. Deleting a segment will remove a lot of parameters so be sure this is what you really want to do.

Modifying Segments (and Child segments)

Once a segment is added, you can move the segment about the File object by using the Node buttons. You can also modify every value in the segment properties list that you are allowed based on the File object type. To move the segment around, just click once on the segment name to highlight it, then use the appropriate Node button.

To modify some properties of the segment, you can double-click on the segment name or right click on the segment name and then choose – Select Node Properties. Either way, you will open the segment properties panel, just like you have seen before in figure 7.7. You can modify or change any parameter here you wish but you still need to be sure your changes are valid for all of the fields you have in the segment.

Adding Fields

To add a new Field, you have to first select the point after which you want your Field to be added. This means if you want your field first, you have to select the segment name. If you want the Field 5th, you select the 4th Field. Once the insertion point is selected, you can then add a new Field to any segment, including Record segments, by using the main menu: Insert – FileField or using the right-click menu of Insert FileField. This process will open the FileField insert panel, as shown in figure 7.8.

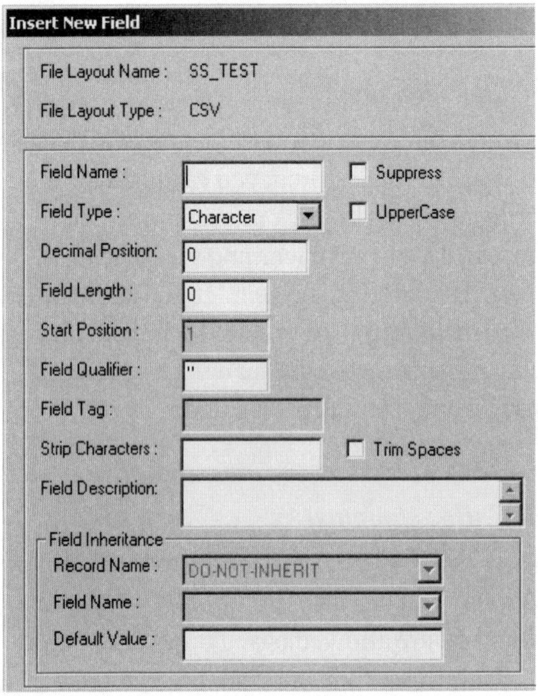

Insert New Field
File Layout Name : SS_TEST
File Layout Type : CSV
Field Name :
Suppress
Field Type : Character
UpperCase
Decimal Position: 0
Field Length : 0
Start Position : 1
Field Qualifier : "
Field Tag :
Strip Characters :
Trim Spaces
Field Description:
Field Inheritance
Record Name : DO-NOT-INHERIT
Field Name :
Default Value :

Figure 7.8 FileField Insert panel.

Again fields on this panel will be grayed out depending on the type of File object you are working on. Each field is explained below including the use.

Field Name **Use** **Description**

Field Name F, C, X This is the name of the field. This is the true Field name if this was copied from the Record. This field is required and must be unique for the segment although different segments can use this same name within the same File object. Maximum is 15 characters.

Suppress F, C, X This is a checkbox that specifies, even though you have defined this field, that it should be skipped in processing. This is a quick way to stop use of fields for a temporary time.

Field Type F, C, X This is a drop down list of valid Field types: Character, Number, Signed Number, Date, Time, Datetime

Uppercase F, C, X This checkbox shows if you have selected Character as a field type. This, if checked, sets all characters to uppercase automatically.

Date Separator F, C, X This field shows if you have selected Date as a field type. It allows you to define the character that is used to separate the day from the month and year. The standard default is /.

Decimal Position F, C, X This field shows if you have selected Number or Signed Number as the field type. It allows you to define the number of decimal positions in the field. Your field length needs to include the number of decimals. Maximum allowed is 31.

Date Format F, C, X This field shows if you had selected Date as the field type. The drop down can be used to specify the date format to be used.

Field Length F, C, X This is the field length. It must be the actual field length if this is a FIXED type File object but for XML or CSV types it is just the maximum allowed value. For Number or Signed Number fields, that maximum is 32. For Date, Time and Datetime field types, this value is set and not allowed to be changed per ISO 8601 standards.

Start Position F This is the number where this field starts within a single row of data.

Field Qualifier C This is the character used to wrap this field. Note that this is set up on the File object and that it can be overridden on the segment properties as well. No matter the settings in the File object or the segment, this is what the field will be using.

Field Tag X This is the tag to be used for this field if the File object is XML type.

Strip Characters F, C, X This inputs all the characters that should be removed from the field prior to processing. This will remove not only a single character but also multiple characters by just entering in many characters.

Trim Spaces F, C, X This, if set, will remove all trailing and leading spaces.

Field Description F, C, X This is a free form text field to describe the field and its use.

Field Inheritance - Record Name F, C, X
If this field is on a child segment, then it can inherit its value from one of the parent segments. Input the parent Record name (parent segment) here as the inheritance is not limited to just one level, but all levels up to the root.

Field Inheritance - Field Name F, C, X
If this field is on a child segment, enter the Field name from the defined

Inheritance Record Name that defines the value to place here by default.

Field Inheritance - Default Value F, C, X
If this field is on a child segment and no value exists for the Inherited Record and Field, you can define a default to be used.

These field types defined above have some special considerations for Date, Time and Datetime fields. Since the format is defined, you have to make sure your input file (if you are reading) is in sync with the format specified. You have some ways to define the format on the date type but you need to understand that 2/2/2002 will give you an error. You must pad all the values to fill the full format. So, in your case, the real date should be 02/02/2002. This meets the standard format and the length for a date field (10 characters length). Time fields are 20 characters long and are to be input in the following format - HH:MM:SS.ssssss[+/-hhmm]. Datetime fields are 31 characters long and in the format of CCYY-DD-MMTHH:MM:SS.ssssss[+/-hhmm]

Once you have defined your new Field, click the OK button to have it added to your segment. If the field was added to the wrong place, you can use the Node buttons to move the field to the correct position.

Deleting Fields

To delete a Field, you first have to select the Field to delete by clicking on it once so that is highlighted. Then, you can just type the delete key or right click to bring up the right-click menu and select delete. This will open a warning message panel to ask if you are sure whether you want to delete a Field. If you answer yes, the Field will be deleted from the segment.

Deleting a Field does not usually change any segment properties since you have less characters being used but this can affect the other Fields. If you are using a FIXED format type and you have Fields after the one you deleted, you may have a problem. With FIXED, you set the start position and field length. Now that a Field is removed, does the next Field start within the flat file on the start position defined for it? The start position may or may not be correct. You may have to modify all the Fields following the Field you have just deleted to correct for this problem (see Modifying Fields below).

Modifying Fields

When you modify a Field, you have to bring up the FileField properties panel. To do this you can right-click on the Field you wish to modify and chose: Select Node Properties Yes, you just did this same menu selection for segments but you should have right clicked on a Field. You can also double click on the Field name as well and this will bring up the properties panel, s shown in figure 7.9.

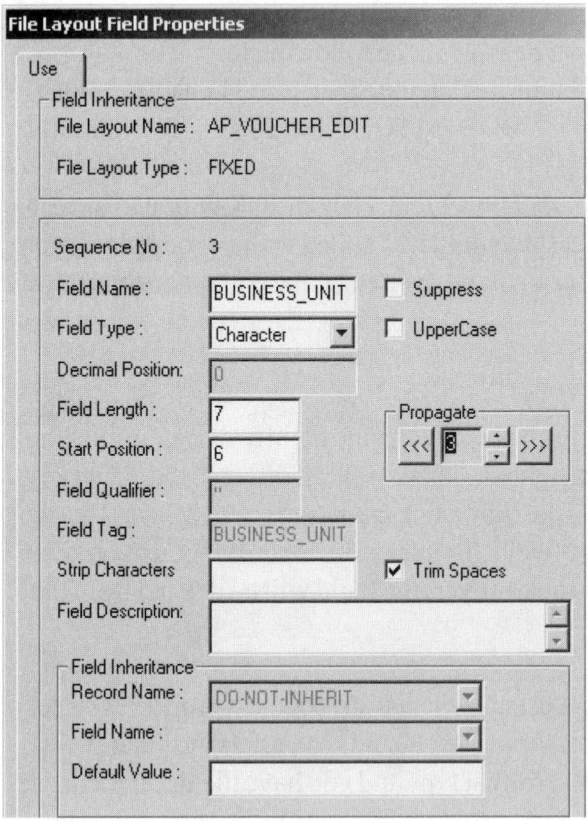

Figure 7.9 FileField Properties panel

This panel looks very much like the Insert panel in figure 7.7 but there are two new fields. The first is the Sequence No. This field is not editable but shows you the order of the fields within the segment. This is just a handy reference for when making changes to the order of the Fields.

This panel also has the propagate set of fields. You will find this very handy if you have to modify the start position or change the field length. The propagate set of fields are only active for the File object type of FIXED. This is because for CSV and XML type File objects you do not define the start position for each field.

To use the propagate process, you first have to enter in a number to change the starting position. The change will occur on the Field you have open. If you are adding length to this Field then you need to change the next Field since the starting position of this Field is not changing, just the length. Once you are on the Field where you wish to change the starting position, you can just directly type in the number; but then you will have to change every field after as well. This propagate feature allows you to do this quickly. You use the up and down arrows just to the right of the number to change the number (you cannot directly type it in). Change the number to the value of the change (you can also use negative numbers since the previous Field may have decreased in length). Once the number is correct, you then click on the triple arrow (>>>)to the right of the number. This will change this Field and every subsequent Field within the segment (not any child segments) by adding this number to the start position. With one simple change you can affect hundreds of Field assignments saving you lots of work.

There may also be cases when you need to affect the Field or Fields in front of this Field; that is what the triple arrow (<<<) to the left is for. Where the right arrow changed all Fields after this Field, this triple right arrow changes this Field and all Fields before this one. This way the propagate can handle just about any change you can think of.

Note: If you change a Field to where the start of some Field becomes negative you will receive a warning to fix the problem before you will be allowed to save the File object.

Saving the File object

Before saving the File object you need to make sure one more time of the names of the Fields and Segments. Later in this chapter you will learn how to make the Record data output through this File object. The PeopleCode process can use methods called WriteRecord, ReadRowset and WriteRowset. If any of these methods are used then you have to make sure of the name of the Fields within the segment and the names of the segments themselves. If you are going to manually write the file, using WriteLine functions, then you do not need to match names.

Once you are ready to save, click on the save button to bring up the save panel. Enter in the name of the File object. You can name it anything you wish but you are limited to 30 characters; and you should follow all of your naming conventions.

Flat File Concepts

You have learned all about Records, Segments and Field but how does this all correlate to a flat file that you are trying to create. This section is to try and help you understand this concept and list some ways that flat files are used. Our first example is where you are loading an item catalog. You will receive a file from an outside system – which has no idea about your PeopleSoft Record structure. This file could be sent through an EDI system, FTP flat file or even XML; but because of the simple structure it is most likely to be an FTP flat file. The received format is shown below.

```
200161   0356700Brass pump 1/4"TFT fitting       YXFJ
3008944  3375500Segement valve                   NXFH
56HGJ47650001250Aluminum Washer                  YAAA
```

This is a simple format with one set of data per row where: the first 9 characters are the item number; the next 7 characters are the list price;

the next 33 characters are the description; and the last 4 are some special codes. To set up this up as a File object you would create a FIXED type with only one segment. The segment would have 7 Fields to capture the item number, price, description and the four special fields.

That example was simple but many times a flat file is not so easy. EDI and XML flat files are in layers with different meanings. This is why child segments were created. Even FTP flat files can be done in layers. Our next example assumes an AP voucher set of data.

```
0100815
01277567847BAY TECHNOLOGIES
110200161      00000299900Brass pump 1/4"TFT fitting
1132002-03-140000115
1132002-04-010000087
11056HGJ4765   00000001250Aluminum Washer
1132002-03-140010000
01286867363RIVERFRONT FURNITURE
1103008944     00003375500Segement valve
1132002-03-280000001
9990815
```

Just a simple look tells you that this flat file is a bit more complicated but it is easy to read, once you understand the structure. The first and last lines are codes that show the begin and end transaction since this flat file could contain multiple transactions. The second line is the start of the first transaction. This line is made up of 3 elements; the first being the code (012) to tell that this is the header information; the second contains the Vendor Id (7756784) and the third Vendor description (BAY TECHNOLOGIES). Remember back on the segment properties the File Record ID? This first element (012) could fit the File Record ID since this value is always seen on the first level of a transaction.

The third line is the information about the item being received, which fits being a child segment of the Header since the qty received line is never without the header information (012). This third line also contains a transaction id (110), which works in the File Record ID on the child segment. Can you start to see how parent and child segments are being used? This third line also contains information on the item number, the prices and description (The information is similar to the previous item catalog example).

The fourth and fifth lines are children of the line (110) showing the receipt dates and quantities for that line. Again you have the code (113) showing the purpose of this line within the flat file. The sixth line contains a transaction code of 110, which is your line code. This means for this vendor, you have two lines to process (and maybe more). The line is followed by another 113 transaction showing the date and qty received.

The eighth line then restarts a new vendor by using the 012 transaction code. You can then see how this flat file works. By using transaction codes in the front, you can define how the rest of the line is to be used and interpreted. Of course, there is a hierarchy at work here with the parent header, child line and child delivery information. If you have created a File object to represent this flat file it would look something like this.

```
File Object Name
      Segment Header
            Vendor ID
            Vendor Name
            Segment Line
                  Item Id
                  Price
                  Descr
                  Segment Schedule
                        Date received
                        Quantity
```

This simple diagram shows the fields and the parent child relationship to be used in creating the flat file. You see, to create a good File object you have to know the flat file structure as well as the Record structure that you are going to be processing. Normally, a File object is created for either reading data or writing data. It is rare for it to be used both ways.

This completes learning how to create a File object but now you need to understand how to use the object within PeopleCode. This is where you learn how to do the actual output or reading of a file with the object you have just created.

Using PeopleCode to read/generate the file output

The File object is only used within PeopleCode and is a class unto itself. This means you need to declare your object and use its methods and properties to access and control the object. The whole purpose of this PeopleCode class is to enable the reading and writing of external files.

Declaring the File object

It is recommended to always declare an object up front in PeopleCode. This is the syntax to use.

```
Local File &APFILE;
```

This code shows using the fixed commands of "Local File" followed by a variable name. This variable name can be anything you wish as long as it is allowed in PeopleCode. The purpose of this code line is to set up a variable with the File object instance so that you can use the functions, methods and properties of the File class.

File object Built-in Functions

The functions are the first code that you will use to set up the object for use. You have to substantiate the object to a file and retrieve information about the flat file; that is the purpose of these functions.

FileExists

This function tests to see if a file exists or not on your system. You can use this process to test to see if a file is ready to be processed (to be read) or has already been processed (written out). You can also use this function to see if an outside process has already retrieved the output of an earlier run so that if the file still exists, you should not continue the process and you can publish a warning or error message. This way you do not overlay files of earlier runs and lose data. Here are a few examples of the function.

```
If FileExists(&FileName) then
If FileExists("R:\PSTMP\APVCHR.TXT",
%FilePath_Absolute) then
```

Normally this function is used in an "IF" statement to make a decision but it is not limited to this at all. Just understand the function returns a TRUE value if the file is found or a FALSE value if not.

The first example shows using a variable name for the name of the file while the second example uses a hard coded value. A bind variable could also have been used just as well for this first parameter. The second example shows you the optional second parameter. This parameter only has two settings: %FilePath_Absolute and %FilePath_Relative. If you do not use this parameter, then %FilePath_Relative is assumed. This second parameter controls how the first parameter is used. If %FilePath_Relative is used, then the process assumes the file is under the defined drive and directory stated in the PeopleSoft PS_SERVDIR environment variable. This means the process will use the value in the PS_SERVDIR and then add the file name parameter you have defined. If this had been done for the second example, you would have had an error since this was using an absolute drive and directory.

This also brings up the issue of directory separator ("/", "\"). If you are using Windows you need to use the "\" while Unix systems use the "/" separator. You will need to make sure you are using the correct separator for your system whether you are running on the client or server. Normally, you will be running your Application Engines on the server. If you are not sure which to use, see your system administrator.

Note: *If you use a %FilePath_Relative you will need to be sure to preface your file name with a "/" or "\" so that your directory path is built correctly.*

A further note, when your Application Engine program runs, you have to understand that the drive and directory structure is not to your local computer but that of the Process Scheduler server, since that is from where the program will be launched. You can easily map drives there for your use but depending on your security these may have to be done by the System Administrator. Also, if you are not sure of the drive and directory to assign – see your system administrator for help.

FindFiles

This function does something similar to the FileExists function but this function retrieves a list of file names based on a search criteria. Since this function returns a list of field names, you should always use this function with an array to load all of the file names.

```
&FileArray = FindFiles(&FileName);
&FileArray = FindFiles("R:\PSTMP\APVCHR.TXT",
%FilePath_Absolute)
&FileArray = FindFiles("R:\PSTMP\AP*.TXT",
%FilePath_Absolute)
&FileArray = FindFiles("R:\PSTMP\APVCHR?.TX?",
%FilePath_Absolute)
```

The assumption here is that the variable &FileArray is a defined string array. Looking over the examples, you will see that you have the file name as the first parameter and %FilePath_Absolute as the second parameter. The second parameter is not required but if you do not define the second parameter it is assumed to be using %FilePath_Relative. All of the same issues exist as on the FileExits function for file name, directory and use of directory separator. You will notice that in example 3 and 4 you will find some new items. These are the wild cards.

You are allowed to use only two wild cards per statement to keep down the processing that PeopleSoft will have to do. The '*' wild card is used to find all values while the '?' is used to replace any one character. You can use these only within the file name itself, not any of the directory structure; so, R:\PSTM?\APVCHR?.TXT is not allowed but R:\PSTMP\APVCHR?.TX? is since both of the wild cards are within the name, which included the name extension (the characters after the '.').

GetFile

This function creates the File object instance within PeopleCode. It verifies the file exists and opens it ready for processing – either to write a record or to read from it. Here are a few examples.

```
&APFILE = GetFile(&FILNAME, "R");
&APFILE = GetFile(&FILNAME, "W");
&APFILE = GetFile("R:\TMP\APVCHR.TXT", "R", "ASCII",
  %FilePath_Absolute);
```

From these examples you can see the basic statement to the full parameter statement. The first two examples show the typical basic statement where you substantiate the predefined variable (&APFILE) to a File object using the GetFile function. The function must have the first two parameters filled in. The first parameter is the file name which can include the drive and directory. The second parameter sets the method of action to the file. You are not allowed to read and write to a file at will but you must set up how you will process the file. There is a defined set of actions that you can perform and they are all listed below.

R Read – This opens a file for reading starting at the beginning of the file.
W Write – This opens a file for writing. If the file does not exist, then it is created. If the file exits, any existing data is deleted and the file is set to start loading new information.
U Update – This opens a file for reading or writing allowing you to update or change data in the middle of a file. This one action is special and requires the use of the GetPosition or SetPosition File object method. Once you open the file with this action type you need to define your starting point. You can read through the entire file but when you perform the first write, all data beyond the point at which you entered data is deleted from the file. ***Warning**: Only use this action type with character sets of ANSI. Other types may not work correctly.*
A Append – This opens a file for writing but will add any new information to the end of the file if it already exists. The information is

appended to the existing file with no older information lost. If the file does not exits, a new one is created.

E Conditional Read – If the file exists, it is set up to read otherwise nothing is processed and the file is not opened. It is a good idea to check the File object property of IsOpen to verify that the file was opened correctly.

N Conditional Write – If the file does not exist, the file opened for writing. If the file does exist – then nothing is processed and the file is not created. It is a good idea to check the File object property of IsOpen to verify that the file was opened correctly.

The third parameter, which is not required, defines the character set that you want to use in the flat file. There are two shortcuts to use here: one being "A" to define an ANSI standard and the other "U" to mean UNICODE. Any other character set you wish to use must be fully spelled out, such as ASCII or UTF8. If you do not specify a character set, then ANSI is used by default.

***Warning**: If you read a file using a different character set than the file was written in, then you will receive a run time error.*

The fourth parameter, which you have already seen before, works just the same; with all the same rules and problems as listed in the FileExists function above, so there is no need to go over this one more time.

You will note that the GetFile function is similar to a method you will learn about in the next section called OPEN. Do not confuse the two as the Open method can only process a File object that has been originally substantiated by the function of GetFile. See the Open method below for more information.

File object Methods

Once you have created a File object, you can then use its method and properties to affect the file itself. Here are all the methods you are allowed to use, showing the syntax and describing how they are used.

Close

This method closes the file so that it is completed and any buffer information is written to the file. It also unlocks the file so that other processes can then access the file. It is highly recommended to close all files since this will flush any buffers to the file output; so that if anything goes wrong later your file will be complete. Here is the syntax.

```
&APFILE.Close();
```

First there is the object variable so that the system knows which file you are closing. Then follows ".Close()". This is all you have to type to perform this method. Once a file object is closed, you can use the object again on a different file or the same file by using a GetFile function command.

CreateRowset

This method creates a Rowset object based on the File layout that has been defined by the previous method of SetFileLayout (see SetFileLayout method later in this chapter). You cannot use this method unless you have first set the file layout to use, otherwise you will not create the Rowset correctly. The purpose for this method is to build a rowset where you can then use all of the Rowset class methods, functions and properties. Typically, you will use the Fill or Select methods to load data into the rowset but you could also use the functions of GetLevel0() or GetRowset. These functions and methods will fill the Rowset buffer with data so that you can process a method called WriteRowSet (see WriteRowSet later in this chapter) that will write the data from the buffer out to the flat file.

Here is an example of the method.

```
&APROWSET = &APFILE.CreateRowSet();
```

The syntax follows the dot notation using the File object variable and the method command without any parameters. No parameters are needed since you are creating a rowset instance based on the File object layout.

This method is used for writing information to a flat file. If you want to read information and use a Rowset, use the ReadRowSet method (see ReadRowSet following).

GetPosition

This method is used when you have set your File object to use the action type of "U" or Update. This method will not work with any other action types and you will receive a runtime error if you try. This method returns a number that represents where you are within the flat file. It returns a number that is after the last read. Assuming your file layout is 10 characters for each row of data - if you have read 3 rows of data in, then the GetPosition method would return 31.

***Warning**: There are some serious issues with different character sets. Only use this method with the ANSI character set.*

The uses of this method are to know where in the file you are so that you can use the SetPostion method (see below) and to reset where you are in the file to update the correct row of data. The use of this method usually requires some complicated PeopleCode since once you perform the first write on the file, all data beyond where you first wrote is deleted from the file. This is why a lot of developers will read a File in, using one object, and have a second File object open to write out the new data with a different name. In this way you can process all updates sequentially and not lose any data in the original file. This method does exist and you may have occasion to use it. Just be sure of the limitations of this method and the use of the action type Update.

This method requires no parameters since you are only the current position in the file. Shown below is the example of the use of this method.

```
&FILEPOS = &APFILE.GetPosition();
```

Open

This method is similar to the GetFile function. The parameters are exactly the same but the use is a bit different. Where GetFile substantiated a File object, Open can take an already substantiated File Object and re-connect it to another external flat file. To better explain, assume you need to process through 5 files. You do not need to process all 5 at one time, but you can process them sequentially – one after the other. You would only need to use the GetFile function once to create the File object for the first file. Then once you are done processing the first, you could use the Open method to close the File object and reset the File object to your second file. In this way, you only need one File object variable and you could potentially write some looping code to process a set of files with only one set of PeopleCode. This would save on time and effort in coding. Of course, if you need all five files open at the same time, you would need to run the GetFile function five times into five different File object variables. The Open method is there for sequential processing to allow one variable to represent a set of files.

Here are few examples of the method in use.

```
&APFILE.Open(&FILNAME, "R");
&APFILE.Open(&FILNAME, "W");
&APFILE.Open("R:\TMP\APVCHR.TXT", "R", "ASCII",
  %FilePath_Absolute);
```

The syntax for this method is to use the dot notation on the substantiated File object with the method of Open. Then the parameter list follows with the first two parameters being required while the third and fourth are optional. The parameters are exactly the same as listed for the GetFile function with the file name, action type, character set and file path control. Since these were all discussed before there is no reason to repeat. If you need a refresher, read the previous GetFile section above.

ReadLine

This method reads the next row of data from the flat file. It reads from the last position through to the end of line character. It then removes the end of line character and places the results into a text string. If there is no more data to read, then the method returns a false result so that you can test for end of file. Review the examples below for syntax and use.

```
If &APFILE.ReadLine(&STRING) then
While &APFILE.ReadLine(&STRING);
```

You can see from the two examples that the method is typically used within a logic decision to check for the TRUE or FALSE return on the last read. This way you can simply process an entire file. The one parameter must be a string variable (be sure to define the variable up front for ease of use). Once the string variable is loaded you can parse the variable based on how the file was put together; such as CSV field separators or knowing the structure based on the first three characters.

ReadRowset

This method is used to read external flat files based on the File object specified in the previously called method of SetFileLayout (see below). It is similar to the WriteRowSet method, which is designed to write to external flat files. The ReadRowset method, when used, will create a Rowset object and immediately populate data into the Rowset from the external file. The entire Rowset will be filled from level 0 through all of the child segments for the one row of data in level 0. The file read point will then be set to the next line of data to load for the entire Rowset (which may not be line 2 since it is for the entire Rowset).

***Warning**: If you do not issue the SetFileLayout method before this method, the Rowset will be set with NULL values.*

Once the end of file is reached, the ReadRowSet method returns NULL values into the Rowset meaning there is nothing returned from the method itself but that you will have to test the Rowset to see if it is NULL, to check for end of file.

Review the example.

```
&APROWSET = &APFILE.ReadRowSet();
```

You can see that the Rowset object variable is loaded with data unless the end of file is reached.

There are some special considerations if you are using multiple File objects to read in the one external file. This process is used in combination with the method SetFileId (see below). The method ReadRowSet will also return NULL when a FileID is encountered. A FileID in the external file is trying to tell you that a different layout is coming so you need to change the File object. You will have to test for this NULL value on the Rowset. Since this is also the same process used to tell if you are at the end of file, you have to check the property of IsFileId to determine the next FileID to use or whether the end of file has been reached (see IsFiled in the property section below).

SetFileId

This method is used when you had to create multiple File objects to define the one external file you are trying to read. This method is used in conjunction with the ReadRowSet and SetFileLayout methods and the CurrentRecord and IsNewFileId properties.

***Warning**: This method cannot be used within any type of file object except FIXED.*

To understand the use of this method you need to understand the required layout of the external file. When the external File Layout changes, there needs to be within the external file a new row of data that consists of a value called the FileID. This value represents that this row is showing there is a File Layout change at this point in the file.. This value should be the same value throughout the entire external file. The next value is the actual File Layout name, which is a combination of two values – a hard code value showing the File Layout change and then the File Layout name to use. This File Layout name is then the one that is used to load the new File object and the name must exactly match the File object name you created in the Application Designer. See the example below of an external file format.

```
...data...
000022784665907567377FRED SCHMIDT196004272578765
777MSTRRCD
2597356767MARY SIMMONS397637736730936369
...data...
```

The example shows that our FileID value would be 777 and the name of our File object would be MSTRRCD. There could be more information after this on this row of data but the PeopleSoft system would just ignore it. Note, this row of FileID information is not considered to be part of any Rowset and is only used by special functions and methods. To see the proper way to make this process work, including the syntax of the method SetFileId, see the code example below.

```
&APFILE.SetFileLayout("BOGUS.TXT");
&APFILE.SetFileId("777", 1);
&APROWSET = &APFILE.ReadRowSet();
&CURRENT = &APFILE.CurrentRecord;
If &APFILE.IsNewFileId then
   &FileLayout = FindFileId(&CURRENT);
   &FileLayout = "Filelayout." | &FileLayout;
   &APFILE.SetFileLayout(@(&FileLayout));
   &APFILE.SetFiledId("777", 1);
End-if;
```

The first line sets the File Layout object to be used as a bogus value. This is to show you that you do not have to initially define the correct layout as once you read the data you will be able to retrieve the correct layout, which this example will show. The second line uses the SetFileId method. The syntax is the File object variable and then two parameters. The first parameter is the value that is used to show this row of data is changing the File Layout. The second parameter is to show where in the sequence of the row, the name of the File Layout begins (777). Using the example, it starts at the first character.

***Warning**: On line one of the example, a name of BOGUS was used. The File layout object defined here must exist otherwise you will get a runtime error. The best thing to use here is a known valid File layout object for the file you are to process; but you do not have to care which one to use since this will be reset by the code, as show in the example.*

The third line then reads the first row of data – which should be the file layout change information. The fourth line uses the CurrentRecord property to assign a value to a variable which you will need to use later to retrieve the File Id information. The fifth line uses an IF statement to see if there is a new File ID. When the code is processed for the first time, The IF will be true since the first row will be the file layout change data. The sixth line extracts the file layout name from the external file. The seventh line builds the variable to be in the format of "Filelayout." plus the File Layout object name for the external file. The eighth line then sets the file layout to be used. The ninth line shows doing the SetFileId method again and this is required. Every time a SetFileLayout method is processed, the SetFileId information is lost so you must reset the value to know what the value is for the file layout change row of data.

At this point you can start reading the file since you have the layout defined. You would do this by returning to line 3 of our example and doing the read. You would have to add more code to the process when the IsNewFileId returns false – meaning you have a new valid row of data to process.

SetFileLayout

You have just seen this method used in an actual example (see SetFileId previously) so you should understand that this method sets the File object that you created in the Application Designer to use, to read the external file. You must use this method on any open File object variables to know how to read the data. See the following examples for the proper syntax.

```
&APFILE.SetFileLayout(Filelayout.APVCHR);
&APFILE.SetFileLayout(@&VARIABLE);
```

These examples do not show it, but this method does return a value of TRUE if the command completes successfully, and FALSE if not. The only reason this should fail is if the File object variable is not open or the File layout object does not exist. The method uses the standard dot notation with one parameter. This parameter is the name of the File layout object. You can hard code the value, as in example one, or use a variable, as in example two. The format of the variable must be in "Filelayout" plus the File layout object name. Assuming a File layout name of APTMP1, you should store in the variable "Filelayout.APTMP1".

SetPosition

This method is used in combination with the action type of Update. This method is used to set the position within an opened external file. This is normally used in error correction or recovery from a problem. You can store the start position in a separate external file or database record. You can then read this record or flat file to determine where you last processed and then use the GetPostion to determine where you are, and start processing again when the values match.

***Note**: You can set the start position to 0 without any issue but if you give a number that exceeds the file length you will receive an error. That is why it is recommended to use the GetPosition method.*

```
&APFILE.SetPosition(0);
&APFILE.SetPosition(77);
&APFILE.SetPosition(&LastPosition);
```

This method does not return any value to say if the process worked or not. The only requirement is a parameter stating where to place the file pointer for the next action you will request. A value of 0 is allowed, as this is the start of the file.

WriteLine

This method writes the supplied string variable to the external file. This method also automatically adds the end of line character to the line being written.

```
&APFILE.WriteLine("This is a string");
&APFILE.WriteLine(&STRING);
```

This method only requires the one parameter; a string value or variable. This method does not return any value so you cannot directly check if the write was successful or not. This method is meant to handle easy files with limited format and does not require a File layout to be defined. This is typically used to add end of transaction or end of file commands that are outside of the normal file format. This means you can write most of the file using the WriteRowSet method but use this method when doing a special string. It is possible to mix the two ways (Rowset and manual) to build the one file.

WriteRaw

This method writes raw data, hence its name, from a binary type field out to the external file. This is used to write out images and other items stored in binary format within the database. Most fields are not binary format but image type fields are. Here is an example of the method in use.

```
&APFILE.WriteRaw(&RECORD.ITEM_PHOTO.Value);
```

This example shows the use of the dot notation on the file object with only the one parameter. This parameter is usually a value from a database record or a rowset. Since raw binary format types cannot be set for variables, this is the most common use of this method.

WriteRecord

This method allows you to write out one row of data from a database Record to the external file. This method is used when the WriteRowSet was just not feasible for some reason, or took too much time to create.

The WriteRecord is a quick and easy way to write information into a flat file quickly and easily for one Record. It can also be used for multiple Records but that is the purpose of the WriteRowSet (see following).

The WriteRecord method requires the use of a File Layout object so this method must come after the SetFileLayout method you learned about earlier in this chapter. This method also assumes that the Record name matches exactly to a segment name defined in the File Layout object. When this method is used only that segment will be used to write out data. Once the Record name is matched, the Field names are matched; and they must match exactly. This is why it is crucial to make sure the File Layout object is written knowing the Record being used to create the external file.

```
&APFILE.WriteRecord(&RECORD);
```

As you can see from the example you only need to list the substantiated Record variable. A special note should be made that not only does the Record have to be substantiated but also you then have to load data in the Record; you can do this through various means such as, SQL fetch, copy from another Record, etc. Once you use this method, the Record information is verified and sent to the external file.

Even though it was not shown, this method does return a TRUE if the write was successful or a FALSE if the write had some problem.

***Note**: If your File layout object is of the XML type, the close tag is not written out after any WriteRecord. You need to use WriteLine or WriteString to output this final tag.*

WriteRowset

This is the recommended method to use to output data to an external file. This method writes an entire Rowset in one statement. If you have an external file needing 3 segments, it would take three WriteRecord statements to equal the one WriteRowSet statement. You should now be able to see why this is the recommended way to process files.

The syntax is similar to the WriteRecord except that the one parameter is now a Rowset object, as shown in the example below.

```
&APFILE.WriteRowSet(&ROWSET);
```

As with the WriteRecord, you can use various processes to load all of the data in the Rowset, so that you when you write it out the entire Rowset is sent to the external file. As with the other methods, this one also requires that you have processed the SetFileLayout method prior to issuing this method. This method also returns a TRUE if the write occurred without any problems, otherwise you will get a FALSE return.

WriteString

This method is exactly like WriteLine except this method does not automatically place an end of line character. Some external systems may require the end of line and some may not. Use this method where the end of line is not required.

***Note**: Typical end of lines is a Carriage Return character.*

```
&APFILE.WriteString("This is a string");
&APFILE.WriteString(&STRING);
```

The examples show how to use this method with either a hard coded string or a variable.

File object Properties

These are the properties for the File object that you can use to manipulate the File or confirm information about it.

CurrentRecord

This property returns the current Record (last read row of data) as a string. This is used when the external file is made up of multiple File layout objects. You need this property to read the row of data into a variable that you can then apply other functions to determine the FileId.

See the following code line (this is the same code from the SetFileId Method previously) for an example.

```
&APFILE.SetFileLayout("BOGUS.TXT");
&APFILE.SetFileId("777", 1);
&APROWSET = &APFILE.ReadRowSet();
&CURRENT = &APFILE.CurrentRecord;
If &APFILE.IsNewFileId then
   &FileLayout = FindFileId(&CURRENT);
   &FileLayout = "Filelayout." | &FileLayout;
   &APFILE.SetFileLayout(@(&FileLayout));
   &APFILE.SetFiledId("777", 1);
End-if;
```

You can see this property is used after the ReadRowSet method to extract the information in the File object variable into a string variable called &CURRENT. Later this variable is used to extract the FileID.

IgnoreInvalidId

This is a property that you can set to change the process. Normally, when the ReadRowset method runs, the process just skips over these problem records, if it encounters an error either through an invalid FileID or not matching the current File layout object. The default setting on this property is TRUE and this allows for skipping records that are problems. If you set this property to FALSE, then the program will not skip over them when records are encountered that are not valid, and will terminate with an error. You can change this process to your error control needs. You can both read and update this property.

```
&APFILE.IngnoreInvalidId = False;
If &APFILE.IngnoreInvalidId then
```

IsError

This property is read only and returns a TRUE value if an error condition is encountered during the last method processed on the File object. If the property returns FALSE, then no errors have occurred on the last method command.

```
If &APFILE.IsError then
```

IsNewFileId

This property returns a TRUE if a FieldID value has been encountered. The FieldID search value is set by the method SetFileId. If a record is read that contains this value, then this property is set to TRUE; so that you can test on it to see if you need to change the File layout object for reading in more of the external file.

```
If &APFILE.IsNewFileId then
```

IsOpen

This property returns a TRUE value if the File object variable has been opened and is ready for the action determined by the Open method or the GetFile function. If this returns FALSE, then there was a problem opening the File variable object. This property is usually checked right after opening the File object.

```
If &APFILE.IsOpen then
```

Name

This property returns the name of the external file. If no file is open or the File object has been closed, then this will return a NULL string.

```
&NAME = &APFILE.Name;
```

RecTerminator

This property contains the end of line or record terminator. You cannot only read the value but you are allowed to change it. The property starts out initialized with the appropriate end of line for the server but you can change it since you may be creating a Mainframe file on a Windows NT file server. This allows you to change the end of line for the receiving system no matter what the requirements are.

```
&APFILE.RecTerminator = "//"
```

Putting It All Together

Here is just a small example of a simple output file utilizing a few of the methods and properties.

```
Local File &APFILE;

&APFILE = GetFile("APVHCR.TXT", "W");
If &APFILE.IsOpen then
   If &APFILE.SetFileLayout(Filelayout.APVCHR) then
      &RECORD = CreateRecord(Record.VOUCHER_HDR_TMP);
      &SQLOBJ = CreateSQL("%Selectall(:1)", &RECORD);
      While &SQLOBJ.Fetch(&RECORD)
         &APFILE.WriteRecord(&RECORD);
      End-While;
   Else;
      Callerror("FILELAYOUT");    JAW STOP HERE
   End-if;
Else;
   Callerror("FILE");
End-if;
```

***Note**: The use of the Callerror function is a user defined function to simplify the code line here to show where to put in the error routines.*

File Security Considerations

For those who are security conscious, you need to be aware that with the creation of external files or the reading of external files, someone could get around your security system. The process of writing the file is not under the person who launched the program but under the server's authority. This means, if a user has access to a Page that launches the Application Engine program that creates a file, the user has rights to create the file. If you wish to prevent users, you will have to be sure of all your Pages that launch these types of programs have been set up with the proper security.

There is also the issue on the reading of files. If a user has access to running the program and they also has access to where the input file is to be placed, then the user can load data into the system around all your security measures. With the use of external files, you need to not only secure who can run the Application Engine program but also who has access to the file directories where programs are run. You also should not allow any user input into the file name or directory, as the user can then change the standard process and load a file not expected nor wanted by the company.

This does not mean you will have security holes in your system, just that you need to think of new things to make sure you are secure in your business.

Next

This completes the File object chapter, covering quite a bit of territory, but this is not all. Application Engine has a great deal to offer you, especially if you can think in terms it knows best. Application Engine is a tool that works best on sets of data. Processing one by one is usually done in reports and Pages that you create for the user. Application Engine programs usually update or process large volumes of data.

To do this effectively, you need to think in sets, not in rows. This takes a different way of thinking than you would normally do for a report. You need to learn what is called by advanced developers, set processing. It is not difficult to learn, it is just a new skill that you need to have to make Application Engine the great tool that it is. This is what the next chapter is all about. Learning how to code and think in terms of set processing.

Chapter 8

Set Processing

In this chapter you will learn the reasons Set Processing is important in Application Engine programs, the most important of which is performance. Then you will be shown the distinctions between Set Processing and Row-by-Row Processing and what the impact of these differences is in your programs. This chapter then reviews some common myths and misconceptions about Set Processing. Then some practical Set Processing techniques are covered to take you from the theory into some actual application of designing for Set Processing.

Set Processing Defined

The word "Set" in Set Processing comes from the mathematical definition meaning a group of elements. In the case of database programming, a row of data is a single element and a "set" would be a group of rows. Processing means to change data in some way such as a calculation. Multiplying Hours Worked times Pay Rate to get the Gross Pay of an employee is an example of processing. Thus, Set Processing means to process data as a group of rows rather than one row at a time.

To get a good grasp of what Set Processing can do for you requires good definitions for both Set Processing and Row-by-row Processing and then to compare the two types.

Row by Row Processing

When the data in your application requires some type of changes, there needs to be some method to get at this information and modify it. In most of the traditional languages the programmer codes a set of statements to accomplish this. Here is an example of how the programmer might code this:

- Begin a loop
- Get the next row of data to process
- If no row available, then exit the loop
- Do the needed update (calculation, modification, deletion, etc.) to that one row
- Continue at the top of the loop

This set of statements is called Row-by-row Processing because it processes data one row at a time. Use of a Do Select Action is an example of row-by-row processing.

Set Processing

Set Processing is built on the concept of handling groups of rows at one time. By contrast to Row-by-row Processing, the coding of Set Processing goes like this:

- Do the needed update to all the rows to process

From the programmer's perspective this is definitely simpler than the row-by-row procedure.

Set Processing is called non-procedural because the programmer tells the program what to do, but not how to do it within the database. The programmer does not specify the procedure used to do the update. Instead this procedure is built into the Relational Database Management System (RDBMS) and it is out of the hands of the programmer. The details of how to do it are left up to the RDBMS, thus various types of built-in optimizations are applied to the update that the programmer need not program or worry about.

***Note**: The term "update" is being used in a fairly generic sense meaning any change to the database. This includes SQL insert and delete statements as well as update statements.*

Row-by-row Processing vs. Set Processing

This section reviews some sample code using Set Processing as well as Row-by-Row Processing.

Here is an example of Set Processing followed by an example of doing the same task using row-by-row processing. You can then see how each process will handle the same problem. In this example there is a simple Record of Inventory Items called ITEM_RECORD that looks something like this:

ITEM_ID	ITEM_GROUP	PRICE
ABC-23	A	32.50
DEF-44	B	14.00
XYZ-99	A	22.00
MNO-56	B	16.23

The example problem is to reduce the price of all items in Item Group A by 10%.

Set Processing Example

The Set Processing SQL statement to handle the example problem would be as follows.

```
UPDATE ITEM_RECORD
SET PRICE = PRICE - (PRICE * (10 / 100))
WHERE ITEM_GROUP = 'A'
```

This SQL Statement tells the database to get the set of ITEM_RECORD rows with an ITEM_GROUP of 'A'. Then to this set of rows apply a 10% reduction. In fact this SQL statement is a very clean statement of the business rule you defined above in English: "reduce the price by 10% of all items from Item Group 'A'".

Row by Row Processing Example

By comparison to the Set Processing example above, the row-by-row code written in SQR is shown below.

```
begin-procedure Update-Item-Record
begin-select
ITEM_ID            &ITEM
      do Update-One-Item

FROM ITEM_RECORD
WHERE ITEM_GROUP = 'A'
end-select
end-procedure

begin-procedure Update-One-Item
begin-sql

UPDATE ITEM_RECORD
SET PRICE = PRICE * .9
WHERE ITEM_ID = &ITEM

end-sql
end-procedure
```

This code starts with the procedure Update-Item-Record that loops through each row to process one at a time. For each row, the procedure Update-One-Item is called and then updates that one row.

As can be seen, this entails quite a few more lines of code. Not only that, but the code lines inside the loop are executed once for each row to be processed. Just looking at these two methods together gives a visual representation of how many extra processing steps there are in the row-by-row processing.

Set Processing Advantages/Disadvantages

There are a number of advantages to Set Processing over Row-by-Row that you will want to know about as well as some disadvantages.

Advantages

The biggest advantage Set Processing has over Row-by-Row is performance. One of the important aspects of computers and computer programs is that they be sufficiently fast for the tasks at hand. Using Set

Processing correctly in your Application Engine programs can reap performance benefits of 10, 20, 30 or sometimes even more than 50 times the speed of row-by-row processing. When you take a batch update Application Engine program that runs in a half hour and change it to run in a minute is of no small consequence. It also will free up needed server resources.

Another advantage of Set Processing is scalability. Since row-by-row executes a set number of lines of code for the processing of each row, the more rows to process adds to the time involved. Set Processing executes one line of code for the whole set so does not have this repetitive execution of code. Although the single Set Processing statement can take longer to execute than a line of code done in row-by-row, the overall time for processing is quicker.

So, whether the program is handling just a dozen or a hundred rows, there may not be very much discernable difference in speed between the two methods. Once you have thousands or tens of thousands of rows to process, the performance advantages of Set Processing become quite clear in the execution times of your programs. Set Processing done correctly with proper indexing and good coding is very scalable. Row-by-Row performance on the other hand is a more linear progression based on the number of rows to process.

Note: *Many other variables can affect performance and scalability such as network performance, server loads, database space and rollback segments.*

Set Processing occurs entirely inside the RDBMS. In row-by-row processing, information is extracted from the database into the application for manipulation and processing through code that executes outside the database. Then the data is inserted, updated or deleted back into the database. Even where this process is occurring over a high-speed connection between the Database Server and the App Server, the need to move data back and forth takes time. This performance hit of data movement across the network is then compounded by the fact data is generally updated back to the database one row at a time.

In row-by-row processing one can get fairly involved with loops inside of loops inside of loops. As you can see from the previous SQR code example, a Set Processing SQL statement does its action all in one statement. The same functionality coded in row-by-row requires multiple Steps and Actions and, therefore, is usually more involved to read and thus to modify.

Another advantage of Set Processing is that RDBMS vendors are constantly competing to optimize their Set Processing commands and are improving performance with new releases. These improvements are then automatically applied to your programs without any programming changes when you upgrade database versions. Your Set Processing statements will automatically benefit over time as newer, faster optimization methods are built into the RDBMS for these commands.

Disadvantages

The prime disadvantage to Set Processing is that there are times where the developer needs to handle a single row of data at a time because there is just no other way to do certain processing. That is why Row-by-Row processing was added to SQL with the addition of SQL cursors. It fills this programming need to handle a row at a time when there is no way to do the processing to a set of rows.

SQL statements can also become quite complex using Set Processing logic. Use of EXIST clauses and sub-queries can make the SQL seem hard to read. It is a skill that needs to be learned that prevents some developers from using Set Processing.

Row-by-Row and Set Processing in PeopleTools

These two different types of processing are available for your use in a number of places in PeopleTools. Looking at how these two types of processing are used in these tools will give you a better understanding how and where you can use these methods.

SQL was originally designed around the concept of Set Processing. Row-by-Row Processing was added to SQL later on and became a part of the ANSI standards (American National Standards Institute) in the 1989 standard called SQL-89. Row-by-Row was added to SQL with an object called a cursor, which is often thought of as a pointer to a row of data. Actually a cursor is more than that. A cursor is an object, which holds the result of a query i.e. a set of rows. The cursor can then "Fetch" (point to) one row at a time so that each row can be handled individually by you in your code. The field values for this row can be retrieved for processing. This is how SQL does row-by-row processing and the ability to use SQL cursors is built into a few of the PeopleSoft tools including Application Engine.

Row-by-Row Processing

- In Application Engine this cursor processing is delivered in the "Do Select" Action where the Action type is either "Select/Fetch" or "RestartRecord". In this Action, your SQL returns a set of rows. Behind the scenes and hidden from your view, a cursor is created to hold this set of rows. Then for each iteration of your "Do Select" loop, one row is fetched for your use. This is how to do Row-by-Row Processing in Application Engine.
- SQR does Row-by-Row Processing in its BEGIN-SELECT / END-SELECT block of code. The FROM and WHERE clauses retrieves a set of data that SQR then creates into a cursor behind the scenes hidden from the developer's view. SQR then fetches through the rows of this set one at a time and allows processing of them.
- The PS SQL Object retrieves rows using a SQL cursor behind the scenes and has its own Fetch method built into it for retrieving one row at a time.
- A big part of online PeopleCode is the handling of rows in a Scroll Area or Rowset Object. The handling and updating of rows in a Rowset or Scroll Area is all done one row at a time. To process the information in a Rowset or Scroll Area requires looping through the rows of data and making changes one row at a time.

Set Processing

- Application Engine, of course, also does Set Processing in its SQLAction and does it exceedingly well.
- SQR also does Set Processing in its BEGIN-SQL / END-SQL block.
- SQLExec can process many rows at once in Set Processing fashion when doing inserting, updating and deleting.
- The SQL Object can do Set Processing for inserting, updating and deleting.
- Scroll Areas or Rowset Objects can be loaded with many rows of data at once in a Set Processing fashion using the ScrollSelect function; similarly in a Rowset Object using the "Select" method.

Set Processing Myths

There are a few myths regarding Set Processing that need to be debunked. These myths are things that tend to interfere with Set Processing gaining an even larger following and being utilized fully.

Set Processing is sometimes slower

The first myth is that Set Processing in not always faster than the same coding done in row-by-row processing. Now it can certainly be seen how poorly designed Set Processing code can be made slower than the equivalent task done in row-by-row processing, if one really worked at it. There are many ways to code the same task, some of which might be of questionable design, construction and efficiency.

Certainly Set Processing is a skill and to some degree an art that takes some practice to design and code well. A skillfully coded Set Processing program will be faster than row-by-row processing doing the equivalent task for the reasons already covered.

Set Processing is too much of an Advanced Skill to learn easily

There is the idea that skilled Set Processing is too difficult for you to learn it, so why bother? There is no question that it is a skill that you will improve over time. There can be room for you to find better ways to structure and code your Set Processing as you progress in this skill, just because there are a number of great ways to get things done in Set Processing.

This does not mean that it is a steep learning curve to get started. If you have reasonable SQL skills, then armed with a fairly small number of key tips and techniques that are discussed later in this chapter, you will easily be able to jump right into Set Processing with good success and start reaping the performance benefits. These techniques are not at all hard to learn, as you will soon see.

Set Processing is only useful in Batch Update Programs

PeopleSoft has added the CallAppEngine() PeopleCode function in version 8. With this call, Set Processing can be done in on-line PeopleCode.

One example is where an on-line page had hundreds of rows to display in a Scroll Area that required many intensive calculations. All these calculations were done using row-by-row processing in PeopleCode. This Page took 10 minutes or more to display information on the screen. Sometimes it even overwhelmed the Application Processor and caused the Page to hang.

An Application Engine program was created to build the data and do the calculations in an Inprocess Record using Set Processing. This program was then called from the PeopleCode replacing the earlier PeopleCode that calculated the Page information using row-by-row processing. The program then inserted all the rows of the Inprocess Record into the Scroll Area. Since this modification, the Page never hangs and displays 10 times faster than before. As you can see,

Application Engine and Set Processing goes beyond just batch update processing. It can be very useful for some online applications as well.

Set Processing is not useful in a Row-by-Row program

Actually, Set Processing can be very valuable in conjunction with a row-by-row processing. SQR is a very powerful tool that, like Application Engine, has facilities to perform both Set Processing as well as row-by-row processing. Some portion of an SQR report must by necessity be done in row-by-row processing, since a row of data is retrieved and printed on a line, then the next row is retrieved and printed on the next line, and so on. Where this data is unchanged from the data row to the print line then this row-by-row processing can move fairly quickly. If a lot of manipulations and calculations start occurring between the data row retrieved and the print line, this can reduce performance quite remarkably.

An easy trap to fall into when coding a report or other row-by-row program is to do ALL your processing on a row-by-row basis because the printing or processing of each line has to be done row-by-row.

You need to move all the calculations from the row-by-row processing and load into a Record using Set Processing. Then this data can be retrieved from the Record and printed out on a row-by-row basis. Where the amount of processing that is moved from row-by-row to Set Processing is significant, performance improvements of 20 times or more are commonly observed. Do not under-estimate the performance gains of doing Set Processing in a Row-By-Row program.

Batch processing jobs often require row-by-row processing anyway

There is another myth that a fair amount of batch update programs cannot be done entirely with Set Processing and that a fair amount of row-by-row will be needed. As you begin to use Set Processing techniques in your programs, you may encounter a number of situations that seem to require row-by-row processing along with Set Processing. However, as you continue developing your Set Processing expertise, you will begin to find that you are less and less dependent on row-by-row processing. You will discover more and more of your programs that can be done with just Set Processing.

Regarding this issue, there is an analogy here to a challenging game in Microsoft Windows called Freecell. Those who get good at this game can win most Freecell games, but still some are so tough that it seems they cannot be won. In the help section for Freecell there is a curious note that says, "It is believed (but not proven) that every game is winnable." Being inspired by this note, a number of Freecell players have gone on a mission to replay every lost game until it was won. Over the years some dedicated players have yet to find a Freecell game that could not eventually be won even if it took a dozen tries or more to do so. The analogy here is that with a strong mindset that the job can be done entirely in Set Processing, you will find many ways to do without any row-by-row processing where you thought this was not possible. You will discover fewer and fewer instances where you just cannot do without some row-by-row processing.

Now there will be some times when you will just have to use row-by-row processing in your batch update programs. One example of needing row-by-row is where you need to add a sequence number to your output where each succeeding row acquires the next higher sequence number. Your database platform may have a vendor specific Set Processing solution for this, but generic SQL Set Processing does not.

With this in mind, you can challenge yourself to assume an aggressive viewpoint and attitude that your program can be done with only Set Processing. With this mindset you will begin to discover many, many things that can be coded in Set Processing and you will certainly begin to enjoy the performance benefits. Even where you absolutely must do some row-by-row processing, keeping this to a minimum and doing the rest in Set Processing will buy you performance gains. With this enthusiasm for making it all work in Set Processing, the next section for you to look at covers some techniques that will help you accomplish this.

Set Processing Design: Techniques, Tools and Tips

Designing and coding Set Processing programs can be a lot of fun but also sometimes fairly challenging. In this section you will see some useful techniques, tips and tools for making Set Processing work effectively. This section covers how to design with Set Processing in mind, then it shows you how that design turns into code. The examples given here are a sub-set of what a complete Application Engine program written with Set Processing might look like. For a full demonstration of these techniques in a complete Application Engine program, see Chapters 11 and 12.

***Note**: These are some basic ideas and techniques that have proven to be quite useful for programming of Set Processing. These ideas are not the only way to design and code your Set Processing programs, but they are offered to you here as a collection of tools to get you started producing efficient Set Processing programs.*

Designing your program

One of the first things to consider is the design of the program to be coded. This is not the design that a functional analyst does in gathering the business requirements and writing the program specs for the technical person. This is the internal design of the program that the technical developer does. It could be said that the two things that many programmers don't do enough of is to a) spend enough time designing their programs and b) spend enough time testing their completed programs.

Input-Processing-Output

To begin your design you need some point of reference to start with. This is where dividing up your task with the concept of IPO (Input, Processing, Output) can come in very handy. IPO is an old mainframe term that can be useful for you here in looking at your design. The flow of data goes in this order; it is input into the database, some processing occurs on this data and the results are output in some way that is useful to the user. An example would be a Payroll system, where data about employees such as pay rate, hours worked and deductions is Input into the computer. Then some Processing occurs based on this input data such as calculating the net pay for the week for each employee. Finally there is some output such as a paycheck being printed.

Actually changing this sequence for designing is very useful. It is very helpful for design work to start with the output of the program because the definition of the output is the requirements of the task at hand. What is required for the output tells you what data is needed for input and then what processing is required of that input to create the needed output. In fact, the output requirements of the program are a good definition of the entire purpose of the program.

This output might take the form of a printed report, information displayed on the screen, output to another process or even sent to another computer system. Even data that is input and/or processed then just stored in some Record somewhere not viewed by a user, is still sitting there for the potential of some type of future output.

So start with the Output as your focal point for design. Secondly, look at what existing data is available (Input) that will contribute to this Output. Then, figure out what Processing will be required of the input data to create the necessary output. As an example, perhaps part of the display of order lines requires the display of the Extended Price for each line. Extended price is not stored in any Record but it can be calculated from the two columns in the Order Line Record called Quantity and Price. So, now for this one piece of your output, "Extended Price", you can clearly see that your Input is going to be the Quantity and Price columns of the Order Line Record and that the processing necessary is to multiply Quantity times Price to get the Extended Price needed for your output.

The above is a very simple example and the full solution for most applications is far more complex than this requiring access to multiple Records and gathering data that exists on multiple rows, etc. So in short:

1. Look first to the required Output
2. Secondly, look at what Input is available to support this Output
3. Then look at what processing of this Input is necessary to deliver this needed Output.

This gives a simple one, two, three framework for organizing the design of the program and the design and use of an Inprocess Record.

In deciding where your input comes from you must know the Records you are dealing with and what the data in them means. Data can flow through various transactional Records and it can have different significance, based on what Record it is in and what its status is, etc. The same field can exist in many different Records. How does the data in that field differ in meaning from one Record to the next? Or from one status to the next? With a good understanding of the purpose of each Record and what the data in it means in your applications, you will make good choices for your input data and how you do your processing. There is just no substitute for knowing your Records well.

Designing the Inprocess Record

Generally a batch update program does not consist of a single Set Processing statement. Such a program usually contains a whole series of Set Processing statements. In the techniques demonstrated here, these statements do not update the regular PeopleSoft Records. Instead these statements update a Record created just for this program. Since it is this Inprocess Record that is the recipient of the bulk of this Set Processing, it is important to design this Record with Set Processing in mind.

***Note**: An Inprocess Record can be a standard Record or a Temporary Table.*

The types of fields that go into an Inprocess Record could be conveniently broken down into four groups.

1. Key fields
2. Output fields whose values exist in a PeopleSoft Record
3. Output fields whose values needs to be calculated from other fields
4. Non-output fields that are needed to facilitate Set Processing.

Key Fields: These are not required but if you do not use keys, you will not get performance scalability and you may allow duplicate rows of data. It is always good to use keys even on Inprocess Records. Keys should be defined based on requirements for performance and uniqueness of each row of this Record. The keys to use come from the data output required in combination with the input data being used.

Note: *Where your InProcess Record is used for the final output, a useful way to design this Record is to have one row in the Record for one row of final output.*

Note: *Although not always required, it is recommended that Process Instance should be a key in Inprocess Records to account for multiple instances and use of Temporary Tables.*

Output fields whose values exist in a PeopleSoft Record: It can be very useful to have all fields needed for output in the Inprocess Record. In the case of outputting a flat file using the File Layout object, then it is required. Where these values exist already in your PeopleSoft Records, then it is easy to use the same named field in your Inprocess Record.

Output fields whose values need to be calculated from other fields: Where the output field value does not exist in your PeopleSoft Records, then you will need to use a field that will hold the results of some calculation that your batch update program will provide. Such a field name may already exist in your system or you may need to create a new field. An example might be "Extended Line Price". This field means the order line quantity times the price on that line. The Order Line Record does not contain this as a calculated value, but it does contain the two fields, quantity and price, that can be used to calculate the extended price.

In designing the Inprocess Record it can be advantageous to flatten some or all of the data. For example, an Inprocess Record that contained one row of data for each order line might contain a field for quantity shipped. Since a single order line can be shipped multiple times, then this data is accumulated from a Record that exists at a sub-line level. This is an example where the calculated data comes from multiple rows in another Record.

Non-output fields that are needed to facilitate Set Processing: There can often be a need to include other fields in your Inprocess Record that are not output fields. These could be fields that are needed in some calculation or other processing. For example, if "Shipped Amount" (the Quantity Shipped times the Price) was required in the output but the Quantity Shipped field was not required for output, the Quantity Shipped would still need to be included in the Inprocess Record. This is because the Quantity Shipped needs to be calculated for each order line, before you can calculate the Shipped Amount. After you load the Quantity Shipped with one Set Processing statement, then a later Set Processing statement can calculate Shipped Amount.

Design Example

Here is an example in how you can use these design techniques in building Set Processing statements. In this example, there is a need to output to a flat file, one row for each active Order Line on open customer orders. Fields required in the flat file are the Business Unit, Order Number, Line Number, Product ID, Quantity Open and the Quantity shipped. The first four fields come directly from the Order Line (ORD_LINE) Record. The last two are output fields and need to be calculated in some way. The quantity shipped is calculated from an inventory demand Record called SHIP_INF_INV. Quantity Open is calculated from Quantity Ordered on the ORD_LINE Record minus the Quantity Shipped. The constructed Inprocess Record looks like this:

Record Name: ORD_LIN_STG

Fieldname	Type	Length	Comments
BUSINESS_UNIT	Char	5	Key and output field
ORDER_NO	Char	10	Key and output field
ORDER_INT_LINE_NO	Nbr	5	Key and output field
PRODUCT_ID	Char	18	Output field
SHIP_FROM_BU	Char	5	Non-output: Used for indexing
QTY_ORDERED	Sign	13.4	Non-output: Used in calculation
QTY_SHIPPED	Sign	13.4	Output Calculated field
QTY_OPEN	Sign	13.4	Output Calculated field

Note*: Process Instance was not included in this example to simplify the explanations. Process Instance should normally be included as part of the Key structure.*

Notice that all the required output fields are present plus two more fields: SHIP_FROM_BU and QTY_ORDERED. Although these two are not in the final output they are included here because they are needed in the course of processing. As you will see shortly, SHIP_FROM_BU is used for indexing speed and QTY_ORDERED is needed for the calculation of an output field: QTY_OPEN.

Populating the Inprocess Record

Now that you have your Inprocess Record designed primarily around your output, it is time to look at the Input side of things regarding where your data will come from.

In this particular example, the choice is fairly simple. If you look at the ORD_LINE Record you will discover that it contains the same fields as the first five fields in the Inprocess Record. Also the ORD_LINE Record is keyed exactly the same way. This makes your choice quite easy. You will populate the Inprocess Record with an insert/select coming from the ORD_LINE Record as your input. The SQL follows.

```
INSERT INTO PS_ORD_LINE_STG
(BUSINESS_UNIT, ORDER_NO, ORDER_INT_LINE_NO,
 PRODUCT_ID, SHIP_FROM_BU, QTY_ORDERED, QTY_SHIPPED,
 QTY_OPEN )
SELECT
 BUSINESS_UNIT, ORDER_NO, ORDER_INT_LINE_NO,
 PRODUCT_ID, SHIP_FROM_BU, QTY_ORDERED, 0, 0
FROM PS_ORD_LINE
WHERE ORD_LINE_STATUS NOT IN ('C','X')
```

There are several items to note here. The first six fields in the Inprocess Record insert straight from the input Record. The last two fields are inserted with zeroes because you don't have the values for these yet. You will be calculating the values for these two fields shortly. The WHERE clause at the bottom weeds out any lines that are marked as cancelled ('X') or closed ('C'). This is where you select which rows go into your Inprocess Record.

Updating the Inprocess Record from another Record using Set Processing

Now that you have your rows in place, it is time to work on the two calculated fields. The QTY_SHIPPED field comes from the SHIP_INF_INV Record, which has a more complex key structure than your Inprocess Record. This key structure looks like this.

Record Name: SHIP_INF_INV

FieldName	Type	Length	Relates to on ORD_LINE_STG
BUSINESS_UNIT	Char	5	
DEMAND_SOURCE	Char	2	
SOURCE_BUS_UNIT	Char	5	BUSINESS_UNIT
ORDER_NO	Char	10	ORDER_NO
ORDER_INT_LINE_NO	Nbr	5	ORDER_INT_LINE_NO
SCHED_LINE_NO	Nbr	5	
INV_ITEM_ID	Char	18	
DEMAND_LINE_NO	Nbr	5	

With this in mind, here is a first draft of the code that will update your quantity shipped:

```
UPDATE PS_ORD_LINE_STG
SET QTY_SHIPPED = (SELECT SUM (S.QTY_SHIPPED)
           FROM PS_SHIP_INF_INV S
            WHERE PS_ORD_LINE_STG.BUSINESS_UNIT =
                                      S.SOURCE_BUS_UNIT
            AND PS_ORD_LINE_STG.ORDER_NO = S.ORDER_NO
            AND PS_ORD_LINE_STG.ORDER_INT_LINE_NO =
                                     S.ORDER_INT_LINE_NO
            AND S.CANCEL_FLAG = 'N'
            AND S.SHIPPED_FLAG = 'Y')
```

Here, you are updating the QTY_SHIPPED in your Inprocess Record through a sub-query to the SHIP_INF_INV Record. The first three lines on the WHERE clause of your sub-query give sufficient information to uniquely identify all the rows in SHIP_INF_INV that relate to the order line in the Inprocess Record. You don't want to join to any fields below the field ORDER_INT_LINE_NO because you want all the shipping rows for each order line row. The last two lines of the sub-query are selection criteria that are there to exclude any rows that are cancelled or not yet shipped.

This looks good for starters except there are some problems with the way this is coded. These problems will be corrected here one at a time so you can look at each issue as this update statement is improved.

The first problem for you to look at here is important because it can adversely affect the performance of Set Processing. If you look at the key fields in SHIP_INF_INV listed above, notice that you only joined using fields 3, 4 and 5 in the key structure. Although this was sufficient to ensure that you got all the correct rows, there can be severe performance issues with omitting the leading key fields. To be sure this is not a problem you can solve this by using all key fields in your joins. See the newly added lines in bold below:

```
UPDATE PS_ORD_LINE_STG
SET QTY_SHIPPED = (SELECT SUM (S.QTY_SHIPPED)
            FROM PS_SHIP_INF_INV S
            WHERE PS_ORD_LINE_STG.SHIP_FROM_BU =
                                          S.BUSINESS_UNIT
            AND S.DEMAND_SOURCE = 'OM'
            AND PS_ORD_LINE_STG.BUSINESS_UNIT =
                                        S.SOURCE_BUS_UNIT
            AND PS_ORD_LINE_STG.ORDER_NO = S.ORDER_NO
            AND PS_ORD_LINE_STG.ORDER_INT_LINE_NO =
                                      S.ORDER_INT_LINE_NO
           AND S.CANCEL_FLAG = 'N'
           AND S.SHIPPED_FLAG = 'Y')
```

This is where you use SHIP_FROM_BU to help fill in the gaps at the top of the keys. Since rows in SHIP_INF_INV that apply to Order Lines always have a DEMAND_SOURCE = 'OM', that is where the second added line comes from. These two rows now fill in your keys and will improve your speed.

The next issue that you need to address is that for each order line (row in ORD_LINE_STG) there can be zero, one or many applicable shipping rows in SHIP_INF_INV. The code above breaks down where a row in the Inprocess Record has zero applicable shipping rows. This is because in this case the SUM statement returns NULL. Since Records designed in PeopleTools have fields that do not allow for NULLs (except Longs and non-required Dates) the SQL fails. One tip on how you can handle this is to replace any nulls with zero. This is done in SQL Server with ISNULL or in Oracle with NVL. This changes the SUM phrase like so assuming SQL Server.

```
(SELECT ISNULL (SUM (QTY_SHIPPED), 0)
```

Note: *The method shown here is a vendor specific extension to SQL. This or its equivalent may not be available on your platform.*

This method keeps your SQL statement from crashing but can cause some performance issues. This is because this causes ALL rows to be updated whether there is some quantity shipped or not. If you have 20,000 rows in your Inprocess Record and only 15 of those rows have some shipping quantity, it would be faster to just update those 15 rows.

A better solution instead is to add an EXISTS clause to the main update statement that causes only those 15 rows that have been shipped to be updated. The SQL code looks like the following.

```
UPDATE PS_ORD_LINE_STG
SET QTY_SHIPPED = (SELECT SUM(S.QTY_SHIPPED)
            FROM PS_SHIP_INF_INV S
            WHERE PS_ORD_LINE_STG.SHIP_FROM_BU =
                                        S.BUSINESS_UNIT
            AND S.DEMAND_SOURCE = 'OM'
            AND PS_ORD_LINE_STG.BUSINESS_UNIT =
                                      S.SOURCE_BUS_UNIT
            AND PS_ORD_LINE_STG.ORDER_NO = S.ORDER_NO
            AND PS_ORD_LINE_STG.ORDER_INT_LINE_NO =
                                    S.ORDER_INT_LINE_NO
            AND S.CANCEL_FLAG = 'N'
            AND S.SHIPPED_FLAG = 'Y')
WHERE EXISTS (SELECT 'X' FROM PS_SHIP_INF_INV S
            WHERE PS_ORD_LINE_STG.SHIP_FROM_BU =
                                        S.BUSINESS_UNIT
            AND S.DEMAND_SOURCE = 'OM'
            AND PS_ORD_LINE_STG.BUSINESS_UNIT =
                                      S.SOURCE_BUS_UNIT
            AND PS_ORD_LINE_STG.ORDER_NO = S.ORDER_NO
            AND PS_ORD_LINE_STG.ORDER_INT_LINE_NO =
                                    S.ORDER_INT_LINE_NO
            AND S.CANCEL_FLAG = 'N'
            AND S.SHIPPED_FLAG = 'Y')
```

An important thing to notice here about this EXISTS clause is that it is almost identical to the sub-query that sums up the QTY_SHIPPED. The only difference is that the SUM(S.QTY_SHIPPED) is replaced with the literal 'X'. The FROM and WHERE clauses are identical.

This 'X' may look odd to the uninitiated. Using a literal is faster than using a column name, because using a column name requires that at least one row is actually retrieved. Using 'X' (or any literal) means that the RDBMS only needs to go so far as knowing that a row exists or not to return its verdict. This is a bit faster than retrieving a row.

This update SQL structure works for any aggregate function. One difference here is that if the aggregate is COUNT(), then the EXISTS sub-query is not needed! This is because COUNT() returns a zero rather than a NULL if there are no rows.

Now that you have finally completed this one SQL update, you can continue with further processing as required.

Updating the Inprocess Record from itself

Where the calculation can be done entirely from values that already reside on your Inprocess Record, then the update can be extremely simple. In the example, the next field to update is QTY_OPEN. It is the calculation of QTY_ORDERED minus QTY_SHIPPED but if QTY_OPEN is negative, then make it zero. This is done in the following Set Processing update statement.

```
UPDATE PS_ORD_LINE_STG
SET QTY_OPEN = QTY_ORDERED - QTY_SHIPPED
WHERE QTY_ORDERED > QTY_SHIPPED
```

Now you have populated your Inprocess Record with all the required output data.

Getting the exact number of rows required

If there was an additional requirement to only output rows that had some shipped quantity then there are several ways you could handle this. At this stage you could delete all the rows where the shipped quantity is zero:

```
DELETE PS_ORD_LINE_STG
WHERE QTY_SHIPPED = 0
```

This works well, except that if your processing updates are extensive and you have a large number of rows where the shipped quantity is zero, then a lot of rows end up being processed unnecessarily. In this case a more efficient way to handle this is to apply your earlier EXISTS clause to your insert/select statement. In this way you only start out inserting the rows needed and there is no need for a later deleting of unnecessary rows. The SQL would look like this.

```
INSERT INTO PS_ORD_LINE_STG
(BUSINESS_UNIT
… )
SELECT
BUSINESS_UNIT,
…
FROM PS_ORD_LINE
WHERE ORD_LINE_STATUS NOT IN ('C','X')
   AND EXISTS (SELECT 'X' FROM PS_SHIP_INF_INV S
    WHERE PS_ORD_LINE.SHIP_FROM_BU = S.BUSINESS_UNIT
   AND S.DEMAND_SOURCE = 'OM'
    AND PS_ORD_LINE.BUSINESS_UNIT = S.SOURCE_BUS_UNIT
   AND PS_ORD_LINE.ORDER_NO = S.ORDER_NO
   AND PS_ORD_LINE.ORDER_INT_LINE_NO =
                                     S.ORDER_INT_LINE_NO
   AND S.CANCEL_FLAG = 'N'
   AND S.SHIPPED_FLAG = 'Y')
```

Once you have done all needed processing and have the exact number of rows in your Inprocess Record ready for output, you can proceed with the output step to populate your flat file from the Inprocess Record. This is done in a PeopleCode step and is not shown here because it is not part of the SQL Set Processing techniques being demonstrated. This process is performed using a File Layout object and is discussed in detail in Chapters 7 and 12.

Using Process Instance

If it is possible that multiple users may run your program concurrently, then you can create your Inprocess Records as PeopleSoft Temporary Tables to handle this. This separates the Inprocess Records for each user so there is no conflict. See Chapters 5 for a complete description of Temporary Tables.

You can also do this without creating your Inprocess Record as a Temporary Table by just adding the field PROCESS_INSTANCE as the first field in the key strcuture of the Inprocess Record. During the populating of the Inprocess Record, load %ProcessInstance into this field. In all your update statements be sure to include in the WHERE clause of the Inprocess Record: WHERE PROCESS_INSTANCE = %ProcessInstance. This includes purging the Inprocess Record at the end of your program if you are using standard Records. This separates out the rows for each user's process and avoids any conflict. See Chapter 9 for more information or issues with multiple instances.

Multiple Inprocess Records

There may be the need for multiple Inprocess Records in a single program. This all depends on the output needed and the complexity of the program. There is no rule as to how many Inprocess Records you need to create. It can be 1 or 100. Create as many as are necessary for your program to accomplish its task.

Skilled Use of Joins

Knowledge of joins is a real skill to develop. You must be fairly skilled in this area when your programs start getting complex. One very important tip here is to know and understand the keys and indexes that you are working with. The purpose of this is both to understand what makes a row unique in each of your Records and for performance reasons. If you don't know the indexes on the Records you are joining, then how can you possibly join them correctly?

Another part of joins is using inner or outer joins. This is useful where you need to join two Records together but one of the Records doesn't have all the associated rows to join; yet you don't want this fact to reduce the number of rows returned in your join. In this case inner or outer joins can be very useful.

Use of EXISTS

EXISTS is a powerful SQL feature to use. It is a test for a non-empty set. It is used as a method to include or exclude (as in NOT EXISTS) rows based on the existence of other rows often in different Records. It was introduced in the design example above for use in an update statement. It can also be useful in the where clauses of delete and select statements. You will find that there can be many applications for EXISTS and it is a common tool to use.

Sub-queries

Sub-queries are a powerful tool to use. You have already seen one use in updating the QTY_SHIPPED in the example above. Sub-queries can sometimes be used to populate a field during insert statements as well. Sub-queries can also be useful in the main where clause of your insert/select, update or delete Set Processing statements.

It is possible to update multiple fields each with its own sub-query (separated by a comma) in a single update statement. See example below.

```
Update PS_EXAMPLE1
Set field1 = (select A.name1 from ps_vendor a
            where ps_example1.set = A.setid
            and ps_example1.vendor_id = A.vendor_id),
Field2 = (select A.vendor_status from ps_vendor a
         where ps_example1.set = A.setid
         and ps_example1.ship_to_vndr = A.vendor_id),
Field3 = (select A.vendor_class from ps_vendor a
          where ps_example1.set = A.setid
          and ps_example1.bill_to_vndr = A.vendor_id)
Where process_instance = %Processinstance
and exists (select 'X' from ps_vendor a
          where ps_example1.set = A.setid
          and ps_example1.bill_to_vndr = A.vendor_id)
```

If an EXISTS clause is used, it is imperative that the EXISTS clause will work for each field updated with a sub-query. There is a performance degradation in updating multiple fields like this. Sometimes two separate update statements each updating a single field with a sub-query is faster than a single update statement updating the two fields with sub-queries.

Updating with Insert/Selects

Instead of updates to the Inprocess Record there is a way to use insert/select instead. In this technique you create two Inprocess Records that are a mirror image of each other with identical keys and fields. Instead of an update statement, the technique is to insert rows from the Inprocess Record to the mirror Record passing all the common field values straight across. This SQL will also be updating or calculating other fields in the mirror Record. You must delete all the rows in the first Inprocess Record that were copied to the mirror Record. Then insert/select from the mirror Record back to the Inprocess Record. This process can be done multiple times with varying SQL to update the Inprocess Record as needed with various SQL statements.

This process is used when multiple updates can be done in one SQL insert statement. This process adds additional overhead in that three SQL statements must be run (one to insert into the mirror Record, one to delete the Inprocess Record and one to insert the data back from the mirror Record into the Inprocess Record). These additional SQL statements take more time to process rather than one Update statement. This mirror Record process should only be used when 3 or more fields can be updated at one time to make the overhead of this process worth the effort.

***Note**: The mirror Record if used multiple times must be deleted prior to being used. This will add a fourth SQL statement adding a bit more overhead.*

Using CASE

The CASE feature in SQL can be very helpful and at times can save you from coding extra SQL statements. If a field in your Inprocess Record needs to be updated in different ways based on some conditions, one way to do this is with a separate update statements for each condition. A more efficient way, however, is to use a CASE statement in a single update or insert statement.

```
UPDATE ...
SET STATUS_DESCR = CASE L.ORD_LINE_STATUS
                     WHEN 'C' THEN 'CLOSED'
                     WHEN 'X' THEN 'CANCELED'
                     WHEN 'P' THEN 'PENDING'
                     ELSE ' ' END
```

In this example, STATUS_DESCR can receive different values based on the value in ORD_LINE_STATUS.

Using Views

A view can be used to bring data together from multiple tables and present the data as if that data resided in a single table. It can also be used deliver a sub set of rows from one or more tables through its where clause. Sometimes calculations can be done in a view and that can relieve you from having to otherwise do this calculation in a separate update statement on the staging table. Occasionally where the output requirements are easy enough, a view can entirely replace the Inprocess Record and the output of your Application Engine program can come from a well-constructed view. It can be very worthwhile to discover where a view can save you work in your set processing statements and incorporate this into your program. A skilled use of views can be a very valuable asset in set processing.

Performance Testing Your Set Processing Statements

When you are coding your Set Processing statement, you may want to try several different ways of coding it and do some performance testing on each way. There are several ways to do this. If your Application Engine program is complete, you can view the Application Engine Trace from the Process Monitor after your program has run. See Chapter 13 for more information on SQL tracing in Application Engine.

Sometimes SQL products have a timing feature to give the speed of a SQL statement. If you haven't yet completed your Application Engine program but still want to test a SQL statement for speed, then a SQL product can be useful to time an individual SQL statement.

This list covers a lot of ground. These tips and techniques will take you a long way into Set Processing and you will soon be building on these techniques; perhaps even developing some techniques of your own.

Next

The next chapter will show you how to prepare your Application Engine to be run in multiple instances. It is important for you to know how to do this so these multiple instances do not collide with each other.

Chapter 9

Multiple Instances / Multiple Programs

Multiple instances is a concept where you have the same Application Engine program running multiple times at the same moment. It does not matter who started the Application Engine program, one or multiple users could have launched it, but that the process allows for multiple running instances at the same time. It is hard to keep an Application Engine program from only running one instance but it can be done (later in this chapter there is a section that will deal with this specifically). Normally, you allow for multiple instances and you have to make sure that your Application Engine program deals correctly with this concept; this will be taught to you in this chapter.

Multiple programs are where you may have different programs running against the same set of Records and data that you are trying to process within your Application Engine program. Not only do you have to be aware of your Application Engine programming running multiple times but there may be other programs that are trying to select, update or insert new Records. You need to be aware of the ramifications of your program, the time it will be locking Records and the other processes you may be affecting. You could be affecting Records that may even be locking PeopleSoft Pages.

There are certain things you can do to handle these issues and of course there are alternatives. PeopleSoft recommends some of these while others may be a matter of personal choice. Each of these will be explained, with the benefits and drawbacks so that you can make your own decision.

Understanding Multiple Instances

When you run an Application Engine program, you start by selecting data, processing it through various steps and possibly saving it into Temporary Tables. Your final output maybe just more updated data or may be newly inserted rows. The main problem with Multiple Instances comes with the updating or inserting of data into Records. There can also be a small issue with selecting data but that has special conditions.

Selecting Data

If your database performs locks when reading, you could lock your database Record just doing a read (such as is the case in SQL Server). Even reading data will block others from reading, updating or inserting data since you have locked pending your completion of the read. This will not affect the initial run of the Application Engine program but it could slow down other succeeding Application Engine programs.

For example, you have an Application Engine program that reads through all of the Employee Records. As your program starts, it locks the Record so that no other updates can affect the data since you are in the process of reading this Record. The lock is not released until the next commit is encountered or the Application Engine program ends. By having this lock you are guaranteeing that the data is not being changed so that you can process it correctly but this has a drawback. You are affecting other programs running after you including PeopleSoft Pages. Pages cannot even select data until your read lock has been released.

If your database allows it, you can do a process called a "dirty" read. This means you select the data without placing any locks. You can setup databases to perform this way but this should not be used as a general rule. This may solve the locking problem but then you have to understand that some Records may not be updated correctly. This can happen with multiple programs running on a set of data. Assume you have program A that runs and grabs data but as it reads each row, program B is updating a field. Because A does not lock it, program B can be updating as you are reading from program A. Program A may load data that has no rows updated, some records updated or all records updated. This can cause your program to fail or process rows incorrectly if program B updates a field when you are going to make some decision or update within program A utilizing this same field. This is why you need to place read locks, to keep the data in sync with your expected program flow.

Even for simple select processes you need to think of the multiple instances or multiple programs that can be running against a set of data. You can even get what is called a "deadlock condition" when program A is reading data from Record A, and then tries to read data from Record B. Meanwhile program B is reading data from Record B (locking it and preventing access to program A) and then tries to read data from Record A (which A has now locked). These two programs are now waiting on each other to release locks but neither can since it cannot continue until the other program has released its lock. There is no way to break this process once it has started but there are things you can do to your program so that this condition does not exist.

Selecting data also has an issue with multiple instances in that when your program starts it wants to get a set of data to process. If your program can be launched multiple times (either by one user or many users) you need to be able to select a specific set of data to work on and prevent the other running programs from affecting your data. This problem is called "walkover". The second program tries to "walkover" and select the same data that the first program has already selected.

Updating/Inserting Data

When you update or insert new data, you are also placing locks on those rows updated or added. The locks exist until the next commit is done or the program ends. These locks affect other programs just as in the select process, holding them until your locks are released. The deadlock and walkover conditions also exist with inserts and update statements. In fact, they are now much more prevalent.

***Note**: With updates and inserts you should never turn off the locking capability as this could cause unknown errors or incorrect values being set into the database.*

PeopleSoft Recommendations

To solve the issue of walkovers and deadlocks, you can use some capabilities of PeopleTools, as well as some development processes.

These are processes that PeopleSoft uses when they create Application Engine programs (and other batch programs as well). You need to know these processes so that you can read PeopleSoft programs easily, as well as using them when you develop.

Using Temporary Tables

To solve the issue of multiple instances, PeopleSoft uses Temporary Tables, which you learned about in Chapter 5. This chapter taught you about how these work, creating a special instance of the Record for every run. Now, when your program runs and uses Temporary Tables, you can be sure that all programs will run in their own instance and not have any conflict with any other program; and the best part is that this will all be done for you automatically. Well, almost automatically in that you have to use some Meta SQL, like %Table.

Even though not all programs done by PeopleSoft use this concept, you will find that this is used more and more. This handles most of the contention issues like walkover and deadlock within the Temporary Tables but what about the first select of data? You still have to get data from the production Records (like the Employee Record) to load into the Temporary Tables. This is why PeopleSoft uses the field called PROCESS_INSTANCE.

Using Process Instance

Many of the main data Records contain a field called PROCESS_INSTANCE. This field is used by batch programs, like Application Engine, to note the rows of data within a Record that are being processed. You will find that many programs will update the process instance field with the process instance of the running program if certain conditions exist and the process instance is 0. This simple logic works to find the rows of data to process that have not been processed before.

There is one thing though, you will need to reset the process instance field back to 0 once you are done because there may be other programs wanting to run against this data that require a 0 process instance. This may cause you a problem in that now you no longer know what you have processed against. If this is a problem and you must reset the process instance to 0, you will need to find another field to use or try the alternate method below.

With just these two items you have prevented most of your problem with multiple instances and programs.

Using Commits

Even though you have been warned many times about doing a commit and causing yourself problems, there are many times when you should do a commit. This of course makes your program a bit more complicated since you have to take into account a re-start; but if you use a simple set of rules, this can be done easily.

First, after you have selected your data using process instance and inserted all the rows to process into your first Temporary Table, you can submit a commit. This will release any locks you have on your production Record and allow other programs and processes to continue. Meanwhile, you can use the Temporary Tables to review, update and process.

You do not have to issue any more commits due to multiple instances since you are now working in your set of Temporary Tables but you may want to because of performance issues. Every update or insert to a database is not stored in the database until a commit is processed. This means all of your updates and inserts are stored in pre-committed tables (these are not the same as PeopleSoft Temporary Tables but are internal database tables). These pre-committed tables can handle a lot of data but as you do more and more this buffer of information increases in size. The buffer can get so large as to dramatically affect performance for not only your Application Engine program but also all processes (including Pages and other batch programs). If you know your program is doing a large amount of data updates or inserts, then it is a good idea to issue a commit to flush out these pre-committed tables and store them into the database.

Other Alternatives

While PeopleSoft uses and recommends a specific way to handle multiple instances and multiple programs, some developers have used an alternative method. Here, you will see these methods shown, including their drawbacks, so that you can see the best way to code your Application Engine program.

Using Standard Records (not Temporary Tables)

While PeopleSoft uses Temporary Tables, you can use standard Records as along as you place the field PROCESS_INSTANCE in the key structure. What you are doing here is developing the same process that PeopleSoft gives you with the Temporary Tables. This requires you to build and create Records but not worry about the number of possible instances. Since all of your programs will be running in this one Record, you will have to be concerned about Record space and proper indexes.

When you use a standard Record, you will not have to use any special Meta SQL to get the correct Record name but you will have to write into all of your select, update and insert SQL where statements the PROCESS_INTANCE field. Luckily there is a Meta SQL variable that you can use.

You will also have to build new SQL statements that will clean out (delete) these standard Records after you are done using them. PeopleSoft Temporary Tables automatically delete all data for you so now you have to build more SQL statements.

Although this is more work, there is a benefit. During the testing phase you can turn off the delete portion of your Application Engine program so that these standard Records are left with data. You can then use it to debug and determine how the process is working, and what you need to do to fix it. Once the program is working fine, you can again, turn the delete steps back on.

***Warning**: To process the delete correctly for this standard Record, you cannot just delete the whole Record (truncate) but you have to delete only the data where the process instance equals to the one you were just using.*

Using Inprocess Status Fields (not Process Instance)

When selecting data from production tables you could use the process instance field but if that field is used or critical to other business processes you may not be able to use the process instance field. Another way to extract data is to create a new Record that contains the keys of the production Record plus any other fields you need, like a status field. Assuming you need a program to process against the Employee Record, you would create a new Record, as listed below.

ST_EMPLOYEE
Employee_id – Key
Process_instance - Key
Status

This simple Record makes it easy to process and to know which Records have yet to be processed. To use this, you would make the following SQL statement.

```
Insert into PS_ST_EMPLOYEE
(Employee_id, Process_instance, Status)
Select a.Employee_id, %processinstance, "U"
from PS_EMPLOYEE a
where a.group_type = '030'
  and not exists (select 'x' from PS_ST_EMPLOYEE  b
               where a.employee_id = b.employee_id)
```

If you look at this SQL statement, you will see that it inserts data into the new Record where a special condition exists in the PS_EMPLOYEE, and it does not already exist in the new Record. Now, the inprocess Record, is loaded with the all the rows that are ready to be processed showing the process instance in this new Record. You can then issue a commit and start to process all rows from the new Record, just as if you had set the Process Instance in the original production Record (PS_EMPLOYEES).

This may seem as if you have more work to do with setting up the new Record but there are advantages. First, you do not have to rely on the process instance being 0 in the initial Record. Second, you do not cause any problems with other batch programs by changing the process instance directly. The drawback for this method is that you have created a subset of data to process that clutters the database with information that could have been kept in the main production table (use of the process instance). This method is shown since PeopleSoft batch programs may not be set up to handle additional batch processes in the middle of steps that were not expected. This method gives you a way to handle this problem.

Special Method for Inprocess Status Fields

There is also one other reason that this method is used and that is for the purpose of data tracing. By using inprocess status Fields, you can store information as it moves through your Application Engine program. One drawback already pointed out was that you then had to create the delete SQL statements to cleanout these standard Records, so that data is not left. If you do not delete the information, these Records will grow in size causing performance problems as well as database storage issues. But what if you did not delete at the end of your Application Engine program but instead at the beginning. This is a radical departure from most programming processes but before you discount it, think this through.

All Application Engine programs do not need to use this method but if you have a complicated process with many steps and you need to trace how the data was built for verifying reports or processes, you might want to consider using this process. You can also use this process to build reporting Records but it is not recommended since reporting Records do not want to allow multiple instances running against them; since you are trying to build a Record or set of Records based on the last run. See the section Preventing Multiple Instances for how to process correctly for reporting Records.

The special method requires that you use standard Records to store data and that you are going to program in the delete in the beginning of the program. This is where it gets a bit tricky. You cannot just delete the whole Record since there may be other Application Engine programs that are in process and may require restart. If you delete all of the data, you may corrupt a program and not allow restart of that Run Control ID. So, you can only delete data in the standard Records that come from a successful previous Application Engine run. This may seem complicated but there is an easy solution using the following SQL.

```
Delete from PS_STANDARD_RECORD
Where process_instance < %Processinstance
and exists (select 'x' from PSPRCSRQST
            where prcsinstance =  process_instance
            and runstatus in ('8', '9')
```

This SQL deletes all the rows in the standard Record (PS_STANDARD_RECORD) where the process instance is less than the one you are currently running (all the old rows) and where it exits in a tools Record called PSPRCSRQST. The status of the tools Record must be in 8 or 9. These statuses mean that the process instance has been completed or cancelled respectively. This means the outside program has completed, to success; or the user has stopped the process and cancelled the program, never wanting to restart it. There are many other statuses but these are the only two that can be used to remove rows. There may also be a condition where the process request row data may not exist. This happens when the system administrator cleans out these old process instance request records so that the Record is not overfull of old data. To remove these rows of data you need to use the following SQL.

```
Delete from PS_STANDARD_RECORD
Where process_instance < %Processinstance
and not exists (select 'x' from PSPRCSRQST
               where prcsinstance =  process_instance)
```

This SQL will remove the row(s) if the process request row of data no longer exists. This will then remove rows from the standard Record where either the user or the system administrator has deleted the process instance.

Now with these two SQL statements you clean up just one Record so you will have to run these two SQL statements for each of your standard Records. This can be quite time consuming but you get an added benefit of having the last run always in the standard Records to verify runs and trace data.

Preventing Multiple Instances / Multiple Programs

Now that you have learned all about multiple instances and multiple programs there may be times when you want to prevent multiple instances from occurring. Preventing multiple instances and multiple programs could be done using this same method, review of the run control status Record, but would require re-working all of the programs.

One of the main reasons for preventing multiple instances is having an Application Engine program that creates a reporting table. A reporting table is just a Record that remains with data, on purpose, after the Application Engine program is complete. Other batch programs, Queries, Crystal reports or user Pages, can then use this reporting table.

There are multiple ways to accomplish this but three of the main methods are listed here.

Process Definition

When you create a new Process Definition for an Application Engine program, you can define the run location. You can set this to Server and include the Server name to use. Then, this process scheduler server can be set up to run all jobs, one at a time. The process scheduler server has a setting that defines how many programs can be launched at the same time. The System Administrator could set this up to be just one. This would guarantee that only one would run at a time.

By setting the process scheduler to allow just one running program, you could even prevent multiple programs, as well as multiple instances.

This does work but requires setting up more than one process scheduler server and requires more maintenance by the System Administrator. This process is also not recommended by PeopleSoft and is shown as a possibility to use at your company site; you have to weigh the benefits with the controls required and the capability of your hardware.

Control Record

This method requires the use of a Record to store information about the running program. This simplest Record would be as shown below.

CONTROL RECORD
Seq Number – Key
Process_instance

Upon the start of the Application Engine program, a row would be inserted here and then committed to the database. The SQL would first have to find the minimum sequence number to use and then insert a record. This would then allow programs (not just Application Engine programs) to see whether their process instance had the lowest sequence number. If the program did, then the program could start; otherwise the program goes into a wait loop. The wait loop should not tax the database system by just making wild SQL select statements but be in PeopleCode that will loop through a simple for-next loop. This still places a load on the Application Server to process the PeopleCode so this should not be used everywhere; only on select Application Engine programs.

You could try to use an update statement directly on the control record, assuming only sequence number one, making your program wait until the previous programs commits but this may not work. Your wait time may exceed the time out settings of your process scheduler. This may mean your program will time out and go to an error status before the previous programs complete.

Process Run Control Record

This method is just a derivative of the Control Record method. Instead of using the Control Record you could use the PSPRCSRQST Record to see if any other programs of the same name (PRCSNAME) are running (RUNSTATUS). If there are, this process then loops and waits until no more exist with a smaller process instance number.

This method does work but only against multiple instances, not multiple programs, since you have to query this Record by the name of the process definition. You could join this process Run Control Record, to a new Record that would contain a list of process definitions names to check, to be able to handle multiple programs.

Next

Congratulations, you have now completed the entire general learning for Application Engine programming. Next up is taking an actual Application Engine program, learning how to read through it and looking for any special considerations. You will also see how these various methods, functions, classes, and codes are used to connect into a viable program. There will also be some new functions to learn as you read through your first program. This will lead to modifying the program and then creating your own working Application Engine program.

Chapter 10

How to Read and Modify an Existing Program

Now that you have learned all about the functions and capabilities of Application Engine, it's time to take all that base information to see how Application Engine programs are put together. This chapter will take you through different programs to show you various ways Application Engine programs are built and how they use the functions and capabilities you now know. You will also learn in this chapter the standard Sections, Steps and Action that most programs use. You will use all of this information to understand the flow of the program and then ultimately the purpose of the Application Engine program itself.

It is best to start at the beginning; that is where you initialize your program.

Initializing the Program

You need to open an existing Application Engine program; open the Application Engine APVCHREDIT. This is an existing Application Engine program that edits through vouchers in the Accounts Payable (AP) module. To open an Application Engine program, click on the Open icon on the toolbar or use the menu: File – Open. This will launch the Open Object panel, which you should be very familiar with. Change the object type to "App Engine Program" and type into the name field "APVCHREDIT". Click the Open button to open the Application Engine program, as shown in figure 10.1

You have already learned that each Application Engine program requires a MAIN Section. This MAIN Section is where the program starts and where you normally set up a few Steps. These Steps are not required but you will find them most of the time in quite a few of the existing PeopleSoft Application Engine programs. Open the Main Section to review the Steps. To open the Section, click on the plus symbol just to the left of the MAIN Section name. This will open the Section, as is shown in figure 10.2.

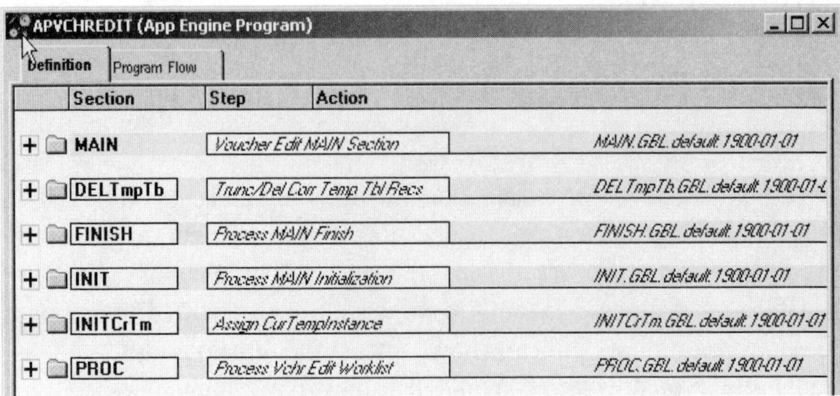

Figure 10.1 APVCHREDIT Application Engine

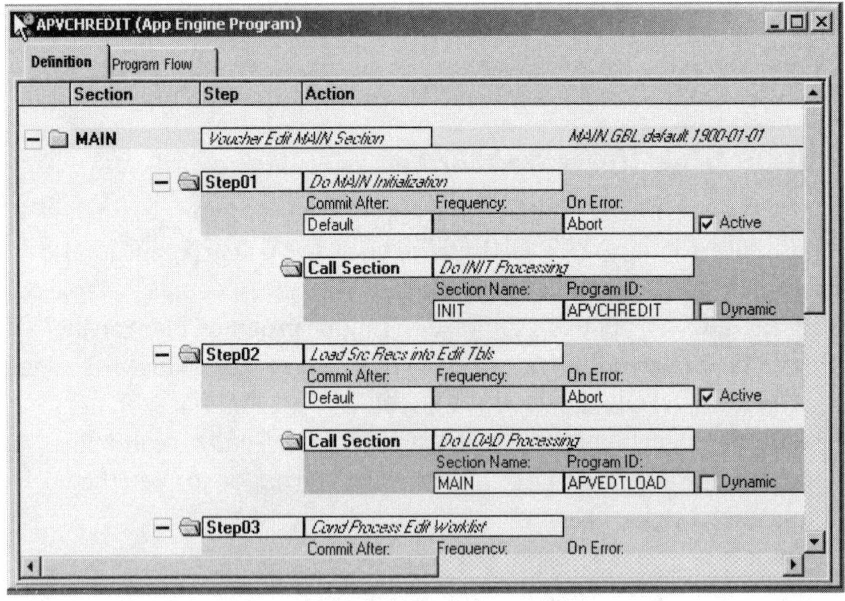

Figure 10.2 APVCHREDIT Main Section open

MAIN Section

Use the scroll bar up and down to see each of the Steps within the MAIN Section. You will see Steps that are repeated over and over in different Application Engine programs. The INIT Step is first and you will see this being called in the Step labeled Step01. The next Step is usually the PROCESS Step. This can be composed of one or many Steps; and is usually more than one. In this program you will find two Steps that perform the main body of work – Steps labeled Step02 and Step03. The last Step is the Final or completion Step, labeled as Step04. This is where you wrap up the program, clean out any standard Records and close any files.

It is not recommended to have SQL within the MAIN Section but you could. It is just proper programming to only have Section calls in the Actions of the MAIN Section, as was shown in this example. This is the proper way to start an Application Engine program so that it is easy to read and follow.

Note, there was one Action with PeopleCode in the MAIN Section, this is fine since you can use the PeopleCode exit process to direct the program into different paths. If you look at the PeopleCode in the Step (just double click on the PeopleCode Action) you will see the following code line.

```
Exit (VED_REQUEST_AET.SELECT_COUNT = 0);
```

Note: *The REM and comment statements were removed in the example.*

This PeopleCode returns a TRUE value if there are no lines to process, this will cause the following Action in Step03 to be skipped; thereby ending any further processing in this Step. Now, if you think about it you can see why there are 2 Steps that do the main body of processing. The first Step (Step02) grabs and filters all of the vouchers to be processed and stores the total number of vouchers to be processed into a Bind Variable. This Bind Variable (VED_REQUEST_AET.SELECT_COUNT) is then used in the following Step (Step03) to see if there are any vouchers to process.

This saves valuable time on the server trying to process a group of vouchers that do not exist.

Now that you understand how to use the MAIN Section and how you build the Sections based on what you need to process, you need to continue and learn what is in the standard INIT Section.

INIT Section

Open the INIT Section by clicking on the plus symbol. You will see various Steps and Actions that are needed to initialize the program. The first Step that is usually done is to retrieve the information from the Run Control Record. Open the SQL in the first Step in the INIT Section. The SQL in this Step is shown below.

```
%Select(OPRID, RUN_CNTL_ID, REQUEST_ID,
CURTEMPINST_FLG, CURTEMPINST_STR,
NEW_SRC_SELECT_FLG, RCY_SRC_SELECT_FLG,
SKIP_VAT_PROC_FLG, SKIP_SUT_PROC_FLG,
SKIP_WHD_PROC_FLG, SKIP_DUPL_INV_FLG,
SKIP_COMBO_EDT_FLG)
SELECT A.OPRID, A.RUN_CNTL_ID, B.REQUEST_ID,
  'N', ' ', B.NEW_SRC_SELECT_FLG,
  B.RCY_SRC_SELECT_FLG, B.SKIP_VAT_PROC_FLG,
  B.SKIP_SUT_PROC_FLG, B.SKIP_WHD_PROC_FLG,
  B.SKIP_DUPL_INV_FLG, B.SKIP_COMBO_EDT_FLG
FROM PS_AERUNCONTROL A, PS_VED_REQUEST_HDR B
WHERE A.PROCESS_INSTANCE = %ProcessInstance
  AND B.OPRID = A.OPRID
  AND B.RUN_CNTL_ID = A.RUN_CNTL_ID
```

You can see the AE run control master Record joined with the VED_REQUEST_HDR Record, which is the Run Control Record for the Voucher Edit process. You will see that the AR Run Control master Record is used since it contains the process instance, which is supplied via a Meta SQL variable. The only fields selected from the AE run control Record are the Operator ID (OPRID) and the Run Control ID (RUN_CNTL_ID). This is the old way to extract data. This is shown since some of the existing PeopleSoft Application Engine programs still use this old process. There is really no reason why the AE run control master Record is used to select the Operator ID and Run Control ID as these are automatically loaded into Meta SQL variables called %Operatorid and %RunControl respectively. So this SQL could have been simplified to only use the Run Control Record of VED_REQUEST_HDR using the Meta SQL of Operator ID and Run Control ID to select the correct row of data. Here is a sample of how the SQL could have been written using all the new information.

```
%Select(REQUEST_ID, CURTEMPINST_FLG,
CURTEMPINST_STR, NEW_SRC_SELECT_FLG,
RCY_SRC_SELECT_FLG, SKIP_VAT_PROC_FLG,
SKIP_SUT_PROC_FLG, SKIP_WHD_PROC_FLG,
SKIP_DUPL_INV_FLG, SKIP_COMBO_EDT_FLG)
 SELECT B.REQUEST_ID, 'N', ' ',
   B.NEW_SRC_SELECT_FLG, B.RCY_SRC_SELECT_FLG,
   B.SKIP_VAT_PROC_FLG, B.SKIP_SUT_PROC_FLG,
   B.SKIP_WHD_PROC_FLG, B.SKIP_DUPL_INV_FLG,
   B.SKIP_COMBO_EDT_FLG
 FROM PS_VED_REQUEST_HDR B
 WHERE B.OPRID = %Operatorid
   AND B.RUN_CNTL_ID = %RunControl
```

You will note that the Operator ID and the Run Control ID were dropped from the select and the %Select areas. This is due to it being unnecessary since these are supplied in Meta SQL, and there is no reason to select and store these values.

No matter which way is used, you still have to get the Run Control Record information to help in selecting the right data and processing the data correctly. This statement also shows you how the select is used to bring in the data and store it into the State Record Bind Variables.

Once the Run Control information is loaded, the next Action in this Application Engine program performs a Log Message. This Log Message Action allows you to write a message with information out to the message log that you can review later, via the process monitor, to see what variables were set or which steps and actions were taken. This is very helpful in tracing problems especially when you are first writing your own program. The purpose of the Log Message Action here is to output the Operator id, Run Control id, request id and process instance - these are all shown in the parameter list of the

Action. This is not a bad habit to be in; using the Log Message throughout your Application Engine program.

Still within the INIT Section, the program is not yet complete. There is still more initialization that needs to be done. In this program a further Step is called to run another SQL Action of the type Do When. This Do When Action runs a SQL statement that will perform the next Action if a row of data is returned. This second Action is a call to another Section. The purpose of this Section call (INITCrTm) is to define the temporary process instance that needs to be used within the Voucher Edit process. Normally, most programs do not have to do this but this is the case in this Application Engine program.

You can see how even within the INIT Section you may call other Sections. The logic to be used is; if you have a unit of work, then you should place this into it's own Section. You can then name the Section making it clear what this Section is and what it does. The reason for this is twofold. First, it makes the program easier to read and follow through the logic; and secondly, it makes it much easier to modify. If each logic unit of work is in it's own Section, then it is easy to write a new Section and change the original Action to call this new Section. This way you can modify the Section without having to change the core program.

The Temporary Tables are now cleaned up within Step03 of the INIT Section. In this Application Engine program there are a lot of deletes to be done so instead of just having the delete SQL here, a Section call was made to locate all of the delete statements into one Section. See how much cleaner this is to review and understand when the developer has taken the time to structure the Application Engine program into logical Sections?

The last Step of the INIT Section performs an update to the Run Control Record of this Application Engine program, to store the process instance. Normally, you do not have to do this but it is needed here because of the special circumstances of the Voucher Edit program; since there could be multiple programs running and the programs need to work without crashing over each other.

Even though you did not see a lot of the functions and commands used, you will learn about those in the next section of this book. The purpose here was to show you how a standard PeopleSoft Application Engine program starts using the MAIN and INIT sections. The process is to learn how to break a program into logical sections and to see how you get a program ready to run, including grabbing the Run Control information.

***Note**: Use of the INIT name for a Section is not required but highly recommended.*

Next, you will learn about the main body and process of the Application Engine program. This is where you will see some of the functions, commands and special logic used to make an Application Engine program.

Processing the Program

Now that the Application Engine program is started and the bind variables are loaded with either the Run Control information or initialized, its time to start the actual data processing. The power of the Application Engine program is in how it manipulates data and that is what this section of the book is about.

There is no set structure and naming convention for the main body of the program. You will probably have multiple Sections, Steps and Actions. The process to learn here is how to flow with the program. This is where the new release of the Application Engine comes in. To flow with the program, assuming you are still reviewing the APVCHREDIT Application Engine program, click the program flow tab. This takes you to the program, sorted in order by how the program will run.

You could have done this same thing when you went through the INIT and MAIN Sections. It does not matter which view you use to follow the program, just as long as you do follow it. It is also known that most

MAIN and INIT Sections tend to be small and are easily read using the definition tab view.

Scroll down through the program till you see Step02 from the MAIN Section, as shown in figure 10.3.

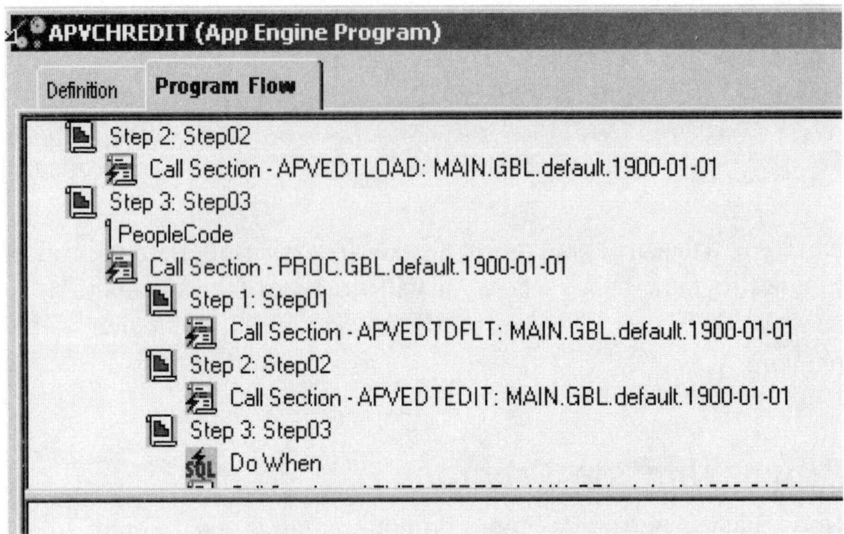

Figure 10.3 APVCHREDIT Program Flow view at Step02

This is where the next two Steps in the MAIN section do all the necessary processing. The first Step (Step02) calls another Section within a different Application Engine program. This is usually done because all of the program logic, SQL and PeopleCode in this other Application Engine Section can be considered a function. All of the logic can be set into its own Section, which could have been included in this Application Engine program; but by placing it into its own program, the called Section can be used by any number of Application Engine programs. That is why it is considered a function that can be called and used by other Application Engine programs.

Another feature to use within this view is that you can see the call to other Application Engine programs, and by clicking on the icon you can then open the Application Engine program directly. Click on the icon to open the called Application Engine program as shown in figure 10.4.

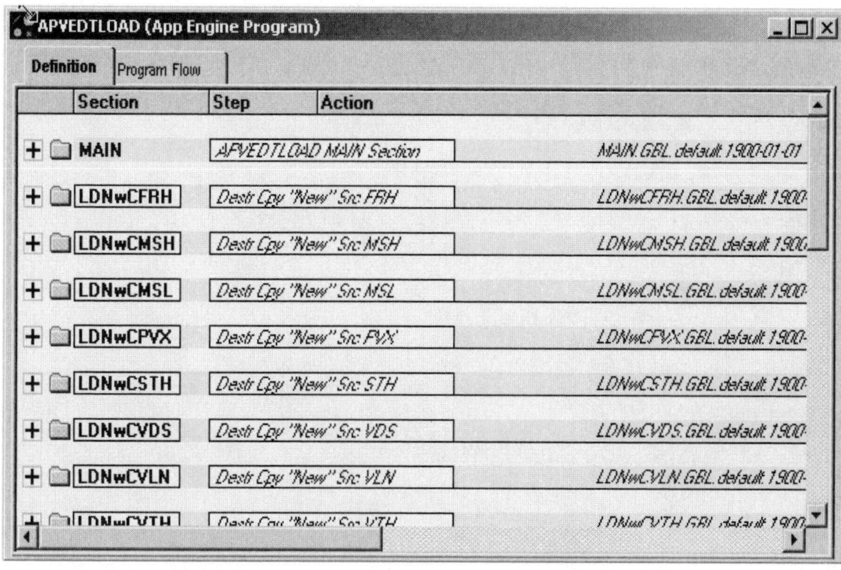

Figure 10.4 APVEDTLOAD Program opened

Note that you are not taken to the Section name being called since this Action only opened the Application Engine program itself. You will need to scroll through to find the Section being called so that you can then review the program from here.

Returning to the original program at Step03, you can see it calls a Section within the Application Engine called PROC after an Action of PeopleCode runs. The PeopleCode checks to see if any Vouchers are to be processed. You can see the PeopleCode directly in the flow view by just clicking on the PeopleCode icon. This will then open the PeopleCode program to display in the area below so that you can review it as shown in figure 10.5. You cannot edit the program here but you can read it to see the conditions and action this code is performing.

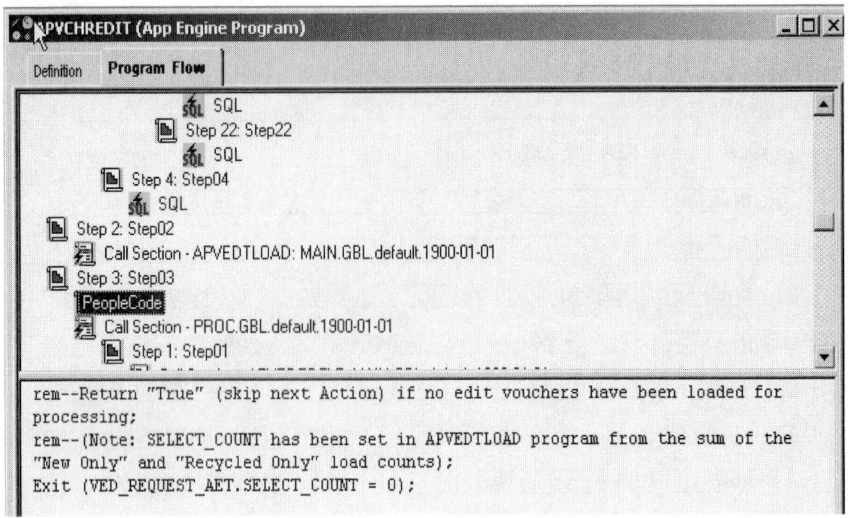

Figure 10.5 APVCHREDIT Program Flow – PeopleCode view

This code reviews a Bind Variable that was stored in earlier program Sections. If the value returns 0, it passes a TRUE value; thereby skipping the following Action within this Step. If this Action is run, it calls a Section called PROC within this same Application Engine. You should be able to see why this flow view is so helpful in reading and following the code.

You have learned that you can see the PeopleCode in the view area below but you can also see SQL, as well. To test this out, just move down further within the Section PROC to find a SQL statement – it's at Step03 within the Section PROC, as shown in figure 10.6. Remember to click on the SQL icon to show the SQL in the view area.

***Note**: SQL Statements are displayed for not only the SQL Actions but other Actions as well.*

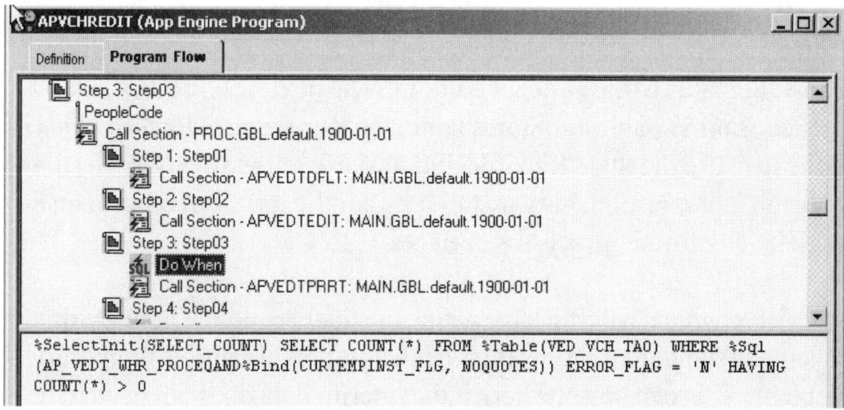

Figure 10.6 APVCHREDIT Program Flow – SQL view

So far you have learned all about the main body in how to read and work through all the Sections, Step and Actions but the program is not complete yet, as you have to run through the Final Section.

Finishing the Program

Using either view (definition or program flow), locate the last Section named FINISH. The name used for the final Section can be Finish, as listed here, or anything you wish; but it needs to be descriptive of the end process, like Close or Cleanup. If you review the Finish Section, as shown in figure 10.7, you will see that this Section only has two Steps.

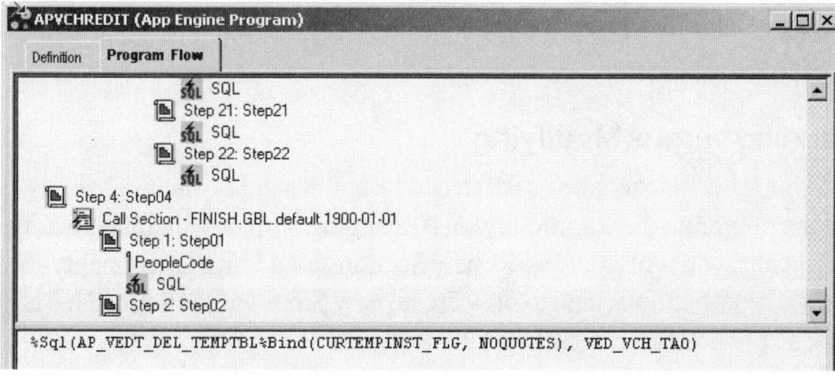

Figure 10.7 APVCHREDIT Program Flow view at FINISH

The first step has two Actions with the first being some PeopleCode. This PeopleCode sets a value in one of the Bind Variables. This is to show the status of the voucher edit run. The next Action takes this loaded Bind Variable and stores it into the Run Control Record. This is done because the State Record Bind Variables are lost as soon as the program completes. This way the status of the run is saved and can be used by any further processes or pages.

A lot of programs will still have within the final Section SQL that will delete the standard Records (not the PeopleSoft classified Temporary Tables). This can be done here if the interim data does not need to be saved between runs.

This completes this program's final Section but more could have been done, if required, for completing an Application Engine program. Now that you have learned how to read and flow through a complete program there are a few items to learn about how to best modify an Application Engine program.

How to Modify an Application Engine Program

While there is no right or wrong way, there is a best way to go about the process of modifying an Application Engine program. First, you must understand the modification you are about to undertake. Are you being asked to add additional functionality, versus just modifying the existing functionality? This is a big difference that you need to understand.

Adding versus Modifying

Adding new functionality is defined as bringing in totally new capability to the program where as modifying is changing or removing functionality. Typically, you will create entire new Sections for adding functionality while modifications tend to only create new Steps and Actions. This is not a hard and fast rule but a generalization.

To give some examples say you have this voucher edit process and you want it to also verify the vendor address against a special flag you have created on the address Record. This process is an addition of functionality since nothing like it exists already in the voucher edits process. Even though you are modifying the voucher edit process you are adding new functionality. A modification takes an existing function or process and changes it. For example, the PO creation process gathers all open requisitions and builds them into purchase orders. If you were asked to modify this process so that it would only take requisitions that were created within the last 10 days this would be a modification since the process already gathers all the requisitions.

The reason you need to understand this is that to make a good modification you have to understand how you are going to modify the program. In adding functionality you will look for places to build in calls to your new Sections while in modifications you look for the place where the data is selected or modified. Now that your frame of mind is set on how you are to modify your program, you need to understand the program flow.

Understanding the Program Flow

This is the most difficult part of making a modification to an existing Application Engine program; you have to understand the flow of the program and the data. This is where you will spend time reading through the entire program. Even if you are only modifying a small function, you will still need to read all the SQL and PeopleCode. You will even need to read all the SQL and PeopleCode that follow your expected change to verify that nothing you have done will break or change the end results of the program.

There is no best way to do this, as you just have to read through the program. Developers have used various methods; such as printing out the program and then spreading it all over the floor, spending hours reading the program from the Application Designer trying to memorize it or making crib notes trying to understand the process. The recommendation is to use what works best for you but most developers end up using the crib note process.

***Note**: The new Application Engine program flow report may be of assistance here as* well.

The crib note process is where you start reading the program and you make comments and notes as you read, as to the purpose of each Section, Step and Action. These comments are usually not longer than a sentence or two, trying to keep it simple. The purpose is to write a road map of the program. If you are lucky, this may already exist for you if the developer made comments in the Application Engine program. Most developers do not do this and it is a terrible loss; but hopefully you will not continue this loss of information as you modify and create your Application Engine programs.

***Note**: If you create a crib document, remember to save it so that others may use it later.*

The best place to modify a program is one where you impact the existing program code line the least. Since each program is unique and some are very complicated, there is no one answer as to the best place. The only thing you can do is to understand the program in full so that you can make the best choice for the customization you need to do, and for the needs of the business using this program.

Now that you understand the program and you are ready to make your changes there are a few things to understand and learn that will help in this modification process.

Modification Process

If you need to modify an Action, you can just change it directly but this does not leave any audit trail of information. This is not the recommended solution. The better solution would be to inactivate the Step so that it is no longer used, then create a new Step with the new Action. Of course the old and new Steps would have comments added to show the reason, developer, date and project number. If you need to delete an Action, the best process is to inactivate the Step and mark with comments.

If you need to modify an entire Step, you use the same process that was used above for an Action. The old Step is inactivated and the new Step and Actions are added. Comments are again placed and the program saved. If you need to delete a Step, then you only have to inactivate and mark with comments.

If you need to modify an entire Section, and there are good reasons for doing this, you can inactivate the entire Section but then when you create a new Section you are able to use the same name, as along as you set the effective date to later than the Section you just inactivated. This way you can see the change history of the Section, including all the Steps and Actions that are within the Section.

If you add a new Action, Step or Section, you can create it normally but be sure to set the right effective date and mark with the appropriate comments.

Project Migration

With your Application Engine modification all complete, you need to place all the necessary objects into a project. First, you should place your Application Engine itself into the project. To do this, when you have the program open in the Application Designer working area and you have it selected, click on the menu: Insert – Current Object into Project. You can also just type the F7 key to have it added as well. Now you need to add the other objects.

If you added or changed any SQL or PeopleCode, you will need to add that to the project. The easy way to do this is to open the SQL or PeopleCode in the Application Designer window (do not use the Program flow view) by double clicking on the Action to have the SQL or PeopleCode display in their respective editor windows. Once the window is open, use the menu: Insert – Current Object into Project; or you can type the F7 key. In either case, the SQL or PeopleCode will be added to the project.

Now, the only other thing you have to be sure of is whether you added or modified any Actions, Steps or Sections. This is where most developers miss getting all of their Application Engine objects into the project; so pay attention. You will need to manually add to the project all Sections that contain a change either in the Section, Step or Action. If you change the active flag on a Step, then you need to include into the project, the Section where the Step is located. If you do not include that Section, then the change you made, and any others within the Section, will not be migrated to the next database. This could also cause errors in the migration when the project is moved.

If you had added a new Action with a new SQL object and then only placed the SQL object in the project, once the project is moved you will get an error stating that it does not know where to place the SQL object, since the new Action does not show in the current Application Engine program. This shows you why you must include the Section to capture all the changes to the Section, Steps and Actions.

These are the only objects of the Application Engine program but remember you may have created a Page to run the program, a File object for output or any number of other objects that you need to include into your program.

Next

Now you should be able to read and modify an existing PeopleSoft Application Engine program, but what if you need to create an entire new program? This is where the next chapter will take you. The next chapter will show you how to build a program using some of the functions and commands you have already learned.

Chapter 11

Creating a New Application Engine Program

Now that you have learned to read and modify an existing Application Engine program, you need to add to these skills. It is one thing to modify a program while it is quite another to write your own Application Engine program. In this chapter, you will learn some valuable steps that are needed to make an efficient Application Engine program. A good program just does not happen but takes planning and order; that is where you have to start. Once you develop your plan, then you can begin writing your program.

To fully learn all of this, you are going to take a given problem and work through the whole process from start to finish. You will define the problem, understand the data structure needs of both the input and the output and finally create the program flow of how you get from input to output; then you can get on with creating the actual program. Each of these steps will be explained in the following sections within this chapter, including writing the actual program.

Defining the Problem

To work on a new Application Engine program, you must understand the problem. This means you need to get valid specifications of what the program is required to do. This is the best situation but you may not get all the information. Even if you receive a specification it may not contain all of the needed detail. If you are lucky enough to receive a specification be sure to read it thoroughly. If you are on your own, be sure to talk with the requestors of the program to obtain the information you need. Now, what is that information that you need?

First, you should find out what you are starting with before you apply any logic or action. Are you working with all the Customer Master Record or just the Customer Master Records that have been set up to be Ship To's? You need to find out not only the data but also the condition of the data such as, vouchers, which have not yet been matched or Employees with salaries less than 50% average of the company. This gives you the starting point.

Next, you need to find out what needs to be done to the data and what logic to apply. What processes do you need to do under what restrictions? In a nutshell, what is the purpose of the program? This is where you really need to dig and discover, as this is the core of the program. This may be a simple process or this can be long and drawn out but you will have to discover what it is required to do. Some Application Engine programs are simple with only a few steps, while others have hundreds of SQL Actions and are quite complicated. You will need to understand the rules and restrictions that will apply to the data.

Finally, you have to understand the output required; i.e. what are the final results? Do you require a file output or updated Records? What is the status of the Records? Is a new Record to be filled in with the data remaining so that other programs can report against this new data? If you have a new Record, you will need to get the full information about the fields required and the type of fields. If you have only to update an existing Record, you will need to get the rules by which the Record is to be updated such as its keys.

One last thing to review would be procedures if an error occurs. This condition may require special processing of removing rows of data, updating a Record with special conditions or even writing information to the message log (remember you cannot do a printout with Application Engine).

To make your learning complete, review the following problem definition, as you will be using this as an example in creating a full Application Engine program. Once you understand the problem, you can move onto the next step of the data structure.

The Problem Defined

Your customer wants a new process that will review all the current unreserved orders that are due to ship within the next 14 days. The unreserved amount for each item will be compared to that Business

Units' available quantity. If the unreserved amount is greater than the amount available, then the missing amount is to be requested from a different Business Unit in the form of an interunit transfer request.

Understanding the Data Structure

Once you have the problem defined and fully understood you can move onto the next process to build an efficient Application Engine program. This next step is to define and fully understand the data structure. At this point you can only define the input or starting point of the data structure since you have not yet defined how the program is to work.

This step entails you reviewing your problem in connection with the Record definitions to define the actual SQL with which you can use to start your program. This SQL can be just one statement or it can be multiple statements. It is more likely to be multiple statements since the start is not just to select the data; you have to get the run control information as well.

First, you have to define the criteria with which you will start your Application Engine program. The Fields you add here are to the Run control Record, which the user will input to start the program. The Fields added to a Run Control Record should be those you need as defaults, such as Business Unit or SetID. These Fields can also be one that allows the user to control the data to be processed. These control fields can be anything you think of, so there are no limitations. However, with more control fields, you may have to spend more time building SQL so only add what you really need. Once you determine all the fields you need to add to the Run Control Record, you need to start work on the initial data select.

The initial data is determined from the definition of the problem. Once the problem is understood then you can use Application Designer or a third party SQL product to review the data Record structure. Sometimes it is better to use a third party SQL product since you can not only see the Record structure but also the actual data being stored into the Records. Spend some time reviewing not only the data structure but also the actual rows of data within the Records. The time spent here will help you when you move onto the next step and actually start to think how to define and flow the program.

The Problems Data Structure

The problem only requires the input of an Inventory Business Unit to process. A Record that contains an Inventory Business Unit is all that is needed and that can be found in an already exiting Run control Record of RUN_CNTL_IN.

The initial data for this program is to be the unreserved orders for the defined Business Unit. This data comes from the DEMAND_INF_INV Record; since it is required to have all of the data, there is no need to restrict the data. The data is selected with the field of BUSINESS_UNIT to select only those records to be issued from the entered Business Unit. The quantity to be summed is the QUANTITY_REQUESTED – QUANTITY_BACKORDER, to get the correct amount still to be reserved.

There is also another requirement to compare the total of unreserved quantity in the DEMAND_INF_INV Record to the items' quantity available. The quantity available is stored in the Record BU_ITEMS_INV in the field QTY_AVAILABLE.

Creating the Program Flow

Now you come to the fun part of developing the Application Engine program – writing the program flow. Some developers use fancy software programs while others use the basic paper and pencil. No matter how you write your program flow, you do need to sit down and think about the process of taking your data from the starting position to the end results. This is an iterative process in that you may restart the process if you encounter a problem in completing the program so don't be afraid if this happens to you. In fact, this is the reason that you need to write the program flow so that you can see your program all laid out, to review whether you can make any improvements or go over areas that do not seem to be working.

To start this process you begin with the data structure you defined previously. First, you begin with the Run Control data you have to capture. You draw a box and then write inside it, "Get Run Control data". Then you need to think about what the next step of logic should be. It may be to take some of the Run Control data and convert it or apply some more logic. For example, if you had to take a date loaded from the Run control Record and add some value, such as a Leadtime value from a Business Unit; you would first have to select the Business Unit value and then apply the logic. This process creates two steps; you draw another box under the first with the text "Get Business Unit leadtime" followed by another box with "Calculate new date value", as shown in figure 11.1.

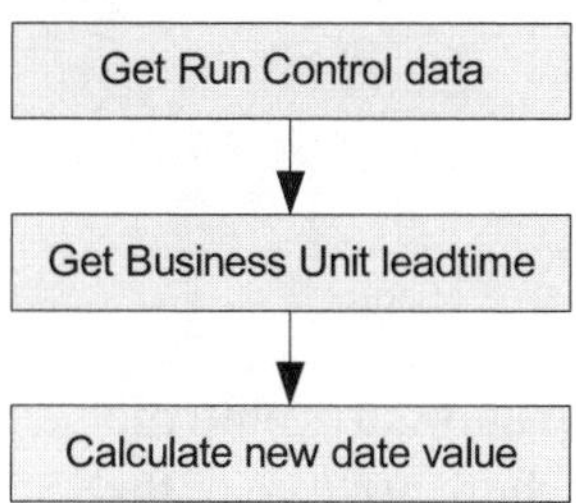

Figure 11.1 Program flow

You will also note that lines with arrows have been added to the program flow to show direction. You can also see that you are not writing any PeopleCode or SQL at this point but just noting actions and flow directions. You continue building this flow noting actions, selects or even updates of data. Also, do not be concerned that one box matches one SQL. This is normally the case but it is not required; the purpose is to just note the actions needed; the steps to be taken and in what order. This program flow becomes your outline to use when you get to writing your actual program.

So far this has been simple and straightforward but some programs can be quite complicated. The Application Engine program allows for looping logic and with PeopleCode you can do just about anything. The idea here is to write the basic flow without worrying about the actual syntax and code you will write. You want to get the flow of how you are going to move from step A to step Z. Instead of trying to write the entire program at once you want to break the program up into simple and understandable steps. To understand a more complicated process, review figure 11.2.

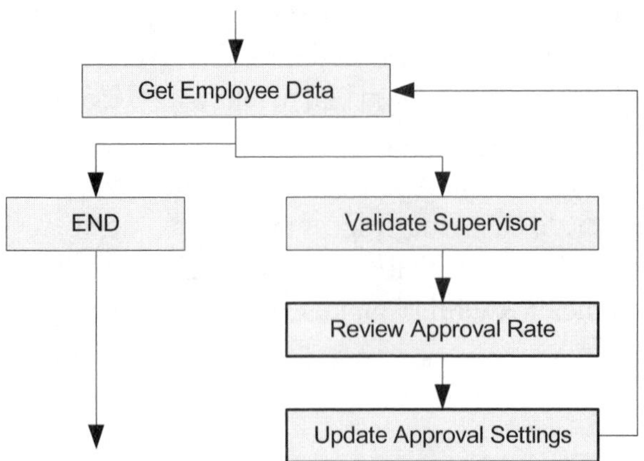

Figure 11.2 Complicated Program flow

The program flow comes into this figure at the top and starts with the process to get employee data. You will note that there are two paths out of the box. If you follow the one to the right, you will see that you have 3 steps to process then it loops back around to the box where you started. This is to show looping logic that could be a Do Select or a Do While Action. The type of Action is not important at this point but to show the flow of the logic. The other path from our initial box is to show the exit process and then onto some other logic or maybe to the completion of the program.

As you work and develop your program flow, do not forget to think about using your Set Processing. Try not to use single rows of data in updating or inserting new rows of data but think in groups of data. Also, do not forget to process all the way from the beginning to the end including the initialization and cleanup of any standard Records.

Do not worry if your program flow is not perfect, it is just a template to start with that you can add to if you wish. There is no right or wrong program flow, it is just an aid that will greatly help when you get to writing your program. To see this completely done, review the following complete program flow of the problem.

The Problem Flowed

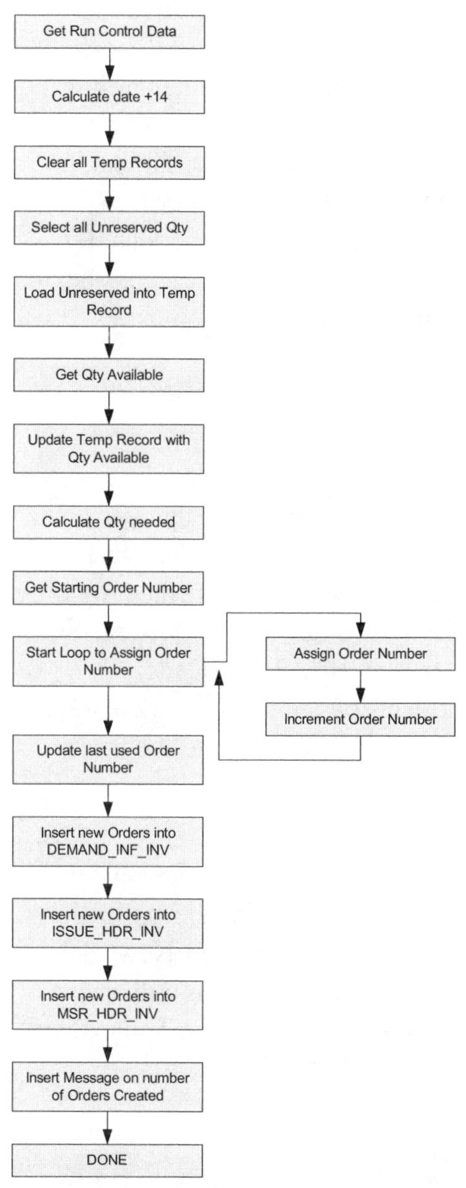

Figure 11.3 The Problem Program Flow

The flow starts with gathering the Run Control Record. Then, a calculation needs to be done to get the date that will be used to select all of the unreserved quantity. The unreserved quantity needs to be selected and then stored into a standard Record. Then, the quantity available needs to be gathered and updated to the standard Record. The next step is to calculate the quantity needed, if any. The starting order number needs to be retrieved so that the order number can then be assigned. Then a loop is performed to assign the order number, incrementing it to be ready for the next loop. Once all the order numbers have been assigned, the last number needs to be updated so that no duplicate orders are created. Finally, the last three steps update the production Records to create the interunit orders.

Writing the Code

With the problem understood and the program flow created, it's now time to apply all of your skills to creating the code. Note that you are not creating just SQL as you will use SQL and PeopleCode. You have to think of all of the tools available to you when you create the program. Some steps are better in PeopleCode while others will be better in SQL - normally you will write 90% SQL to only 10% PeopleCode. PeopleCode should be used for logic decisions and special calculations, such as for date fields; while SQL is used to select, update and insert volumes of data.

To begin writing the code, you start with the first block in the program flow. First, you need to open a new object in the Application Designer. Click on the new button or use the menu: File – New. Select the type of object as an Application Engine program. This will open a new Application Engine program in the working area of the Application Designer, as shown in figure 11.4.

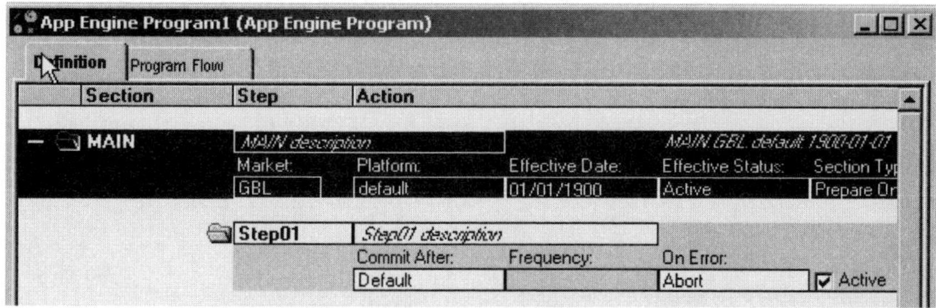

Figure 11.4 New Application Engine program

You start with a Section of Main and one Step to build your program. If you remember back in the earlier chapters, you learned the basic sections that most PeopleSoft programs contain. The Main Section can contain more than just Section calls but this is not normally done; making it easier to read and follow programs. Before you can add new Actions to this Main Section, you have to first create the Sections that you will be calling. This is where you break your program up into workable sections. You could even then split the work up among various developers, each working on their own Section and with the program flow document each would know how their Section begins and ends.

For the problem you are working on you will need to add at least 3 Sections; INIT, CLEANUP and PROCESS. The INIT section is of course for initializing the program, setting up the standard Records and any initial calculations. If you have read through the program flow carefully you will see that there is a step that states "Get Starting Order Number". Although this is not at the start this step could be thought of as an initializing step since you only capture this data once. You could also place this into the PROCESS section, as shown in the program flow, but it is recommended that all initializations be placed into the INIT section. This is done so that your program is easier to read or modify. The CLEANUP Section is just what the name implies. This closes the program and does any cleanup necessary, including issuing any messages of the process completion or errors encountered. The PROCESS Section is the one that can be broken up into many Sections depending on the length and complexity of the program. There is no right or wrong number here. For this simple program you will start with just this one PROCESS Section and see, as you develop, if more are needed. Now, add the three Sections as described so that your program looks just like figure 11.5.

***Note**: You will need to not only add the Sections but also change the names of the Sections as well, as you learned in Chapter 2.*

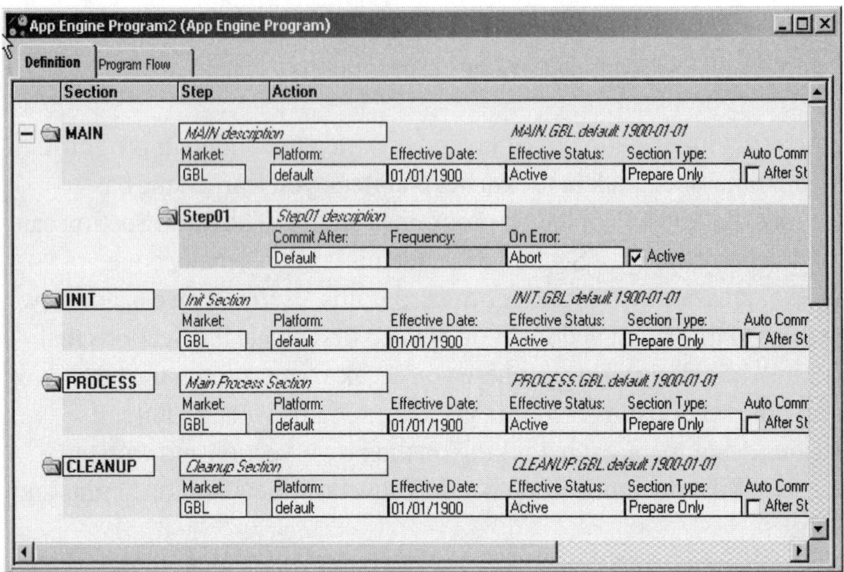

Figure 11.5 Application Engine program with initial Sections

This gives you the core of the program to complete but you need to tie your new Sections to the Main Section. Add a new Action to Step01 to call the Section INIT. Then add a new Step and Action within the Main Section and call the Section PROCESS. Add a third Step and Action and set up to call the Section CLEANUP. Your Application Engine program should now look just like figure 11.6.

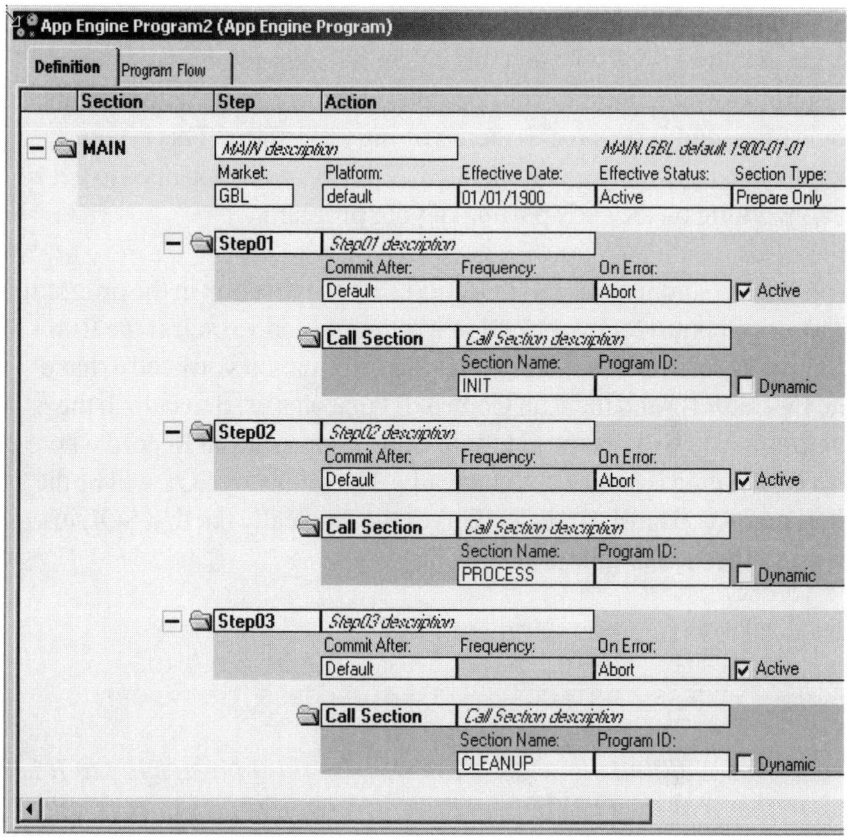

Figure 11.6 Application Engine Main Section complete.

Before you get too much further along in the program you need to understand that something more can be done. Even though you have created some of the program using names that mean something, this may not be the case later in the program or if the program has many more steps. The need for comments does not diminish even if you have a simple program like this one. You should still think in terms of what would help the developer after you or even yourself if you have to modify this program 5 years from now. You have a small amount of text in the description of each Section, Step and Action that you should fill in as you go. You also have the capability to add longer and more thorough comments to each Section, Step and Action. Remember that you can show these comments by using the right click menu or the menu on the toolbar (View – Show All Comments). These large comment fields should be filled with text that will most likely come from your program flow document. You can note a Step or Action with what the logic of the code you have written is trying to perform. This is very helpful and it is highly recommended. With that said, you need to get onto working on the code portion of your program.

You need to start in your INIT Section with the first box in the program flow document. Here you need to write some code to select the Run Control Record information. To get this information you need to have the Operator ID and the Run Control ID that was used to launch the program. You will first need to select this from a special Record where this information is loaded automatically. The following SQL will be the first Action you have to create. This SQL is typically the first SQL in most Application Engine programs.

```
%Select(OPRID, RUN_CNTL_ID)
Select OPRID, RUN_CNTL_ID from PS_AERUNCONTROL
Where PROCESS_INSTANCE = %Bind(PROCESS_INSTANCE)
```

Note: *You will find many program still use this above SQL but it is not required as the OPRID and RUN_CNTL_ID can be accessed via Meta SQL variables.*

Create the first Step and Action in the INIT Section. It is now time to add some SQL and if you have not yet done this yet you will have to save your program. You cannot add any SQL or PeopleCode to a program unless you have first saved the program. Save the program using your naming convention (this problem will use SS_INV_RPLN) and then add the SQL to the first Action in the INIT Section.

Note: *To add the SQL just double click on the Action itself to open the SQL Editor.*

You also might want at this point to change the name of the Step to more closely match the purpose of the Action SQL you have just typed in. If you do change the name, and it is recommended that you do so, you will receive a warning message that changing this Step name will require the Application Engine program to be saved, as shown in figure 11.7.

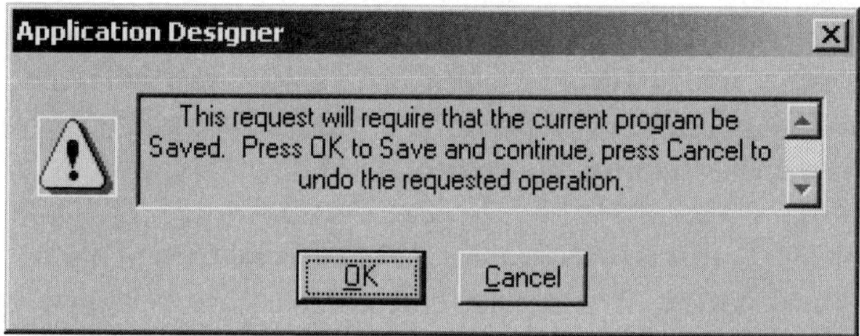

Figure 11.7 Save Warning

If you do not wish to save at this time, click the Cancel button and this will not save and your input will be lost on the Step name. Otherwise, click the OK button to change the Step name and save the Application Engine program.

If you assume to use the Run Control Record of RUN_CNTL_IN on the Page, which launches your program, you would create the next SQL statement to retrieve the business unit value that you need.

```
%Select(BUSINESS_UNIT)
Select BUSINESS_UNIT from PS_RUN_CNTL_IN
Where OPRID = %Bind(OPRID)
  and RUN_CNTL_ID = %Bind(RUN_CNTL_ID)
```

You can see that you now have to use the bind variables that you just loaded in the previous SQL to get the correct value. This reads the proper row within the Run Control Record, selects the business unit value and stores into the bind variable.

***Note**: You have not yet designed the AET record to use. This can be done as you create your program or can be created in one pass after you have built your entire program.*

Now, add a second Step and Action to the INIT Section and add this SQL to the second Step's Action. Be sure to update the name and description fields as well. If you change the name of the Step first, before you do anything else, you will not receive that warning message you have just seen while changing the first Step's name. This is because you have one chance to change the name without penalty as you have done here. The Application Designer understands that you will want to change the names so if you do it first, then all the links to the Action and its appropriate SQL can be maintained without forcing you to do a save. It's just a neat feature to be aware of.

This completes the first box. Note that you had to create two SQL Actions for this one box. This is perfectly acceptable since there is no direct correlation between a program flow box and one Step or Action. Now, you need to tackle the code for the next box in our program flow. This is to calculate a date. It is assumed to take today's date and add 14 days to it. This could be done in SQL using some specific database parameters or by the use of Meta SQL that you learned in Chapter 6.

```
%Select(Due_date)
Select %DateAdd (%CurrentDateOut, 14)
from PS_INSTALLATION
```

This would work but why go to the trouble to talk to the database and select from a one row Record just to get a date? This SQL is a trick that PeopleSoft uses to perform a SQL operation that is quick and fairly painless. The Record PS_INSTALLATION has only one row of data so any select on this Record returns very quickly. This way when you are not selecting any data from the database you can use this SQL to perform processes but this places additional overhead on the system and the database server when this would be done much simpler in PeopleCode, as shown below.

```
SS_INVRPLN_AET.Due_Date = AddToDate(%Date, 0, 0, 14)
```

Since you want your program to be as efficient as possible, add a new Step and Action to the INIT Section. Change the type to PeopleCode and enter the PeopleCode just listed above.

Before you can save your PeopleCode you will have one issue to resolve. Since you are using PeopleCode and it will try and validate all

Records, Fields and syntax, you will have to create the AET Record now before you can save your PeopleCode.

Creating the AET Record

To create the AET Record you first need to open a new Record object. You can than add the necessary Fields manually or you can use a trick where you open an existing AET Control Record to drag and drop some of the necessary fields. No matter which you use, your Record will need to have the following Fields:

```
Process_instance  Key
Run_cntl_id
Oprid
Business_unit
Due_date
Order_number
Inv_item_id
Quantity_new
```

Once you create and save your Record, it should look just like the one in figure 11.8

SS_INVRPLN_AET (Record)

Record Fields | Record Type

Num	Field Name	Type	Len	Format	Short Name	Long Name
1	PROCESS_INSTANCE	Nbr	10		Instance	Process Instance
2	RUN_CNTL_ID	Char	30	Mixed	Run Cntl	Run Control ID
3	OPRID	Char	30	Mixed	User	User ID
4	BUSINESS_UNIT	Char	5	Upper	Unit	Business Unit
5	DUE_DATE	Date	10		DelivDt-PO	Delivery Due Date fron
6	ORDER_NO	Char	10	Upper	Order No	Order No
7	INV_ITEM_ID	Char	18	Upper	Item	Item ID
8	QTY_NEW	Sign	11.4		Qty	Quantity

Figure 11.8 AET Record SS_INVRPLN_AET

This may not be the full Record yet since you have not completed the programming of the Application Engine code, but this is a start. You can always come back and change this Record by adding and dropping Fields as required. Do not forget that before you can run your program for testing you will need to Build this Record and attach it to the Application Engine.

There may seem to be more fields than you think you need but later in the process you will need them. Since it is not worth your time to come back and update a Record object it is thought best to just create the Record in full the first time.

Once you have saved the AET Record, you can then save your PeopleCode. This completes the second box in the program flow. The next box tells you to clear all standard Records. What Record is this? Well, since you have not created the standard Records yet it is unknown as to which or even how many. This could be one Record or many Records depending on the complexity of the program. The best thing to do here is to set a placeholder, that you can come back to later and add more Steps or Actions as needed. So, add a new Step and Action changing the name to CLEAN. You will come back later and add the SQL to this Action once you have determined what and how many standard Records need to be cleaned up.

Inserting Unreserved Demand

The next step in our program flow selects the unreserved demand and this is part of the main process. You could move onto the process Section but there was a step later in the program flow that was talked about being placed into the INIT Section – "Get Starting Order Number". If this step was loaded into the INIT Section you could have a functional problem. The order number that you are going to use is a general order number that is used by many processes. If you select the next order number now, it may be seconds before you apply the number. You need to reserve this number and block others from using it. The problem is also in that you may not only need one number but many. To prevent the program from allowing multiple orders to be created with the same number, you need to have the selection and update of this order number as close to the use as possible. Even though you should place all processes that are initializing values into the INIT section you may not always be able to do this.

If this program were a real life situation, there would be two recommendations to make to relieve this duplicate order number problem. One would be to create a new order number that is only used by this process, so that no user from another system could cause a duplicate order number. The other would be to see if only one order number could be applied and then the order line number changed for the each row. Even with these great suggestions, your customers demand changing order numbers and will promise that no other users will be on the system when this program runs, so the duplicate order number is not considered a problem for this situation.

Not moving the "Get Starting Order Number" to the INIT Section is decided and this does truly complete the INIT Section for now. You will come back to fix the CLEAN Step later. Remember to save your Application Engine program itself every so often so that in case any problems occur you do not lose too much work. With the INIT done, you need to open the PROCESS Section so that you can add more Steps and Actions here. Expand the PROCESS Section and add a new Step and Action. The type of Action will be SQL since the program flow shows selecting data.

The program flow shows you to create a select SQL statement but if you did this you would have an issue. This would force you to load one row of data at a time into some Bind variables to process but you do not want to use row-by-row processing. You want to be using Set Processing. This example was put here specifically to show you that sometimes you will need to combine program flow steps into one Action. This is the case here with the program flow boxes; "Select All Unreserved Quantity" and "Load Unreserved into Standard Record". These two can be combined into one logical SQL Step that inserts data into a standard Record using an insert/select statement. Sometimes you, the developer, have to step back and think about how you will apply SQL to this program flow. You are not set to having one box being one SQL. You can make one box be many SQL statements or many boxes be one SQL. You are in control of the program to use proper set processing logic.

With you fully understanding the issue, you need to write an insert statement using an insert/select to get the unreserved quantity as shown below.

```
Insert into PS_SS_INVRPLN_TMP
(Business_Unit, Inv_Item_Id, Qty_Requested,
 Qty_Available, Qty_New, Order_Number )
Select
BUSINESS_UNIT, INV_ITEM_ID,
Sum(QTY_REQUESTED - QTY_BACKORDER),
0, 0, ' '
from PS_DEMAND_INF_INV
where BUSINESS_UNIT = %Bind(Business_unit)
  and SCHED_DATE <= %Bind(Due_Date)
Group by BUSINESS_UNIT, INV_ITEM_ID
```

You can see that to get the correct number of the quantity unreserved there has to be a calculation. This is to get the correct number based on the functional use of the Fields. This is very important for you the developer to know. You have to understand how the data is used and how Fields are used to get the number that you wish. You have to be comfortable with the process and all the potential uses. You will also see a SUM is used since an item can have more than one order or even order line that is unreserved at any one time.

You also see a few other Fields input with hard coded values. These values are just placeholders for use later in the program. The Qty_Available field will be where you will load the quantity available that you are to later select. The Qty_New field is to be the one to calculate the amount needed and the Order_Number field will contain the order number to be used. By having the program flow available, you could scan through the whole process and develop the needs for the standard Record.

Input this SQL into the first Action of the PROCESS Section.

Having the program flow is very helpful in creating the standard Record but do not think that it will be perfect. There may be other reasons to add fields that you have not discovered, especially with complex programs, but by having the program flow it makes it easier to do. Before you go any further, you should create the standard Record.

Creating the InProcess Record

This is a standard Record to be defined. If you had used a Temporary Table, you would not have to clean up the Records as you have to do in this program, but the data is stored between runs so that any debugging or review can be done. This is the benefit to using your own standard Records. You will find throughout PeopleSoft that, depending on the developer, the use of Temporary Tables varies. PeopleSoft recommends using the Temporary Table and you should make this choice depending on your needs.

To create your Record, open a new Record object and add the following fields:

Field Name	Key	Default
Business_Unit	Key	
Inv_item_id	Key	
Qty_Requested		Default 0
Qty_Available		Default 0
Qty_New		Default 0
Order_Number		Default 0

***Note**: Keys are important even on InProcess Records as they will set a primary index and make sure you do not have duplicate rows.*

Save the Record with the name of SS_INVRPLN_TMP. You do not have to create this Record now could build it later. If you wanted to test your SQL as you build, you would need the Record built.

Update Qty Available

With your first Action in the PROCESS Section complete, review the next box in the program flow. This is where you "Get Quantity Available" which is in the Record PS_BU_ITEMS_INV. Of course, again, just selecting the data is not enough, as you need to store it. In fact if you review the next program flow box you will see the action to be done with the information – "Update Standard Record with Quantity Available". So, you should combine the two program flow boxes into one SQL statement, as you did before.

You could make a process where you select each row and then update the standard Record one at a time; but this is slow and takes too many resources. Meanwhile you might also be placing read locks (depending on your database) into a live production Record that could affect performance of other processes and users. You need to be aware of this so that you create the most efficient program possible.

Here is the SQL to place into the next new Step and Action of the PROCESS Section.

```
Update PS_SS_INVRPLN_TMP
set QUANTITY_AVAILABLE = (select A.QUANTITY_AVAILABLE
   from PS_BU_ITEMS_INV A
   where A.BUSINESS_UNIT = "SS01"
   and PS_SS_INVRPLN_TMP.INV_ITEM_ID = A.INV_ITEM_ID)
Where exists (select 'X' from PS_BU_ITEMS_INV A
   where A.BUSINESS_UNIT = "SS01"
   and PS_SS_INVRPLN_TMP.INV_ITEM_ID = A.INV_ITEM_ID)
```

Note a hard coded value used in the where clause for the business unit. You have to retrieve the inventory available from the Business unit where you will be creating the transfer orders. Normally, you would have retrieved this value from a Record or maybe even the Run Control Record.

You will see that not only is the update done matching a row within the BU_ITEMS_INV but that it also must exist. This is done so that if the item has not been setup in the other business unit you will not try to insert a null value, which the database will issue causing an error and aborting your program.

This brings up an issue about error processing. You need to have your program aware of errors and then determine how to report them. You cannot print errors in Application Engine but if you leave your standard Record with data after processing you can set an error status condition (now you can see why this may be important to leave data in the standard Records). You can then write a simple Query or Crystal report to print out the errors. You can also issue a message to the Application Engine log to store that an error occurred. The only issue with the message log is that it is not that easily visible to the users.

Update QTY_NEW

The next box in your program flow states "Calculate Quantity Needed". The program needs to calculate the Qty_New value. To do this you only need to apply this simple SQL. Again remember to think and work in sets of data.

```
Update PS_SS_INVRPLN_TMP
set Quantity_new = Quantity_Requested
Where quantity_available >= quantity_requested
```

This SQL will set the Qty New to the value in the Qty Requested where there is enough in the Qty Available to meet the Qty Requested. But what if there is some available but not enough? This is a second condition and so requires a second SQL.

```
Update PS_SS_INVRPLN_TMP
set Quantity_new = Quantity_Available
Where quantity_available < quantity_requested
  And quantity_available > 0
```

You now need to add these two SQL statements to the Application Engine program under the Section PROCESS. Since these are both SQL statements you will have to create two new Steps and Actions and add a SQL statement to each one. The order for these two SQL statements is not important since they operate independently and one statement does not rely on the other.

With this complete, you now come to where the order number assigning needs to occur. Since each row needs to be assigned a unique number, you are forced at this point to use row by row processing. There may be special commands that some databases can use to do this in one SQL statement but not all databases that use PeopleSoft can do this; so this book will teach the generic way. If your platform supports special commands, do not hesitate in using them as long as you understand the ramifications of using the program in other locations or on other systems.

Creating the Loop

The first box says to get the Start order number, which is a simple select to the business unit "SS01". This can be done in the next new Step and Action to add to the PROCESS Section.

```
%Select(order_number)
Select BEG_SEQ + SUBSTRING('0000000000' +
LTRIM(STR(LAST_AUTO_NBR +1)), LEN((STR(LAST_AUTO_NBR
+ 1)), MAX_LENGTH)
from PS_AUTO_NUM_TBL
where SETID = 'SS01'
  and num_type = 'MSR'
  and default_beg_seq = 'Y'
```

This SQL captures information from the Auto Numbering sequence record to determine an Order Number per the entered controls on the Business Unit specified to the Setid of SS01. This gives you the starting order number where you will be adding to it as you build your interunit transfer orders.

According to the program flow, it's time to start your loop to insert your first interunit order. To do this loop, you are going to need to process using a special Action type. So far you have only used SQL and PeopleCode but now here is where you use a special Action type called Do Select. A Do Select is a SQL statement that for every row returned in the SQL it will process the remaining Actions within the Step. This will work for you in that you have to select all the rows to be created into an interunit order and then the next Action can do the actual insert.

Add another Step and Action, changing the name and description of course, and place in the following code after you have set the Action type to Do Select.

```
%Select(Inv_item_id, quantity_new)
Select INV_ITEM_ID, QUANTITY_NEW
from PS_SS_INVRPLN_TMP
Where QUANTITY_NEW > 0
```

***Note**: If you change the Action Type after entering in the SQL, you will be forced to save the Application Engine to accept your changes.*

Now you need to add another Action to this same Step that will process for each row of the first Action Do Select SQL. You will note that you have captured the item id and the quantity to enable you to perform the next action and that is to insert the interunit order number. Add the SQL below to a new Action in the same step using the Action type of SQL

```
Insert into PS_DEMAND_INF_INV
Values (%Bind(Business_unit), 'IN', 'SS01',
%Bind(order_number), %Bind(INV_Item_ID), 1, 1,
%Bind(Quantity_New))
```

***Note**: This SQL is not complete since the Record has over 150 fields. Due to space just the basic keys were shown.*

The only thing left to do now is to update the Order Number variable. This will take another SQL statement but since you have already used one here you cannot just add another SQL Action to this Step. You are now stuck with two choices.

First, you can add another Action here but one that uses the CallSection type. Then you have to create a new Section that has one Step and Action to perform the update, and another Action that increments the counter in your bind variables. This increment is not easy since the value in the order number is made up of characters in the beginning sequence that is followed by a set of numbers. You would have to write some SQL to break apart the order number, increment it and then re-build it.

The other possibility is to rewrite the loop process. Why do you even want to think of this? This is because sometimes the program flow will not match how you have to work within the Application Engine program. You may decide on some simple logic that looks good on paper but you need to understand how Application Engine works with it's Set Processing. This may require you to re-build certain Steps as well. To re-write the looping logic, review figure 11.9 to see the new program flow.

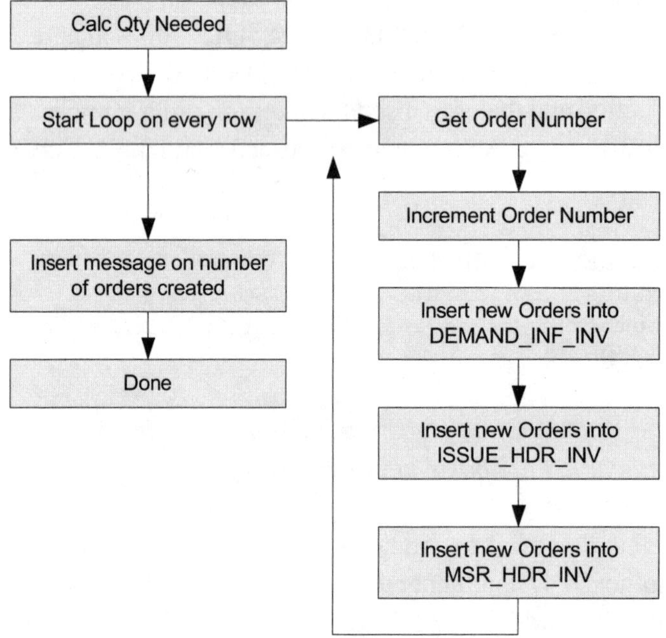

Figure 11.9 New Program flow – loop section

This is not a big change but will require some re-write of your Application Engine program. The process is to better understand how to create looping logic and how to build this logic into your program flow diagrams; and to also show that sometimes you just have to change your program mid stream.

To change your program you have to do a bit of work. First, create a new Section called INSERT. This is where you are going to place all of the SQL within the loop that will be doing mostly the inserts – hence the name. Now, go to the Step that was selecting the beginning order number. Cut this Step out and the copy it into your new INSERT Section. Take the SQL Action step right after the Do Select and cut out the SQL. Add a new Step and Action to the Section INSERT and add the SQL here. The fix is almost done; add one more Action right after the Do Select and set the Action to Call Section. Set the Section to be INSERT.

This change will set up the process so that when the Do Select runs, for every row of data returned, the INSERT Section will perform the necessary SQL. Now, you need to complete the work inside of the INSERT Section. To keep everything in order you need to add a new Step and Action between the two Steps already added to the INSERT Section. Remember to select the Step before you wish to add your new Step (a.k.a. the first Step) and then click the Insert Step button.

To this new Step and Action add the following SQL to update the order number.

```
Update PS_AUTO_NUM_TBL
Set last_auto_nbr = last_auto_nbr + 1
where SETID = 'SS01'
  and num_type = 'MSR'
  and default_beg_seq = 'Y'
```

Having this SQL here allows you to keep the auto sequence number updated to the most current, to reduce the possibility of making a duplicate order. Since you are also handling one order at a time, you can simply do the update by adding one to the number sequence. Then when the loop repeats, the first Step, which contains the select process, will get the next number value.

You should now have 3 Steps in the Section INSERT. You will have to add 2 more Steps and Actions, one for each of the SQLs below.

```
Insert into PS_ISSUE_HDR_INV
Values (%Bind(Business_unit), 'IN', 'SS01',
%Bind(order_number), %Bind(INV_Item_ID))
```

```
Insert into PS_MSR_HDR_INV
Values (%Bind(Business_unit), 'IN', 'SS01',
%Bind(order_number), %Bind(INV_Item_ID))
```

***Note**: Neither of these two SQL statements is fully functional – they have been shortened due to space.*

Now your program is almost complete. You only have to update the message log with the number of orders you have just inserted in the demand Records. To perform this, you need to select a count of how many orders were created. You can do this through a simple SQL statement. Add a new Step and Action to the Section CLEANUP and place the SQL listed below in there.

```
%Select(QUANTITY_NEW)
SELECT COUNT(*) FROM PS_SS_INVRPLN_TMP
WHERE QUANTITY_NEW > 0
```

You now have the Count of orders but need to add this information to the message log. Add another Action to this same Step, with the type of Message Log. Then you can set a message set and number that you will add later. Be sure to set the %Bind(NEW_QUANTITY) in the Parameters to have the count displayed.

This should complete your Application Engine program but you need to go back to the INIT Section and update the placeholder Step and Action you created to hold the SQL to clean out the InProcess Record information. Here is the SQL you should add.

```
DELETE FROM PS_SS_INVRPLN_TMP
```

Since there have been many changes to the program flow, review this table to show all the Sections, Steps and Actions that your Application Engine program should contain.

Main

INIT

GetRUNOR Get Operator ID and Run Control

GetRUNCN Get Run Control info

CalcDate Calculate Date in PeopleCode

CleanTMP Delete all TMP

PROCESS

GetUnRes Get UnReserved Demand

GetAvail Get Available onHand

CalcQuantity1 Calculate Quantity needed

CalcQuantity2 Calculate Quantity needed 2

InsrtOrd Select Quantity to be inserted

INSERT

GetOrdNR Get Order Number

UpdOrdNR Update Order Number

InsrtDII Insert Demand Inf Inv

InsrtIHI Insert Issue Hdr Inv

InsrtMHI Insert MSR Hdr Inv

CLEANUP

GetCount Get count of orders inserted

Insert Message log

Your Application Engine program is now complete and ready to test but there are a few things that you need to review and think about.

Completing the Program

You should now spend some time reviewing your program and checking a few points.

- Make sure you have set all the standard Records to be cleaned in your cleanup or init section.
- Check to make sure the AET Record is complete – all fields are added.
- Make sure to build the AET Record
- Check to make sure all standard Records are complete – all fields added
- Make sure to build the standard Records

You will also have to attach the AET and Temporary Tables (if your program requires them) to the Application Engine program. Open the Application Engine properties window by clicking on the toolbar properties button or use the menu: File – Object Properties. To add the State Record (AET Record) to the Application Engine program, click on the State Record tab and enter in the information, as shown in figure 11.9.

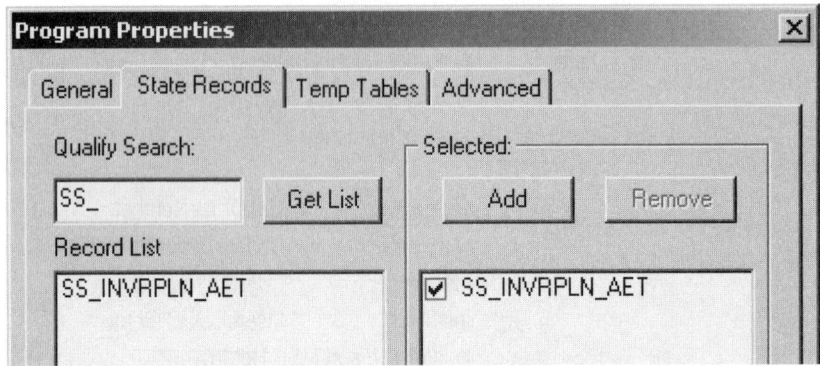

Figure 11.9 Application Engine properties – State Record

Now, click over to the Temp Tables tab to add the Record(s) to the Application Engine program, if any are required. There are none required for this program but you may need to do this in the future, so you should always check to make sure that all necessary Records are added.

Test your SQL

Now you come to the part most developers hate. This is to test the SQL that you have just written. You can test the entire program but this just adds a level of complexity to figure out if you have any problems. It is much easier to test based on each SQL statement but it does take some time, and a bit of effort. This is the recommended process to guarantee a great working program, as you cannot only test to see if the SQL works but also if the SQL is optimized properly. This is a very key point.

Most Application Engine programs are used to process large batches of data and so needs to be optimized. This means to review the SQL to make sure you are using all the keys or even proper indexes. The only way to be sure on this process is to copy the SQL out of each Action and then into a SQL product like Query Analyzer or SQL Plus. You can then run the SQL; but of course you have to change the bind variables to a literal value. You should not only be looking to see if the SQL runs correctly but returns the expected values and works efficiently.

Once you have run all your SQL statements you can run the program in total. There are settings you can change to help with this full program testing and these are all discussed in Chapter 13.

Next

You have completed the process to write a full Application Engine program that does some database updates but there is another class of programs where you want to output data in flat files. This is what the next chapter is all about. There you will learn how to use the File object to output data into a text file which many interface programs require.

Chapter 12

Creating a New Program using the File Layout object

Since you have already built an Application Engine program, back in Chapter 11, the basics will not be covered. This will allow this chapter to fully cover the use of the new File Layout object in acceptiung input from a flat file or writing an output file. A separate section is written below that explains the specific controls for writing each type of file processing both input and output Application Engine programs.

Output Program

This section covers the process of building an Application Engine program that will output a flat file to a specified directory. This program will extract data from the PeopleSoft system, process the data as required and then output the data into a specified format in a specified directory location.

The Problem

To start this program, you need to understand the problem that this Application Engine program is trying to solve. This problem involves exporting the Sales Orders that have been shipped to an outside commission system. This process is to run every night with the daily shipments, then on the first day of each month, determined by the fiscal calendar, a special flag is to be set so that the outside system knows a new month is to be processed.

The output file is to be in a comma separated format (CSV – comma separated values) with the Order Number, Customer ID, Item Id, Quantity and New Month flag.

Program Flow

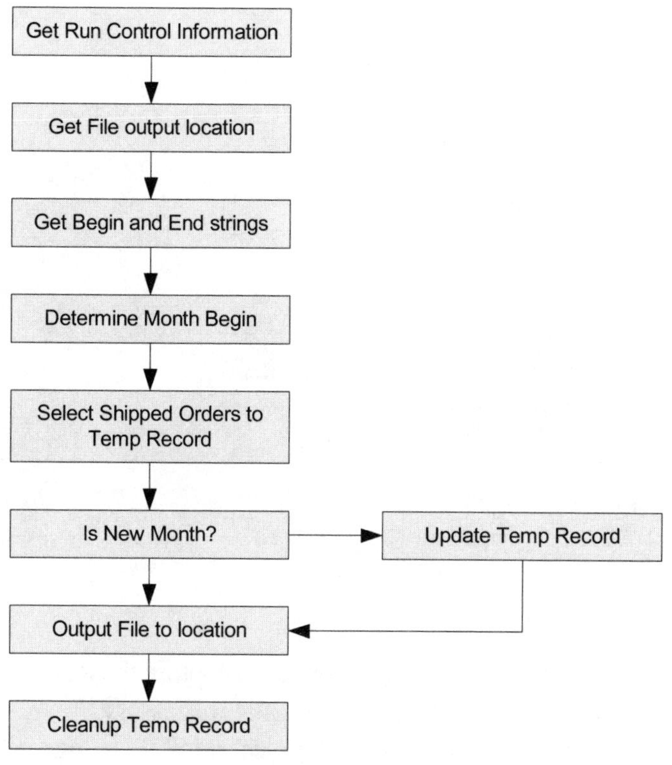

Figure 12.1 Program Flow output program

Writing the Code – INIT Section

To start this program, first create the core. Add Sections INIT, PROCESS and CLEANUP to the Application Engine program. Next, add Steps and Actions of type Call Section to the Main Section, calling each of the newly added Sections (just as you did in Chapter 11). Now, add the following SQL, each in it's own Step and Action, using the type of SQL to the new INIT Section.

```
%Select(OPRID, RUN_CNTL_ID)
select OPRID, RUN_CNTL_ID from PS_AERUNCONTROL
where PROCESS_INSTANCE = %Bind(PROCESS_INSTANCE)

%Select(BUSINESS_UNIT)
select BUSINESS_UNIT from PS_RUN_CNTL_OM
where OPRID = %Bind(OPRID)
  and RUN_CNTL_ID = %Bind(RUN_CNTL_ID)

%Select(Filename, Filepath)
select Filename, Filepath from PS_BUS_UNIT_TBL_OM
where BUSINESS_UNIT = %Bind(Business_unit)

%Select(meta_sql_string)
select STRING_TEXT from PS_STRINGS_TBL
where PROGRAM_ID = %Bind(Business_unit)
  and STRING_ID = 'BEGIN'

%Select(meta_sql_string1)
select STRING_TEXT from PS_STRINGS_TBL
where PROGRAM_ID = %Bind(Business_unit)
  and STRING_ID = 'END'
```

The first SQL gets the bind variables that allow us to capture the Run Control Record – note that this statement is no longer necessary through the use of the Meta SQL variables. The second SQL, using bind variables from the first SQL, loads the information from the Run Control Record – which is only the Business Unit. The Third SQL selects the file name and directory path from the business unit Record for the business unit that you are using in running the program. The fourth and fifth SQL statements retrieve the begin and end text strings from the strings Record. With these five SQL statements, you have covered the first three boxes within the program flow.

The next box, to determine the month begin date, could be done all in PeopleCode but if you remember the earlier warning; you should try to not perform any SQL statements in PeopleCode as it is not as efficient as using the Application Engine SQL statements. So to determine if this is a new month, you will need to use a combination of SQL and PeopleCode Action types.

First, you have to get the last run date of this program. You cannot assume this program will run every day; there may be times when the program fails and so misses a day or the program only runs on weekdays, and so might miss the start date of a month if it was assigned to a Sunday or Saturday. To do this you need to create a one row Record that will hold the last process date. Since you are creating a Record, you can at this point create the AET Record that you will need for this program as well. Create the following two Record definitions.

Last Selection Record – Name: SS_OMLOAD_ACT

Field Name	**Key**	**Prompts**	**Default**
Last_Activity_Dt	Y		%Date

AET Record – Name: SS_OMLOAD_AET

Field Name	**Key**	**Prompts**	**Default**
Process_instance	Y		
Run_cntl_id			
Oprid			
Business_unit			
Filename			
Filepath			
Meta_SQL_string			
Meta_SQL_string1			
Last_Activity_Dt			
Month			N

Note*: Be sure to assign the AET Record to your Application Engine program.*

With the Records complete, you can now write the next SQL statement to go into the INIT Section. Add another Step and Action with the type of SQL and add the following SQL text to it.

```
%Select(Last_Activity_dt)
Select LAST_ACTIVITY_DT from PS_OMLOAD_ACT
```

***Note**: You will note that no where clause condition is added since this Record is assumed to have only one row in it at all times.*

***Warning**: The last SQL assumes that a value will be in the Record but this may not be true the first time you run this program. You can either add code/SQL here to account for this issue or be sure to run a script to define the initial value.*

Add one more Step and Action but this time set the type to PeopleCode. In this Action you will place the PeopleCode that will determine whether a new month has elapsed between the last select date and today's run date. The PeopleCode is listed below.

```
&date_temp = SS_OMLOAD_AET.LAST_ACTIVITY_DT;
&testM = "N";
While &date_temp < %Date
   &date_temp = AddToDate(&date_temp, 0, 0, 1);
   &YEAR = Year(&date_temp);
   SQLExec("select 'Y' from PS_CAL_DETP_TBL
            where setid = 'MODEL'
             and CALENDAR_ID = '01'
             and BEGIN_DT = :1
             and FISCAL_YEAR = :2 ",
          &date_temp,  &YEAR, &testM);
   If &testM = "Y" Then
      SS_POLOAD_AET.MONTH = "Y";
   else;
      SS_POLOAD_AET.MONTH = "N";
   End-If;
End-While;
```

The code takes the value of the last activity date and compares it to today's date. If it is less, one day is added to it and then a SQL Exec is done to determine whether this date matches a start date of the calendar. You will note a use of the SQL Exec command even when you had been warned not to do this. This is to show that sometimes it is acceptable since you see the loop of the logic is inside the while clause of this PeopleCode. You could have rewritten this to place all SQL in a separate Action but then you would have had to create more steps with more logic. This process, even though breaking the SQLExec rule, is still simpler.

The end result of this PeopleCode is to set the value in the Field called MONTH. This value will be used later in the program to change the direction based on the value within this Field. This last PeopleCode also completes the INIT Section. Now you need to move onto the PROCESS Section to write the necessary SQL statements.

Writing the Code – PROCESS Section

The program flow starts by selecting data from a Record into an standard Record. The standard Record will have to be modeled after the File format output. This means you must have all the Fields that are in the File output in the standard Record. This does not mean that you cannot add even more Fields to the standard Record, its just that you must have all the values to be output in the File object within the standard Record.

If you remember back to Chapter 7, the File Object Chapter, you could create multiple levels within the File Object but you do not have to put these in multiple Records. You see there is no forced correlation between the File object levels and standard Records. Now with that said, you should understand that most developers expect there to be a natural match between a level on the File object and an standard Record. This is not a requirement but it is the recommend way to keep the idea of a level within a File object matched to one Record.

For your needs here, create the one Record with the following fields, as listed below:

Record – Name: SS_OMLOAD_TMP

Field Name	**Key**	**Default**
Process_Instance	Y	
Order_No	Y	
Cust_ID	Y	
Inv_item_id	Y	
Quantity		
Monthly_type		N

***Note**: The use of a new field MONTHLY_TYPE is not the same as MONTH, as was stored in the AET Record. This is done since the Field character length did not match the File layout requirements of only one character.*

Now it's time to put in the first Step and Action into your Process Section. Set the Action type to SQL and add the following SQL.

```
Insert into PS_SS_OMLOAD_TMP
Select %Bind(Process_Instance), Order_no,
 Ship_to_cust_id, Inv_item_id, sum(Qty_shipped), 'N'
from PS_SHIPPED_INF_INV
where DEMAND_SOURCE = 'OM'
  and SOURCE_BUS_UNIT = %Bind(Business_unit)
  and SHIPPED_FLAG = 'Y'
  and CANCEL_FLAG = 'N'
  and SHIP_DATE <= %CurrentDateIn
  and SHIP_DATE > %Bind(Last_Activity_dt)
Group by Order_no, Ship_to_cust_id, Inv_item_id
```

This SQL selects data from the shipping record based on today's ship date and the last extract date, and stores it into your standard Record. Note the use of the sum command in case there are multiple rows of data returned.

With the data loaded, there is only one decision to make as to setting the new month flag (stored in the field Monthly_type). There are a few ways to make this process happen and each will be explored in detail.

The first way is to add a new Step and Action with the Action type of PeopleCode. You will also need to set the On Return value to Skip Step. In this Action you will place PeopleCode that based on the setting of the bind variable will exit True or exit False.

```
If SS_OMLOAD_AET.MONTH = 'Y' then
   Exit(0);
Else;
   Exit(1);
End-if;
```

The PeopleCode here checks the value of the bind variable to see it matches Y. If it does match, then the PeopleCode is forced to exit with a False setting. This will cause the setting on the On Return to be ignored and the processing will continue at the next Action. If an exit of 1 is set, meaning the month is not set to Y, then the On Return is used and the next Action will be skipped.

To make this work correctly, this same Step would have a second Action added to it with the type set to SQL. Here is the SQL that will be in the Step.

```
Update PS_SS_OMLOAD_TMP
Set MONTHLY_TYPE = 'Y'
Where PROCESS_INSTANCE = %Bind(Process_instance)
```

Now you can see how these two Actions work together to give the correct results. If the PeopleCode finds the bind variable MONTH set to Y, the exit is forced with a false so that the On Return is ignored. This causes the next Action to run and set all of the values to Y. If the PeopleCode exited with a 1 value (TRUE) then the On Return setting is used and the next Action is skipped leaving the values set to N.

The second way you can use is to place in the PeopleCode the actual SQL statement, as shown in the example below.

```
If %bind(month) = 'Y' then
   Sqlexec("Update PS_SS_OMLOAD_TMP
            Set MONTHLY_TYPE = 'Y'
            where PROCESS_INSTANCE = :1",
          SS_OMLOAD_AET.PROCESS_INSTNACE );
Else;
   Sqlexec("Update PS_SS_OMLOAD_TMP
            Set MONTHLY_TYPE = 'N'
            where PROCESS_INSTANCE = :1",
          SS_OMLOAD_AET.PROCESS_INSTNACE );
End-if;
```

You might think this is better since you now have only one Action and not two to go through, but this is not true. The amount of overhead to do a second Action is nothing compared to the amount required to create a SQL statement within PeopleCode. Since this is not a loop but a single SQL statement, it is not best to put the SQLExec here; although this may work but you need to follow good programming practices.

The last way and most simple is to have the information loaded into the MONTH field upfront. In the previous SQL, where you are loading the standard Record, you could have changed the hard code value of 'N' to use the %Bind(MONTH). This is true in this case since MONTH does allow two characters, but you have loaded it with only one character.

For now, add the one Step and two Actions so that you can get used to creating a decision point in your Application Engine program.

You are now down to the last step of the PROCES Section that is to output the data into the File format required. To do this, it requires the use of a File object that you now need to create in the Application Designer.

Create the File Object

To create your file object, open a new object by clicking on the open toolbar button or use the menu: File – New. Select File Layout as the type and click the OK button. This will open a new empty File object, as shown in figure 12.2

Figure 12.2 File Layout object – new

First, you need to set the type of File object this will be. Click on the Properties button on the toolbar. This is where you should enter the title of your File layout and your project information. After you input that information, click over to the Use tab and change the file layout format field to CSV. This should then ungray the definition qualifier and delimiter fields so that you can change them if you have to. Since you need to have a standard CSV file, you can leave these alone for now. Your settings should look the same as in figure 12.3.

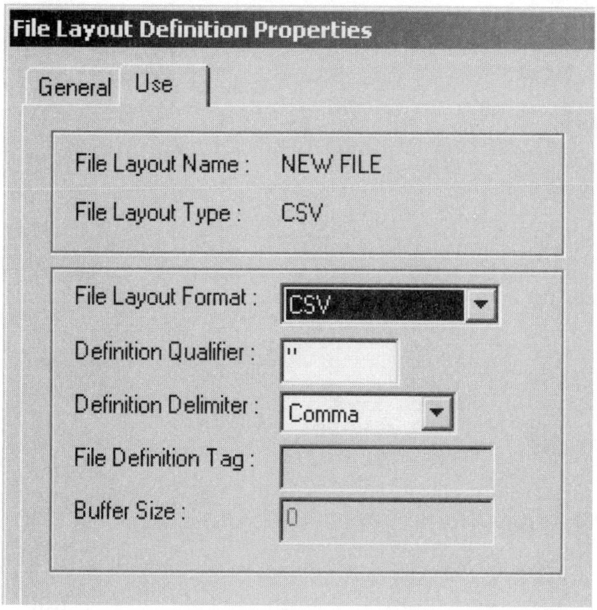

Figure 12.3 File Layout Properties – Use Tab

Now it is time to build the File Object from the definition of the problem. You could build your File object manually but you have already created the Record where the data will be loaded. You can build it very easily from here. Of course, you will have to make some changes since there are fields in the Record definition that you will not want in your flat file. To add the Record to the File object, right click on the NEW FILE object name to get the menu and select Insert Record, or use the main menu: Insert – Record. This will open the panel, as show in figure 12.4.

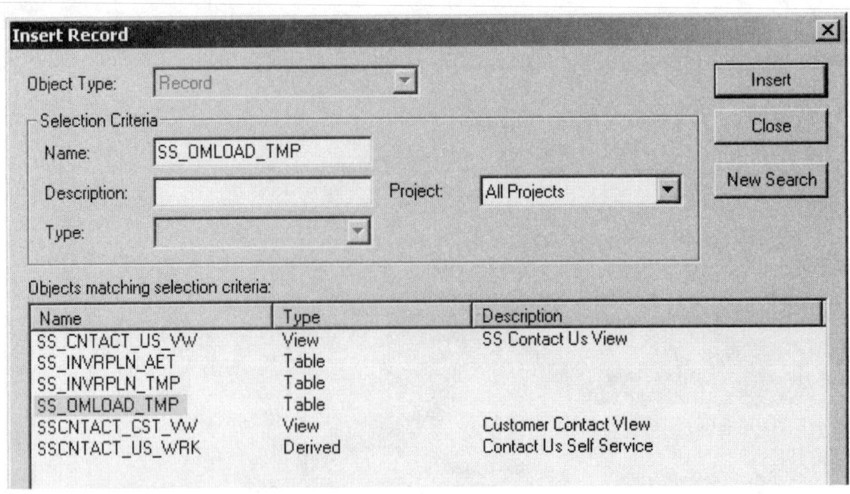

Figure 12.4 Insert Record panel

Here, you input the name of the Record to add to the File Object (note it is shown in figure 12.4 – SS_OMLOAD_TMP) and then click the Insert Button. The figure was done by typing in just SS and then clicking the Insert button. Once you see the Record you want to add in the list box, just double click on SS_OMLOAD_TMP. This will load all of the Record information into the File Object and it should now appear as in Figure 12.5.

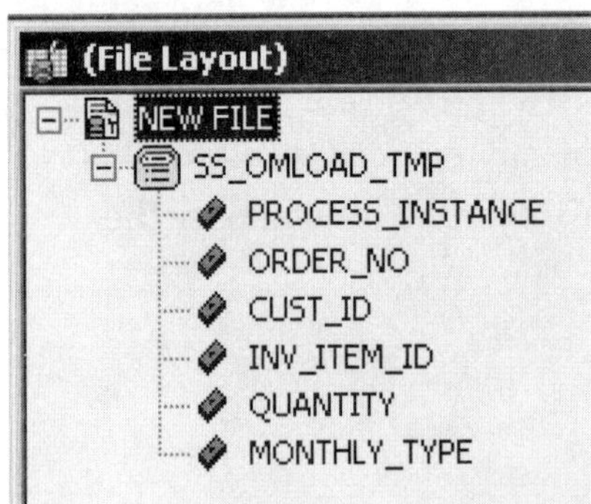

Figure 12.5 File Layout with Record added

You are almost done but there is a bit of clean up to do. First, you have the Process Instance field that is not required in the output of the flat file.

This field will have to be removed from the Record. You do this by clicking just once on the Process Instance name and then typing the delete key, or the menu: Edit – Delete. This will open a warning message asking whether you are sure you want to delete. Click OK if you want to delete the field or NO if you do not. Your File Object is now complete so remember to save it and add it to your project.

You can, if you wish at this time, check out the File Object – in some cases you may even want to change some of the values as to the length of the fields or the order. You can just double click on the Field name or Record name to have the property panel open for you.

With this File Object complete, you can now write the last Step and Action for the PROCESS Section. This last Action is going to be PeopleCode so add a new Step and Action to your Application Engine program changing the Action type to PeopleCode. Double click on the Action to open the PeopleCode editor and type in the following PeopleCode.

```
Local Record &RECORDSS;
Local File &FILE;
Local SQL &SQL;

&FILE = GetFile(RTrim(SS_OMLOAD_AET.FILEPATH) |
  RTrim(SS_OMLOAD_AET.FILENAME), "W",
  %FilePath_Absolute);
If &FILE.IsOpen Then
   If &FILE.SetFileLayout(FileLayout. SS_OMLOAD_TMP)
     Then
     &RECORDSS = CreateRecord(Record. SS_OMLOAD_TMP);
     &FILE.WriteLine(SS_OMLOAD_AET.META_SQL_STRING);
     &SQLSTR = "%SelectAll(:1) where PROCESS_INSTANCE
        = :2 ";
     &SQL = CreateSQL(&SQLSTR, &RECORDSS,
SS_OMLOAD_AET.PROCESS_INSTANCE);
     While &SQL.Fetch(&RECORDSS)
        &FILE.WriteRecord(&RECORDSS);
     End-While;
    &FILE.WriteLine(SS_OMLOAD_AET.META_SQL_STRING1);
  Else
     /*error processing that file layout not found*/
     &FILE.Close();
```

```
      Exit (0);
   End-If;
Else
   /*error processing that file not found*/
   Exit (0);
End-If;
&FILE.Close();
Exit (1);
```

This PeopleCode program is responsible for reading the data from the standard Record and then outputting the data into the flat file based on the File object. To understand the process, review each line of the PeopleCode. The first three lines define the object variables for the Record, File and SQL object that will be used later in the program. The next line creates the File object by using some bind variables concatenating to build the directory and file name. Then a check is made on the File object to see if was opened correctly. If it was, then the File Layout object is attached to the open File object. If the File Layout is attached correctly and returns a positive result, the next line of code creates the Record object with the standard Record that contains all of the data from the previous Steps and Actions of the Application Engine program. The next line writes a special one line data to the flat file because it is required. The next two lines create the SQL object. Then starts the loop process that reads a row of data from the SQL object. For each row read from the SQL it is written out to the flat file. After the last line is read, the loop ends and again another special one line record is written to the flat file.

The next steps of the code are the else clauses where the File Layout object is not found or attached correctly, and the File object is not opened correctly. These else clauses exit with a 0 value allowing further processing to specify an error, if required. For these exit clauses to be used correctly, you would have had to set the On Return type to Skip Step. Then add a new Action to this Step to issue a message log stating a file error was found. You could also pass other information such as necessary to the log to state the type of error. In this way, when the program exits with a 0 value, then the message log Action is not skipped and is performed.

If all was successful, the file close is done since you never want to end a program without closing your open File objects. The last line exits PeopleCode properly. If all were successful, your output would look something like the example below.

File Output Example
"PDF0001", "ACT01", "ZDF00045-GH", "36", "N"
"PDF023875", "N31", "ZDF0364-BK-FX", "4.55", "N"
"RWK03", "ACZGHY", "ZDF00045-GH", "1576890", "N"
"PDF0004", "ACT01", "SERVICES", "36", "N"

You will note that field size is variable up to the maximum allowed by the field as defined in the File Layout object. If the field length is less, then it is shortened. You will also note the quantity field (4th value), may or may not have decimal displaying. The system is trying to be helpful by only showing decimal precision if the value has any.

Note *– The decimal precision and field length within the File Layout have no affect when using the CSV format. This was tested on version 8.16 first release.*

This simple PeopleCode program is all you need to make an output file work. If the file object had multiple Child Segments, you might have needed to develop more loops for each child segment or you could have used the Rowset object to output the file. It is recommended to use the Rowset process versus multiple loops for each child segment because the PeopleCode required for the Rowset is simpler.

Here is an example of the PeopleCode based on a 2 level (one parent and one child) FileLayout object.

```
Local File &file1;
Local Rowset &RWSHDR, &RWSLIN;
Local Record &ORDHDR, &ORDLIN;
Local SQL &SQLHDR, &SQLLIN;

&ORDHDR = CreateRecord(Record.ORD_HEADER);
&ORDLIN = CreateRecord(Record.ORD_LINE);
```

```
&SQLHDR = CreateSQL("%selectall(:1) where
BUSINESS_UNIT = :2", &ORDHDR,
SSJAW_AET.BUSINESS_UNIT);

&RWSHDR = CreateRowset(Record.ORD_HEADER,
CreateRowset(Record.ORD_LINE));

&file1 = GetFile("p:\temp\ssjaw.txt", "W",
%FilePath_Absolute);
If &file1.SetFileLayout(FileLayout.SSJAW) Then
   If &file1.IsOpen Then
      &file1.WriteLine("This is the beginning");
      &K = 1;
      While &SQLHDR.Fetch(&ORDHDR)
      &ORDHDR.CopyFieldsTo(&RWSHDR.GetRow(&K).ORD_HEADER);
         &L = 1;
         &SQLLIN = CreateSQL("%selectall(:1) where
BUSINESS_UNIT = :2 and ORDER_NO = :3", &ORDLIN,
SSJAW_AET.BUSINESS_UNIT,
&RWSHDR(&K).ORD_HEADER.ORDER_NO.Value);
         &RWSLIN = &RWSHDR.GetRow(&K).GetRowset(1);
         While &SQLLIN.Fetch(&ORDLIN)
           &ORDLIN.CopyFieldsTo(&RWSLIN(&L).ORD_LINE);
            &RWSLIN.InsertRow(&L);
            &L = &L + 1;
         End-While;
         &RWSHDR.InsertRow(&K);
         &K = &K + 1;
      End-While;

      &file1.WriteRowset(&RWSHDR);

      &file1.WriteLine("This is EOF");
   End-If;
End-If;
&file1.Close();
```

The program here creates two Rowset objects inside the PeopleCode program and then fills data from an outside Record. The process then inserts rows into each level of the RowSet object as needed. This is required so that the Rowset objects can maintain the connection from one level to the other. If this code was within a Page or Component you could have used other methods and properties to fill the Rowsets and output the file.

Note: Only one WriteRowset command is used. This will output the entire Rowset both Header and Line.

Here are two samples of the output from the above program. The first sample shows where a File Record ID was added to each level – having 100 for the top level (HDR) and 200 for the lower level (LIN). The second example below also shows if you have used the inherited feature that tells the File Layout if this field is on the upper level and the value is the same as the one on the lower level, then do not display it for the lower levels.

```
Sample 1
"100","082","SSR0700000","100040"
"200","082","SSR0700000","9","200060"
"200","082","SSR0700000","10","000025"
"100","082","SSR0700001","553206"
"200","082","SSR0700001","11","A66705"
"100","082","SSR0700002","502890"
"200","082","SSR0700002","1","207594"

Sample 2
"100","JJJ","SSR0700000","100040"
"200"," "," ","9","200060"
"200"," "," ","10","000025"
"100","JJJ","SSR0700001","553206"
"200"," "," ","11","A66705"
"100","JJJ","SSR0700002","502890"
"200"," "," ","1","207594"
```

The program is not yet complete, as you have to finish the CLEANUP Section, which is what follows.

Writing the Code – CLEANUP Section

Since your program outputs a file format of the data in the standard Record, there is no need to leave the data in the system. Add a new Step and Action of the type SQL to the CLEANUP Section and then add the following SQL.

```
Delete from PS_SS_POLOAD_TMP
Where Process_instance = %Bind(Process_instance)
```

The last process you have to do is to update the last select date with today's date. This is done with another SQL statement so you need to add a second Step and Action with the type of SQL.

```
Update PS_SS_POLOAD_ACT
Set last_activity_dt = %CurrentDateIn
```

This completes the writing of your output Application Engine program. Be sure to save all your SQL, PeopleCode, Record and Application Engine objects. Then you can get on with the testing process, which will be covered in more detail in Chapter 13.

Now you need to learn how to read in files using the File object and Application Engine. The process is very similar so you should be able to pick this up quickly after having completed reading the Chapter this far.

Input Program

The following section covers the processes where an outside system is sending a flat file of information that you want to load into a PeopleSoft Records. This is not the recommended PeopleSoft way since they would recommend you use the Business Interlink process or Messaging tools. These other tools allow you to enter data as if you were a user inputting data into a Page, which allows the process to validate and perform all the edits. These tools are beyond the scope of this book although they are mentioned here. This book will concentrate on a simple problem to take flat file data and load it to an interface Record that exists in PeopleSoft.

The Problem

You have an outside system that is creating purchase orders that you need to have loaded into PeopleSoft. There is an interface Record to do this – PS_PO_ITM_STG – and its purpose is to accept purchase order information so that these rows of data can be turned into PeopleSoft purchase orders. Many other PeopleSoft process use this same Record to create purchase orders so PeopleSoft is built to handle the needs of your problem.

***Note**: This is one of many Records that are required to make this process work. There are two other stage Records that you must use if you are to make this successful. The problem stated here is being simplified to show you how to build Application Engine programs and not how to create outside purchase orders.*

Your flat file is coming in from a Mainframe system in a fixed format, as shown below:

Field Name	Length	Type
Item	15	Character
Sign	1	Character (+ or – only)
Quantity	10.2	Number (filled with 0's)
Vendor Name	25	Character

Your program is to read this file and load into the PS_PO_ITM_STG Record one row for every row in the flat file.

You will also need to create a File Layout object, as shown in figure 12.6.

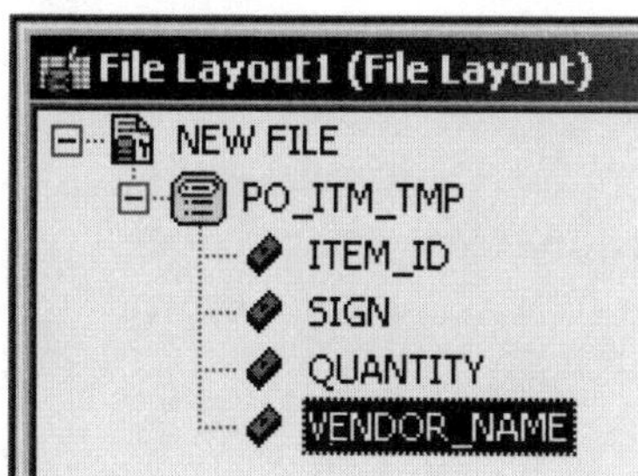

Figure 12.6 File Layout object

To create this File Layout object, first, you need to add a Segment – you can use any name you like since it is free form but it is recommended to use the name of the Record that you will be loading the data into. It is not required, it is just good sense and follows the basic PeopleSoft process. When you add the Record, you only have to set the maximum record length, which should be set to 54.

Next, you need to add the FileFields, as shown, in the proper order. Be sure that you set the parameters Field Properties of this File Layout object, as shown in the table below then save the File Layout object as SS_PO_LOAD.

Field Name	**Type**	**Decimal Position**	**Field Length**	**Start Position**	**Default**
Item	Character		15	1	
Sign	Character		1	16	+
Quantity	Number	2	13	17	
Vendor Name	Character		25	29	

Here is the expected program flow that your new program will follow.

Program Flow

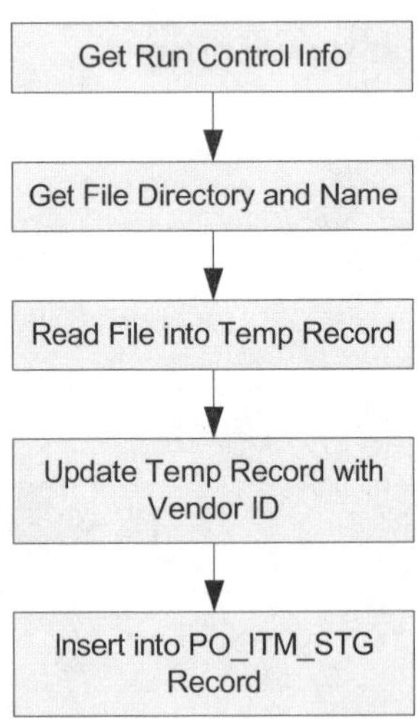

Figure 12.6 Program flow input program

Writing the Code – INIT Section

To start this program, first create the core. Add Sections INIT, PROCESS and CLEANUP to the Application Engine program. Next, add Steps and Actions of type Call Section to the Main Section calling each of the newly added Sections. Now, add the following SQL each in its own Step and Action using the type of SQL to the new INIT Section.

```
%Select(OPRID, RUN_CNTL_ID)
select OPRID, RUN_CNTL_ID from PS_AERUNCONTROL
where PROCESS_INSTANCE = %Bind(PROCESS_INSTANCE)

%Select(BUSINESS_UNIT)
select BUSINESS_UNIT from PS_RUN_CNTL_PO_AE
where OPRID = %Bind(OPRID) and RUN_CNTL_ID =
%Bind(RUN_CNTL_ID)

%Select(Filename, Filepath)
select Filename, Filepath from PS_BUS_UNIT_OPT_PM
where BUSINESS_UNIT = %Bind(Business_unit)
```

This program is a bit simpler so you can just jump right into the main body of the program.

Writing the Code – PROCESS Section

The first step in this program is to read the flat file into a data Record so that further Steps and Actions can process against it. Add a new Step and Action to the Process Section being sure to change the Action type to PeopleCode. Now, enter in the following PeopleCode.

```
Local File &filess;
Local Rowset &RWSTPO;
Local Record &RECTMP;
Local SQL &SQLPOTMP;

&RECTMP = CreateRecord(Record.PO_ITM_TMP);
&SQLPOTMP = CreateSQL("%Insert(:1)");
&filess = GetFile("p:\temp\ssjaw.txt", "R",
%FilePath_Absolute);
```

```
If &filess.IsOpen then
   If &filess.SetFileLayout(FileLayout.SS_PO_LOAD)
        Then
     &RWSTPO = &filess.ReadRowset();
      While &RWSTPO <> NULL
      &RWSTPO.GetRow(1).PO_ITM_TMP.CopyFieldsTo(&RECTMP);
         &SQLPOTMP.Execute(&RECTMP);
         &RWSTPO = &filess.ReadRowset();
      End-While;
   Else
      REM Error Handling on File Layout
   End-if;
   &filess.Close();
Else;
   REM Error Handling on File
End-if;
```

***Warning**: Where the WriteRowset command took the entire Rowset and wrote it out to a file, the ReadRowset only processes one record at a time. A ReadRowset Record consists of one level 0 Record and any child levels below it.*

The program here, although fairly short, does a lot in a little space. First, the Record object and the SQL objects are created. You need to create a Record and SQL object since the data read from the file; even though it will be loaded into a Rowset, is not saved to the database. Since the Rowset is created within the PeopleCode space and not directly tied to a Record within the database, you will have to copy the data into a valid Record and then have it inserted into the database. Next, the File object is created, ready to Read with the File Layout defined to the File object. The first read of the Rowset is done and the start of the while loop. If the Rowset is NULL – meaning that no data is loaded into the Rowset – the program exits and closes the File. If there is data, the Rowset copies data of the one Record you have in your File Layout to the Record object created here in this PeopleCode. Then the SQL object is run to perform a SQL insert to the database based on the Record data loaded into the Record object. The next Rowset is read and checked to see if it is NULL.

This program will loop through all the data within the flat file and write to the Record in the database so that the data is saved. If there were multiple levels, you would have had to perform more CopyFieldsTo and Execute commands for each Record level.

If the flat file had been a CSV type, you could have used a different method to read in the data. Here is a short example.

```
If &filess.SetFileLayout(FILELAYOUT.SS_PO_LOAD) Then
   While &filess.ReadLine(&STRING);
      &ARRAY = Split(&STRING, ",");
      For &I = 1 To &RECTMP.FieldCount
         &RECTMP.GetField(&I).Value = &ARRAY[&I];
      End-For;
      &RECTMP.Insert();
   End-While;
End-if;
```

The code shown here sets the FileLayout to the File object. Instead of using the ReadRowset command the ReadLine command is used. This reads the data into a string variable (&STRING). The data in the variable is just one line string of text and so needs to be "cutup" into the Fields that are going to be inserted into the database. An array is loaded based on using the Split command, knowing that each Field is separated by the listed value (","). Then, a For-Next loop is done to move through all the fields of the Record object and insert the data from the array into the Record objects. After all the Fields are loaded into the Record object, the data is inserted into the database via the Insert method.

This is how you handle simple flat files but PeopleSoft gives you the capability to handle complex files. These complex files are made up of a single file that contains multiple different layouts

Processing Complex Flat Files

To process complex files, it is required that the flat file be in FIXED format; CSV and XML formats are not allowed. There is also another requirement in that the flat file must contain an indicator that tells you that a new File Layout needs to be used and what File Layout that should be. This special indicator is typically set in the File Record ID on the Record level within the File Layout object. You do not have to set this File Layout value but it is a good place to store it for future reference.

The indicator and its layout name must also be on a separate line since these values are not considered part of the Rowset data. You will see how this indicator is used once you write the PeopleCode.

To give a good example, here is what a flat file would look like using multiple layouts and the indicator.

```
SSS POLOAD
ITEMAA          +000000001500Thrifty Barn
ITEMAB          +000000051100Steves House of Stuff
ITEMGHJ6        +000000008700Joes Place
SSS ITMLOAD
ITEMAA          Copper Pipe 1/4in threaded
ITEMAB          Laser Filter Blue
ITEMGHJ6        Wood Garden Rake XL
SSS PRCLIST
ITEMAA          +00004555
ITEMAB          +00023599
ITEMGHJ6        +00000070
```

The Indicator in this example is "SSS" but it could have been anything. This will tell the program that a new File Layout needs to be used. The indicator is followed by the name of the Layout to be used – again this is just free form text. You will have to coordinate with the creator of the flat file to make sure your Application Engine program will read the file correctly. This is because the flat file will contain the layout name which will need to match the File Layout object name that you saved in PeopleSoft Application Designer or you will have to code in a process to understand the name within the flat file that corresponds to a known saved File Layout object name.

Now, you can create the PeopleCode that will read this flat file, assuming you have already created all the necessary File Layout objects.

```
&filess = GetFile("p:\temp\ssjaw.txt", "R",
      %FilePath_Absolute);
If &filess.SetFileLayout(FileLayout.SS_PO_LOAD) Then
```

```
    &filess.SetFileID("SSS", 1);
    &RWST = &filess.ReadRowset();
    &LAYOUT = &filess.CurrentRecord;
    &LAYOUT = Substring(&LAYOUT, 5, 10);
    &filess.SetFileLayout(@(FileLayout." | &LAYOUT));
    &RWST = &filess.ReadRowset();
    while &RWST <> NULL or &filess.IsNewFieldID
       If &filess.IsNewFieldID then
          &LAYOUT = &filess.CurrentRecord;
          &LAYOUT = Substring(&LAYOUT, 5, 10);
          &filess.SetFileLayout(@(FileLayout." |
               &LAYOUT));
          &filess.SetFileID("SSS", 1);
          &RWST = &filess.ReadRowset();
       End-if;
       Evaluate &LAYOUT
       When "POLOAD"
          &RWST(1).RECORDX.CopyFieldsTo(&RECORDX);
          &SQLX.Execute(&RECORDX);
       Break;
       When "ITMLOAD"
          &RWST(1).RECORDY.CopyFieldsTo(&RECORDY);
          &SQLY.Execute(&RECORDY);
       Break;
       When "PRCLIST"
          &RWST(1).RECORDZ.CopyFieldsTo(&RECORDZ);
          &RECORDZ.ExecuteEdits();
          If &RECORDZ.IsEditError then
             &SQLZ2.Execute(&RECORDZ);
          Else;
             &SQLZ.Execute(&RECORDZ);
          End-if;
       Break;
       End-Evaluate;
       &RWST = &filess.ReadRowset();

    End-While;
End-if;
&filess.Close();
```

The first two lines open the flat file and assign a known File Layout object. The third line assigns the indicator value of "SSS" as the FileID. The first Rowset is read from the flat file. This program assumes the first row of data is going to be a FileID record. Otherwise, you would need to program in here more validations and checks. Lines 5 and 6 take the value in the FileID record (the whole line in the flat file is read as one record) and then substrings the value, taking only the layout name and placing it into the &LAYOUT variable. This program also assumes that the names of the layout in the flat file will match exactly to the names of the File Layout objects you saved in the Application Designer. The 7th line assigns the correct File Layout to use and then the next Rowset is read. A check is made to see whether the Rowset is NULL, meaning that it has reached the end of the file, or if it has reached a new FileID. You cannot just check for NULL here in that if you find a new FileID the Rowset will return a NULL. The next seven lines are for checking whether there is a new FileID and then getting the next File Layout to use, and reading the next row of valid data.

If a new FileID was found, then the program evaluates which Layout you are using so that the proper data rows can be read into the proper Records. Note, in the "PRCLIST" layout process, Edits can be performed.

Once all the Rowsets have been read, meaning a return of NULL and no new FileID, the program will close the File object.

Continue with Process Section

Now that you have the file read into a data table (PS_PO_ITM_TMP) you can perform the necessary edits, as are required. In the process flow the next step is to assign the vendor id to the Record using the Vendor name from the flat file, as shown in the next SQL example.

```
Update PS_PO_ITM_TMP
Set Vendor_id = (Select B.Vendor_id
      from PS_VENDOR B
      where B.vendor_name_short = PS_PO_ITM_TMP.DESCR
      and B.SETID = %Bind(VNDR_SETID))
Where exists (Select 'X' from PS_VENDOR B
      where B.vendor_name_short = PS_PO_ITM_TMP.DESCR
      and B.SETID = %Bind(VNDR_SETID))
```

The next step is to insert the data from the standard Record into the PS_PO_ITM_STG record. Of course, this program would not work in real life as this record requires many more values to be set or defaulted in. This is just used as an example to show how to get from the flat file into a PeopleSoft database Record.

```
Insert into PS_PO_ITM_STG
Select * from PS_PO_ITM_TMP
```

Writing the Code – CLEANUP Section

This is the last section to complete and that is to remove all data from the PS_PO_ITM_TMP Record.

***Note**: The standard Record did not contain a Processs_Instance so when you delete all its rows, you may crash other running programs. Be sure you write your program based on the needs of the user.*

Add a new Step and Action to the Cleanup Section making sure the Action type is SQL, then add the following SQL.

```
Delete from PS_PO_ITM_TMP
```

Your program is now complete. Remember to save the Application Engine program and add all the various objects to your project: Application Engine program, Application Engine Sections, PeopleCode and SQL.

Next

The book has now shown you just about all there is to know about Application Engine programming except how to test and debug. There are special details to know in how best to debug a program you have just written or an existing PeopleSoft delivered Application Engine program. That is what the next chapter will now cover for you.

Chapter 13

How to Test, Debug and Trace your Application Engine program

Now that you have learned all about the functions and methods of Application Engine programming, from SQL to PeopleCode, there may come a time when you have a problem with an Application Engine program. You could have written the program yourself or it could be a delivered PeopleSoft program. In either case, you need a way to debug the program, following it through all of the Steps and Actions. PeopleSoft gives you a few ways to accomplish this debugging or tracing. There are also other ways to test and debug your program that you accomplish by how you write your program. All of this and more will be taught within this chapter so that you can be an expert on how to test, debug and trace all Application Engine programs no matter who wrote them.

This Chapter is broken up into three sections: Testing, Debugging and Tracing. Testing covers how you can write your program in such a way as to help test your program. Also covered will be the commit and roll back issues as it relates to testing. Debugging covers how to review your program online, as it is running, to test variables and values within the code, both for SQL and PeopleCode. Tracing covers the batch output results of Application Engine programs. This output can show you not only the SQL that was run but also the time it took (a.k.a. timings) which is essential for proper testing of performance.

Testing your Application Engine program

When you created your Application Engine program, you may have used standard Records for processing data. If you did, you can use the data left in these Records to review the progress of your program. Make sure you inactivate the Section or Step(s) that clears the standard Records so that data is left in them after the program completes, unless you have written your program to clean these standard Records at the start of your program. You should then be able to review the data in the standard Records, following the data to the expected end results. If you have multiple standard Records, you can check the data in each Record as it is processed through the entire program.

***Note**: If you turn off the cleanup Section and/or Step(s), your program may have issues when you rerun the program so be sure the program can handle multiple instances or remove the data from the standard Records prior to starting the next program run.*

***Note**: If you used PeopleSoft Temporary Tables then when the Application Engine program completes the Records are deleted of all data from the run; so you cannot use this process to help in testing your program.*

Once you have completed your review, be sure to re-activate any Sections or Steps that you deactivated during your testing phase. You may also have to delete any errant data left in your Standard Records.

There are also some special tricks you can do if you are processing data using SQL. These tricks do not work in processing logic with PeopleCode and some of the special SQL Action types but you can try to simulate the logic. What you do is to use your database's online SQL program: Query Analyzer for Microsoft SQL Server or SQLPlus for Oracle, to name just a couple. Contact your database administrator to have your specific online database program installed so that you can use it. Once you have this program open and logged into your development database, you can then run your actual SQL statements. You can start at the beginning of your program or if you have data left in your standard Records you can start somewhere in the middle. You can then run each SQL statement in the online database program to see the effect in the standard Records. This way you can do step by step testing even making some adjustment to the SQL if you find a problem. Just remember to copy your SQL changes back into you original Application Engine program.

***Warning**: Using this trick, depending on your online database program, you may be auto-committing data upon each SQL. This is not a problem; you just need to be aware of it.*

Later in this Chapter you will learn how to do online debugging where you can follow each SQL step but you cannot make any online adjustments.

Commits and Rollback

Some issues with the commit process need to be addressed now, especially in context with programs that are aborting in the middle of the program. If an Application Engine program completes successfully, then all database Records are committed. If an Application Engine program aborts at some Action, either from PeopleCode or SQL, then the database will rollback to the last Step where a commit occurred. If you remember, the Section and Step control when and if a commit is performed. If you do not specify it, the normal default is to NOT commit until the end of the program. If you do not set any commits, then when your program fails in the middle, it will rollback to the very beginning and all of your data in any standard Record will disappear.

For testing purposes, it may be very valid to set the commit to occur on many Steps or Sections, then once your testing is complete you can go back and turn the commits back to the way you wish your program to run in production. You will need to make these decisions as you test and debug your Application Engine program.

***Note**: The commits will also affect your restart capability, which you will learn all about in the next chapter, Chapter 14.*

Debugging your Application Engine program

Now that you can test your Application Engine program, you need to learn the tools that PeopleSoft gives you to resolve problems. This online debugging allows you some freedoms but not as much as you just learned about. Of course, many times you will only need to use the debugging process to fix or understand an Application Engine program so you need to learn how to use this tool.

Starting the Application Engine Debugging process

The Application Engine debugging process is made up of two parts. The first part is called the Application Engine debugger, which reviews all of the SQL Action types. The second part is the PeopleCode Debugger that you should know about from your normal PeopleSoft development. You will use the standard PeopleCode debugger to debug your Application Engine PeopleCode. These two parts make up the entire Application Engine debugging process.

Application Engine Debugger

To start the Application Engine debugger, you need to set up some parameters so that when you launch the Application Engine program you want to debug, the program will automatically start up in debug mode.

***Warning**: The debug process is not considered a batch-oriented process. You can only do this process using two-tier or running the program on your client. If you wish to run using a process server or through the Internet client, then you must use the tracing options in the next section of this chapter.*

There are two ways to launch an Application Engine program on your client. The first is using two-tier access and the second allows you to run your Application Engine program directly using a Command line. Both of these scenarios require special setup of the PeopleSoft application on your PC. See your system administrator for help with this set up if you are unable to continue.

Two-Tier Access

To set up the debug option, you need to open the Configuration Manager loaded onto your client. You do this by using the windows menu and clicking on the Client Configuration Manager icon that is within the PeopleTools menu that was loaded by your system administrator.

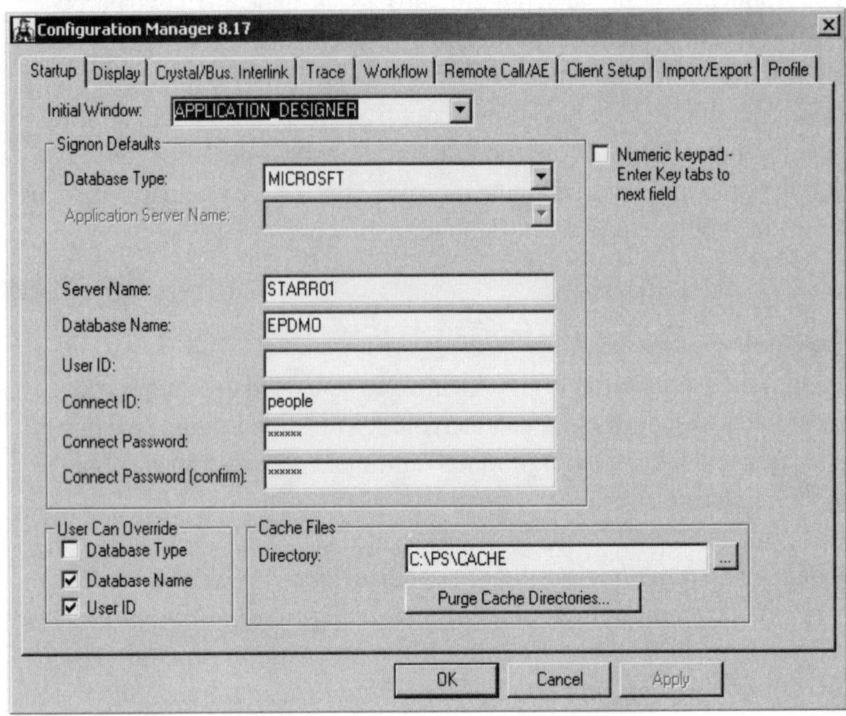

Figure 13.1 Configuration Manager

Now click over to the Profile tab, as show in figure 13.2.

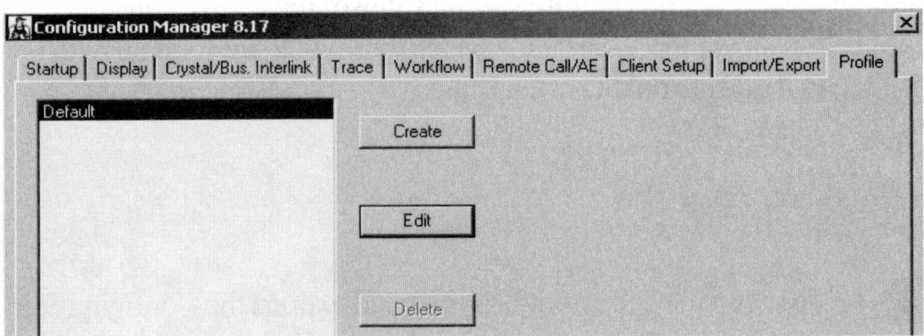

Figure 13.2 Configuration Manager – Profile tab

Here you may see the default or a special profile. Your system administrator establishes all this when they setup your PC with the

PeopleSoft Tools application. Normally the default profile is the only one used. If you see more than one, you will need to determine the correct profile that is being used since the settings you will be changing are connected to that profile. Contact your system administrator to determine the correct profile to use.

Be sure to highlight the correct profile and then click on the Edit button. This will open the profile editor, as shown in figure 13.3.

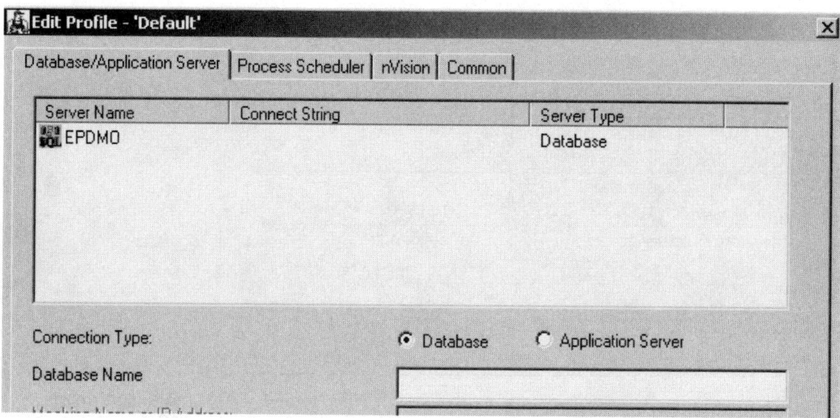

Figure 13.3 Configuration Manager – Profile Editor

Next, click over to the Process Scheduler tab, as shown in figure 13.4.

This panel shows you a lot of information but you are only interested in the checkbox in the upper right-hand corner. There are two checkboxes within the group outline of Application Engine. The first checkbox is for debug; that is the setting that controls whether the debug process will be used or not. If this is set ON – then any Application Engine program run with this profile will be launched within the debugger. Click on the Application Engine debugger by clicking once in the checkbox and then click the OK button to save your settings. If you had already launched the PeopleSoft Application, you would need to click Apply to change your settings for the already open application. Now, click OK in the Configuration Manager to save the profile changes. Your settings are now changed so that when you launch an Application Engine it will open in the debug option.

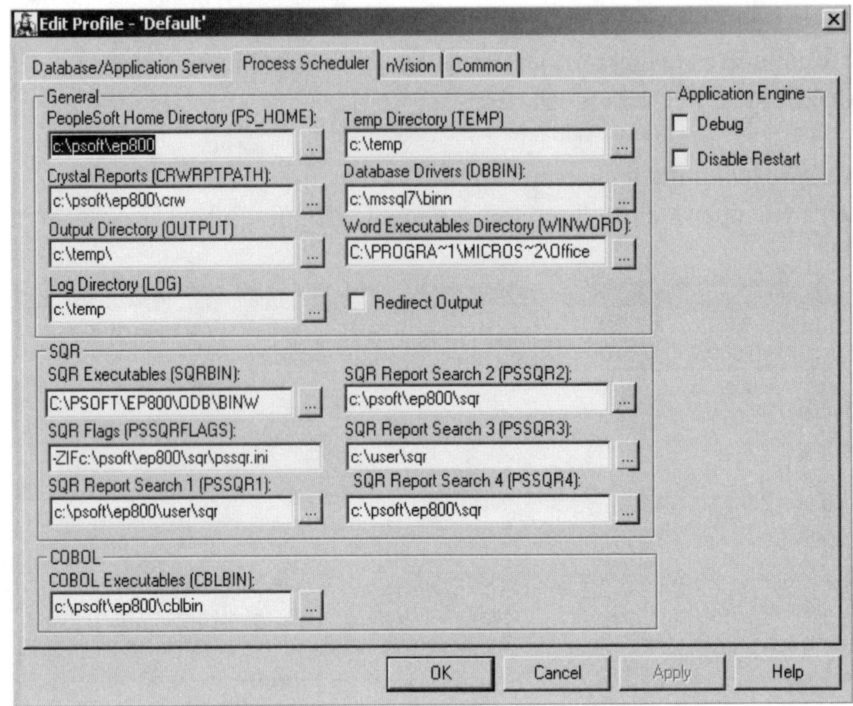

Figure 13.4 Configuration Manager – Process Scheduler tab

***Warning**: You have just set the debug option ON and now ALL Application Engine programs run on this client using the specified profile will start in debug mode.*

You can now open the PeopleSoft Application in two-tier mode to launch Application Engine programs to use the debugger if you run them on your client. You will have to use the Run icon on the two-tier application toolbar to launch the Application Engine program, not the new Run button on the page itself.

Command Line

This process allows you to launch your Application Engine program completely outside of PeopleSoft. This is a handy way to run

Application Engine program without having to create all the Run Control Records and Pages. You can also use this method to run an Application Engine program that does have a Run Control Record and Page but you have to understand that data will be expected in the Run Control Record, so your program may have unusual results if you have not loaded this information. You can also use this method to restart a failed Application Engine program.

Note: *To load the Run Control information, use the Internet client to access your Page just as if you were to run the program. Enter in all the necessary Run Control information and save. This will load the Run Control Record and now allow you to use the command line process.*

To start an Application Engine program using the Command line process, you first have to open the Command window. This depends on your windows operating system, but assuming you are using Windows you can do this by running a program called command.exe. You then need to type the statement into the command window to launch the Application Engine program.

The command string is the program name followed by a long string of parameters. You can type the parameters directly or use a text file. The command string is as follows:

```
psae {parameter string}
psae ${name of parameter string file}
```

The parameter list can contain many different settings. Some of these settings are required but others are optional. Review the following table for the full list of parameters.

Name	Value	Description
-CT	Database Type	Required. This is the database type name with only the following values allowed: MICROSFT, ORACLE, SYBASE, INFORMIX, DB2UNIX, and DB2
-CS	Server Name	Only required for Informix and Sybase. Server name for signon validation.
-CD	Database Name	Required. Name of the database to run the program against.

-CO	Operator ID	Required. Name of the operator that is running the program.
-CP	Operator Password	Required. Password of the operator that is running the program.
-R	Run Control ID	Required. Run Control ID value.
-AI	Application Engine program name	Required. Name of the Application Engine program to run.
-I	Process Instance	Required. Process Instance number to use. If not known, use 0 to have assigned next number. Default is 0.
-DEBUG	Yes/No	Optional. Setting to determine whether to launch program within debugger. Default is No.
-DR	Yes/No	Optional. Setting to disable restart. Yes means to disable restart. Default is No.
-TRACE	Number	Optional. Value to control the Application Engine trace. See Below (1)
-DBFLAGS	Number	Optional. Setting to disable the %UpdateStats meta-SQL construct. To disable use 1 otherwise 0.
-TOOLSTRACESQL	Number	Optional. Value to control the SQL trace. See Below (2)
-TOOLSTRACEPC	Number	Optional. Value to control the PeopleCode trace. See Below(3)

(1) Trace Parameter settings.
The value used here is a combination of the settings that you wish to activate.
1 – Activates the Step Trace
2 – Activates the SQL Trace
128 – Activates the Timing statements
256 – Activates the PeopleCode Detail Timing statements
1024 – Stores the Timing information into the results Record
2048 – Activates the database explain information output. This is valid only for Oracle, Informix and Microsoft database platforms.
4096 Stores the database explain information into the results Record. This is valid only for Oracle DB2 and Microsoft database platforms.

If you wish to activate 1, 2 and 128, then you would use a value of 131 (1+2+128).

(2)Tools Trace SQL

The value used here is a combination of the setting that you wish to activate.

1 – Show SQL statements processed
2 – Show SQL Statement variables
4 – Show connect, disconnect, commit and rollback commands
8 – Show Row Fetch (shows it occurred, not data)
16 – Show All other API calls except ssb
32 – Show Set Select Buffers (attributes of columns)
64 – Show Database API specific calls
128 – Show COBOL timing statements
256 – Show Sybase Bind information
512 – Show Sybase Fetch information
4096 – Show Manager information
8192 – Show Message Agent information

Most of these settings you will not use to perform a trace. You will mostly use the settings of 1, 2 and 4.

(3)Tools Trace PC (PeopleCode)

Again this setting is a value where you combine the features you want to show in the trace.

1 – Display all instructions
2 – List the program steps
4 – Show all variable assignments
8 – Show all fetched values
16 – Show stack usage
64 – Show start of all programs
128 – Show all external function calls
256 – Show all internal function calls
512 – Show all parameter values
1024 – Show all function return values
2048 – Show each statement in program

Here is an example of a complete Command line.

```
psae -ct MICROSFT -cd EPDMO -co VP1 -cp VP1 -r
 SS_RUN_IN -i 0 -ai SS_PO_LOAD -DEBUG Y
```

Application Engine Debugger Started

With all the parameters set and the Application Engine program launched on the client, the Debugger program starts. This program will open a DOS window on your client assuming you are running Windows. The Application Engine program will start and then hold, pending input from you at the First Step and Action. If you look at the DOS window you will see the following text.

```
PeopleTools 8.0 - Application Engine
Copyright (c) 1988-1999 PeopleSoft, Inc.
All Rights Reserved
Application Engine Debugger - enter command or type ?
for help.
SS_PO_LOAD.MAIN.INIT>
```

The first Action within your Application Engine program is now holding, pending your review. You have some commands you now need to supply to the debugger to tell it what to do. The basic command is "?; this will list all of your available commands. A description of each command follows so that you can determine what you need to do.

Note: *Each command is listed in Upper case but the debugger does not care about case, so either is valid here.*

B – (Break)

The Break command enables you to set a breakpoint within your program. This allows you to process through other lines of code without stopping until your breakpoint is reached. This is exactly the same process you will use to set break points within your PeopleCode, except here you can set where in your Application Engine program to set the break. This is a very effective technique when debugging a large Application Engine program.

When you issue the break command you are then offered sub-commands; Set, Unset or List.

S – (Set)
The Set sub-command allows you to set new break points. The debugger will ask you the program name, Section, and Step as to where to apply the break point. The debugger will assume that the current program name, Section and Step are to be activated but you can easily override. If you want to set the current program name, Section and Step, just type the enter key to each prompt.

```
SS_PO_LOAD.MAIN.INIT>B
(Set), (U)nset, or (L)ist? S
Program [SS_PO_LOAD]:
Section [MAIN]: PROCESS
Step    [INIT]: STEP03
Breakpoint set at SS_PO_LOAD.PROCESS.STEP03

SS_PO_LOAD.MAIN.INIT>
```

In the example listed here, you input the command B, followed by the subcommand of S (note that all of your entries have been underlined for the purpose of clarity). Then, the program asks for the program name, which you leave blank and type the enter key. This defaults in the value displayed in the square brackets. You could have assigned another program here as you remember that an Application Engine program can call another Application Engine program; so you may need to change this value in the future. Next, you enter in the Section of PROCESS and the Step of STEP03. The debugger program then displays where the break point has been set and is ready for another command.

U – (Unset)
This subcommand allows you to unset a break point. This is used when you determine the break point you were using is not the right one or you wish to change the focus of your debugging. Once you input the subcommand you will be given a numbered list of previously set breakpoints. All you have to do is to input the break point corresponding number and that break point will be removed.

```
SS_PO_LOAD.MAIN.INIT>B
(Set), (U)nset, or (L)ist? U
(1) SS_PO_LOAD.PROCESS.STEP03
(2) SS_PO_LOAD.PROCESS.STEP12
```

```
(3) SS_PO_LOAD.CLEANUP.STEP01
Remove which breakpoint? 2
```

This example will remove the breakpoint at SS_PO_LOAD . PROCESS . STEP12.

L – (List)
This command will list all available breakpoints.

```
SS_PO_LOAD.MAIN.INIT>B
(Set), (U)nset, or (L)ist? L
(1) SS_PO_LOAD.PROCESS.STEP03
(2) SS_PO_LOAD.CLEANUP.STEP01

SS_PO_LOAD.MAIN.INIT>
```

C – (Commit)

The Commit command forces a database commit to the system even if your program did not call for it. This is used so that all changes are committed, so that you can then use other programs to review the data in the actual database records. This command can only be given when the program has completed the entire Step (a Step may contain multiple Actions).

X – (Exit)

The Exit command will abort your running Application Engine program but prior to aborting it will force a database commit, so that all the work is saved. You can use this process to test your re-start logic as well as ending the program, so that you can use other programs to review the results and make any necessary changes. This command can only be given when the program has completed the entire Step.

You will be asked to confirm whether you wish to Exit and commit all of the work done so far. Enter Y to have the program commit and exit. If you enter N, then the debugger program will continue to wait for input.

See the command QUIT for another alternative for ending your program.

G – (Go)

The Go command tells the debugger to execute the next Action. The program will then run until the next breakpoint is encountered, the next watched field changes or the end of the program is reached. This command cannot be stopped (unless by a breakpoint or watched field change) so it should be used in concert with breakpoints and field changes or if you just want the program to complete.

L – (Look)

This command will display all values within a State Record (a.k.a. variables) associated with this program. This command will ask the State Record to display (the default will automatically be displayed) and then ask which field you want to display. The field list default is "*", which means to show all values.

```
SS_PO_LOAD.MAIN.INIT>L
Record Name [SS_PO_LOAD_AET]:
Field Name [*]:
SS_PO_LOAD_AET:
  PROCESS_INSTANCE     = 1183
  BUSINESS_UNIT        = 'US01'
  SETID                = 'MODEL'
SS_PO_LOAD.MAIN.INIT>
```

***Note**: Both of the values to input, Record Name and Field Name, allow the use of wild cards and partial input. "*" means to display all values and "SS*" means to display all values starting with SS.*

M – (Modify)

The Modify command allows you to change a value within a State Record that is associated to the running Application Engine program. This is used to correct a problem that you have discovered and you want to test out the remaining program to see whether the value is set correctly. This way you can continue to debug even if you have found one problem.

Once you issue this command, you will have to tell the debugger which AET Record and Field to use and then the value to change it to. This command will show you the current value so that you can make the correct determination of what the value should be.

```
SS_PO_LOAD.MAIN.INIT>M
Record Name [SS_PO_LOAD_AET]:
Field Name [none]: SETID
Current Value:  SS_PO_LOAD_AET.SETID = 'STD'
Enter new value (do not use quotes around text
strings):
MODEL
```

This example changes the value in the SETID field from STD to MODEL.

I – (Step Into)

The Step Into command allows you to start into the Step and stop prior to running the first Action. You can then review the State values or other parameters. If this command is used and you are within a Step, meaning that you are about to run an Action, this command will run that Action and then hold, pending the next Action or next Step. If the next Action to be run is a Call Section type and you use this command, you are taken to the new Section and stop at the first Step. Review the flow chart to help understand the use of Step Into.

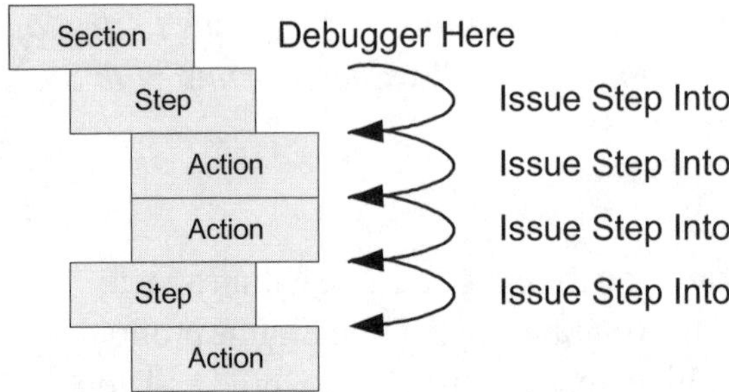

Figure 13.5 Step Into flow diagram

When you are stepping through a program this is the most commonly used command.

O – (Step Out of)

The Step Out of command is used commonly where you have entered into a Step to the Action level, meaning you have issued the Step into command once, and then you want to run all of the Action code within that one step without stopping. Once the next Step is encountered the debugger will hold, pending input.

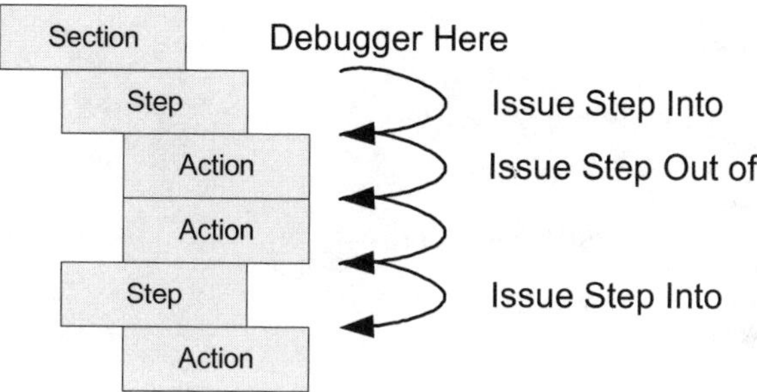

Figure 13.6 Step Out of flow diagram

If the Step Out of command is issued when the debugger is at the Step level, then all Steps and Actions are completed within the Section, as shown in the following diagram. If the Section is MAIN, then the program will complete just as if you had issued the GO command.

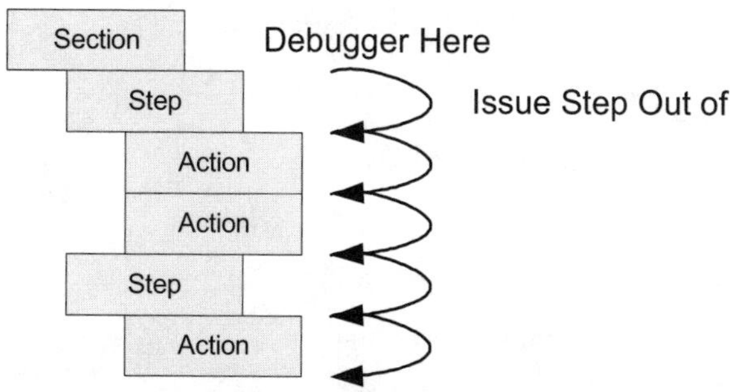

Figure 13.7 Step Out of flow diagram

***Note**: The Step Out of command can run multiple Steps and Action but if any of these have a breakpoint or there is a Watched field change, then the debugger will halt. The Step Out of command does not override these settings.*

S – (Step Over)

The Step Over command, if used from the Action level, will process the next Action and wait for input. If there are no more Actions, then the process is taken to the next Step and the debugger waits, as shown in the following diagram.

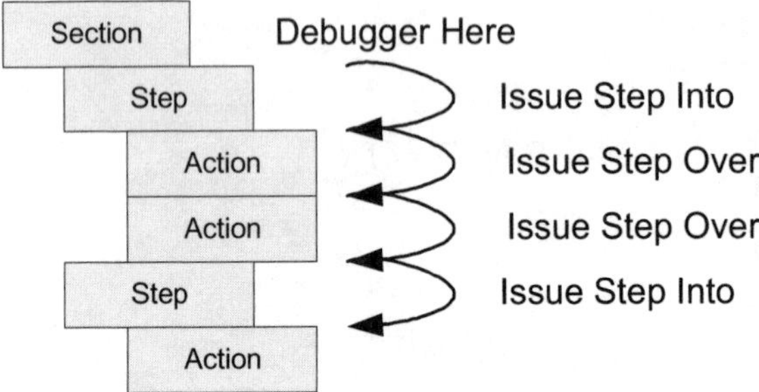

Figure 13.8 Step Over flow diagram

If the Step Over command is issued when at the Step level, then all of the Actions within the Step are executed and the debugger will then position at the next Step pending user input. If the process is at the end of a Section, the debugger will return to the calling Section pending the next command. Review the following flow diagram for review of the process.

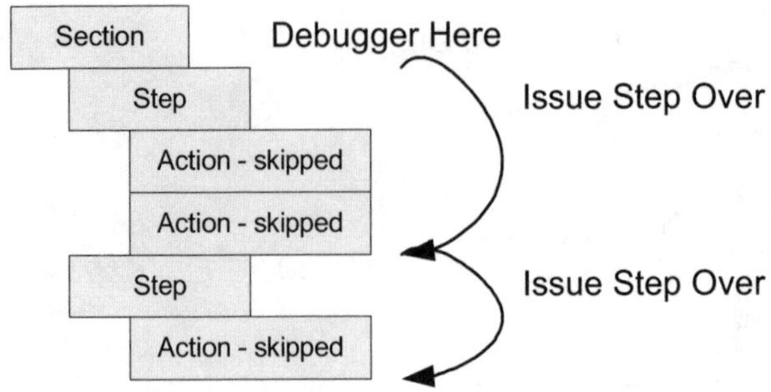

Figure 13.9 Step Over flow diagram

This command is similar to Step Into but allows you to process through an entire Step at once. This assumes you are not going to have any problems within the Step.

R – (Run to commit)

This command will act just like the GO command but will stop after the next database commit that you have set within your program. You can use this to quickly debug a program or review your database commit plan.

Q – (Quit)

The Quit command will abort your program and not force a database commit, so that all data will roll back to the last commit. This works very closely to the Exit command but without the database commit. You can use this to end a program to fix the problem and then restart, or to test out your restart logic and capability.

You will also be asked to confirm your selection in that you wish to rollback your data and exit the program. "Y" will exit the program and rollback while "N" will return the debugger to waiting for user input.

W – (Watch)

The Watch command allows you to define a field, within an AET Record assigned to this program, to be watched. Then, when this field value changes, the debugger will stop at the Action where the value changed. You will only see the changed value and your program will be stopped, pending your further command.

There is a set of sub-commands to make this command work; Set, Unset and List.

S – (Set)

The Set sub-command allows you to set a Watched field. The debugger will ask you the AET Record name and Field name as to where to apply the Watch. The debugger will assume the default AET Record but you can override it by typing in a new value. You will have to set the Field name as no default can be given.

```
SS_PO_LOAD.MAIN.INIT>W
(Set), (U)nset, or (L)ist? S
Record Name [SS_PO_LOAD_AET]:
Field Name [none]: SETID
Watch set on SS_PO_LOAD_AET.SETID

SS_PO_LOAD.MAIN.INIT>
```

In the example listed, a Watch is set on the field of SS_PO_LOAD_AET.SETID. Now, whenever this value changes from what it is currently defined, you will get a break in the program; meaning the debugger will stop the program so that you can review using the other debugger commands.

***Note**: You are not allowed to set a Watched field with the type of LONG.*

U – (Unset)

This subcommand allows you to unset a Watch. This is used when you determine the Watch you were using is not the right one or you no longer need it. Once you input the subcommand, you will be given a numbered list of previously set Watches. All you have to do is to input the Watch corresponding number and that Watch will be removed.

```
SS_PO_LOAD.MAIN.INIT>W
(Set), (U)nset, or (L)ist? U
(1) SS_PO_LOAD_AET.SETID              = 'MODEL'
(2) SS_PO_LOAD_AET.BUSINESS_UNIT      = 'US01'
Remove Watch on which field? 1
```

This example will remove the Watch on the Record SS_PO_LOAD_AET Field SETID.

L – (List)

This command will list all Watched Fields.

```
SS_PO_LOAD.MAIN.INIT>W
(Set), (U)nset, or (L)ist? L
(1) SS_PO_LOAD_AET.SETID              = 'MODEL'
(2) SS_PO_LOAD_AET.BUSINESS_UNIT      = 'US01'

SS_PO_LOAD.MAIN.INIT>
```

This completes the debugger for Application Engine. You will notice that there were a lot of settings talked about when running the Application Engine from the Command line. These trace commands are all covered in the next Section entitled "Tracing your Application Engine".

There is one more piece to cover in the debugging process and that is to go over the PeopleCode Debugger.

PeopleCode Debugger for Application Engine

To activate the PeopleCode debugger to trace your Application Engine program, you need to start PeopleTools using the same Operator ID that you will be using to launch the Application Engine program. This is necessary so that the Application Designer PeopleCode debugger can communicate with the Application Engine program.

Once you have logged onto the system in two-tier mode, you need to start the PeopleCode Debugger. You do this by selecting the menu:Debug – PeopleCode Debugger mode. This will start the process but now you have to tell it how you want to debug. You could have placed a break point in your Application Engine PeopleCode program or you can just have it trace from the start.

In either case, once the program starts, the tracing will begin. You can also have the debugging just output a trace file. All of this follows the standard PeopleSoft debugging which you should know already from developing with PeopleCode. If you do not yet have this experience, see the PeopleBooks or the book "Developing PeopleSoft Applications with PeopleTools 8.1" published in Feb 2002 by STARR Software Inc.

With the debugging process known for both the Application Engine and PeopleCode, you need to learn the batch-oriented process called tracing. Tracing involves printed or database record outputs of information. The tracing is faster yet not as dynamic. There are many levels of tracing and you need to learn how to read the output; this is all what is covered in the next section.

Tracing your Application Engine program

Tracing your Application Engine program can be done with the debugger you have just learned about or it can be used alone - most of the time it is used alone. It is primarily used to understand the performance of your program but it can also be helpful in understanding the program flow, based on real world conditions and data. The trace output has many components that you set up prior to running the Application Engine program. Each of these components is for a specific task so you need to learn each one, and it's specific capabilities. There are four components: Step Trace, SQL Trace, AE Timings, and Database Optimizer Trace.

***Warning**: Each of these component traces do affect the overall performance so should not be left on after the review is complete.*

Step Trace

You can use this trace component to see the path followed by your Application Engine program as it processes the logic using the data in the selected database. You can tell from the output which path or logic was taken including good and bad exits. It does not however tell you what the data was, just the path the program took.

This is best understood by reviewing a typical output.

```
PeopleTools 8.16 – Application Engine
Copyright (c) 1988-2002 PeopleSoft, Inc.
All Rights Reserved
Database: EPDMO8(SqlServer)
16.33.1 2002-07-12 Tracing Application Engine program
SS_PO_LOAD
```

```
16.33.1  . (SS_PO_LOAD.MAIN.Step01) (Call Section
                                      SS_PO_LOAD.INIT)
16.33.1  ..(SS_PO_LOAD.INIT.Step01) (SQL)
16.33.1  ..(SS_PO_LOAD.INIT.Step02) (SQL)
16.33.24 . (SS_PO_LOAD.MAIN.Step02) (Call Section
                                   SS_PO_LOAD.PROCESS)
16.33.24 ..(SS_PO_LOAD.PROCESS.Step01) (SQL)
16.33.24 ..(SS_PO_LOAD.PROCESS.Step02) (SQL)
16.33.2 ..(SS_PO_LOAD.PROCESSS.Step02) (Log Message)
16.33.3 . (SS_PO_LOAD.MAIN.Step03) (Call Section
                                     SS_POLOAD.CLEANUP)
```

This output follows a test Application Engine program using standard logic. The first three lines are just the standard output. The fourth line tells you the database being used and its type. The fifth line shows the time using the format of HH.MM.SS (H = Hour, M = Minute, S = Second) with the date and the name of the program being traced. Now you get into the meat of the trace. Each of the following lines is made up of sets of data.

First, is the time in the same format of line five. This is the start time and not the amount of time for a particular Step or Action. You can however make some base judgments about time, subtracting the next line from the line you are on to get how long a specific line took. This is not very accurate but you can get a good idea of what is going on. If you need more accurate timing, see the SQL Timings section below.

Next, you will find a series of period or dots. These periods show you the level you are on as you work through your Application Engine program. This example only goes through two levels. You can see the program starts at level 1 and then by calling a Section you move to a lower level, as shown in lines 6 to 7. Then when the Section is complete you move back to level one as is shown on lines 8 to 9.

The next set of data is the Application Engine program name (remember that you can call another Application Engine program so you do need to see this) with the Section and Step name separated by periods. The last set is the type of Action that was performed. If you look at lines 11 and 12 you will see the same program, Section and Step name but with a different Action type. This shows you how multiple Actions within a single Step are displayed.

SQL Output Trace

This component trace shows you the actual SQL statements used including bind variables, commits, and rollbacks. The output follows the program flow as each statement is processed. The output is easy to read, as is shown in the following example.

```
PeopleTools 8.16 – Application Engine
Copyright (c) 1988-2002 PeopleSoft, Inc.
All Rights Reserved
Database: EPDMO(SqlServer)

%Select(SS_POLOAD_AET.DOWNLOAD_TO_FILE,
SS_POLOAD_AET.BUSINESS_UNIT) SELECT DOWNLOAD_TO_FILE,
BUSINESS_UNIT FROM PS_RUN_CNTL_IN WHERE OPRID =
‘JWEESSIES’ AND RUN_CNTL_ID = ‘jawtest’
/
– Buffers:
–    1) Y
–    2) 00701
/
Restart Data CheckPointed
/
COMMIT
/
DELETE FROM PS_SS_POLOAD_DETTMP
/
DELETE FROM PS_SS_POLOAD_HDRTMP
/
Restart Data CheckPointed
/
COMMIT
/
INSERT INTO PS_SS_POLOAD_HDRTMP (PROCESS_INSTANCE,
BUSINESS_UNIT, ORDER_NO) SELECT DISTINCT 327556,
h.BUSINESS_UNIT, h.ORDER_NO FROM PS_SS_POLOAD_DETTMP
l WHERE l.ORD_LINE_STATUS <> ‘X’ AND
l.SCHED_ARRV_DTTM >= ‘2002-07-17 00:00:00.000’ AND
l.SCHED_ARRV_DTTM <= ‘2002-07-16 23:59:59.000’ AND
NOT EXISTS ( SELECT ‘X’ FROM PS_SS_ORD_HLD j WHERE
l.BUSINESS_UNIT = j.BUSINESS_UNIT AND l.ORDER_NO =
```

```
j.ORDER_NO AND j.EFF_STATUS = 'A' AND j.STATUS_DT <=
'2002-07-16' )
/
UPDATE PS_SS_POLOAD_HDRTMP SET RECV_DATE = ( SELECT
MAX(RECV_DATE) FROM PS_RECV_HDR  RECV WHERE
PS_SS_POLOAD_HDRTMP.BUSINESS_UNIT =
RECV.BUSINESS_UNIT AND PS_SS_POLOAD_HDRTMP.ORDER_NO =
RECV.PO_ID AND RECV.CANCEL_FLAG = 'N' ) WHERE
PROCESS_INSTANCE = 327556 AND EXISTS (SELECT 'X' FROM
PS_RECV_HDR  RECV WHERE
PS_SS_POLOAD_HDRTMP.BUSINESS_UNIT =
RECV.BUSINESS_UNIT AND PS_SS_POLOAD_HDRTMP.ORDER_NO =
RECV.PO_ID AND RECV.CANCEL_FLAG = 'N')
/
UPDATE PS_SS_POLOAD_HDRTMP SET RECV_QTY = ( SELECT
SUM(QUANTITY) FROM PS_RECV_LINE_SHIP  RECV WHERE
PS_SS_POLOAD_HDRTMP.BUSINESS_UNIT =
RECV.BUSINESS_UNIT AND PS_SS_POLOAD_HDRTMP.ORDER_NO =
RECV.PO_ID AND RECV.CANCEL_FLAG = 'N' ) WHERE
PROCESS_INSTANCE = 327556 AND EXISTS (SELECT 'X' FROM
PS_RECV_LINE_SHIP RECV WHERE
PS_SS_POLOAD_HDRTMP.BUSINESS_UNIT =
RECV.BUSINESS_UNIT AND PS_SS_POLOAD_HDRTMP.ORDER_NO =
RECV.PO_ID AND RECV.CANCEL_FLAG = 'N')
/
/
Restart Data CheckPointed
/
COMMIT
/
```

This example is just a portion of code to show most of the output. The first 4 lines you have seen before (in the Step Trace above) as to the copyright, name and database of the running Application Engine program. Then follows the SQL trace of the first Action. Note that you cannot tell which Action, Step or Section you are running. This is just the SQL output and why most developers will use the Step and SQL trace in combination.

The first SQL line is loading values into the bind variables. You will see the full SQL syntax including the PeopleSoft commands to load the bind variables. You will also note that in the where clause of this first SQL the %bind() constructs are not displayed but the actual value used. The trace option shows all of the resolved bind variables so that you do not have to determine them.

The next lines show the Buffers:. The Buffers: are values that are being stored into the bind variables so that you can see the resultant output of the SQL statement. In the example here, "Y" will be loaded into the bind variable DOWNLOAD_TO_FILE.

The next line shows a restart checkpoint that if the program fails after this line and no further commits are done, then the program will rollback to this point. The next line shows you the COMMIT processed to the database.

The next two lines are update statements. These statements are in separate Actions but you will notice that no Commits or Rollback information is in between them. This is due to the fact that the Application Engine program was developed so that no commits were done here. You can see that you move from SQL to SQL working through the statements.

After the two delete SQL statements, a commit is done and another rollback checkpoint is established. Three more SQL statements run showing inserts and updates to be done to your data, followed by the last commit.

This trace output is easy to read and very helpful in finding SQL errors in that it shows the resolved bind variables within each SQL statement.

AE Timings

This component trace captures and displays the time it takes to process your SQL statements, as well as PeopleCode Actions. This time is very accurate as compared to the simple Step Trace process listed above. You can use this data to find statements that are slowing down your program, causing bottlenecks or just finding the overall health of the Application Engine program.

It is recommended that you perform this trace on every Application Engine program that you create, at least once. The reason is that a good Application Engine program should not only work correctly but also perform quickly. This trace process will show each statement and the time it takes to complete. A test is also not complete with just a limited amount of data. You may need to load a large amount of data to simulate a real world situation. Hopefully, you will have access to a database, which has this data, or you can easily build the amount of data. You need to do this since SQL performance does not increase sequentially but rather exponentially. This means 100 rows processed in a test Application Engine program may take five minutes, you might then expect 200 rows to take ten minutes but it may end up taking 1 hour. This does not necessarily mean large amounts of data will take time, it means you need to review each SQL to see the impact on the real amount of data expected for your program.

There are a few concerns about this trace process. First, the timing numbers are rounded to the nearest tenth of a second for display but the total uses the true value before it is rounded, so that the total is an accurate value. Second, the trace does not work with the CallAppEngine PeopleCode launch process when you are sending the output to a Record. For a trace of an Application Engine program called with the CallAppEngine function, use the standard tracing for SQL and PeopleCode supplied via the Application Designer.

The timing trace process has two output formats. You can send the data to a standard output log, which you can display online; or you can send the data to a Record where you can report on it, or use any process to extract the data.

Online Display

This output is either sent to the report manager so that you can review this online in a Page, or to an output file. In either case, the output is the same. Below is an example of the format, to review and understand each section.

```
PeopleTools 8.16.03 - Application Engine
Copyright (c) 1988-2002 PeopleSoft, Inc.
All Rights Reserved
Database: EPDMO(SqlServer)
                          PeopleSoft Application Engine Timings
                                (All timings in seconds)
                                 2002-07-16  06.32.02
                          Compile    Execute    Fetch       Total
SQL Statement             Count Time Count Time Count Time  Time
------------ -- -- -- -- -- -- --

PeopleCode
SELECT PS_SS_POLOAD_DETTMP                   1  6.7 42853  7.3 14.0
SELECT PS_SS_POLOAD_HDRTMP                   1  0.0  2061  0.2  0.3
                                                                ---
                                                               14.3
Application Engine
CHKPOINT                     0  0.0     23  0.1     0  0.0  0.1
COMMIT                       0  0.0     23  0.4     0  0.0  0.4
LOGMSG                       0  0.0      2  0.2     0  0.0  0.2
                                                            ---
                                                            0.7
AE Program: SS_PO_LOAD
CLEANUP.Step01.S             1  0.0      1  0.0     0  0.0  0.0
CLEANUP.Step02.S             1  0.1      1 17.2     0  0.0 17.3
CLEANUP.Step03.S             1  0.0      1 10.8     0  0.0 10.8
CLEANUP.Step04.S             1  0.1      1  0.7     0  0.0  0.8
INIT.GETBIND2.S              1  0.0      1  0.0     1  0.0  0.0
INIT.GetRunDt.S              1  0.0      1  0.0     1  0.0  0.0
INIT.RmvRunDt.S              1  0.0      1  0.0     0  0.0  0.0
INIT.SetRunDt.S              1  0.0      1  0.0     0  0.0  0.0
SSUPDATE.Step01.S            1  0.1      1 15.6     0  0.0 15.7
SSUPDATE.Step02.S            1  0.1      1  5.8     0  0.0  5.8
SSUPDATE.Step03.S            1  0.0      1  0.5     0  0.0  0.5
                                                            ---
                                                          213.5
-----------------------------------
                             Call     Non-SQL  SQL      Total
PeopleCode                   Count    Time     Time     Time
------------ --- ---- ---- ----
AE Program: SS_PO_LOAD
INIT.DtrmnDat                    1        0.0       0.0       0.0
WRITEOUT.PRNTHDR                 1       26.3      14.3      40.6
                                      ---- ---- ----
                                         26.3      14.3      40.6
-----------------------------------
                                   E x e c u t e
PEOPLECODE Builtin/Method          Count    Time
------------------ --- ---
String(Type 1) BuiltIns             152163       4.1
Date(Type 2) BuiltIns                    8       0.0
Any(Type 4) BuiltIns                257113       6.3
Boolean(Type 5) BuiltIns                 1       0.0
DateTime(Type 11) BuiltIns              12       0.0
Integer(Type 17) BuiltIns               24       0.0
File(Type 129) Methods               87774       8.3
File(Type 129) BuiltIns                  1       0.0
SQL(Type 130) Methods                44914      13.3
SQL(Type 130) BuiltIns                   2       6.8
Record(Type 131) BuiltIns                2       0.4
-----------------------------------

Total run time                      :      257.9
Total time in application SQL       :      228.6
Percent time in application SQL     :       88.6%
Total time in PeopleCode            :       26.3
Percent time in PeopleCode          :       10.2%
Total time in cache                 :        2.7
Number of calls to cache            :          9

-----------------------------------

PeopleTools SQL Trace value: 0 (0)
PeopleTools PeopleCode Trace value: 0 (0)
Application Engine Trace value: 128 (0x80)
Application Engine DbFlags value: 0 (0)
```

Note*: This example is a reduced portion of an entire output so the totals will not match.*

To review this output you need to understand each section. The first section is called SQL Statement. This contains all of the SQL applied in your Application Engine. Within this section you will find three areas that cover the SQL as applied to PeopleCode, Application Engine database control commands and the SQL statements you wrote.

The PeopleCode area shows, here in this example, two select statements done to two different Record names. This area also reports the Execute and Fetch information. Compile time is not calculated here but is considered part of the Execute time. The Execute information shows the number of times the SQL was done and the time it took to complete. The time for an Execute is from the start of the SQL command until the set of information is built – that is the set of data is ready to be fetched. The Execution time is just the time it takes to gather the rows of data but not process through them. The Fetch count is the number of rows processed and the Fetch time is the time it took to process through all of the rows.

The next area shows the Application Engine database control commands such as the work done to make Restart checkpoints, database commits and any messages that were logged. Basically, this is the entire overhead necessary to run your Application Engine program. This area shows the Compile, Execute and Fetch information. The Compile information shows the number of times the SQL was compiled and how long it took the database to do so. Then, you have the Execute and Fetch, as explained in the PeopleCode area.

The last section is all of the SQL that you wrote into your Actions. You see each SQL with the name of the Section and Step followed by one letter showing the Action type. This area shows the Compile, Execute and Fetch values, as already explained.

Note: *The timing values are rounded to the nearest 10th but the totals use the full time value, so you can get an accurate number. This means that sometimes the numbers displayed here will not add up exactly.*

Note: *The timings here are not perfect since there is some extra overhead applied to perform the trace but this should be minimal.*

The next section is entitled PeopleCode. This section displays information about each Action that was called of the PeopleCode type. The output displays the number of times this Action was called, the time for non-SQL activity and the time for SQL.

PeopleCode Built/Method is the next section in this output. This section displays a summary of all generic method and built in functions. It's a simple summary to see where most of the PeopleCode time is spent.

The Summary section is where all of the total time is shown and compared for reference. A new value here is the Cache. Cache time and number is used when accessing any cache such as memory cache, file cache or database cache. Cache also includes resolving any Meta-SQL data. The time in cache is the amount of time it took processing to analyze, retrieve and ready the cache for use while the number of calls refers to how many times the cache was accessed.

The last section is the Environment. This shows you the settings of the trace values so that you can fully understand the overhead applied in creating this output file. You can also see which traces you were running, to verify you have all the information you need.

Record Storage

This output process allows you to store the information into defined PeopleSoft Records. This allows you to run reports or use other programs to report the data. You cannot only review one Application Engine program but you can compare many run times throughout a period of time. To best understand, review the list of Records that the information is loaded into.

PS_BAT_TIMINGS_LOG – stores the main information and the totals.
PS_BAT_TIMINGS_DTL – stores the detail information for every section.
PS_BAT_TIMINGS_FN – stores just the detail execute information.

The key to each Record is the Process Instance.

Warning: *Application Engine programs launched by the PeopleCode function CallAppEngine cannot have their timing information stored into the database since no Process Instance is assigned; and this is key to these Records.*

You can use these Records to create your own Report but PeopleSoft gives you a basic report already built. This SQR program is called BATTIMES.SQR. You can use this report to build on and create your own, or just use it as is.

To use the basic report as is, you need to launch the SQR program by using the menu: PeopleTools – Process Scheduler Manager – Use – Batch Timings.

You can also review online the batch timings for your Application Engine if you have turned on the process. This is seen from the Process Monitor when you click on the Details button. The details page will show a hyperlink called "Batch Timings" which will take you to a page to review that particular program's data that was stored when it ran.

Database Optimizer Trace

The database optimizer section works similarly to the Timings output in that you can store the information to a hard copy output or into a Record. There are some limitations, depending on your database platform, as to whether you can use the online output or the Record. There is also a concern with starting an Application Engine program via CallAppEngine. See the table below for the detail information.

Database	**Output**	**Record**	**PeopleCode**
SQL Server	Yes	Yes	No
DB2	No	Yes	No
Oracle	Yes	Yes	Partial *
Informix	Yes	No	Partial *
Sybase	No	No	No

* The issues with the PeopleCode are that you will get an output trace for all of the SQL that runs after the first SQL Action.

The process works specifically for each database platform so read each section below for your specific database.

SQL Server

The hard copy output will be sent to the database server in the directory %TEMP&\psms<queueid><spid>.trc

For the Record output, the data will be stored in the Record PS_OPTIMIZER_TRC.

For either of these traces, you will need to use the SQL Server profiler utility. For the hard copy output, after opening the SQL Server profiler utility, you need to use the menu: File – Open – Trace File. This will open the file so that you can review the data. For the Record output, you will need to define some parameters based on the Source Table window, as shown in figure 13.10.

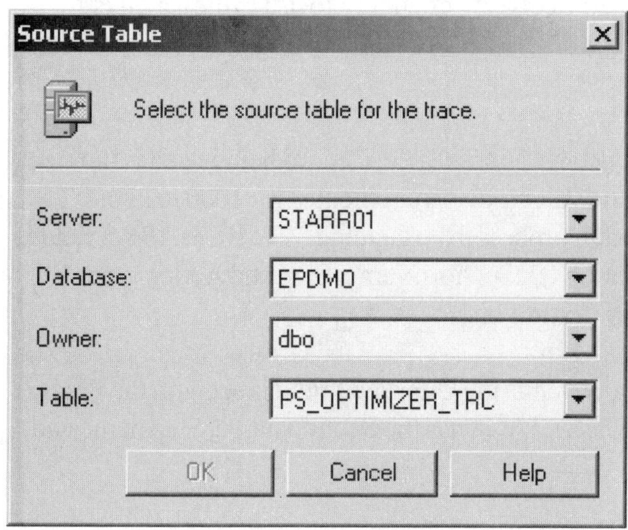

Figure 13.10 SQL Server profiler utility – Source Table window.

You need to define the server and database that you are using. The Owner and Table both need to be as displayed, as shown in figure 13.10. This will open the trace Record for you to review.

See Microsoft's SQL Sever Profiler Utility for more information on how to use this product.

There is a major issue if you are tracing that could lead to problems. If the Application Engine program crashes while you are tracing you need to review the trace output to verify whether the program was tracing a SQL statement at the time. If the program was, then you must kill the trace manually. If you do not, the SQL Server database will continue to trace and lock the trace file or Record, adding more and more information. To stop this trace you must use the following SQL Server command in Query Analyzer.

```
xp_trace_destroyqueue <queueid>
```

To determine the proper <queueid> you cannot just use the <queueid> that was listed in the file name. Each SQL statement processed creates its own <queueid>. You will have to use the SQL Server system administrator to find the correct <queueid> to use in the statement.

DB2

For the operating system of OS/390 the Record being used is the PLAN_TABLE. The QueryNo is incremented by 1000 to avoid clashing with any other process that is tracing. The REMARKS field is set with the Application ID, Section Name, Step and Action type followed by the Run Control ID.

For UDB operating systems, the QueryNO field is set with the Process Instance and the QUERYTAG with the Section name, Step name and SQL statement.

Oracle

The hard copy output writes to the default Oracle trace directory specified on the database server. To read this file you will need to use the TKPROF utility.

To use the Record output you will need to create the PLAN_TABLE with the statement_id field of varchar(254). For all the necessary information for creating this Record, PLAN_TABLE, see the Oracle documentation. The Record output also will not capture the optimizer plan for the %UpdateStats and %TruncateTable unless the %TruncateTable resolves to a SQL delete command.

Informix

Since Informix only allows the hard copy output, the only changes are based on the type of operation system. For Unix systems, the output is written to the sqexplain.out file. For NT systems, the file is written to %INFORMIXDIR%\sqexpln\username.out.

Controlling of the Database Optimizer process

Being that the Database optimizer requires working with your database server as well as PeopleSoft, additional controls have been given to prevent unwise use of this setting.

If you use the Internet client following the menu: PeopleTools – Utilities – Use – PeopleTools Options, this will take you to a page, as shown in figure 13.11.

Home > PeopleTools > Utilities > Use > PeopleTools Options

PeopleTools Options

Language Settings

Language Code: English
Translations Change Last Updated Information

General Options

Disconnect Cursors After: 30 Seconds (0 = Never)
Temp Table Instances (Total): 3
Temp Table Instances (Online): 3
Multi-Company Organization
Multi-Currency
*Maximum App Message Size: 10,000,000
Use Business Unit in nVision
Multiple Jobs Allowed
Base Time Zone: PST
Allow DB Optimizer Trace
Last Help Context # Used: 2245
Grant Access
Platform Compatibility Mode
*Data Field Length Checking: Others
Style Sheet Name: PSSTYLEDEF

Help Options

F1 Help URL:
Ctrl-F1 Help URL:

Save

Figure 13.11 PeopleTools Options

On this page there is a setting called Allow DB Optimizer Trace. This setting will control, for a database, if the database optimizer trace can be done. If the value is not checked here, then you are not able to run the database optimizer no matter the settings in any of the methods in starting Application Engine programs.

This allows the system administrator to block the database optimizer process for any reason. This is typically done on production databases.

Turning on Application Engine Tracing

Now that you have learned about all the types of Application Engine tracing, you need to know how turn on and off the tracing. As with the debugger you learned about earlier, how you start your Application Engine programs define where you need to set up some values to perform the type of tracing you desire. You can launch this via the Command line, Two-tier access, Three-tier access and through the Internet client. The tracing process allows you to easily modify some parameters in the Process Scheduler and Application Server to allow three-tier and Internet client access that you did not have with the debugger program. All of these launch processes are discussed in the following sections.

Command Line

You have already learned about this process in the Application Engine Debugger section above. The only new item is how to turn on and off the trace process.

```
psae -ct MICROSFT -cd EPDMO -co VP1 -cp VP1 -r
  SS_RUN_IN -i 0 -ai SS_PO_LOAD - TRACE 131
```

Assuming this sample of code, you are launching the Application Engine program called SS_PO_LOAD with the Trace turned on. The Trace will perform the Step Trace, SQL Trace and display the Timing statements.

In case you have forgotten, here are the settings for the Trace parameter.

Trace Parameter settings

The value used here is a combination of the settings that you wish to activate.

1 – Activates the Step Trace
2 – Activates the SQL Trace
128 – Activates the Timing statements
256 – Activates the PeopleCode Detail Timing statements
1024 – Stores the Timing information into the results Record

2048 – Activates the database explain information output. This is valid only for Oracle, Informix and Microsoft database platforms.
4096 Stores the database explain information into the results Record. This is valid only for Oracle DB2 and Microsoft database platforms.

Once you launch your program, the trace will be output to a file or stored in the Record, as defined by your parameter.

If you wish to not trace this Application Engine program where you may have the trace turned on via other methods (the ones listed below), you need to define the trace parameter as 0. This will force the trace off, no matter the other settings.

Two-Tier

The two-tier method requires you to set the Configuration Manager prior to running your Application Engine program. This is similar to the two-tier debugging process but you need to go to a new panel. Once you have your Configuration Manager open, you need to click over to the Trace tab, as shown in figure 13.12.

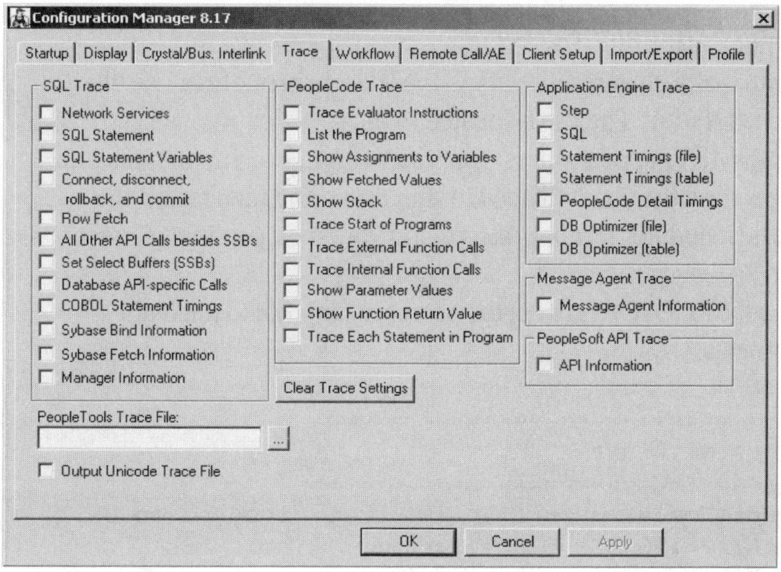

Figure 13.12 Configuration Manager – Trace tab.

Review the group area entitled – Application Engine Trace. This is where you can turn on and off via the checkboxes for each type of trace you wish to perform. Remember that specific databases may not be able to perform the type of traces you ask.

Once you have your settings entered, click the Apply button if your PeopleSoft client is already open, or click the OK button to save your settings. Then, open your PeopleSoft client if it is not already and launch your Application Engine program. The trace will complete as you have defined.

Three-Tier and Internet Client

The Three-Tier and Internet client are set up the same. They both require the change of settings on either the Process Scheduler or the Application Server. You can make the changes directly in the configuration file or use the PSADMIN program. The PSADMIN program is used by your system administrator in configuring your Application and Process Schedule servers.

Process Scheduler Server

You can make changes directly to the file – psprcs.cfg or use the PSADMIN tool. The file is located in the %PSHOME%\appserv\prcs\<prcs server name>. If you make the changes directly, you will need to shut down and then restart the Process Scheduler server to start using your new parameter's settings.

Locate the [TRACE] area in the psprcscfg.cfg file to make the adjustments.

```
[Trace]
;=================================
; Trace settings
;=================================
; PeopleTools trace file (NT only, ignored on UNIX)
TraceFile=%PS_SERVDIR%\logs\PeopleTools.trc
TraceSQL=0
TracePC=0
TraceAE=0
```

You will want to make changes to the TRACEAE setting, using the value table below.

Value	Description
1	Trace STEP execution sequence to AET file
2	Trace Application SQL statements to AET file
128	Timings Report to AET file
256	Method/BuiltIn detail instead of summary in AET Timings Report
1024	Timings Report to tables
2048	DB optimizer trace to file
4096	DB optimizer trace to tables

You add up the values for the type of tracing you wish to perform and place that number in the TRACEAE value, as shown below.

```
TraceAE=3
```

This example will perform the Step and SQL traces to the standard online file.

***Warning**: The TRACEFILE setting does not control the Application Engine Trace output. See the section below entitled "Locating the Trace File" for information on where to locate the actual output.*

The use of the PSADMIN program is not going to be taught here as system administrators, not developers, use this tool. If you need to use this program, contact your system administrator for help.

Application Server

The application server controls are on the psappsrv.cfg file located in the %PSHOME%\appsrv\<app server name\. As with the Process Scheduler server, if you change the file directly you will need to stop and restart the Application server to have your changes take affect.

Locate the [TRACE] area in the psappsrv.cfg file to make the adjustments.

```
[Trace]
;=========================================
; Server Trace settings
;=========================================
TraceSql=0
TraceSqlMask=12319
TracePC=0
TracePCMask=4095
TracePPR=0
TracePPRMask=4095
TraceAE=0
Write crash dump to separate file=Y
```

Modify the setting of TRACEAE using the values in the table below.

Value	Description
1	Trace STEP execution sequence to AET file
2	Trace Application SQL statements to AET file
128	Timings Report to AET file
256	Method/BuiltIn detail instead of summary in AET Timings Report
1024	Timings Report to tables
2048	DB optimizer trace to file
4096	DB optimizer trace to tables

Again, you add the values to get the setting you wish.

You can also use the PSADMIN tool to make the changes as well. Either case will work but be sure to work with your system administrator, so that you do not adversely affect your production environment.

Locating the Trace File

The trace file for Application Engine programs do not follow the standard trace process where you can define the name within the Process Scheduler server configuration file, Application server configuration file or Configuration manager. The file output is based on how you launched the program and on what platform it is running.

Client workstation
%UserTemp%\PS\<database name>\
CallAppEngine PeopleCode on NT
%SystemTemp%\PS\<database name>\
CallAppEngine PeopleCode on Unix
$PS_HOME/log/<database name>/
Command line on NT
%SystemTemp%\PS\<database name>\
Command line on UNIX
$PS_HOME/log /<database name>/
Three-tier or Internet client
Log/Output Directory as defined by the Process Scheduler configuration file.

To review the Process Scheduler directory, you open the psprcs.cfg file and locate the Process Scheduler section. In this section there is a value called Log/Output Directory. This is where you input the value to have the files output directory defined. A sample is shown below.

```
[Process Scheduler]
;=========================================
; General settings for the Process Scheduler
;=========================================
ProgramName=PSPRCSRV
PrcsServerName=PSNT
DBBIN=c:\MSSQL7\Binn
Max Reconnect Attempt=12
Reconnection Interval=300
Log/Output Directory=%PS_SERVDIR%\log_output
```

The file name always starts with "AE_" and ends with ".AET". Then depending whether a Process Instance was used, the name would be:

AE_<program name>_<process instance>.AET
AE_SSPOLOAD_37115.AET

If no process instance was used, such as in the case of running via the command line, then the name would be:

AE_<datetime stamp>_<os_pid>.AET
AE_0717150901_1080.AET

Note: *the datetime stamp is in the format of mmddhhmmss.*

Next

This completes all the information in regards to the tracing and debugging of Application Engine programs. There was a lot to cover to show all the various sections, areas and ways to process. Do not worry if you cannot remember them all for you can always refer back to this book. You will also find that you will only use one or two ways most of the time and so you will become very familiar with it and be able to do your job.

The next chapter covers any special issues involved with re-starting an Application Engine program. There are a few rules to learn to help this process along. You will need to re-start an Application Engine once you are developing these programs, as there are always failures. You can use the information here to debug the process and once you fix the program, you can restart to complete your program.

Chapter 14

How to Restart Application Engine programs

Application Engine has a unique ability, some developers would call this a liability, in that when a program aborts, crashes or halts for any reason, it holds the status of the program run. This allows the program to be restarted where it ended which gives both positive and negative issues. You will learn in this chapter about these issues, both positive and negative, as well as how to restart the Application Engine program. A frank discussion on Application Engine restart ability will be given as well to show ways to develop and write your program. You will also learn how to enable and turn off the Restart process, since that needs to be done first that is what you will learn next.

Setting the Restart Process

As a default, all Application Engines are set up to allow restart. Only under specific circumstances should you not allow your Application Engines to restart. Some of these reasons may be: your program is performing row by row processing, your program needs to be ultra fast and you do not want the overhead of applying restart checkpoints or your program is doing looping logic with commits after every 'X' number of loops. These are just some of the reasons why you might want to force the restart off.

If you had previously turned off the restart ability and now need to turn it back on, you first need to open your Application Engine program in the Application Designer work area. Click on the menu: File – Object Properties or use the toolbar properties button, as you have seen in Chapter 11. This will open the Application Engine Properties window, as shown in figure 14.1.

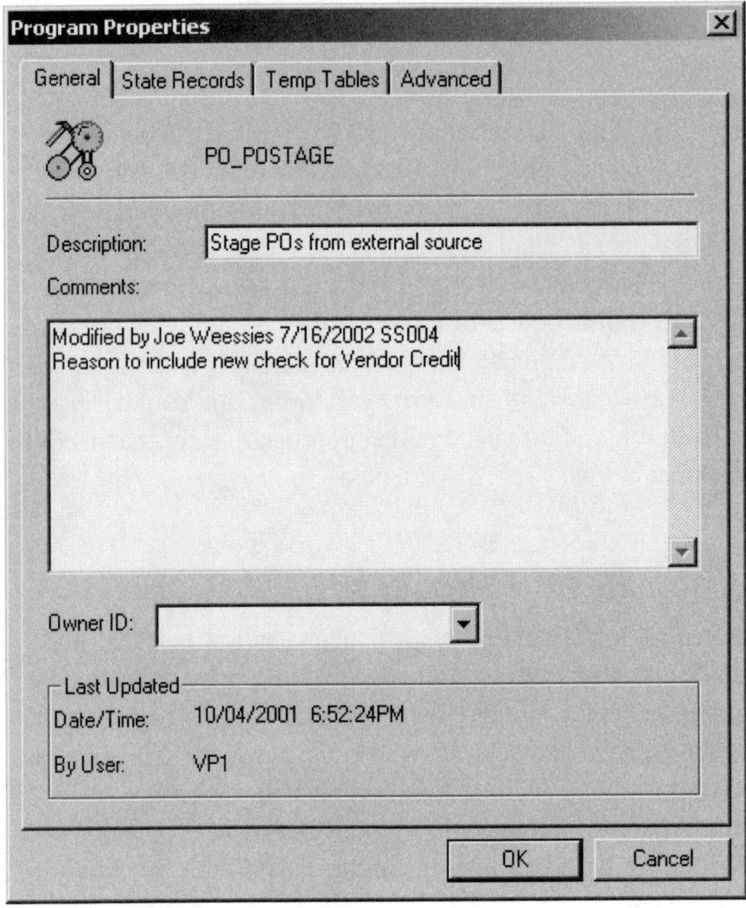

Figure 14.1 Application Engine Properties

You then click on the Advanced tab to show the advance settings, as shown in figure 14.2.

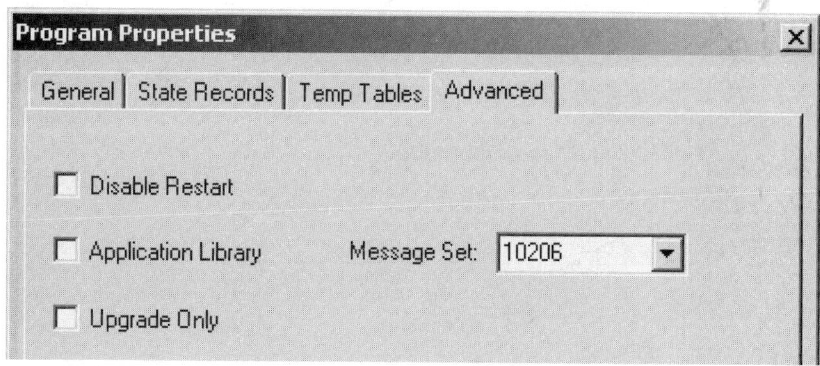

Figure 14.2 Application Engine Properties – Advanced tab

The checkbox marked Disable Restart in the example here is unchecked; meaning that this Application Engine program is allowed to restart. You have to make sure this checkbox is unchecked to enable or allow the restart ability of Application Engine. If you check this box you have just set this program to not allow restart.

This is normally all you would have to do but if you are running Application Engine programs in two-tier you will have to make sure that your Configuration Manager also has this setting turned off. If either one, being the Configuration Manager setting or the Application Engine properties, is set to disable restart then your Application Engine program will NOT be allowed to restart.

To set Disable Restart in the Configuration Manger, launch the Configuration Manager program. Next click on the profile tab. Select the profile under which you want to be sure that your Application Engine program will allow restart, and then click the Edit button. This will open the Profile Editor window you have already seen back in Chapter 13. Now click on the Process Scheduler tab and you will see the window, as shown in figure 14.3.

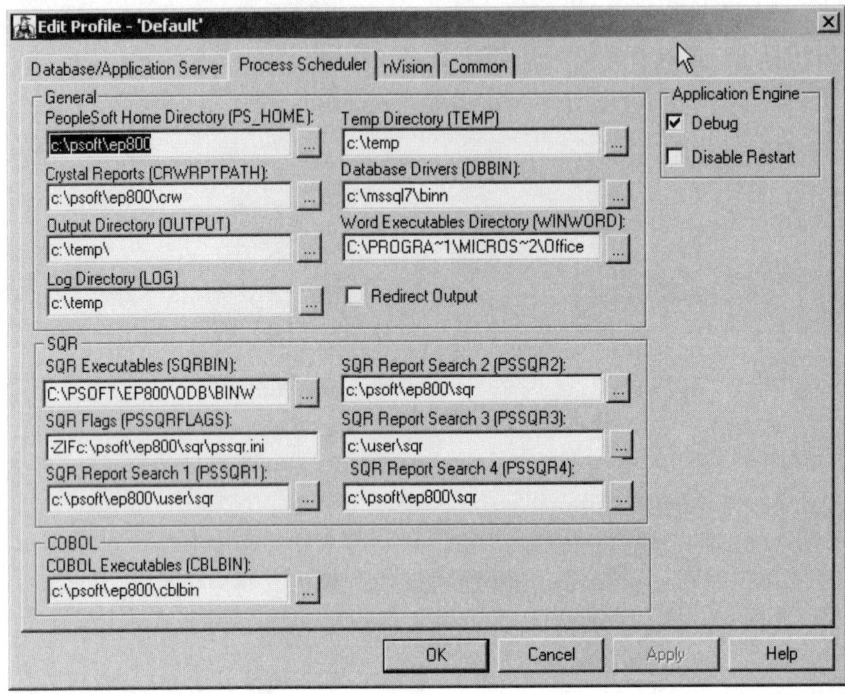

Figure 14.3 Profile Editor – Process Scheduler tab

In the upper right corner there are two settings for Application Engine. You have already learned about the Debug setting in Chapter 13 but the other setting, Disable Restart, is the one you are concerned about now. In this example, the setting is off; meaning that any programs run on this client will be allowed to restart. You can just easily click in the checkbox and then any Application Engine program running on this client would not allow restart.

The last way to control the restart ability is if you launch Application Engine programs via a command. All of the controls for the command were given in Chapter 13 but to set the Disable Restart to Y you would issue the following typical command.

```
psae -ct MICROSFT -cd EPDMO -co VP1 -cp VP1 -r
 SS_RUN_IN -i 0 -ai SS_PO_LOAD -DEBUG Y -DR Y
```

This is a sample launch of a program but note the last parameters given (-DR Y). This is the parameter that sets the Disable Restart to Y; meaning that this program is not allowed to restart. A value of N can be supplied, meaning to allow restart, but mostly developers would just not include the parameter, since the default is N.

As with the Configuration Manager and the Application Engine properties, setting a value of Y for the Disable Restart works the same as the command line. If any Disable Restart parameter used is found to be Y, then the Application Engine program is not allowed to be restarted.

If you leave the Disable Restart flag on, you can still restart your Application Engine program using the Command line but you do not start where you left off. The Disable Restart forces the program to begin all over again at the beginning. It is like the program has never run. This can cause you issues if you decide to leave the Disable Restart flag on and you perform commits within your Application Engine program. Data will be saved half done and then the program will restart from the beginning, and causing data to be processed twice.

A special note should be made that turning on the Disable Restart does not prevent you from still processing commits within your Application Engine program. The commits will still perform as intended; it is just that the restart checkpoint process will not be done. If the program does abort, then you will have data potentially in a partially completed process. This is why it is imperative you study carefully and make your decision, knowing the issues and concerns.

***Warning**: If you try to restart an Application Engine where the Disable Restart is set to "Y", you will receive a "bad restart" error in the Process Monitor.*

What Happens When Application Engine Aborts?

If your Application Engine program aborts, there are two levels to be concerned about. First there is the abort where you program gets the status of ERROR on the Process Monitor. The other abort is where the program stops processing and the error was unable to be trapped by the system. These un-trapped errors leave the Application Engine with a status of PROCESSING in the Process Monitor.

Error aborts are due to three reasons: SQL code errors where you have set the Action control of On Error to Abort, PeopleCode errors where you have set the Action control of On Return to Abort and SQL statements that returned, updated or inserted 0 rows of data where the Action control of No Rows was set to Abort.

Un-trapped aborts are caused by all other problems including, but not limited to: DBA kills the process, memory violation, database crash, process server crash, network problems, etc. These errors are beyond the ability of PeopleSoft to trap since they can be caused by many different factors.

Once your program does abort, a series of things happen. This is not listed in any specific order. This abort example also assumes you have not turned on the Disable Restart.

- The Process Monitor is updated with the an error status if PeopleSoft captures the abort.
- The database will roll back all of the database inserts and updates to the last time a commit was done.
- Any SQL select pointers are dropped (so you cannot restart on a specific row of data in the middle of a SQL select as an example).
- PS_AERUNCONTROL Record is updated and committed with the last checkpoint.

The PS_AERUNCONTROL Record is where all Application Engine programs store the information about where the program was last check pointed. This Record holds the information about where the program will restart. You can use this information to change the restart point or review the status.

When you want to restart your Application Engine program, it will use this Record to find the begin point and it will start processing there. All previous Sections, Steps and Actions will not be done but are essentially skipped over, starting at the last commit.

When your program aborts, there are a few issues to go over to make sure you understand the full ramifications of your program being in a restartable state. There are some positives and negatives that you need to learn.

In this Record, PS_AERUNCONTROL, you will also find the value for AE_CRITICAL_PHASE. This is the setting on the Section controls called Section Type that you learned back in earlier chapters. There is no reason why you would treat an abort differently when the Section is critical or not. This is just a key indicator to let you know the severity of the problem.

Negative Issues

Once your program aborts, the Run Control ID that was used to launch the program is now in a locked state. You cannot use this Run Control ID to launch this specific Application Engine program again until you have either cleaned out the abort or you have restarted and successfully completed the program. You can use this Run Control ID for other Application Engine programs and other processes as well. This may seem a small point but if you understand how users operate, this can be a big issue. Users tend to use the same Run Control ID for launching a specific program over and over. This is because by using the same Run Control ID, all of the parameters are already set up. Do not be surprised that you will encounter the situation where a user has run an Application Engine program that aborted and they immediately launch the same program again using the same Run Control ID.

Since the program has halted, your staging Records may be full of data. If you have not programmed your Application Engine to take into account multiple instances running, having a half completed program can be a problem to other programs.

If an Application Engine program does have an abort, then only that Run Control ID is held. While this one Run Control ID is held, other users, or even the same user if using a new Run Control ID, can still launch this specific program. An abort does not stop the programming from being launched again and again.

Positive Issues

With your program aborted, it is held in partially complete status. This means there are Sections, Steps and Actions that will not have to be run again since they had no errors. This allows you to fix the problem and restart your Application Engine program right where it left off. This saves a lot of valuable processing time and speeds up the process for the user who may be waiting for the data output.

Not only does your program hold, but the database is committed as well so that you can see the actual data the program is about to use. This helps immensely with debugging and finding the root cause problem.

Restarting Application Engine programs

Assuming your program has stopped and if it allows to be restarted, there are two ways to restart your program: through the Process Monitor or via the command line.

Warning: *It is assumed that you have fixed the problem that caused the abort in the first place. If you have not, the program will just Error out as before.*

Process Monitor

The Process Monitor is typically used by the users to restart their failed Application Engine programs. You, the developer, can also use the Process Monitor to see and update other user's process information, but you will have to have the security settings allowing you to do this. To restart a failed Application Engine program, you first need to open the Process Monitor page by using the Internet client menu: PeopleTools – Process Monitor – Inquire – Process Requests, as shown in figure 14.4.

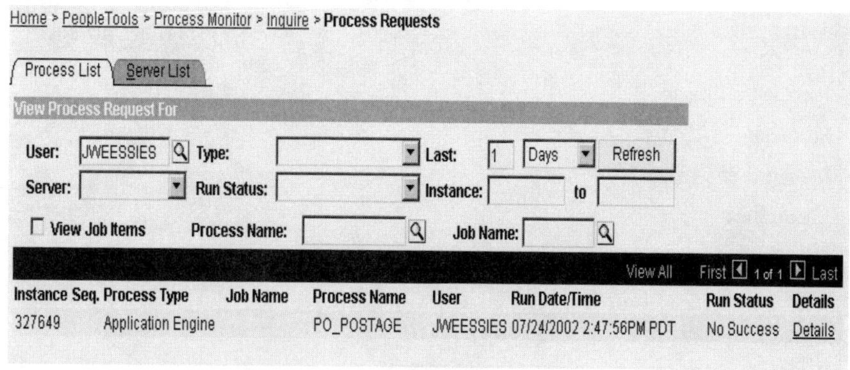

Figure 14.4 Process Monitor

Click on the hyperlink of Details. This will take you to the Page, as shown in figure 14.5.

This is where you make the changes to either Delete or Restart the process. If you choose to delete, then the process request is removed from the Process Monitor and PeopleTools Records are updated allowing you to re-use the Run Control ID again. This Delete process does not clear up any database commits or roll back the program to the start. You should only Delete Application Engine programs where you are sure there will either not have any problems with data left partially complete, or the program never committed and so has rolled back to the beginning already. Normally, you would click the Restart radio button. After making your selection on the Radio button, you click the OK button and your program will either be Deleted or Restarted, as you have selected. It is possible that your Application Engine program will restart and then fail at a later step due to another problem. PeopleSoft does not have any limit on the number of times a restart can be done.

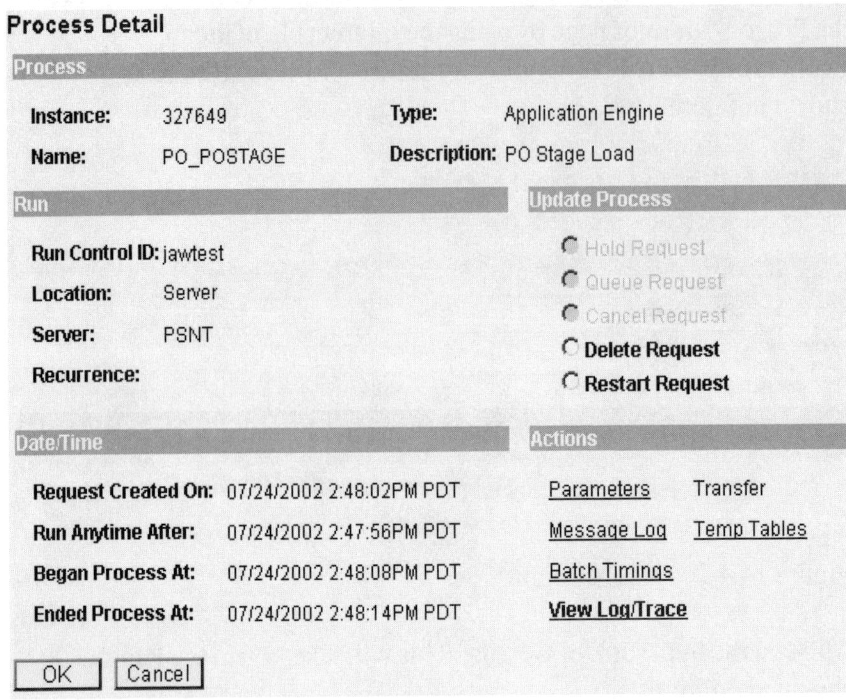

Figure 14.5 Process Monitor Detail Page

***Note**: If you launched the Application Engine via two-tier connection onto your client, you will need to use the two-tier access to restart. Restarting Application Engines via the Internet client can only process those programs, which were run on the Process Scheduler servers.*

Command Line

This is a more technical process to restart and usually takes some special operating system knowledge. This is typically used by the system administrators and some developers to launch and also restart failed Application Engine programs. This process allows you to launch the Application Engine program in a different location. Where the Process Monitor will launch the program via where it was run, the command line allows you to restart a program on the server where it was originally launched on the client, and visa versa.

To use the command line, it requires that you collect some information upfront. You will need to know the database type, database name, Operator ID, password of the Operator, Run Control ID, Application Engine program name and the Process Instance. All of these values can be found within the Process Monitor. If your Application Engine program was not launched via the Process Scheduler, such as you used the command line, then you will have to find these out manually.

You use the same command line parameters that you learned about in Chapter 13 (review Chapter 13 Debugging for all information needed). Here, is a sample of a typical command line.

```
psae -ct MICROSFT -cd EPDMO -co VP1 -cp VP1 -r
  SS_RUN_IN -i 33784 -ai SS_PO_LOAD
```

You do not need to do anything else as the program will launch and use the PS_AERUNCONTROL Record to restart at the specific location necessary.

Developing for Restart

If you allow restart, and most Application Engine programs will, you need to be aware of some issues with restart and how it handles specific issues. You need to know this so you can write your Application Engine program to be able to handle these issues. This means you need to anticipate program errors occurring at any point within your program. You are not concerned with how and why the error occurs, you will for fixing the error later, but only that if it occurs how is your program going to react when it is restarted. You need to be aware of this issue at every Section, Step and Action.

You, as the developer, have to write your program knowing when your commits are occurring and where potential problems could occur leaving you with data half processed. You have to plan for this event knowing how commits are done and how the restart is processed.

When your Application Engine program first starts, a new row is created within your State Record(s) using the Process Instance as the key. Then, every time a commit is done, this specific row is updated and stored to the database. If the program completes with SUCCESS, then the row is deleted from the State Record(s). If the program ERRORS out, the State Record(s) are not deleted but left in the last commit condition. This way when the restart happens, all of the data, (State Records, standard Records and Temporary Tables), are in a condition in sync with each other. If, however, you had used a Derived type of Record for your State Record(s) you have a new issue to contend with.

Every time a commit is done, Derived type State Records are re-initialized to a blank state. This also happens when an abort occurs within an Application Engine program. If you are on Step3 when the abort occurs and your last commit was right after Step2, your program will restart on Step3 but any value in the Derived State Record will be blank; and this could cause problems. To counter this issue, you must have at least one State Record be a standard Record type to maintain any values necessary upon an abort or you will have to create a process where after every commit you re-build your Derived State Record.

You can also have issues if you use the Action type of Do Select. This type retrieves rows of data from a SQL select statement. Each row is then processed as required. If in the middle of the processing an abort happens where you had a commit occurring within the loop, you may have an issue when the program is restarted. A restart will not pick up where it left off within the loop. It will use the original SQL select statement and if you had not planned on this occurrence, you could cause more problems or even have the program abort again. It is good programming to include an Action where you update a status flag on the original select row to show that the row has been processed. Then, in your Do Select SQL statement, you would include this status flag with the off condition in the where clause.

How to Start Over

There may come a time in your development where you have an Application Engine program that has aborted. You could restart but you do not want to for various reasons. These reasons could include: the user cannot restart the process, you need to fix some earlier Steps and Actions to have the program work correctly or the process was launched via the command line and the parameters were forgotten. No matter the reason, you need to be able to reset the Run Control so that you can use it again.

You can do this through the Process Monitor by going to the Detail page. You can click on the Cancel radio button and then click the OK button (review figure 14.5 for reference). Once this is done, the Delete radio button becomes active. You can then click the Delete radio button and then the OK button to have the Run Control ID deleted from the process Records. This will allow the Run Control ID to be used again.

If you are unable to use the Process Monitor, you can also perform these same actions manually via a third party SQL product. You will want to run the three following SQL statements.

```
Delete from PS_AE_RUN_CONTROL
Where Oprid = 'JWEESSIES' and RUN_CNTL_ID =
'jawtest99'

Delete from PS_AERUNCONTROL
Where PROCESS_INSTANCE = 33718
  and Oprid = 'JWEESSIES' and RUN_CNTL_ID =
'jawtest99'


Delete from PS_SS_POLOAD_TMP
Where PROCESS_INSTANCE = 33718
```

The first SQL goes to the Run Control Record for all Application Engine programs. The second statement cleans out the "memory" of where the last Application Engine program last committed. This second step is not mandatory but it is recommended, since this clears out a Record of bad information. The last statement can be one more many depending on the number of standard Records you have. This example shows clearing one standard Record. You will need to clean all of the standard Records since having a row of data in this Record is not normal unless you are going to restart. If you did not use standard Record but used Temporary Tables, you will have to clean these Records as well – see Chapter 5 on Temporary Records to review the Records to be cleaned.

Next

The last chapter of this book covers the new features in 8.4. While the book was being completed, a new release by PeopleSoft was being released. Rather than ignore the new release, a special chapter was added to show the differences; and there are a few. The main being that the window client is no longer active. Depending on your situation, you may need the 8.4 differences or you may be able to just use the 8.16 version. In either case, it is good knowledge to have as you build your skills within PeopleTools.

Chapter 15

Updates to Application Engine version 8.4

This book was written based on PeopleTools version 8.16. PeopleSoft, in March of 2002, released a new updated version – PeopleTools 8.4. This new release contains a number of improvements to Application Engine and they are all listed here.

Tuxedo Service

Application Engine is now a Tuxedo service. This was done to increase performance in that the program itself (Application Engine) does not have to start and stop. Performance is also increased by use of memory caching for the program and the variables used within the program. This saves on trips to the database to read the next line of the program or store the last variable.

PeopleCode: Exit function

The exit function within PeopleCode now requires the use of only a numeric value. True or False Boolean values that were allowed in earlier versions are no longer allowed.

PeopleCode: Database Commit Required

Two functions and one method used within PeopleCode now require that you commit all changes prior to using them. These are: StoreSQL function, DeleteSQL function and AESection.Save method. This is required due to locking on specific PeopleSoft tools tables. This will prevent other processes and users from progressing within the system. They may be stopped by being a deadlock victim.

PeopleCode: Declaring Variables

You are now required to declare all variables in PeopleCode. If you do not, then the editor will issue a warning message.

PeopleCode: FieldChange and Database Updates

The PeopleCode FieldChange event now allows you to perform database changes (inserts or updates) from Record, SQL Objects and Application Engine programs. At the end of the FieldChange event, all database updates and inserts are committed to the database. This capability is new for Record and SQL objects. Application Engine programs, however, performed a commit once the program completed, if the program was launched using the function of CallAppEngine PeopleCode. With the release of version 8.4, some minor changes may need to be made to your PeopleCode within the FieldChange event for this new capability to work properly.

In a FieldChange event, if a database change is followed by a think-time function, a user interaction such as a Secondary Page or an Error Message, then the changes must be committed by the use of the CommitWork function. The CommitWork function must be issued between the database change and the think-time function. This also now allows the use of more than one CallAppEngine function within a single FieldChange event by issuing a CommitWork between each CallAppEngine. See a simple example below.

```
CallAppEngine("MYAPPID1", &strecord1, &strecord2);
   CommitWork();
CallAppEngine("MYAPPID2", &strecord1, &strecord2);
   CommitWork();
CallAppEngine("MYAPPID3", &strecord1, &strecord2);
   CommitWork();
```

Warning: *If you fail to place the CommitWork function properly within the FieldChange event, you will receive a runtime error.*

If you are upgrading to PeopleSoft version 8.4 and you have CallAppEngine calls in FieldChange events, you will need to review your code for this situation and correct this with the insertion of CommitWork() functions.

Note: To find and fix PeopleCode in your system, you can run the process to compile all PeopleCode. The output of this process will be a listing of all invalid statements that you can easily change to the required value.

Application Engine Property Field: Program Type

There is a new field in the Application Engine properties panel called Program Type. It is found on the "Advanced" tab of the program properties dialog box. There are five values to select from, as follows.

Standard

This setting is for standard Application Engine programs. This is the setting you will use most and is the default.

Upgrade Only

This setting is used for PeopleSoft upgrade programs. This setting allows you to understand that this Application Engine program is only to be run for an upgrade process.

Import Only

This setting is used for special import utilities.

Daemon Only

This is a new type of Application Engine program that works with the new Daemon process. The Daemon process runs continuously within the Process Scheduler Server. It is called PSDAEMON. This Daemon process polls the system looking for specific conditions and if True, launches a defined Application Engine program group that you set up to respond to this condition. A group is one or more Application Engine program that run in a serial fashion. Such an Application

Engine program must have a type of "Daemon Only" to be assigned to a group.

Transform Only

This type of program is used in connection with PeopleSoft's new Integration Broker. It is covered in PeopleBooks on Integration Broker. This type of program is used for XSLT transformation programming, data translation and filtering. This program type is used to translate the data from a proprietary format to your internal format so that you only have to make one program to load the data. You can then create as many transform programs as necessary to handle just the data translation.

Application Engine Property Field: Batch Only

Applications Engine has a new property called "Batch Only". You will want to select this option for any Application Engine program that is intended only for running in batch mode and is using Temporary Tables. This means this program will never be launched using the CallAppEngine PeopleCode function. When this option is selected, online instances of Temporary Tables are not created. This is done to save tablespace within the database and reduce the overhead for maintaining Records that will never be used.

Review your custom Application Engine programs to see where this new property ought to be turned on. It does not hurt your Application Engine program if you leave this setting turned off. You will just have extra Records within the database.

Temporary Table Statistics

There are now new statistics shown regarding Temporary Tables, which is found at the menu: PeopleTools – Application Engine – Inquire – Review Temporary Table Usage. Where you would have found only one Page you will now find two. The first Page, "Temp Table Usage by Record" is the same as it was in Version 8. This Page is fully described in Chapter 5. The second Page, "Temp Table Settings by Program" is a totally new Page.

The Temporary Table Settings by Program Page shows the following information by Application Engine program name: Total Instances, Batch Only, Abort Flag and Disable Restart. Total Instances is the number of instances for the Record searched. Batch Only, Abort Flag and Disable Restart are the Application Engine property settings for the program displayed. The View Records hyperlink will take you back to the Record Page (first Page).

Application Engine Called from COBOL

PeopleSoft is continuing in the direction of replacing its COBOL programs with Application Engine programs. In version 8.4, PeopleSoft has added capability for COBOL programs to call Application Engine programs to help achieve this goal. This is as easy as adding a new COBOL include file (PTCCBLAE.CBL) to your COBOL program and supplying some variables. This is all fully explained in the PeopleBooks for version 8.4.

Process Monitor Details Page

On the Process Monitor Details Page under the Run section for an App Engine process, there is a new field called Current Step. While your App Engine has a status of Processing, this field will display the current Section, Step and Action of the program. This way you can verify where an Application Engine program is at and if it is still progressing through more Steps (you will have to refresh on the main Process Monitor Page to do this).

Process Scheduler: Process Type

There is also a new process type – Optimization Engine. This is an Application Engine program but has some special PeopleCode, which is using the new Optimization logic. This type has the same parameters as a standard Application Engine type but this new type is needed to allow the program to run under the USS.

Data Mover: Temporary Record command

Data Mover has a new command "CREATE_TEMP_TABLE". This is used to create Temporary Tables used by Application Engine. If you need to have Data Mover create Temporary Tables, you can now use this new command to perform the process to build the correct number of Temporary Tables, as defined by your system. This way you do not need to build each Record but can issue the one command, and have the correct number of Records built with the correct name.

File Layout Object

Creating a File Layout object for an Input process allows you to automatically build an Application Engine including the PeopleCode. There used to be a tool called Import Manager that would do this, but that tool has been discontinued. This new capability has been added to fulfill this role.

To have this process work, you need to create your File Layout object. It is very important that your flat file matches the Record and Field names within the File Layout object as well as the order. The data formats too must match from the flat file to the File Layout object. It is also assumed that each Record within the flat file ends with a new line character. The File Layout object is also assumed to only contain those Fields within the flat file, this means that no extra Fields exist within the File Layout object. The flat file however can contain extra fields.

This type of import typically only works on a single Record and not a set of Parent and Child Records. In fact you are not allowed to use the Rowset process to input in from the flat file and the File Layout object must have only one Record at the lowest level in this import process. You could however write and process your own Application Engine to do this. Do not think you cannot create a multi-level File Layout object, it is just that you will only be able to load one Record at a time. In fact, you may want to create a multi-level File Layout object so that you can define Inheritance and defaults to accurately reflect the data.

Previewing Flat File data

Once you have your File layout object created and you have your flat file, you can run a preview of the data load. With the File Layout object open in Application Designer, click on the Preview tab. This will show a panel with a lot of blank fields. You now need to define the location and name of the flat file you are going to use. Click the browse button in the upper right corner and find your flat file. Click the OK button when found.

Next, you will select the Record segment that corresponds to the flat file you are going to be previewing. Use the Segment name drop down field to set the correct segment and this will fill in the Field information for the File Layout object. If you now click on the Refresh button on the main toolbar, the preview area will fill in with data based on the flat file and the segment you have selected. Of course, it will only fill in if the selected segment matches the data within the flat file.

Note: *XML type File Layout objects cannot be previewed.*

If you need to make some minor adjustments, you can click on a Field name within the segment list and then make changes directly here to see the results instantly.

Running the Import process

Once your File Layout object is accurate, you then click on the AE button on the main toolbar. This will create a fully capable Application Engine program to read the flat file and load into the File Layout segment you have defined. This will open a panel where you have to input the Application Engine program name because it is automatically saved.

Now all you have to do is to click on the Run Program button in the main toolbar. This will launch the Application Engine program on your PC and start the import process.

Windows Client

This feature of PeopleSoft has been turned off completely. You are now no longer allowed to use the Windows client to access your Menus, Components and Pages; you will have to use the Internet client. This does not affect the Application Designer, which remains a Windows program. This does, however, affect your capability to trace and debug. You cannot launch an Application Engine program via the Windows client to have it run on your local PC and use the step tracing feature. You can launch using the command line process on a server and trace from there, or use the Process Scheduler settings.

Application Engine Testing

You can now launch Application Engine programs directly from the Application Designer for purposes of testing your program. The only requirement is that you have signed in using two-tier mode and you have your Application Engine program open in the work area. To launch your program, click the menu: Edit – Run Program. This will open a special Run Control panel. Here, you will enter the Run Control ID for the program to use. Since most Application Engine programs start off this way, it is expected that you will have this data already set up within your system. You could have done this from the Page that normally launches this Application Engine program, or you could manually add the data to the Run Control Record with a specified Run Control Id. You can also select whether the Application Engine program is to be launch minimized (your program will start in two-tier mode on your PC). You can also set if your program is to output a log file and where this log file is to be stored. The last parameter is the Process Instance to use. Since this program is being launched via the command line, you need to supply this information so that it will run correctly. Just click the OK button to launch your Application Engine program.

Next

Congratulations! You have completed Developing with PeopleSoft's Application Engine 8. There is an appendix to read that goes through the simple step of attaching an Application Engine program to a Page, in case you needed a refresher. The authors hope you enjoyed learning this enhanced tool and that the book will serve as a guide that you will continue to use in the future.

If you have found errors or have questions on anything within this book, you can email the authors at authors@starrsoftware.com. Your questions will be answered promptly. Also review the STARR Software Inc. web site (www.starrsoftware.com) for corrections on this book as well as new and upcoming books on the suite of PeopleSoft PeopleTools.

Appendix A

How to Connect an Application Engine Program to a Page

The purpose of this Appendix is to show you how to setup your Application Engine Program to run as a batch program through the Process Scheduler. This entails other parts of PeopleTools outside of the Application Engine designer, such as creating a Record, Page, etc. This appendix expects that you already have some familiarity with these tools and is not meant as a tutorial or a replacement for complete text describing these tools. For a full description of PeopleTools, a recommended book is "Developing PeopleSoft Applications with PeopleTools 8.1" by Joe Weessies.

This appendix is meant as a quick guide giving the overall steps necessary to setup and run your Application Engine programs.

Creating a Run Control Record

If your Application Engine program has user-supplied parameters, then a Record is needed to store these parameters. If your program has no parameters then you can skip this step. The Run Control record is always keyed by OPRID and RUN_CONTROL_ID. The additional fields on the record are the parameter fields, in this example BUSINESS_UNIT and AS_OF_DATE. Replace these fields with the actual parameter fields of your program. Since an Application Engine program running in the Process scheduler always knows its own runtime OPRID and RUN_CONTROL_ID, this will allow you to write the code to read this record and get the parameter values for your program.

By standard PeopleSoft convention, the Record name is "RUN_" followed by the name of your Application Engine program. In this example the Application Engine program name is MYAPP, so the record name is RUN_MYAPP.

Record Name: RUN_MYPGM

Fieldname	Type	Length	Parameters
OPRID	Char	30	Key
RUN_CONTROL_ID	Char	30	Key
BUSINESS_UNIT	Char	5	
AS_OF_DATE	Date	10	

Create this as a Table in Application Designer and then build it.

Creating a Run Control Page

Your next step is to create a page to run your Application Engine program. Create this as a standard Page in Application Designer. The naming convention here is the same as for a Run Control Record: "RUN_" followed by the name of your Application Engine program. In this example it is named RUN_MYAPP.

The first object to add to your page is a Sub-Page called PRCSRUNCNTL_SBP or any one of its variants such as PRCSRUNCNTL_LC_SBP that also contains the Language controls if you need it. If your program has no parameters then this is all that you need. If you do have parameters then drag them from your Run Control Record onto this new page as shown in figure A.1. Save the page and go onto the next step.

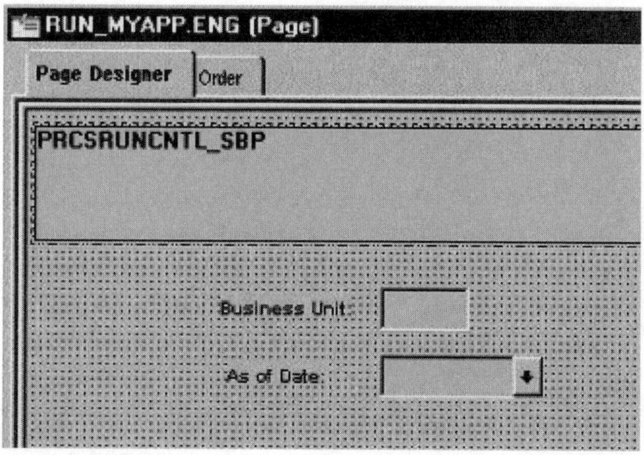

RUN_MYAPP.ENG (Page)

Page Designer | Order

PRCSRUNCNTL_SBP

Business Unit:

As of Date:

Figure A.1 Page

Adding a Page to a Component

The next task is to create a Component and add your Page to it. Again by convention this will have the same name as the Page and Record: RUN_MYAPP. When you drag the Page onto the Component it will look like figure A.2.

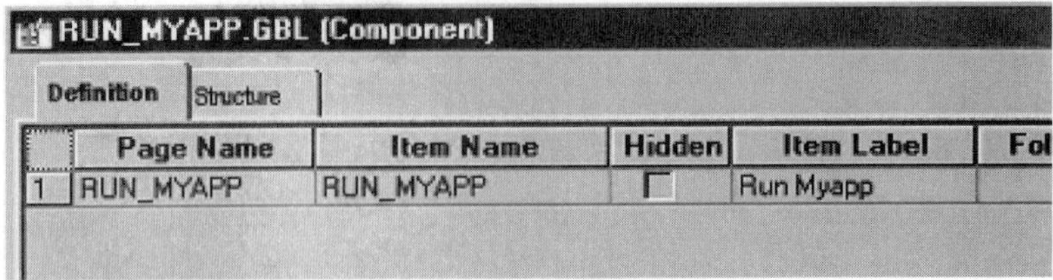

Figure A.2 Component

In the Component properties check the Add and Update/Display Actions. Enter PRCSRUNCNTL as the Search record, as shown in figure A.3. Be sure to save the Component.

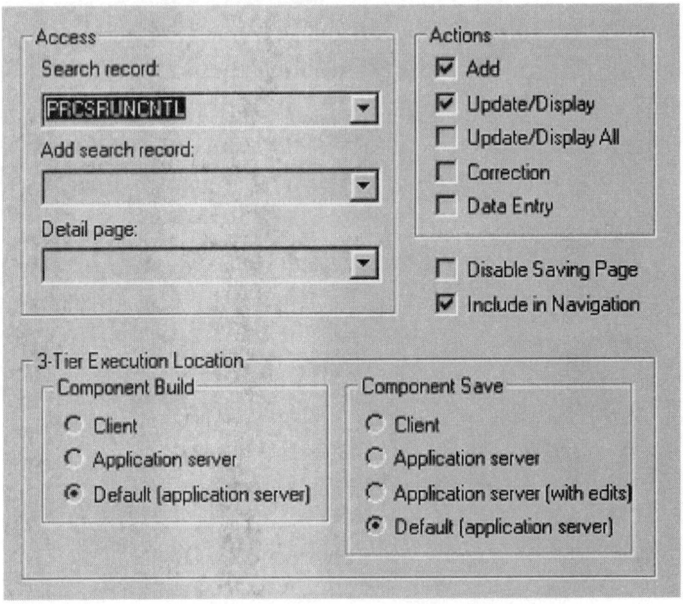

Figure A.3 Component Properties

Adding the Component to a Menu

In Application Designer, open the Menu from which you would like this program to run. When you drag your component onto the Menu under "Process" it automatically loads onto the Menu. You may double click your new Menu item to modify the label, as shown in figure A.4.

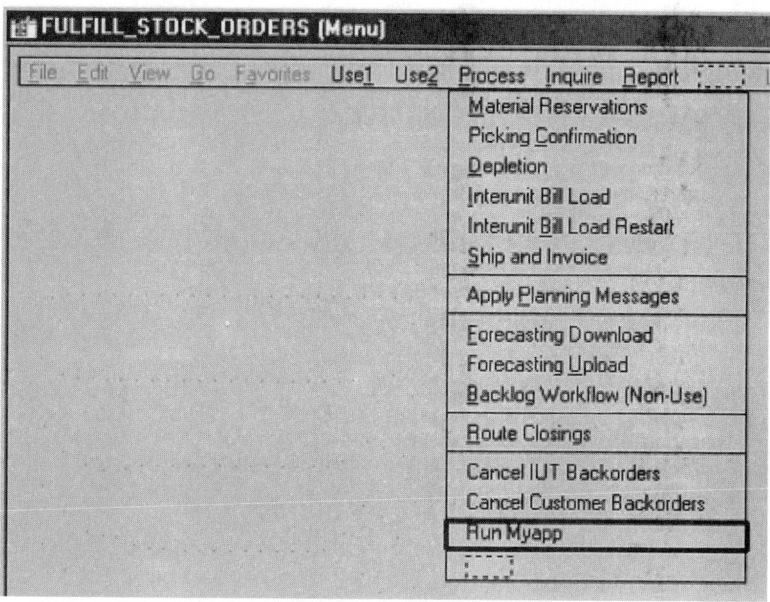

Figure A.4 Menu

Assigning Security

This new Menu entry will not show on the menu at runtime until Security is assigned. Navigate, using the Internet client, to the menu: PeopleTools – Maintain Security – Use – Permission lists. Select a Permission List that is associated to a Role or User ID that will be used to run this program. In a development database (not your Production environment), a handy permission list to use is ALLPNLS. Select the Pages tab and locate the name of the Menu where you added your Component. Click on the Edit Components hyperlink next to the Menu name. Then click on the Edit Pages hyperlink next to your new Menu entry. This will open the Page as shown in figure A.5.

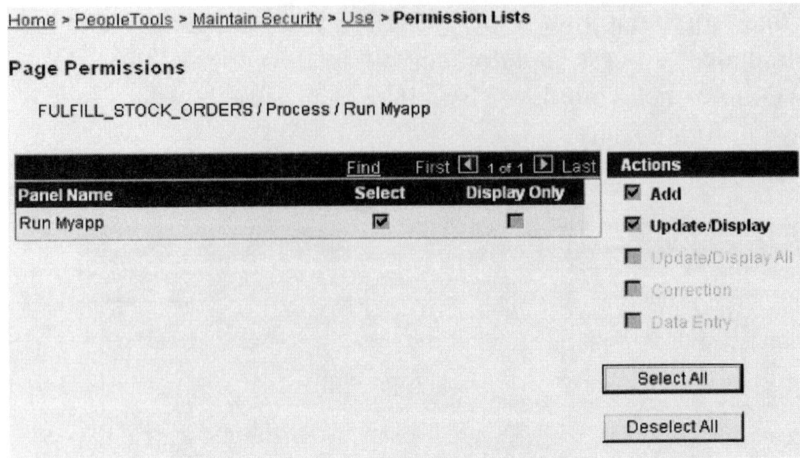

Figure A.5 Page Permissions for RUN_MYAPP

Be sure to save your Security changes.

Now Sign Out and Sign back in. Your new menu entry is now available, as shown in figure A.6.

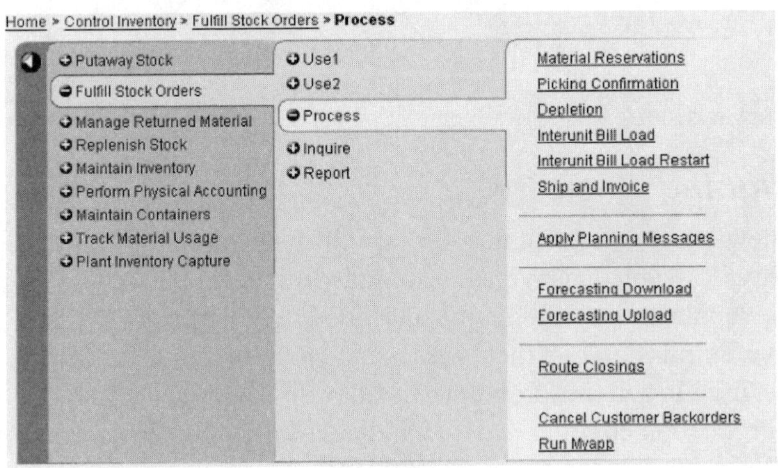

Figure A.6 New Menu Installed

Creating the Process Definition

The last setup step is to create a Process Definition for your new Application Engine Program. Using the Internet client menu: PeopleTools – Process Scheduler Manager –Use – Process Definitions to open the Page. You will then need to click on the hyperlink Add a New Value to be taken to the Add Page, as shown in figure A7.

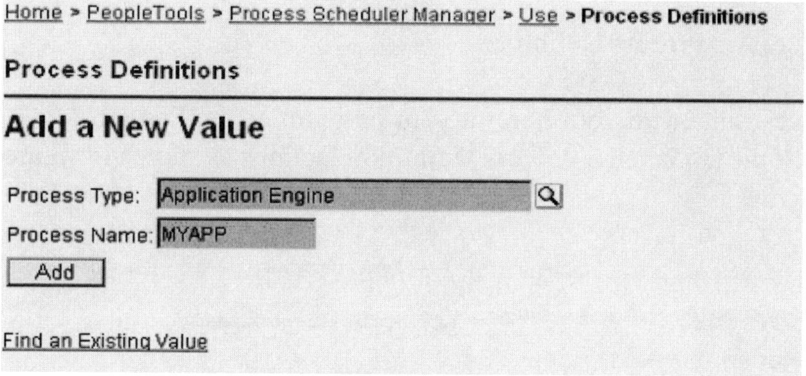

Home > PeopleTools > Process Scheduler Manager > Use > **Process Definitions**

Process Definitions

Add a New Value

Process Type: Application Engine

Process Name: MYAPP

Add

Find an Existing Value

Figure A.7 Process Definition Entry

Under Process Type enter "Application Engine". It must be spelled exactly including upper and lower case. You can also do it the easy way by entering "A", clicking on the search button and then selecting "Application Engine". Enter your new Application Engine program name in the Process Name field and click the Add Button. This will take you to the Page shown in figure A.8.

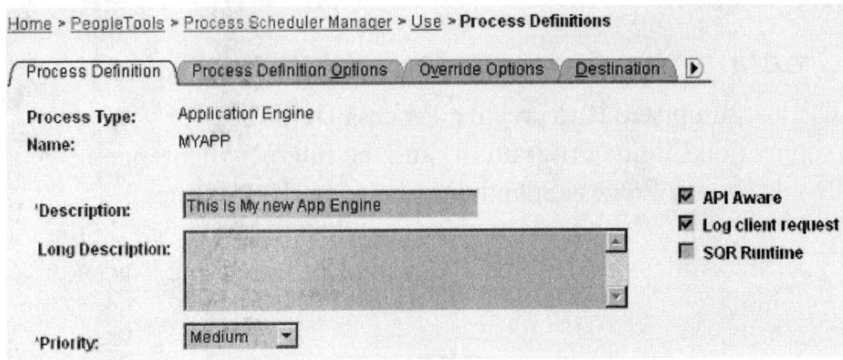

Figure A.8 Process Definition

Enter a suitable description for your program on the first tab. Click the tab labeled Process Definition Options as shown in figure A.9.

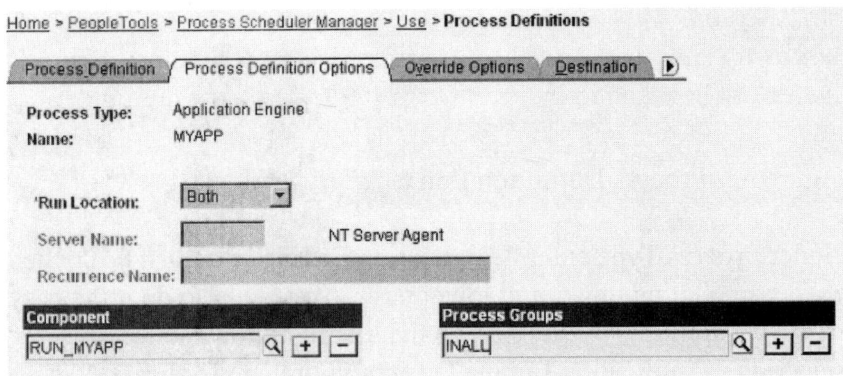

Figure A.9 Process Definition – Options tab

Under Component, enter the name of your new Component. This is what ties your program to your new Component and Page. Under Process Groups enter a suitable security value. For Inventory programs, INALL is commonly used. Click Save.

Starting your Application Engine Program

To launch your Application Engine program, navigate to your new Menu. Enter an existing Run Control or create a new one as shown in figure A.10.

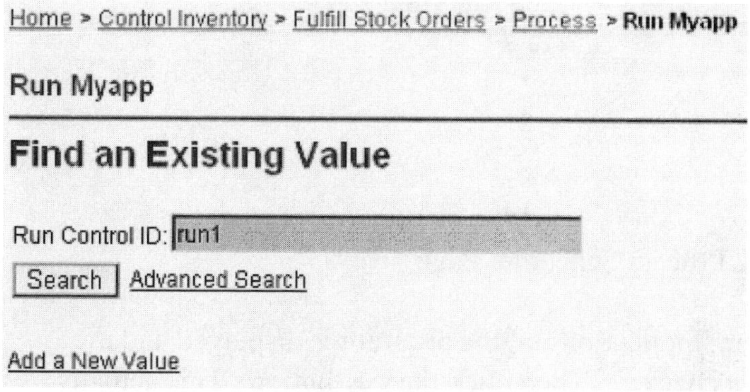

Home > Control Inventory > Fulfill Stock Orders > Process > Run Myapp
Run Myapp
Find an Existing Value
Run Control ID: run1
Search
Advanced Search
Add a New Value

Figure A.10 Run Control Entry

Once you have found your Run Control ID, click the Search or Add buttons to be taken to the Run Control Page as shown in figure A.11.

Home > Control Inventory > Fulfill Stock Orders > Process > Run Myapp
Run Myapp
Run Control ID: run1
Report Manager
Process Monitor
Run
Business Unit: 001
As of Date: 10-18-2002

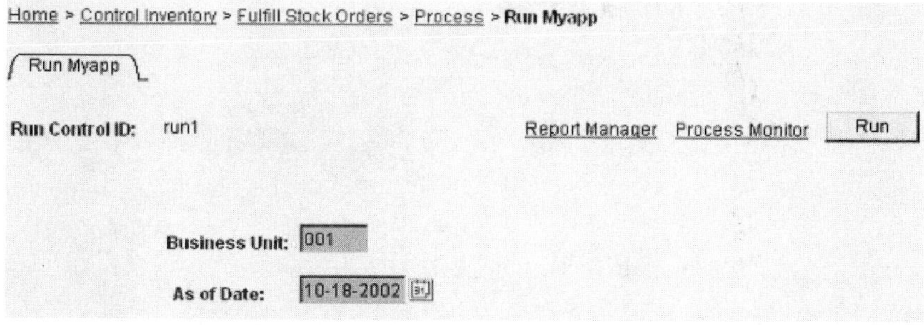

Figure A.11 Run Control Page

Enter your parameters and click the Run button. This will open the Process Scheduler Request page a shown in figure A.12.

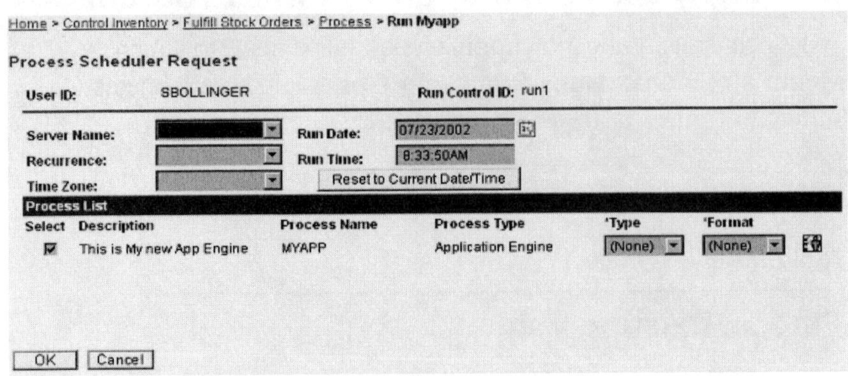

Figure A.12 Process Scheduler Page

Be sure your Application Engine program is displayed and the select box is checked. Then click the OK button. This actually launches your Application Engine program within the Process Scheduler server.

You will be taken back to the Run Control page – figure A.10. Now, click the Process Monitor hyperlink to see the progress of your program as it runs.

Index

Symbols

A

B

C

Q

R

S

T

U

V

W

X

NOTES:

NOTES: